Ninth Edition

THE OTHER WORLD

ISSUES AND POLITICS
OF THE DEVELOPING WORLD

D1166308

Ninth Edition

THE OTHER WORLD

ISSUES AND POLITICS
OF THE DEVELOPING WORLD

Joseph N. Weatherby
Craig Arcenaux
Emmit B. Evans, Jr.
Dianne Long

California Polytechnic State University,
San Luis Obispo

Ira Reed

Trinity University,
Washington, D.C.

Olga D. Novikova-Carter

Howard Payne University,
Brownwood, Texas

Longman

Boston   Columbus   Indianapolis   New York   San Francisco   Upper Saddle River
Amsterdam   Cape Town   Dubai   London   Madrid   Milan   Munich   Paris   Montreal   Toronto
Delhi   Mexico City   São Paulo   Sydney   Hong Kong   Seoul   Singapore   Taipei   Tokyo

Acquisitions Editor: Vikram Mukhija
Editorial Assistant: Toni Magyar
Marketing Manager: Lindsey Prudhomme
Production Manager: Stacey Kulig
Project Coordination, Text Design, and Electronic Page Makeup: S4Carlisle Publishing Services
Senior Cover Designer/Manager: Nancy Danahy
Cover Image: Commuters in Mumbai's Victoria Terminus train station. Benjamin Lowy/Corbis.
Senior Manufacturing Buyer: Roy Pickering
Printer and Binder: R.R. Donnelley and Sons
Cover Printer: R.R. Donnelley and Sons

Library of Congress Cataloging-in-Publication Data

The other world: issues and politics of the developing world / Joseph N. Weatherby . . . [et al.]. — 9th ed.
    p. cm.
Includes index.
ISBN 978-0-205-77887-4
1. Developing countries. I. Weatherby, Joseph.
D883.O87 2011   2009050855
909'.09724—dc22

1 2 3 4 5 6 7 8 9 10—DOC—13 12 11 10

Longman
is an imprint of

www.pearsonhighered.com

ISBN-13: 978-0-205-77887-4
ISBN-10:   0-205-77887-9

BRIEF CONTENTS

DETAILED CONTENTS

Part 2   Other World Regions

PREFACE

In the game of nations there are no winners only losers. The objective of each player is not so much to win as to avoid loss. Problems do not get solved. They are managed. Success is achieved if disaster is avoided or postponed until the next administration.

FORMER EGYPTIAN VICE PRESIDENT ZAHARIA MOHIEDDIN

We live in an era of rapid change. During the nineteenth and most of the twentieth centuries, the West was able to dominate the Other World by using superior technology. One of the fundamental changes taking place in the world today is the expansion of advanced technology to the Other World. Today even the most out-of-the-way places are electronically connected. The result of this growth has been that advanced technical knowledge is available everywhere to everyone. The relative advantages that the West formally enjoyed have either diminished or been eliminated. The playing field between the Western powers and the Other World is becoming level.

Many Other World states are taking advantage of this technical revolution. No longer will the traditional Western powers be able to hold sway over the rest of the world without challenge. The world of this century promises to be a very different place. It is hoped that *The Other World*, 9th edition, will help readers to understand this important development. Whether we like it or not, all of us must prepare for the new world of the twenty-first century.

NEW TO THIS EDITION

In the ninth edition, more emphasis is given to how the global financial crisis is affecting the Other World. Another recurring point of analysis is the new Obama administration, including how similar or different its policies are in comparison with those of the Bush administration and how the new administration may affect specific countries. Specific updates and additions to chapters, "Case Studies," and "Flashpoints" include

- Chapter 2, "The Old and the New," now includes a section on the war on terror and discusses how to define terrorism, the Bush doctrine, and the new Obama doctrine, including how developments in the war affect relationships between developing countries, Europe, and the United States.
- Chapter 3, "Political Economy," contains updates and new analysis of neoliberal economics and globalization to explain recent economic trends and show how they affect developing countries.
- Chapter 4, "Women and Development," considers women as part of the global village and how modernization and globalism affect women's lives, including discussions of finance, technology, and international objectives like the United Nations' Millennium Development Goals.

- Chapter 5, "Latin America," provides a retrospective on Bush's economic policies in the region, considers Latin American economies in light of the global financial crisis, and includes updates on elections and political life in Mexico and Brazil.
- Chapter 6, "Sub-Saharan Africa," provides new insights through discussions of popular culture. It also gives a thorough overview of ongoing and settled conflicts in the region.
- "Case Studies and Flashpoints" sections in the regional chapters have been updated to include recent events and issues, including
  - Shifting power in Cuba and the Obama administration's policies
  - The 2009 election in South Africa
  - Islamic militants in the oil-rich delta of Nigeria
  - Charges against al-Bashir in Darfur and the controversy surrounding them
  - Piracy emerging from Somalia
  - The economies of China, India, Taiwan, Hong Kong, and Singapore after the economic downturn
  - North Korea's nuclear ambitions
  - The recent election in Iran and its aftermath
  - Jewish settlements in the West Bank and the relationship between Israel and the Obama administration

It is our hope that the readers of the new edition of *The Other World* will gain insight into the major issues and changes that affect much of the world's population. If we are to comprehend the political turmoil in the Middle East or the food crisis in Africa, we need to be aware of the dynamics of life in those regions. Finally, we believe that issues in the Other World do not respect borders and that global interdependence will be a fact of life in the future.

FEATURES

This book aims to help students grasp the main dimensions of change in the Third World, which we term the "Other World." This term is intended to present that part of our world that is considered non-Western in its orientation. To appreciate the Other World in today's international climate, we need to know more about its geography, culture, traditions, and political and historical development.

The Other World is a primer on changing Third World issues, using an interdisciplinary focus. We make no apology that this book is what it appears to be: a descriptive introduction to selected world issues. It is descriptive because we emphasize basic information on geography, culture, and political tensions in the Other World. This book targets general education students rather than specialists. Our position is that these students are better served by a book that emphasizes issues, events, and places in a clear, jargon-free way, rather than by one written for political science majors and graduate specialists.

We hope that our analysis will be welcomed by readers who are looking for a supplementary textbook to use in international relations, comparative government, history, and geography courses in which coverage of the Third World is needed. Our point of view is that in the twenty-first century, the focus of world politics has shifted away from an East-West dimension to a North-South dimension.

Two traditional approaches dominate the study of global politics: the comparative approach and the area studies approach. The former addresses the political situation in selected countries with an emphasis on their values, institutions, levels of modernization, and types of government. A deficiency of this method is that it often fails to provide an overview of the geographical areas in which the separate states are located. However, comparative studies are dominant in the social sciences because of their ability to account for similarities and differences among political communities.

The second approach, area studies, centers on the study of geographic regions. This perspective focuses on a region's general characteristics, including geography, climate, economics, political and social structures, culture, religion, and history. Instead of contrasting the differences among states with dissimilar backgrounds, this method promotes an understanding of the people and countries in geographical proximity to one another.

This book combines both perspectives. First, it gives an overview of issues relative to the understanding of contemporary problems common to the Other World. Second, it provides regional coverage of Latin America, Africa, Asia, the Southern Near Abroad, and the Middle East. It then describes the similarities and differences within these regions. Third, it traces events and issues in selected countries in each region.

All the chapters have been rewritten to take into account the effects of changing conditions as the people of the Other World enter the twenty-first century. We have attempted to keep the topics as relevant and up-to-date as possible. Time does not stand still, so we apologize in advance for any illustrations that may become dated because of the rush of events.

SUPPLEMENTS

FOR INSTRUCTORS

MyPoliSciKit Video Case Studies   This DVD series contains video clips featured on MyPoliSciKit for this and other Longman political science titles. Featuring video from major news sources and providing reporting and insight on recent world affairs, this DVD helps instructors integrate current events into their courses by letting them use the clips as lecture launchers or discussion starters.

FOR STUDENTS

MySearchLab   Need help with a paper? MySearchLab saves time and improves results by offering start-to-finish guidance on the research/writing process and full-text access to academic journals and periodicals. To learn more, please visit www.mysearchlab.com or contact your Pearson representative. To order MySearchLab with this book, use ISBN 0205798608.

Longman Atlas of World Issues **(0-321-22465-5)** Introduced and selected by Robert J. Art of Brandeis University and excerpted from the acclaimed Penguin Atlas Series, the *Longman Atlas of World Issues* is designed to help students understand the geography and major issues facing the world today, such as terrorism, debt, and HIV/AIDS. These thematic, full-color maps examine forces shaping politics today at a global level. Explanatory information accompanies each map to help students better grasp the concepts being shown and how they affect our world today. Available at no additional charge when packaged with this book.

Goode's World Atlas **(0-321-65200-2)** First published by Rand McNally in 1923, *Goode's World Atlas* has set the standard for college reference atlases. It features hundreds of physical, political, and thematic maps as well as graphs, tables, and a pronouncing index. Available at a discount when packaged with this book.

ACKNOWLEDGMENTS

All involved in this book benefited from the comments made by the following reviewers: Roger Durham, Aquinas College; Trace Lasley, University of Kentucky; Anjana Mishra, Florida International University; Harry Mokeba, Louisiana State University; Waltraud Morales, University of Central Florida; Sunil Sahu, DePauw University; and Jose M. Vadi, California Polytechnic University, Pomona.

We believe that this text is stronger because of the help of others:

Jane Weatherby provided aid in overcoming the technical difficulties of this project. Jordan Humphreys worked many hours to generate information found in many of the tables. Bobbie Jo Sims helped with proofreading and editing early drafts of the manuscript.

Special thanks to the staff at Pearson Longman for their guidance throughout the editorial and production stages. We would also like to specifically acknowledge the help of Eric Stano, Vikram Mukhija, and Toni Magyar, all of whom who were indispensable in getting this edition into print.

Randal Cruikshanks, Earl Huff, Reg Gooden, and Richard Kranzdorf made important contributions to the success of earlier editions. Their work provided the basis for the current text. Without their help, the later editions of *The Other World* would have been difficult, if not impossible, to write.

Earl Huff, Richard Kranzdorf, and John Stewart generously loaned their photographs to us from personal collections. Because of the number of coauthors, we each have the luxury of blaming the others for whatever errors may have gone unnoticed.

Joseph N. Weatherby

Craig Arceneaux

Emmit B. Evans, Jr.

Dianne Long

Ira Reed

Olga D. Novikova-Carter

1

The Other World

Dianne Long

I am a citizen, not of Athens or Greece,
but of the world

SOCRATES

Socrates was a man of wide vision and understanding, a "citizen of the world" who knew about the great Babylonian, Assyrian, and Egyptian empires that had dominated "the world" long before his time. But his world included only the Mediterranean regions and the area we now call the Middle East. He would have had little awareness or knowledge of the Far East and the complex civilization of the Zhou dynasty that was in existence during his lifetime. Even if he had some fragments of information about China, certainly the Mayan civilization, flourishing on the other side of the world, was totally unknown to him.

Like Socrates, we have all seen the maps and globes that represent our world. We tend, however, to have limited perspectives based on our small knowledge of much of the world and its peoples. Many of us are not aware that the United States makes up less than 5 percent of the world's population. One-fifth of the human race is Chinese, 22 percent live in India, and hundreds of millions of others live in states that have only recently gained their independence. Almost all of the 750 million people added to the world's population since 2000 live in the developing world. The developing world comprises more than two-thirds of the world's states, the vast majority of which are economically less developed and less industrialized than the Western economies.[1]

The world of ancient Greece consisted of a small portion of what we now call Europe, Africa, and Asia, and included less than one million people. Today we know that approximately 6.75 billion people inhabit six massive continents. Sophisticated communications and complex social, economic, and political interactions increasingly link them into a "global village." These linkages bring Americans into increasing contact with those parts of the earth about which we have little knowledge or awareness—the "Other World."[2]

This chapter looks at Other World definitions and characteristics. The following chapters consider colonial domination, economic development, and conflict resolution. The final chapters consider the major regions and suggest important issues.

DEFINING THE OTHER WORLD

The Other World is often described as the have-not, underdeveloped, developing, less-developed, South, nonindustrialized, or Third World countries. Although political scientists, economists, and geographers do not always agree about which specific countries make up this area, the term *Other World* refers to most of the countries in Latin America, Africa, Asia, and the Middle East. These countries include more than three-quarters of the world's population, yet our daily references to them tend to include little more than sparse observations about a cultural orientation or a few generalizations about national politics.

The term *Third World* arose in the Western industrialized community, during the years when it referred to itself as the *First World* and to the Soviet republics and satellites as the *Second World*. These were the nonaligned states, neither siding with the West nor with the Soviet bloc. The term *Third World* had historically been used in reference to those states that were late to develop industry or to adopt modern economic structures. Outside major cities, the peoples in these areas continued to have persistent and overwhelming socioeconomic problems. For the most part, the Third World countries often lacked stable political structures and had characteristically been dominated by First or Second World countries. Their currencies were unstable and not easily convertible into American dollars, British pounds, or Japanese yen. However, over the past two decades, many countries—especially China and India—have made significant progress in modernization, development of industries and international markets, and advancement in information technology. It is not uncommon to place a telephone call in the United States or Europe and find that the customer representative is in India or another part of this developing world.

The discussion in this text includes some developed countries that, because of location, history, or culture, are distinct. For example, Kuwait, South Africa, and Israel attract special attention because of their regional importance and relationships with powerful sponsors outside their areas.

THE CHANGING WORLD

The world today is rapidly changing. Western concepts and traditions of political systems based on competing parties dependent on popular support have been arrayed against the centralized systems of radical socialism in the Soviet sphere. In the 1990s, however, the Soviet Union fell apart, and many of its constituent and satellite countries are remodeling themselves to fit into the Western system. At the same time, many states of Western Europe have moved even more closely together into an economic entity called the European Union, and much of Europe uses a common currency, the euro. Germany reunified into a single state that includes both the Western element and the formerly Communist element and is clearly included within the European Union. Some of the countries of Eastern Europe are undergoing changes as well; however, old ethnic rivalries have emerged, resulting in conflict and bloodshed, as in the Croatia-Serb-Bosnia political crisis.

Terrorism rooted in ethnic and religious beliefs has grown exponentially. The tragedy of the destruction of the World Trade Center in New York on September 11, 2001, brought home the realities of the have-not world that is unhappy with U.S. involvement in Middle East affairs. American military action in Afghanistan (2002) and Iraq (2003) in response to terrorist threats has escalated anti-Western sentiments at the same time that the United States seeks democratization of institutions and privatization of economies of the Middle East. Support for some nations and regimes, such as Israel, and economic embargoes on others, such as Iran, have fostered hatred toward the United States and other Western powers. That hatred finds its expression in hostile acts of terrorism. The growth of Islamist terrorism revealed itself in bombing attacks of commuter trains in Madrid, Spain (2004), and London, England (2005). Hundreds of people were killed or wounded. Terrorism continues to threaten those seen as the enemy. Continued military engagement of U.S. and allied forces agitates terrorist cells worldwide.[3]

Poverty, homelessness, disease, and destruction caused by natural disasters are not isolated to one area of the world alone. Natural disasters, such as the tsunami in Asia in 2004, with its massive tidal wave flooding coastal communities, remind us of the fragility of the manmade environment and the challenges governments face with destruction and reconstruction. Deadly hurricanes struck the Caribbean and the U.S. Gulf of Mexico in 2004 and 2005. In Haiti alone, the death toll climbed to over 3,000. Hurricane Katrina devastated the gulf coastal communities in 2005. A massive cyclone devastated southern Myanmar (Burma) in 2008 with 125,000 deaths and hundreds of thousands of people displaced.[4]

Increasingly, developing states are moving toward democratization and free markets. Countries in today's world that claim to follow a democratic and capitalist model acknowledge the importance of individual rights and free markets. *Democratic* assumptions include a belief in the equality of political and economic rights possessed by all people in the society. Free markets take on the values of capitalism. *Capitalism* assumes private ownership of production and trade combined with a largely unrestricted marketplace based on the belief that the market is self-regulating and should be free of government intervention unless it fails. The individual is assumed to maximize self-interest, to privately own property, and to compete with others to achieve efficient production, distribution, and consumption of goods and services. The individual is important—both economically and politically. People are free to own property, start businesses, trade, and make profits with minimal government intervention.

In reality, however, markets sometimes fail. When they do, the people demand government intervention and regulation to ensure that suitable products are available at tolerable prices. The global crisis of 2008 and 2009 was marked by economic failures for both industrialized and developing countries. Investment in real estate and bad loans led to solvency problems for banks. Spending and investments were immediately affected on a global scale. Financial integration and expanding trade in global markets spread the financial chaos, causing businesses worldwide to fail and unemployment to soar. Governments quickly intervened to prop up national economies. Extended borrowing by the United States made it a debtor nation to China, whose economy boomed in the beginning of the decade. China expanded its manufacturing capabilities, and India likewise expanded customer service operations. Both nations balanced government intervention with free market capitalism. At the same time, the United States and the United Kingdom both aggressively intervened in the marketplace to prop up businesses and to check high unemployment.[5]

Socialist values suggest government intervention in the marketplace. These values include the belief that society and markets need to be controlled by government to minimize abuses by the powerful and greedy. The society, or *collective*, holds property for "the common good," and individuals are encouraged to cooperate with one another rather than to compete against each other. In some societies, both sets of values coexist. Government may regulate the mail system, the phone system, roads and waterways, railroads and other transportation systems, health care, the education system, and other elements important to the economic life of a society. At the same time, private ownership of homes and businesses is tolerated but regulated according to community interests.

The radical form of *socialism*, called *Marxism*, is based on the writings of Karl Marx and Friedrich Engels, who saw human history as a struggle between the exploiting and the exploited classes. Although the former Soviet Union states and China have opened markets considerably, a Communist political system plays a dominant role in controlling economic affairs. *Communism*, modified in various ways with segments of capitalist markets, still exists in North Korea, China, Cuba, and Marxist-led Eastern European states.

In reality, neither the socialist nor the capitalist model seems to produce optimal results. As a result, no economy is purely capitalist or socialist. Today, mixed economies prevail. In such economies, there are places where government intervention is appropriate. For example, government is often responsible for national defense and providing services to victims of poverty, but private firms provide consumer goods and services. Mixed economic systems require political frameworks that not only encourage markets to develop but also allow regulation when markets fail. They provide opportunities for, as well as safeguards against, private individuals and groups that control communications, transportation, banking, and other vital parts of the political economy.

As ideologies blur and international agreements bring industrial states closer, predicting political and economic changes is difficult. The evolution into a global economy causes changes in the power relationships. These changes may lead to increasing international conflict as nations form regional trading blocs driven by the pursuit of profit rather than by political ideology. Control of labor and raw materials may become the principal source of conflict in the post–cold war era as First World nations and trading blocs compete with one another, and as developing nations and masses attempt to resist increasing domination. The 1991 Persian Gulf War indicated the kind of conflict that characterized a New World order. The Iraqi attempt to establish strong leadership of the Arab world by its invasion of Kuwait threatened the supply of oil to, and therefore the economic stability of, the United States, the European Union, and Japan. The Soviet Union appeared to protect Iraqi interests in the cold war. In response, the United States was able to persuade the Soviet Union, and most members of the *United Nations* (UN), to accept using massive military force to end Iraq's occupation of Kuwait.[6] In 2002, the United States initiated military action in Afghanistan, and in 2003, in Iraq. The United States saw itself as an international cop using a preemptive strike foreign policy to crack down on terrorist activity and rumored weapons production. Many powerful nations, including France and Germany, opposed such action, noting that the UN should police states for international law infractions, not the United States. In the aftermath of toppling the leaderships in both Afghanistan and Iraq, the task of rebuilding continues to be challenged by terrorists, ethnic rivalries, failing infrastructures, and staggering socioeconomic inequalities. As the decade ends, struggles in these parts of the world continue, with U.S. troops continuing to be engaged.

UNDERSTANDING THE OTHER WORLD

Consideration of economics, technology, and political structures is important when trying to understand the world's peoples. Geography is also a significant factor. The view of the earth from the first *Apollo* spacecraft revealed it as a small marble of three colors: the blue of oceans, the brown of continents, and the changing swirls of white clouds that envelope its climates. The earth's topographical and geographical features, in continuous dynamic balance with its climates, have influenced much of the destiny of the peoples occupying these fragile lands and traversing its seas. What the *Apollo* photos do not show is the proliferation of national divisions and boundaries. They do not show sharp economic or cultural differences between areas, nor do they indicate quality of life.

This discussion of the developing Other World is descriptive and explanatory. We observe the social, political, and economic conditions in various geographic locations, and we attempt to explain events and untangle relationships among factions within states and conflicts between states. The developing world looks to the West for *modernization* but seeks its own brand of political, social, and economic framework.

Modern social systems are specialized and interdependent. Much of this specialization occurred in the modern world as a result of the Industrial Revolution at the turn of the nineteenth century, when the factory and the workplace away from home became characteristic and symbolic of modern life. More complex and intricate machinery and processes were invented, driving us into a world where computers urge us to act at a faster pace. Today, the spread of technology, especially in communications and transportation, is accelerating the pace of change.

In 1945, when the UN was founded, 31 of its 51 members, or 61 percent, could have been described as developing states. Since then the UN has grown to include 192 members;[7] most new members are developing states. Their entry into the UN has shifted the balance of influence and voting power in the General Assembly from Western to non-Western dominance. For many new states, the move from colonial status to independence was gained through political and social upheaval. As discussed in later chapters, however, ethnic and regional loyalties are still strong and impede the development of national unity in many of these states.

Today, violent conflict prevails in various locales in the world and involves millions of people. Because of these conflicts, over 14 million refugees are displaced from their homelands. More than three decades after the U.S. military withdrawal from Southeast Asia, battles still occur in the Vietnam-Kampuchea-Laos area. Tensions also continue between India and Pakistan. The war between Iran and Iraq during the 1980s was one of the more bitter conflicts in recent years, taking more than one million lives. The Iraqi occupation and annexation of Kuwait became a global crisis. Sporadic fighting is endemic among other countries in the Middle East, as well as in the former states of the Soviet Union. In addition, the Afghanistan conflict has pushed people across the borders into Pakistan, where they live in holding camps in cold temperatures at near starvation. In 2007 alone, over six million refugees were displaced from the Middle East and North Africa, and over 26 million were considered internally displaced persons, people who were forced to flee their homes due to armed conflict or human rights violations.[8]

Africa is also a troubled continent, where civil strife exists in almost every country. Diverse ethnic groups divided by language, culture, and ancient rivalries vie for power and wealth. The crossroads of Africa, the Congo, is beset by such chaos and bloodshed that trade routes and economies are being severely disrupted. Military conflict between Ethiopia and Somalia has continued for years, as has the military and economic disruption in Uganda, Angola, Mozambique, South Africa, Sudan, Somalia, and their respective neighbors. In Latin America, struggles continue in Guatemala, El Salvador, Honduras, Peru, Chile, and Ecuador.[9]

The current situation in Afghanistan highlights the troubling circumstances of the population. Afghanistan has occupied a favored invasion route since ancient times. Foreign empires ruled over tribal peoples until the mid-eighteenth century. Although the country achieved statehood since that time, Afghanistan has remained a tool of her more powerful neighbors. As an example of this, most of the turmoil and human suffering that currently exists is the result of more than 25 years of outside interference that has totally destroyed any political legitimacy within the country. The Afghanistan of regional warlords, each backed by a rival neighbor, created a situation of instability in central Asia. Terrorist camps prompted the United States with British assistance to bomb the country. Whether the weak regime that has emerged in Afghanistan can eventually take its place as a contributing member of the new states in this part of the world is an unanswered question.

CHARACTERIZING THE OTHER WORLD

The great diversity of the peoples and cultures of the Other World means that it is impossible to speak of any significant uniformity among them. The following generalizations, however, describe common features of many of these countries.

1. Dependence on Western powers
2. Delayed modernization
3. Population explosion
4. Unequal distribution of wealth

In general, the Other World faces a variety of significant problems. Our task in this book is to outline the major themes and give specific examples.

Dependence on Western Powers

Most Other World countries have historically been colonies of major Western powers. Their economic, educational, religious, and political systems are now heavily influenced or dominated by their histories and resulting patterns of *neocolonialism* or indirect control over one country by another. Although nominally independent, emerging countries usually maintain economic and political ties with their former colonial masters, preserving many of the established patterns of commerce, politics, and daily life. Such patterns, however, tend to perpetuate the dependence of the new nation on its former rulers. Political and economic institutions designed to extract resources from the colonies are slightly modified and carried into the post-independence era. These institutions, now occupied by indigenous politicians and business leaders, still primarily serve the interests of the industrial powers. These political and economic elites depend on First World governments and corporations for power and position. Dependency exists in varying degrees. Some are still almost completely dependent on other powers, whereas others are moving away from dependency. In the 1990s, private capital from the West flowed into emerging markets of the Other World. Foreign direct investment to the developed world has grown from $25 billion in 1990 to about $250 billion today.[10] Asia and Latin America, participating heavily in the ups and downs of investment, brought about upheavals in global economies, which affected the financial markets of the United States and

Western nations. At the same time, massive financial flows from the West have outgrown regulatory frameworks and have caused such negative effects as increased ecological damage and threats to local cultures as their traditional values and strengths become displaced by Western consumerism. Today economic integration in various regions is growing. The World Bank's *2009 World Development Report* suggests that urban centers in Africa develop cooperative strategies for enhancing free trade across boundaries so that poor countries can improve their economies.[11]

Inflation (rising prices without corresponding increases in goods and services) creates additional hardships. Many peoples not only have low incomes but also find that inflation decreases the value of what little they have. In attempting to support and stabilize economic development, Other World governments have borrowed heavily from First World banking institutions. The World Bank began providing extensive debt relief to poor countries in the last decade, acknowledging that large debt levels constitute a risk of general economic instability for the entire world. The World Bank has forgiven loans and its debt relief totals $25.3 billion.[12]

Delayed Modernization

Sanitation of food, water, and environment is a crucial factor in human health, but only one-third of the Other World has access to adequate sanitation. Facilities for adequate disposal of human wastes are especially inadequate in rural areas, where billions of people live. In Ghana, for example, only 10 percent of the population used adequate sanitation facilities in 2006.[13] Poor sanitation in urban areas is a serious threat to public health because bacteria, viruses, and parasites in human wastes contaminate public drinking water. In Afghanistan, only 22 percent of the population had access to improved water.[14]

Although communication linkages are growing, Other World peoples have little access to telephones, newspapers and magazines, television, and the Internet. In China, for example, only one in a hundred people have Internet access in comparison to 70 in a hundred people in the United States.[15] The Internet is primarily a tool in industrial countries—home to 90 percent of subscribers. Internet use, however, is catching on, particularly in China and India. Some use it for telecommuting and educational services, and others for protesting human rights and environmental violations and maintaining cultural ties. Cellular phones are quickly catching on worldwide as a flexible resource to a community, even with those who are illiterate. China has 547.3 cell phone subscribers and the United States has 255.4 million.[16]

Most developing states have high rates of illiteracy and a shortage of experienced and skilled teachers, technicians, managers, scientists, and engineers. Moreover, the limited number of technologists is usually isolated in a few population centers in each country. Industrialized nations have four times as many managers and technicians per capita. Some countries, such as South Korea, now have intensive training programs to assist in the development of exports and industrialization. Many other countries, however, are unable to mount such training programs. Sometimes they are unable to pay wages appropriate to certain levels of training (e.g., to physicians), so that the danger of a "brain drain" to the higher-paying rich countries always exists.

Management and technological know-how are critical to industrialization and modernization. Because of a lack of capital and appropriate technology, developing countries have difficulty installing and maintaining sanitation systems, energy systems, transportation and communication networks, national security, and government services. The potential for agricultural and industrial progress is also curtailed. Even when financial and technical aid is imported to these areas, there is often little capability to maintain systems and provide inventories of replacement parts and equipment. Technological projects depend on efficiency, punctuality, organization, centralization, and productivity, but often these values conflict with those that are culturally dominant in the developing areas of the world. Local autonomy and interdependence, individual community status, decision by consensus and traditional tribal authority, and personal cooperation are usually more highly regarded than industrialized, organizational values. This situation produces conflict within a larger traditional developing society. Erosion and displacement of values also may bring chaos to previously stable and self-sufficient Asian, African, Middle Eastern, and Latin cultures, leading to serious social and psychological disruptions. Development raises very fundamental ethical questions about meddling in peoples' lives. One thing is certain: Once change has been introduced to a developing country, there is no going back.

Population Explosion

It took 2 million years for the world's population to reach 1 billion, but it took only 100 years to reach the second billion. Today, the world's population is exceeding 6 billion and is growing still. Each year, 90 to 100 million people are added. If the present rate continues, over 9 billion people will populate the earth by the year 2050. The greatest majority will live in the Other World, where the population is growing at two to three times the rate of the population in the industrialized world. Some of the dramatic increases are due to better sanitary conditions and medical technology in some areas, which have led to increased infant survival and increased longevity.[17]

Birthrates and poverty are closely linked. In poverty-level cultures, families face the dilemma of needing workers but also having too many mouths to feed. In larger families, each person's share of the family resources is small. The poorer the family, the more likely the adults will find it desirable to add new family members as future caretakers and workers. Poor societies are dependent on children, adolescents, and young adults to care for the elderly and to support family unit economies. In addition, in poor families, inadequate nutrition and medical care may lead to low birth weights and infant deaths. The higher the likelihood of early death or disability, the more likely new workers must be born into families to ensure that the work gets done and there are providers for the elderly. When the fittest survive to learn traditional skills and values, and when those survivors stay in the clan and village to provide for all, including the very young and very old, the pattern of life continues. However, if young workers find it desirable to move from farms to cities, or if drought or war diminishes food supplies, life hangs on a thread for the children and the elderly left behind in rural areas. In many nations, food production has increased with improvements in farm management and crop techniques. Without an adequate infrastructure to allocate and distribute these increased supplies, more food does not necessarily mean more food on the tables for the bulk of the population.

Disease continues to reduce populations. The number of people living with human immunodeficiency virus (HIV) and acquired immune deficiency syndrome (AIDS) worldwide is estimated to be over 33 million, with the largest number living in sub-Saharan Africa and Asia. Children, who are believed to acquire the disease from mothers before birth or after birth through breastfeeding, make up 2 million of these cases. As this disease continues to spread, primarily through sexual contact, governments and pharmaceutical industries argue over who will pay for costly medications.[18]

Unequal Distribution of Wealth

The most compelling similarity among developing states is the severe poverty of most of their people, who generally live at a subsistence level. Over half of the world's population survives on an annual per capita income of $800 (U.S.) or less. Haiti, for example, is one of the most impoverished countries in the Western Hemisphere. Its per capita gross domestic product (GDP) is approximately $1,300 (U.S.). Poverty has important impacts on quality of life as well. In Haiti, over 40 percent of the population is under 15 years of age, about 40 percent is illiterate, and life expectancy is only 56 years for males and 59 years for females. By contrast, the per capita GDP in the United States is $45,800, 99 percent of the population is literate, and life expectancy is 75 years for men and 81 for women.

The World Bank continues to study the world's poor. The World Bank's 2009 *World Development Indicators* publication indicates that progress is being made toward overall economic growth in the developing world. Fewer people are falling below the poverty line in countries like China and Indonesia, and increases in life expectancy have occurred in the Middle East, Asia, and Latin America. These gains can be attributed to foreign aid and productive use of labor, as well as increased basic social services in education, health care, and family planning for the poor. Still, 20 percent of the world's population, 1.4 billion people, live on less than $1.25 a day.[19] People at these levels are deemed unable to have access to adequate food, shelter, and other necessities of life. The World Bank reports that between 1990 and 2004 the number of people living on less than $1 a day in developing countries declined by 260 million people. Conditions in Africa, however, continue to run contrary to the worldwide decline in poverty. During this same period, the number of impoverished people in sub-Saharan Africa grew by almost 60 million people. That continent faces intractable problems such as high population growth; weak basic economic infrastructure; and wars that have devastated Liberia, Angola, Namibia, Mozambique, Ethiopia, Somalia, and the Sudan. The nations of sub-Saharan Africa have an average poverty rate of over 40 percent.[20]

THE DILEMMA OF THE OTHER WORLD

Everywhere national, cultural, and political systems are shifting in response to complex internal and external pressures and conditions. In the Other World, however, change is occurring at a speed never before seen and in a context of inadequate structures and resources, while leaders express uncertainty about development goals and management strategies for handling chaos.

When the United States became independent in 1776, the world was changing, but it was changing slowly. Events happened and news spread at the speed of sailing ships and a foot's pace. As things changed, the fundamental patterns of rural and city life evolved slowly. However, in the developing world, centuries of change have occurred in only 30 years or less. A person whose grandparents had never traveled more than 10 miles from their birthplace may now be on a flight to London or New York. While the father plows with oxen, a brother may be operating a diesel tractor, and a sister may be learning the intricacies of world economies. Countries are being pulled rapidly in one direction or another by contending political, social, and economic forces over which they have little control. Deeply felt religious values and beliefs that gave stability to people's lives in the past are crumbling, to be replaced by new and alien philosophies.

During recent years, there have been attempts by the world's major financial agencies, particularly the World Bank, to help developing nations relieve persistent poverty and participate in world markets. Large loans have been made to such countries. These loans do not always accomplish their purposes. In some countries, the money is diverted and stolen by corrupt rulers or governments. Other countries continue to be severely handicapped by their lack of technology, education, and effective leadership, or by their particular geographic circumstances. Whenever large loans have been made, economic improvement did not result. Countries were unable to repay loans and were further crushed by high interest costs. This dilemma is now being addressed by an increasingly concerted international action by which loans are forgiven. Help for developing nations can succeed, but there needs to be good diagnosis of the circumstances that face each nation. When a major obstacle is corrupt leadership or government, that problem must be addressed. If a nation is landlocked and mountainous, such as Bolivia, development will be difficult and transportation systems will need to be designed.[21]

As we continue into this century, witnessing regional wars and military threats within various regions, it is difficult for the world to ignore the need for development and the impact the lack of it has on stability, world security, and international trade. New patterns of cooperation and conflict originate from the human experience and interplay with politics, geography, culture, history, economics, and human behavior.

The international community has an unprecedented agreement on the goals for reducing poverty, the eight Millennium Development goals. Created in 1990, each goal's projected accomplishment date was set at 2015.[22] They are

1. Eradicate extreme poverty and hunger.
2. Achieve universal primary education.

3. Promote gender equality and empowerment of women.
4. Reduce child mortality.
5. Improve maternal health.
6. Combat HIV/AIDS, malaria, and other diseases.
7. Ensure environmental sustainability.
8. Develop a Global Partnership for development.

These goals are paving the way for significant action in the years to come to combat poverty and make real progress in human development. International nongovernmental organizations (NGOs) have begun strategies for working toward the realization of these goals, and many have set targets for improvements to come in the areas of the world where important work to eradicate poverty is underway.

Summary

The Other World is marked by dependence on Western powers, delayed modernization, population explosion, and unequal distribution of wealth. The rapid social and economic changes have been hard on some populations. Women, minorities, and the poor suffer more than others in the sea of change as social and economic structures change. Democratization has had many promises for developing peoples, but struggles remain as old social, governmental, and economic systems change. Although improvements have been made, war, human rights violations, disease, and poverty disrupt the lives of many. The prevailing violence across the globe involves millions of people and displaces many from their homelands. Lack of a stable currency and extensive borrowing for creating and building infrastructure contribute further to the struggles of peoples of the developing world.

ISSUES FOR DISCUSSION

1. Will the world population explosion crush us all?

Predictions about population growth have been alarming. Demographers have projected astounding growth rates for the world—particularly for the Other World. Recently, however, they lowered their estimates by 4 billion. New trends show a global stabilization with a target population of 9.4 billion people by 2050 instead of the 11.9 billion originally anticipated. What accounts for this lowered projection?

One answer is global conflict, in which thousands die annually across the troubled nations of the world. Yet another is the increased number of HIV/AIDS deaths, which are growing dramatically. Human casualties also result from changes in the earth's climate, causing natural disasters and affecting food supplies. Another answer is social change, such as family planning practices that significantly contribute to slow population growth. For example, China in the early 1970s had one of the highest population growth rates in the world. At almost one billion people, making up one-fifth of the world's population, China introduced stringent family planning policies. The "later, longer, fewer" campaign of 1972, for example, focused on lowering the birthrate from six children for each woman to one. By 1979, fertility had fallen to 2.7 children, and the one-child policy led to even further reductions, especially in cities.

Social change causes disruption in other areas of life. In China, the pattern of one child in cities and two children in rural areas has caused shortages in services for the aged because fewer young adults are available to care for their parents. In addition, preference for male children, increased longevity of the elderly population, and fragmentation of the extended family have fractured the society. Are these family planning policies desirable?

2. Should the West intervene when abuses occur in the Other World?

It is not easy to generalize about ethnic and religious differences among peoples. Geographic and historic diversity divides people into separate and conflicting ethnic and religious groups, each with its own customs and traditions.

In some areas of the world such groups are mixed together and have managed to coexist. But some contemporary national boundaries include populations that are in long-standing conflict with each other. Also, some ethnic/religious populations live on both sides of national boundaries. Examples are seen in the Middle East. Turkey, Iraq, and Iran are contiguous, but in Turkey there is a dominant population of moderately religious Muslims and a minority population of Kurds. The Kurds live on both sides of the border with Iraq. Kurds are Sunni Muslims, but in Iraq they are a minority in a country dominated by Arabic Shia Muslims. The Sunni Muslims have been in conflict with the Shia Muslims since the seventh century. At the other end of Iraq is Iran, which has a Persian, not Arabic, culture with a very conservative government dominated by Shia Muslims. However, in the area where Iran has a boundary with Afghanistan and Pakistan. there are many Sunni Muslims. Some of these countries also contain populations of Armenians, Jews, Assyrians, and Zoroastrians straddling national borders. Each country has its own traditions and laws affecting religious belief and practice. They range from tolerant to aggressively intolerant.

Different examples are observable in India and Pakistan, which have high proportions of females. Women have little value and are regarded as financial burdens on families, who must provide wedding gifts (dowries) to shift the financial responsibility elsewhere. The murder of female babies and young wives by poisoning, burning, and neglect is frequent but officially hidden. In contrast, many Chinese villages have alarmingly few females of marriageable age because of abortions and infant deaths. In some geographic areas of India and China, ethnic cleansing of religious and ethnic minorities is systematically practiced, though rarely reported.

Among the Bedouin people of Saudi Arabia, family honor is esteemed and cultural codes are very important. The father is central to the family and society, and both young men and women are expected to obey family wishes. Marriages are arranged to protect desert wells and to cement relationships between families. Although Bedouins have moved to cities in large numbers, rather than following the nomadic life of the desert as they have for centuries, traditional values have changed little. Family honor is valued, and women are excluded from modern production. This exclusion has served to trivialize women's decision-making role and minimize their influence within the society.

Since the creation of the UN in 1945, over 100 major international or ethnic conflicts have left 20 million dead. The UN was powerless to intervene because proposed interventions were vetoed in the Security Council—300 such vetoes occurred. During recent years, following the cold war, such vetoes have ceased, and demands for UN action have accelerated dramatically. When conflicts arise, nations seem to depend on others to intervene.

As some parts of the world clamor for global governance, there are also increasing expressions of nationalism. Other World peoples are establishing sovereignty under ethnic, religious, social, or linguistic identities. This fragmentation of the previous nation-state system causes a vacuum of international power and effectiveness, thus threatening economic and social well-being in various geographic areas. How can we protect human rights and preserve national autonomy?

3. Can poor people prosper when a wage economy is introduced?

Over one-half of the world's people exist in subsistence economies. To many, the coming of a wage economy and the elimination of subsistence are positive features of modernization. With wages, one may argue, greater possibilities exist for improving family conditions and for trade with other peoples.

As men in previously subsistent societies begin to earn cash wages, however, they do not always spend them in ways that benefit the family. They may buy alcohol or attractive merchandise. At the same time, women continue to have little access to resources. Women often are prevented from owning land, entering into contracts, or engaging in business enterprises. Over time, women's traditional contributions to family survival are discounted. Activities such as planting and harvesting crops, gathering forest products, husbanding of food supplies, crafting clothing and household products, and caring for children and elderly family members seem to have less value than cash wages. These activities are discounted not only by wage-earning men in the family but also by government statisticians and economic experts unaccustomed to costing out women's work.

World Bank studies show deterioration in children's nutrition even though wages and purchasing power have increased through development projects. When cash crops such as coffee, bananas, tobacco, cotton, cocoa, or specialized foods are introduced, the disparity between wages and child nutrition worsens. Both men and women tend to focus on earning cash. Women work on family cash crop lands instead of in family gardens, which provide food for the table and food to sell at market. As families seek to maximize acquiring cash, the best lands are used for that purpose, and only deteriorated soils are used for family gardens. Women, therefore, work harder, but families do not always benefit. What should be done to relieve this situation?

Review Questions

1. What are the characteristics of the Other World?
2. How have social structures changed in the Other World?
3. How has modernization changed people's lives in the Other World?

Key Terms

Capitalism—A system of private ownership of property, with little or no government intervention, with emphasis on the individual.

Communism—A system with extreme government control, the most radical of which is called Marxism.

First World—Western states, primarily the United States and Europe.

Modernization—Introduction of systems for sanitation, communication, industry, transportation, management, and technology.

Second World—Former states of the Soviet Union.

Socialism—A system of collective ownership of property with considerable government intervention, with emphasis on the common good of all.

Third World—States with limited development, primarily in the Southern Hemisphere.

United Nations—International governing body established with 51 countries in 1945 has increased to 192 countries today. Members are dedicated to reducing global conflict.

Useful Web Sites

Carnegie Council for Ethics in International Policy: *www.cceia.org*
Center for Third World Organizing site: *www.ctwo.org*
United Nations sites: *www.un.org* and *www.undp.org*
United Nations Development Fund for Women site: *www.unifem.org*
World Bank site: *www.worldbank.org*

A Guide to Useful Reference Materials on the Other World

Most college and university libraries maintain government documents with reports on countries and the issues that concern them. Documents are available in paper form, and they are available on the World Wide Web, where governmental agencies have Web sites and newspapers have ongoing news briefs and articles covering global issues. Increasingly governmental agencies and advocacy organizations offer online papers, publications, data sets, and videos. Videos present speakers on important global topics and coverage of events. One such site is the Carnegie Council for Ethics in International Policy (www.cceia.org/education). The Global Ethics Corner is a weekly segment devoted to newsworthy ethical issues. There is a link to its YouTube site where comments or videos can be posted in response to material online. Case studies and instructional supplements are available as well.

The many reports published by the UN are invaluable, particularly the *Statistical Yearbook* and *Demographic Yearbook*. Some autonomous UN agencies that maintain data on specific issues include the World Health Organization (WHO), the Food and Agriculture Organization (FAO), the International Monetary Fund (IMF), and the International Fund for Agricultural Development (IFAD). Reports and publications can be accessed from the home UN site, www.un.org. Similarly, the World Bank's site, www.worldbank.org, has a wealth of publications, press releases, and data describing the developing world and explaining bank policy. Newspapers and periodicals also have excellent Web sites, and individuals can subscribe to regular news releases.

The *U.S. Statistical Abstract* has data on U.S. aid to foreign states, trade statistics, and other information. The State Department also publishes annually a *Status of the World's Nations*.

Several other useful sources include the *Political Handbook of the World*, Arthur S. Banks, ed. (New York: McGraw-Hill, 2009); *New State of the World Atlas*, Michael Kidron and Ronald Segal, eds. (New York: Simon & Schuster, 2009); Charles L. Lewis and Michael C. Hudson, *World Handbook of Political and Social Indicators* (New Haven, CT: Yale University Press, 2009); and *Student Atlas of the World Politics, 2009* (New York: McGraw Hill, 2009).

Many countries publish their own statistical abstracts on a regular basis. General information can be obtained in any quality almanac, such as *The World Almanac*, published annually by the Newspaper Enterprise Association (New York).

Notes

1. *The World Almanac and Book of Facts 2009*, p. 715.
2. Ibid., p. 715.
3. Ibid., pp. 48–70.
4. Ibid., pp. 353–355 and 811.
5. Ibid, p. 47.
6. *World Almanac 2009*. pp. 745–835.
7. Ibid., pp. 725–728, for a brief sketch of the UN.
8. Ibid., pp. 745–835 covers conflicts in each country.
9. Ibid., p. 720.
10. Ibid.
11. World Bank. *World Development Indicators 2007* (Washington, D.C.: World Bank, 2007), p. 314.
12. World Bank. *World Development Report 2009* (Washington, D.C.: World Bank, 2009), pp. 260–282.
13. http://web.worldbank.org. *Issue Briefs: Debt Relief.*
14. *World Almanac 2009*, p. 721, quoting World Health Organization data for 2006.
15. Ibid.
16. *World Almanac 2009* (New York: World Almanac Books, 2009), pp. 745 and 831.
17. Ibid., p. 315.
18. Ibid, p. 717.
19. Ibid., pp. 765 and 831.
20. http://web.worldbank.org. New Brief: Poverty at a Glance.
21. Ibid.
22. http://www.un.org. *Millennium Development Goals.*

2

The Old and the New: Colonialism, Neocolonialism and Nationalism, and "The War On Terror"

Joseph N. Weatherby

*We the English seem, as it were, to have
conquered and peopled half the world in a fit
of absence of mind*

JOHN ROBERT SEELEY, NINETEENTH-CENTURY HISTORIAN

*It is easier to conquer an empire than it is
to keep it*

JOSEPH CHAMBERLAIN, BRITISH COLONIAL SECRETARY

The West has been involved in colonial activity for almost six centuries. No area of the world has managed to avoid being affected completely by this experience. Places as diverse as Gibraltar and the Falkland Islands are still areas of contention.[1] The dismantling of the major colonial empires held by the Western powers has been one of the key political developments since World War II. The postwar period has witnessed the rise of both neocolonialism and nationalism as major features of the Other World. This chapter discusses Western colonialism, neocolonialism, and the Other World's reaction to those events, that is, nationalism.

COLONIALISM

Few subjects in international politics evoke as much emotional reaction as *colonialism*. Most people have a general idea of what the term means, but attempts to establish a definition agreeable to all are frustrating. One need not trace its inconsistent use to determine that its meaning is in the eye of the beholder. To avoid confusion, however, we need to describe some of the more important aspects of colonialism.

In earlier times, the term *colonialism* simply described a country's foreign settlements, or colonies. Writers in the complex world of the later twentieth century used *colonialism* interchangeably with the word *imperialism* to describe the extension of control by one state over another. Used in today's context, both of these terms have an anti-Western bias.

Colonialism and imperialism have slightly different meanings. Colonialism is a relationship in which a group of people located in one country is subject to the authority of the people of another country. This authority can be exercised through direct control by the dominant country, as in the most typical form of colonialism, or through indirect influence, as in neocolonialism. *Neocolonialism* is the process by which rich, powerful, developed states use economic, political, or other informal means to exert pressure on poor, less powerful, underdeveloped states. Neocolonialism also is an expression of global power by the dominant state. In both direct colonialism and indirect neocolonialism, the dependent community can be made up of an indigenous people, immigrants, or a combination of the two. Imperialism, however, is the act of acquiring or holding colonies or dependencies. While colonialism describes a relationship between the dominant and the dependent, imperialism is the process of establishing that relationship.

Sixty years ago political scientist Frederick Schuman described imperialism this way, "In the loose usage of historians, the term often refers to any instance of a state acquiring colonies or building an empire, particularly when the lands involved are overseas and/or the peoples affected are alien in culture and race."[2]

Through the years, the terms *imperialism* and *colonialism* have evoked a wide array of emotional responses. Western countries in the last generation of the Victorian period rationalized that colonialism was a beneficial process that would help to bring a "backward" Other World into the light of the modern age. Their leaders often argued that the highest calling of society was to extend the benefits of Western civilization to its "black, brown, and yellow brothers" in the rest of the world. Brian Moynahan states, "The essence of empire—a prodigious self confidence, and the nerve to treat other people's houses as one's own— . . ."[3] Sir Winston Churchill put it this way, "The act is virtuous, the exercise invigorating, and the result often extremely profitable."[4]

In addition, Westerners were certain that they were destined by history to act as the trustee for a less fortunate colonial world. It was in this spirit that President William McKinley justified the annexation of the Philippines on the grounds that the United States would bring Christianity to the islands. For many Westerners, the expression *white man's burden* was both a challenge and an honor.[5]

Today, colonialism no longer implies honor. There is little doubt that the Other World considers it a disparaging word. Using this contemporary tone when speaking of the American and French experience in Vietnam, General Vo Nguyen Giap said, "The Americans were on the side of the colonialist—the American generals are not very good students of history. Dien Bien Phu paved the way for us to defeat not only the French but later the Americans and now to defend our country against the Chinese."[6]

HISTORY OF COLONIALISM

Many critics charge that colonialism is both a recent development and a result of the expansion of exclusively Western power into the less technically advanced areas of the world. If judged by its definition, colonialism, apparently, is neither new nor exclusively Western in origin. History is full of examples of one people exercising control over another. Even the history of Western Europe has been colored by the invasions of Huns, Mongols, and Turks. Most of the world's peoples have been guilty of practicing some form of domination at some time in history.

For almost all of the last 600 years, the West has played the leading role in the colonial drama. In Western colonialism's early stages, Portugal and Spain were the major European participants. They were so powerful that in 1494 a papal settlement, the Treaty of Tordesillas, divided the colonial world between them. Under the terms of this agreement, the Portuguese had largely a free hand in Africa, Brazil, and parts of Asia, and the Spanish were free to conquer the rest of the Americas and the Pacific. Soon the colonial fever had spread to the Netherlands, England, and France, each of which carved out great empires of their own in the sixteenth and seventeenth centuries. All of these European actors converged in the Americas, in general, and the Caribbean basin in particular.[7]

Speaking romantically of this period of Christians, conquistadors, and buccaneers, William Lyle Schurz wrote,

> The conquest was a thing of superlatives and the men who took part in it were supermen. For never has sheer human will and force of personality accomplished so much through the efforts of so few on so vast a stage. The conquerors not only gave a new world to Castile, their discoveries and conquests resulted in a worldwide social and economic revolution that radically changed the whole pattern of life in Europe and its overseas dependencies.[8]

The first phase of Western colonialism ended in 1781 at Yorktown, Virginia, when American rebels won their independence from the British. At that time, many people in England and other parts of Europe believed that colonies were no longer worth the effort required to hold them. This view was confirmed by the early nineteenth-century withdrawal of the Spanish and French from many areas in Latin America.

Because of perceived needs created by the industrial revolution, colonialism evolved into a new phase during the second half of the nineteenth century. Markets and minerals became the driving forces that led Europeans to establish new colonies throughout the Other World. During this period, many states attempted to acquire colonies. Although the old imperial powers were in the forefront of the new colonizing activities, they were soon joined by Italy, Germany, Japan, and eventually the United States.

Maps at the end of the nineteenth century showed Britain with an empire that included Hong Kong (1841) in the east, India (1661) in South Asia, and African holdings almost too vast to contemplate. France's empire included Algeria (1830), Tunisia (1881), and Indochina (1884). In the twentieth century, France would acquire Syria (1920), Lebanon (1920), and part of Morocco (1912). Although Spain lost its American empire by 1898, it still maintained modest colonial enclaves in North Africa (1470–1580), West Africa (1860), Fernando Po (1778), and Guinea (1844). Portugal's empire included the ancient enclaves of Macao (1557) and Goa (1510) along with the more profitable colonies of Angola (1484) and Mozambique (1498).

Lesser colonial powers included the Netherlands, Belgium, Germany, Italy, and the United States. The Netherlands controlled the Dutch East Indies (1610–1641). Belgium's king owned the Congo (1884) until 1908, when he ceded the territory to the people of Belgium as a colony. The Italians were established in the horn of Africa (1889), and in the twentieth century they carved out an empire in Libya (1911). The Germans held major colonies in Southwest Africa (1884), New Guinea (1884), and Tanganyika (1885; now called Tanzania). The United States acquired the Philippines, Cuba, and Puerto Rico through its victory over Spain in the Spanish-American War of 1898. In the twentieth century, the United States leased the Panama Canal Zone (1903), purchased the Virgin Islands (1916), and gained control over the Pacific Trust Territories (1947). These territories were named the Northern Marianas Commonwealth in 1986.

Although few people realized it at the time, traditional colonialism was a dying movement when the twentieth century began. Spain's day in the imperial sun was already over, and the decline of the other powers was soon to follow. As if by apology, even those colonies acquired by Western states in the early years of the century were called *protectorates*, a legal fiction, rather than *colonies*.

When the end finally came to traditional colonialism, it occurred with swift finality. Germany lost its African possessions with its defeat in World War I. Italy and Japan were forced to follow the German example at the end of World War II. In the aftermath of World War II, most of the former possessions of England, France, Belgium, the Netherlands, and the United States won their independence. The impact of independence on the Other World can best be understood if one considers that these territories included, among others, India and Pakistan (1947), the Dutch East Indies (1949), French North Africa (1956–1962), the Belgian Congo (1960), and the Philippines (1952). Today, only a few quaint anachronisms remain to remind the world of almost 600 years of Western colonial rule. Examples of these out-of-the-way places include St. Pierre and Miquelon, Madeira, St. Helena, and Aruba, which are still closely associated with France, Portugal, the United Kingdom, and the Netherlands, respectively.

As an epitaph to this period, the peoples subjected to colonial rule in the nineteenth century were both non-Western and nonwhite—characteristics that were not important at the time, but have been used by contemporary critics in the Other World to present their grievances with the West in racial terms. The former Soviet Union largely escaped criticisms of this type. Even though it contained vast amounts of territory and encompassed millions of people, the Soviet empire was masked by a Marxist ideology to which many in the Other World were sympathetic. To them, the stigma of colonial racism applied only to Western powers.

Since 1994, the Russian government has been involved in a "dirty war" with Islamic separatists in the breakaway republic of Chechnya. This conflict, combined with new knowledge of how the Soviet Union treated non-Russians in the past, makes it clear that the earlier Other World views of the Soviet Union and colonialism were incorrect.

MOTIVES FOR COLONIALISM

In view of the long period and large number of Western nations involved, no one should be surprised to learn that colonies were established for a variety of reasons. Many of the stated reasons for establishing colonies were only cover-ups for the real motives. Still, there must have been powerful incentives to induce nations and generations of adventurers to risk hardship and death to establish and hold colonies.

If we look back in history, we can identify at least five motives that led the Western states to establish colonial empires. The participants neither simultaneously nor universally subscribed to these motives. Their importance varied depending on the Western country involved and the land selected for occupation. Any list, however, should include the following motives:

1. The crusading ideal
2. Economic incentive
3. Military motives
4. Outlets for surplus population
5. Prestige

Religious and Cultural Motives

Certainly, the desire to spread the Christian faith induced the nations of Western Europe to establish colonies in the Other World. This movement had its birth in the successful reconquest of Spain and Portugal from the Moors in 1492. The natural extension of this proselytizing zeal was to follow the retreating Moors into Africa and from there to conquer a new world in the Americas. For these Iberians, the introduction of Catholicism was as important as the accumulation of resources in their early colonies. At the time when a continent's wealth was to be had in the Americas, the religious crusade was also vigorously pursued. Today, centuries after both the gold and the colonies have disappeared, Latin America's Roman Catholic population, second in size only to Europe's, stands as a legacy to the serious purpose of the religious crusades of Spain and Portugal.

The cultural motivation was also important, affecting both the colonizers and the colonized. One has only to visit former colonies along the North African coast to see the cultural impact of the English, French, Italians, and Spanish, which has survived long after their departure. The Spanish, Portuguese, and French each believed that the highest gifts they could bestow were their language, their culture, and their religion. This cultural "gift" was part of their colonial policy until almost the end of their overseas adventure.

The special emphasis on the importation of culture meant that the indigenous culture of the colony was not considered worthy enough to be maintained. In many places, the native culture virtually died out. Modern Egyptians, referring to the French contact with their country in 1798, say with cynicism that the French were in Egypt for only three years, but if they had been allowed to stay for 15, Egyptians would "say their prayers in French." Similarly, Muammar al-Qaddafi, the leader of Libya, has ruefully remarked, "Any personal action on our part springing from our personality or from our values is cast into doubt, and we ourselves have begun to doubt. That precisely is how colonialism has affected us."[9]

Economic Motives

Religious and cultural colonialism often went hand in hand with economic colonialism. From the very beginning of the Western colonial experience, colonies were seen as a business and the aim of the colonizers was to produce a profit. The desire to become rich was certainly in the mind of almost everyone who dared to tempt fate by joining in any colonial enterprise. Colonies were always used for the profitable import and export of goods by the mother country. In the nineteenth century, economics became the spur that led to the redrawn maps of the Other World.

One might wonder if colonies were actually profitable. The answer depends on the time in history, the location, and the conditions in the colony. For example, in the latter part of the eighteenth century, the French colony of Saint Domingue, whose economy was based on a slave-powered sugar monopoly, was so lucrative that British claims to vast territories in Canada were considered for possible exchange. Today, almost 200 years after independence, the French have gone; the great plantations are no more; there is a worldwide surplus of sugar; and part of the territory—now known as Haiti—is the poorest country in the Western Hemisphere. The boom and bust of this plantation legacy was repeated in Brazil with natural rubber and in other parts of the world with cotton, tobacco, and coffee. At times, colonies held by Belgium in the Congo, the Netherlands in Indonesia, France in Indochina, and Britain in Africa, China, and India were very profitable.

One can easily summarize some of the reasons colonies were economically desirable for their mother countries. They furnished food, minerals, and even

Fort San Juan De Ulu'a: Bult in 1565, the fort was established to protect the Mexican port of Veracruz from pirates. In 1569, the English Pirate Sir John Hawkins was defeated at Veracruz. Recently, the fort was used in the film *Romancing the Stone.*   *Source: Joe Weatherby*

human labor. In return, the mother country supplied the dependent territory with finished products. This arrangement, often monopolistic, gave the mother country's industries preferential trading opportunities unavailable to others. Economic colonialism, however, was not exclusively a one-way street. The countries most successful with their colonies were able to strike a balance between their own desire for economic advantage and the needs of their subject peoples.

Strategic Motives

Following in the footsteps of those who carried the flag for gold and gospel were others who saw the need to protect the mother country's investments. These colonies were established to support more valuable possessions, such as the Spanish occupation of the Caribbean Islands to protect and support the mineral-rich colony of New Spain (Mexico). In the nineteenth century, Britain adopted a foreign policy based on the establishment of a world empire dependent on control of the seas. To be successful, the British had to establish a string of *strategic colonies*—including such diverse outposts as Hong Kong, Aden, Malta, Gibraltar, and the Falkland Islands—for the defense of major colonies and for refueling and repairing the fleet. The importance of strategic colonies to the survival of the British Empire was reaffirmed at the beginning of World

War II, when Winston Churchill said that if the Spanish had attempted to neutralize Gibraltar he would have been forced to seize the Canary Islands to keep the sea lanes to Australia free from German U-boats.[10]

Another type of strategic colony was established to serve as a defense for the mother country itself. The British Crown's 1000-year association with the Channel Islands, located just off the French coast, has provided a first line of defense against a second Norman conquest of the home islands. In the same way, much of Spain's North African enclave empire was established to guard against a repeat of the Moorish invasion of the Spanish mainland.

Finally, some strategic colonies were established by nations pursuing a world balance of power. The value of these colonies is understandable only when analyzed in the context of the great-power politics that existed at the time they were established. For example, the nineteenth-century German occupation of the Marshall Islands and Nauru was probably motivated more by international politics than by hopes for economic gain. Certainly, the visit of the German gunboat *Panther* to Agadir in 1911 provoked Allied fears of German power that led to the Franco-Spanish partition of Morocco in 1912. In that event, France and Britain invited Spain to occupy northern Morocco to prevent the possible establishment of a German military presence in North Africa, which might upset the balance of power in Europe. Clearly, the importance of strategic colonies cannot be evaluated by normal standards for other colonies. They may have been costly to hold, as in the case of the Falklands, and their importance lay primarily in their ability to help maintain or safeguard other interests of the mother country.

Nineteenth-century Shock and Awe: The Rinella Battery was built on the strategic island colony of Malta in 1878. At the time the 100-ton gun there was the largest that could be constructed. This battery was established by the British to protect their supply lines to Egypt and India. *Source: Joe Weatherby*

Strategic colonies have been the most difficult to deal with in the age of decolonization. Many of them had little or no economic worth. Often they were established and settled by the mother country as territories carved out of another land. In Gibraltar, Ceuta, and the Falklands, establishing military bases also involved the expulsion of the indigenous population and resettlement by immigrants considered loyal to the imperial authorities. Today, in the face of Other World pressures for independence, which party has the right to make the decision that determines a colony's future is questionable. Should it be determined by the territory's current residents or by the descendants of the original inhabitants? The question is more complex than it appears.

Spaniards have lived in Ceuta since the fifteenth century, Italian immigrants have inhabited Gibraltar since the beginning of the eighteenth century, and Scots have resided in the Falklands since the early nineteenth century.[11] If one accepts the notion that ancient claims to colonial lands may be pursued in opposition to the present inhabitants, it raises the specter of calls for resettlement in many areas of the world. Yet this is precisely the argument advanced by those who wish to see colonial territorial fates based on historic ties rather than current reality.

Before ending this discussion, we should not overlook those strategic enclaves where the people have no wish for separation from the mother country. One example of this type of colony is Gibraltar, which has been in British hands since it was taken from Spain almost 300 years ago. Originally maintained to protect the trade routes to British East Africa and South Asia, Gibraltar has lost its strategic purpose. With the 1997 British withdrawal from Hong Kong, the Spanish government renewed the call for a return of the 1,396-foot-high rock to Spanish rule.

In February 2009, as the dispute continued, Spanish diplomat, Javier Ruperez, raised Spain's objections stating, "Gibraltar has always been an outpost imperial—now post imperial—or, if you wish, mini-imperial—interest of Great Britain." He further pointed out that in the case of Hong Kong, China never hid its readiness to take things to their logical conclusion; if the British did not leave, to him, the parallelism with Gibraltar is clear.[12]

The 27,000 Gibraltarians, however, have repeatedly opposed any efforts to join Gibraltar with Spain. The British problem is that the two issues are not comparable. On the one hand, the British held 90 percent of Hong Kong on a 99-year lease. Legally, that land reverted back to China when the lease expired in 1997. Britain was forced to hand over Hong Kong at the end of the lease regardless of the views of the residents.

The case for a British Gibraltar is different: The Treaty of Utrecht in 1713 awarded Britain sovereignty over Gibraltar in perpetuity. Should territories such as Gibraltar be returned against the will of the inhabitants merely because the land is contiguous to a larger state?

The issue is complex, and postwar solutions to similar disputes are inconsistent. Usually, the colonial power has attempted to arrange the best deal possible for the inhabitants before agreeing to abandon the colony. This was the case with the British withdrawal from Hong Kong. They negotiated a promise from China to let Hong Kong maintain internal autonomy for 50 years in a policy called "one China, two systems." Portugal and China then agreed to a similar arrangement regarding Macao. However, the British were willing to fight a war with Argentina in 1982 to maintain their control over the Falkland Islands. Each time the British and Spanish have attempted to reach an agreement on co-sovereignty that effort has failed because of opposition coming from Gibraltar's residents.

This dispute argued before the United Nations (UN) Special Committee on decolonization in 2005 centered around two opposing positions. Spain argued that the governing principle for Gibraltar should be historic territorial integrity of Spain. Gibraltarians countered that the most fundamental right of people in the decolonization process must be self-determination, not territorial integrity. The UN's position established in 2004 is that, "Where there is no dispute over sovereignty, the principle of self-determination is a fundamental human right."[13]

In 2006, the people of Gibraltar again held a referendum that was recognized by the United Kingdom as an act of self-determination creating a modern relationship between the two entities. This act was followed in June 2007 by a call from the United Kingdom to have the UN delist Gibraltar as a colony.

The representatives of Spain immediately expressed their opposition to the status change for Gibraltar citing the Treaty of Utrecht (1713) that gave Spain a voice. The Spanish argued that any referendum only involved Gibraltar's internal affairs. The final status of Gibraltar could be decided only between the United Kingdom and Spain with the concerns of the people of Gibraltar being considered.

Responding in 2007, the British Ambassador to the United Nations, Jones Perry, sent a letter to the Secretary–General which stated that in the opinion of London, the clause in the Treaty of Utrecht giving Gibraltar back to Spain was nothing more than an outdated formula.[14]

The UN Special Committee on Decolonization action also agreed to hear from the Gibraltarians themselves. The Gibraltarian leaders stressed that while they welcomed better relations with Spain, they were not willing or would ever be willing to share sovereignty with Spain.

The future is still unclear for places like Gibraltar, where the residents are not Spanish and do not wish to become Spanish. Whether Britain would go to war to defend Gibraltar as they did in the Falkland Islands is an unanswered question. Clearly, the British are prepared to do anything short of war to protect the stated interests of the residents of Gibraltar.

The status of Puerto Rico remains a continuing problem for the Special Committee on Decolonization. For a number of years, the Committee has called on the United States to speed up Puerto Rico's self-determination process.

In response, both the United States and the government of Puerto Rico stressed that a desire for independence was unclear. The American authorities pointed out that most Puerto Ricans treasured their U.S. citizenship. However, other desires were unclear. In recent polls, 46 percent of the population supported annexation, 49 percent supported the status of an associated free state, and only 5 percent supported independence.[15]

In 2008, Hillary Clinton campaigned for the Democratic nomination in Puerto Rico. The Puerto Ricans have an ambivalent position in American life. Since 1952, the island has been a commonwealth. Puerto Ricans can vote in primaries but not in the U.S. presidential election. They serve in the armed forces but have no vote in Congress. They have federal social programs but pay no federal taxes. The sport of politics centers around statehood or enhanced commonwealth status versus a minority who want independence. At present, the majority of Puerto Ricans do not want independence. They want more attention from the mainland.[16]

Finally, over the years many strategic colonies have developed artificial economies and large populations. If suddenly granted independence or absorbed by surrounding territories, these enclaves and their inhabitants would not be able to survive. The mother countries are often forced to maintain and support them long after the empires they were designed to protect have disappeared. Some of the Pacific and Caribbean islands are examples of this type of misfortune, and many of the flashpoints featured throughout this book illustrate the disputes that occur over their fates.

Surplus Population Motive

At different times, the argument that colonies would serve as outlets for a mother country's surplus population has been advanced to justify colonial enterprises. In the past, Britain and France sent convicts, debtors, and other undesirables to Australia and the Americas; and as late as the 1930s, the Japanese talked about relieving their population problem by sending surplus people to Manchuria. Although immigration has often been used as an argument for expansion, finding cases in which the exportation of a surplus population was the primary motivation for establishing a colony is difficult.

Finding cases in which immigration was used to justify territorial expansion is easier—for example, the nineteenth-century territorial expansion of the United States and Russia. Some critics of Israel's past settlement policy have charged that Jewish immigration into Jerusalem and the West Bank of the Jordan River was encouraged by the government to justify the expansion of Israel's borders.

In 2009 the United Nations Office for the Coordination of Humanitarian Affairs reported that because they can't get building permits, about a third of Palestinian homes in East Jerusalem are built without a permit and subject to demolition.[17] On the same day, Israel's Association for Civil Rights said that the government used planning regulation to curb Palestinian construction. The IACR charged that as Palestinian houses are destroyed, Israeli Jewish citizens are moving into those areas. To Palestinians, these demolitions could mean the end of their dream to have East Jerusalem as the capitol of their own state.[18]

Prestige Motive

Probably the most enigmatic motivation for colonization was the establishment and maintenance of colonies as symbols of greatness. If one looks at the world's remaining colonies, it is evident that many are still held for the purpose of prestige. Spain continues to hold the North African enclaves of Ceuta and Melilla long after the justification for them has ended. These colonies have little economic value, and their existence weakens Spain's claims to the British-held enclave of Gibraltar. To Spain, however, these small possessions form a link to a glorious overseas tradition. For modern Spaniards, the crusading ideal, the empire, the civil war, and the tradition of military service in Africa far outweigh any political and economic liabilities that these colonies may bring.

In July 2002, a dozen Moroccan policemen were expelled from the uninhabited Mediterranean islet of Perejil located off the Moroccan coast by members of the Spanish Foreign Legion based in the enclaves. As the *Irish Times* put it, "Madrid's annoyance with the 'invasion' undermines its position on a land issue closer to home. Such a forthright response left Spain with this tricky job of justifying its presence in Morocco while at the same time insisting Britain quits Gibraltar."[19] Because of the rise of anticolonial feelings throughout the Other World, few other powers continue to maintain colonies purely for prestige, although it may partially explain the French role in Martinique and Guadeloupe and the British hold on the Falkland Islands.

THE LEGACY OF COLONIALISM

Sir Winston Churchill expressed a justification for traditional colonialism when he wrote,

> To give peace to the warring tribes, to administer justice where all was violence, to strike the chains from the slaves, to draw the richness from the soil, to plant the earliest seeds of commerce and learning, to increase in whole peoples their capacities for pleasure and diminish their chances of pain—what more beautiful or valuable reward can inspire human effort.[20]

Most of the Other World has achieved independence during the past 60 years. Because the colonizers inevitably justified their empires with the claim that they were bringing the benefits of Western civilization to a backward world, assessing the results of their efforts is appropriate.

Government

The primary interest of the colonial powers was economic, and the quality of preparation for independence varied. In many places, the British left a class of native civil servants who were prepared to keep the machinery of government running after the British had gone. However, where the evacuation was not amicable or where the mother country's own civil servants had governed, little native expertise existed after independence. This sad state prevailed in many of the colonies of France, Belgium, and Portugal. When Belgium recognized the independence of the Congo in 1960, there were fewer than a dozen university graduates in the country. The highest position held by Patrice Lumumba, the Congolese leader, had been postmaster general.[21] Even under the best of conditions, the bureaucratic transfer from colony to independence was not easy. More often than not, coups, corruption, and dictatorships—not Western-style democracy—were the legacy of colonialism.

Education

One of the claimed benefits of colonialism was access to modern education. Since the beginning of the nineteenth century, Other World students have studied in Europe and the United States, and Western schools teaching modern science and mathematics have been established throughout the Other World. Unfortunately, the results of Western education has not met initial hopes and expectations. There have been generations of Western-trained elites who are not accepted in the West and who are viewed with suspicion in their own countries. It was said in the nineteenth century that the Ottomans sent their best young people to Paris to learn to become soldiers and engineers. Once they learned French, they read the writings of Hobbs, Locke, and Rousseau instead of artillery manuals. These young people then returned home as "Young Turk" revolutionaries dedicated to the overthrow of the Ottoman Empire. This destabilizing process has been repeated thousands of times in many countries in the past 150 years. For example, many members of the first cabinet established in Iran after the Shah was deposed in 1979 were Western-trained and held Western passports. For years, these leaders had been working from exile in Europe and America for the downfall of the Shah. Many other Western-trained elites have become anti-Western as their education has given them the perspective to see the hypocrisy of Western policies when applied to their own countries. These elites become disenchanted when they realize they would have better spent their time studying the foreign policies of Britain, France, and the United States rather than utopian Western philosophers. Their disillusionment with the motives of the West has been matched only by their dissatisfaction with conditions at home. Overeducated for the economy, unable to adjust to their own country, and resentful of the West, many of these educated elites become a major source of instability in the Other World.

Economics

The economies of the Other World are invariably tied to the needs of the developed world. Agriculture in the former colonies is oriented to crops like coffee, tea, and sugar, and industry is oriented to the export of raw materials. For example, after independence from France, the Algerians found that one of their major industries was the cultivation of grapes for wine, a beverage that they were forbidden by their Moslem religion to drink. To compound the problem, the postcolonial French had developed new sources for grapes so there was little market for Algerian wine. The Algerians were forced to destroy many of their vineyards and replant with crops more suited for domestic consumption. The Algerian experience has been repeated as a sad economic fact of postcolonial life throughout much of the Other World.

The years 2008 and 2009 witnessed a global economic downturn not seen in many years. Again, the old saying proved true: "If the developed world had an economic cold, the developing world had pneumonia." With economics geared to the old export system, developing countries experienced setbacks that may take them years to overcome.

There were states like China and India that had domestic populations large enough to absorb much of the falloff in export demand for their products. In these cases the decline was only in certain sectors of their economies.

Health

One of the undeniable legacies of colonialism has been the extension of modern health practices to areas in which they had not been available. Even where the health care needs of the impoverished still overwhelm the available clinics, the situation has improved during the past three decades. Western-initiated improvements in medical care, hygiene, and clean water have dramatically increased life expectancy everywhere in the Other World. The result is that adults are living longer and fewer infants are dying. Unfortunately, these advances have outstripped social practices geared to a more brutal age. The result is a population explosion in the Other World that threatens to destroy any chance for people to enjoy the material gains of the twenty-first century. Egypt, which only 100 years ago had no population problem, now has a growth rate that requires an increase in water storage capacity equal to the construction of a new Aswan High Dam every 10 years, just to irrigate enough land to feed its people. With no change in social policy, Other World countries, such as Egypt, are leaking lifeboats; the inhabitants bailing water but doomed ultimately to sink in a sea of humanity. In one way or another, the population explosion, brought on in part by modern health practices, threatens the future of almost every government in the Other World.

Stability

Unlike nations in the West, many states of the Other World have failed to achieve internal unity. The boundaries of most are the result of balance-of-power decisions rather than any desire by Westerners to create states containing the seeds of geographic or cultural unity. The result is a postcolonial world that has few of the economic, social, or political elements generally thought necessary to establish stable governments.

The colonial experience must be judged to have had a generally negative impact on the peoples of the Other World. Although significant material benefits have been inherited from the West, they are offset by the economic, social, and political problems that are the legacy of colonialism.

NEOCOLONIALISM

Today, the great colonial powers of the past no longer occupy the center stage of world affairs. The fate of the world is not determined by traditional colonial powers like Spain, Portugal, Holland, or Belgium. Because colonialism was a primary force in the affairs of nations for nearly six centuries, this question can now be asked: Is colonialism dead or is it merely reappearing in a new form? If traditional colonialism is the only type to be considered, it must be concluded that this era of history has probably come to a close.

The second half of the twentieth century was characterized by the arrival of almost 100 Other World states on the international scene. This rapid evolution of colonies into sovereign states led to a situation in which many former colonies fell under the influence of "new" imperial powers.

The old imperial powers laid the foundations for the Other World as it exists today. They drew the arbitrary boundaries that continue to be a source of conflict. They developed an economic system geared to the provision of needed products for the developed world. They created a leadership caste, which now perpetuates an unfair economic system that exploited the majority for the benefit of the few. The result was the creation of a new colonial system that allowed one-fourth of the world to acquire the major portion of the world's resources.

Sixty years after formal independence, much of the Other World is characterized by hunger, poverty, overpopulation, political instability, and economic dependence. Most of these problems are the legacy of a colonial world that emphasized economic return to the mother country with little regard for the needs of the indigenous inhabitants. Much of the economic, cultural, political, and social institutions of the Other World still serve the interests of the developed world, which is the successor to colonial rule. The economic imbalance between rich and poor, the production of crops for export while children go hungry, and the exportation of bulk raw materials while luxury consumer items are imported are only some of the many problems of the new dependent relationships that evolved between the developed world and the Other World. As previously stated, the leading colonial powers during the great period of Western expansion were also leaders in world politics. Since World War II, the major neocolonial states have shaped most political events. Today, the United States, Germany, and Japan play dominant roles in the economic affairs of many Other World states. These neocolonial powers and their older allies, Britain and France, are now the developed world's political leaders. In this context, traditional colonialism is dead, but neocolonialism is very much alive.

What Is Neocolonialism?

Neocolonialism differs from traditional colonialism in at least two respects. First, there is no official acknowledgment of colonial ties because the subordinate government has established legal independence. Unlike traditional colonialism, the control exerted here is indirect. Second, this influence is exercised through the interaction of the dominant nation's banking, business, cultural, and military leaders with the Other World's elites. This process results in relationships that are dependent on the wishes of the dominant power. The political, military, and economic requirements of the controlling state drive the relationship between the two entities, whereas the needs of the subordinate country are secondary. Today, the Other World has become a dumping ground for consumer goods and military hardware exported from the developed world. Often these imports must be paid for with borrowed funds, which mortgage the future for people in the Other World.

The influence exercised by a dominant power over a dependent state ranges from the activities of multinational corporations to the approval of international bank loans. In an independent world market, it is not unusual for the

TABLE 2.1   2008–09 Comparison of the Gross Sales of Seven Major American Corporations with the GDP of Selected Other World States

Corporation	Sales in Billions	Equals Approximate GDP of State or States
Wal-Mart	404	Egypt
Chevron	263	Peru, Paraguay, and Senegal
Conoco Phillips	230	Singapore
General Electric	178	Kazakhstan and Laos
AT&T	118	Israel and Jordan
IBM	98	Iraq
Verizon Communications	88	Syria

Source: Capital IQ on Yahoo Finance, 2/24/2009, Fortune 500 ranking of America's largest corporations, 5/4/2009, Fortune 500 Issue, 7/21/2008, *The World Almanac and Book of Facts*, 2009 edition. Gross domestic product (GDP) is defined as the market value of all goods and services that have been sought for final use during a year. The GDP covers all workers and goods employed within a nation's borders.

value of an American corporation's sales to exceed the gross domestic product (GDP) of a medium-sized state. Many Other World states are particularly vulnerable to multinational economic pressure (see Table 2.1). In this environment, externally provoked domestic economic problems lead to political instability. Other World leaders go along with a neocolonial relationship to survive.

In most cases neocolonialism is not driven by malice but by the marketplace. It is not a matter of illegal exploitation, but rather a case of the rich, through superior purchasing power, being able to influence Other World economics. This process occurs because the wealthy can outbid the poor for goods and services. The neocolonial relationship is manifested in at least four unequal associations: cultural, political, economic, and military dominance. Taken together, they constitute a degree of control exercised by the developed world that exceeds anything thought possible during the original fight for independence.

The American government reports that, "World trade is on track in 2009 to record its largest decline in eighty years, with the sharpest losses in East Asia."[22] The developing world's only hope is large infusions of credit from the developed world. With at least 121 states needing help, the developed world will be able to expand its economic influence even more.

Cultural Domination

Traditional imperial powers established colonies based on the assumption that their cultures were superior. The Spanish, Portuguese, and French took steps to destroy the indigenous cultures of the colonies and to replace them with a culture imported from the mother country. This policy resulted in the total destruction of many societies in the Other World. Although they took a more benign view, even the British spoke of "the lesser breeds." Colonial policies created a Westernized upper class throughout the Other World. Two hundred years after independence,

Latin American culture is still dominated by Spanish and Portuguese tradition. Forty years after the French withdrawal from Tunisia, Tunisian elites still speak French. In 2009, the upper-class children of the Egyptian revolution talk of London while they play polo and croquet at the British-founded Gezira Club. These Western-oriented elites have become the transmission lines for foreign cultural domination in the Other World. They tend to imitate their former colonial masters in the way that they dominate the people of the former colonies.

Radio, television, advertising, newspapers, magazines, books, and the Internet present a seductive message of Western cultural superiority. From Mexico City to Rabat, from Manila to Lima, young people have been conditioned to want jeans and rock music. Schools that are often patterned after systems from abroad further reinforce this cultural dominance.

In a society of scarcity, such as exists in much of the Other World, the obsession of the elites to create a native version of Western society has caused scarce resources to be diverted from the country's real needs to serve the interests of the few at the top. This practice leaves the developing nations vulnerable to other forms of neocolonial domination.

Political Domination

Much of the Other World is made up of unstable systems of artificially created states, each of which is fearful of its neighbors and, therefore, continually preparing for war. Thus, many developing states seek the aid of other states to achieve political goals that otherwise would be impossible, making them prime candidates for outside influence.

Other World leaders need financial, technological, and military support from the developed world. To get this help, many are willing to submit to varying degrees of outside political influence. In 2009, the Obama administration supported a Pakistani aid package that would triple economic aid from the $450 million level. At the same time, several news sources reported that the military aid program could grow from the current $400 million level to around $700 million. The funding increase would be designated to train the Pakistani military in counterinsurgency warfare. The aim of this effort is to further engage Pakistan in fighting insurgents on the Afghan border. Over time, this kind of unequal relationship could undermine the popular legitimacy of the government in question.[23]

During the cold war, Western intervention in the political affairs of Other World states was rationalized as a necessity to "contain Communism." In the aftermath of this struggle, foreign interventions will be more difficult to justify. In recent years there has been less emphasis on maintaining the balance of power and more concern about securing access to Other World markets, resources, and cheap labor. In the twenty-first century, these goals may be uncomfortably similar to those of the imperial powers of an earlier age.

Economic Domination

Economic neocolonialism may be pursued as the dominant country's formal policy, or it may occur subtly as the result of informal private activities. For example, whereas Western economic aid is clearly policy-driven, the activities of such great multinational powers as Exxon Mobile and General Electric operate largely outside the control of both the dominant and dependent countries. On occasion, the dominant government and private corporate policies may coincide, but this is not always the case. Such ambiguity makes the Other World charge that there is always a link between the policies of the neocolonial power and the multinational corporation, but this charge is difficult to prove. Some American corporations have used their foreign operations to frustrate their own government's policies on trade. The bottom-line strategy for multinationals is profit, not foreign policy.

The multinationals advocate free-trade policies that enable them to buy as cheaply as possible and sell for the highest price, regardless of where the market is located. They maintain that a policy of free trade will eventually result in the establishment of a system that will provide the greatest good for the greatest number of people.

No matter the intentions, people in the Other World believe that the economic impact of neocolonialism has a negative effect on their independence. In their eyes, the history of foreign trade has been the promotion of activities that work almost entirely to the advantage of the developed world. Its policy of keeping markets open to free enterprise virtually guarantees that it will continue to maintain a stranglehold on the wealth of the Other World. The rules of the game of trade have been made by the developed world and benefit the developed world. Economic neocolonialism is a legacy of this modern system of trade.

Military Domination

Much of the Other World is politically unstable. To survive in this hostile environment, the weak have had to pursue a policy of nonalignment or seek the protection of a powerful ally. After World War II, the United States and the Soviet Union courted these countries in an effort to structure a favorable balance of power. The result was the creation of military client-state relationships that involved most of the Other World. Since that time, the neocolonial powers have supplied massive amounts of sophisticated weapons to Other World countries. Weapon availability, parts, and training are all indirect methods for major powers to affect the behavior of their clients. The final outcome of the Falklands War (1982) was influenced by the U.S. spare parts embargo, which denied service to equipment supplied earlier to the Argentine Air Force. Without spare parts, the Argentineans were severely handicapped in both the size and the number of air strikes that they could mount against the British. This deficiency was one factor that ultimately helped to turn the tide of battle in favor of the British forces.

The militaries of the Other World form the life-support system for the arms business in the developed world. Arms sales have been significant sources of income and influence for the United States, the former Soviet Union, South Africa, and a number of states in Europe. Years ago, former U.S. president Jimmy Carter expressed concerns about U.S. arms policy when he stated, "We also need to change our weapons production and weapons sales overseas as a basic foundation for jobs in this country."[24]

In the guise of offering a helping hand to friendly nations, developed states are able to tie clients to their arms industry. During the cold war, this policy allowed sophisticated military hardware to fall into the hands of Other World leaders. In many cases, balance-of-power issues took precedence over the consideration of local issues when decisions on arms sales were made. On more than one occasion, leaders of selling countries were shocked to find that client states were fighting each other in local conflicts with the weapons that were intended for use in the cold war—for example, the hostilities between India and Pakistan and between Iran and Iraq.

The 1990 Iraqi invasion of Kuwait demonstrated the folly of indiscriminate sales of advanced military technology to the Other World. To the surprise and horror of leaders in the developed world, the Iraqis showed that their acquisition of military technology had a level of sophistication that made a military response from the developed world difficult. In the end it took a half-million troops and a war to force the modern Iraqi army to leave Kuwait.

Developed nations have found that once their most advanced military technology is in the hands of a foreign leader, they can no longer control its use in the low-intensity conflicts that occur in the Other World. The development of sophisticated arms industries geared to exports by China, Brazil, South Africa, Turkey, Israel, North Korea, and South Korea has introduced a new dimension to this problem. The end of the cold war and the "build down" of the military forces in the United States and the former Soviet Union caused a "fire sale" of surplus military hardware, further complicating the issue (see Table 2.2).

In the wake of the 1991 U.S. victory over Iraq in the Persian Gulf, American arms sales to the Other World exploded. The U.S. government was placed in the embarrassing position of condemning Russian arms sales while, at the same time, increasing sales of its own.

Of course, military spending far exceeds military arms transfers. In April 2009, The Stockholm International Peace Institute issued a report claiming that major military spending increased by 20 percent during the last five years. The United States far exceeded the military spending of others. The world's largest suppliers of conventional arms to the Other World were the United States and Russia.[25]

TABLE 2.2 Approximate Value of Arms Transfers to Other World by Suppliers in 2006

Country	Sales in Billions of Dollars
United States	10
Russia	8
United Kingdom	3
Germany	2
China	800 million

Source: Congressional Research Service and *The World Almanac and Book of Facts 2009*, p. 173.

In summary, neocolonialism, like traditional colonialism, describes a process in which one people exerts power over another people while, at the same time, enhancing its own status and power. In neocolonialism, the subject people are legally independent, so the dominant power's influence is indirect. Because the practice of neocolonialism is now so widespread, it must be considered one of the two major influences on contemporary politics of the Other World. The second is nationalism.

NATIONALISM

Like modern colonialism, nationalism is largely a Western invention. With the rise of the nation-state in Europe during the eighteenth century, Europeans abandoned their traditional loyalties to clan, church, and crown.[26] No longer were political leaders successfully able to command large followings purely on the basis of divine right, family ties, or papal decrees. For the first time, Europeans started to confer legitimacy on what was to be called the nation-state. This entity would have authority over a group of people, called a nation, who believed that they had a common cultural identity. Leaders who emphasized this linkage to reinforce the legitimacy of their rule strengthened the sense of identity between the nation and state. Commonly proclaimed symbols of nationhood included racial, linguistic, religious, and historical ties that separated one people from another. In time, the nation's flag, anthem, special days, and other traditions assumed a quasi-religious character that was almost unquestioned. Like the mystics of ancient times, the modern leader who successfully captured these images was able to rule. Today, leaders wrap themselves in the national colors at every opportunity to establish legitimacy in the minds of the people. Modern nationalism represents the idea that the merger of the nation and the state creates an entity that is more than the sum of its parts. The individual's personal interests are subordinate to the interests of the nation-state. What makes the nation-state different from states of the past is the transference of the people's loyalties to the state instead of to the crown, religion, city, or clan, establishing the desired legitimacy.

Nationalism is based on the notion of exclusivity and, therefore, the superiority of one nation over another. Conversely, one of the features of nationalism is the use of fear of others to encourage unity. The "foreign devil" is one of the primary motivations for modern nationalism; that is, leaders in both the East and the West portray other leaders as foreign devils to secure popular support for their own policies. The perception of an Osama bin Laden, Kim Jong-il, Barak Obama, or Fidel Castro as a foreign devil depends on one's location.

Nationalism in the Other World is part of the legacy of colonialism. As colonial administrators, teachers, soldiers, and missionaries sought to replicate the culture of Europe, they inadvertently planted the seeds of nationalism. Students learning about Magna Carta rights, the French Revolution, and American independence could not avoid drawing parallels between their own situations and the struggles of young Westerners of another age. Nationalism appeared in the hearts and minds of Western-trained elites long before it became the mass movement that it is today. For example, Western-educated intellectuals formulated the beginning of a theory that all Arabs form a single nation. At the time, their purpose was to create unity for a common Arab struggle for independence. Similar nationalists led movements in many Other World locations during the nineteenth and twentieth centuries.

For many years the Marxist-Leninist model was seen by nationalists as an alternative to the Western approach to development, with its neocolonial implications. However, the collapse of the economy in the former Soviet Union has discredited much of this effort in the eyes of many in the Other World. There is doubt about whether the Marxist-Leninist approach will continue to have much influence.

Some nationalists sought to chart a new course between the push-pull approaches of the East and the West. For them, nonalignment was the only way for the individually weak but collectively strong states to avoid the reimposition of colonialism in a new form. During the 1950s, Nkrumah in Ghana, Sukarno in Indonesia, and Nasser in Egypt effectively used the East-West rivalry to play one side against the other. With the end of the cold war, Other World nationalists had little to bargain with when they were forced to deal with the developed nations. It is questionable whether nonalignment will be a viable policy for them to pursue in the future.

"THE WAR ON TERROR"

Can a terrorist be a freedom fighter?

> There cannot be good and bad terrorists, our terrorists and others . . . All those who resorted to arms in order to resolve political disputes, all those organizations, all those structures and individuals who carry out these policies should not be tolerated.
>
> RUSSIAN PRESIDENT VLADIMIR PUTIN[27]

> The international community cannot tolerate states which assist and harbor terrorists and use terrorism as an instrument of their state policy.
>
> FORMER INDIAN PRIME MINISTER ATAL BEHARI VAJPAYEE[28]

The U.S. government, in presidential Executive Order number 13224, defines terrorism as an activity that:

a. Involves a violent act or an act dangerous to human life, property, or infrastructure, and
b. Appears to be intended,
c. Intimidates or coerces a civilian population,
d. Influences the policy of a government by intimidation or coercion, or
e. Affects the conduct of a government by mass destruction, assassination, kidnapping, or hostage taking.[29]

A terrorist group is a structured organization . . . of more than two persons, acting in concert to commit terrorist offenses. . . . These offenses are committed with the aim of intimidating and seriously altering or destroying the political, economic, or social structures of countries.

EUROPEAN UNION DEFINITION OF TERRORISM[30]

Avoid using the term "Global war on terror." Please use the term "Overseas contingency operation."

2009 DEFENSE DEPARTMENT OFFICE OF SECURITY REVIEW[31]

Wrong a man, deny him all redress, exile him if he complains, gag him if he cries out, strike him in the face if he struggles, and at the last he will stab and throw his bombs.

GEORGE KENNAN, POLITICAL ANALYST AND DIPLOMAT[32]

Who Is the Terrorist? The Traditional View

The subject of who is a terrorist is as confusing as the preceding statements are contradictory. Were the French, Dutch, Danish, and Norwegian resistance fighters who sought to end the World War II Nazi occupation of their countries terrorists? Were the supporters of the Russian, Yugoslav, and Greek partisan movements also terrorists? What about the members of the Irish Republican Army and their opponents, the various protestant paramilitaries: Are they also terrorists?

Two old clichés still apply when labeling who is a terrorist:
One person's terrorist is another person's freedom fighter.
History tends to get written by the winners.

In the past, it could be said that terrorism was a strategy, not a movement. It was and is a strategy used by the weak against the strong. Terrorism involves the use or threat of violence against innocent people to influence political behavior. It is a strategy of conflict that involves a low risk to the perpetrators. It is inexpensive and it works. Terrorists rely on the intimidating effects of assassinations, random bombings, or airplane hijackings to accomplish their goals.

Individuals, groups, and some states use terrorism. The decision to do so is mostly the result of having no other realistic chance to affect political outcomes. In the case of the September 11, 2001, attack on the World Trade Center, an airplane hijacking became an option because the terrorists knew that after the American military victories over Iraq and Serbia they could not hope to confront the military power of the United States directly. What the terrorists hoped to do was demonstrate to the Other World the vulnerability of the United States to this kind of strategy. If one looks at the loss of life, the loss of jobs, the general economic damage, including the collapse of the travel industry, one would have to conclude that the terrorists' attack was successful.

The Bush Doctrine on Terrorists

After the September 11 terrorist attacks on the United States, President George W. Bush broadened the fight against terrorism. In a State of the Union address, he declared that as part of the war on terror, the United States was opposed to an "axis of evil" made up of Iraq, Iran, and North Korea. He drew a linkage between this axis of evil and the American effort already being waged against nonstate terror groups in the Other World. He made good on his threat to oppose these states by leading a "coalition of the willing" in a war that toppled the government of Iraq.

While the evil of the Iraqi regime cannot be denied, many people have difficulty finding a link between the axis of evil states and a more traditional view of the use of terrorism as a strategy.

In an address delivered at the National War College in November 2002, James Woolsey made clear what the linkage was. He stated that he agreed with Professor Eliot Cohen of Johns Hopkins University in arguing that America was now fighting World War IV. If World Wars I and II were conventional wars and World War III was a cold war lasting 40 years, then World War IV was the war on terror. "What is different after September 11th is not that these . . . groups came to be at war with us. They've been at war with us for some time. It's that we finally may have noticed and decided, in part, that we are at war with them."[33]

When the war on terror is viewed as a world war, the axis of evil statement comes into clear focus. This war may have been going on since the Iranian hostage crisis of 30 years ago. It would not simply end with a short military victory over Iraq. To be successful, the war against terror would have to be fought with the same dedication, vigor, and courage that we displayed in World Wars I, II, and III.

Because the conflict was different, World War IV would not require "the collection of pots and pans, the planting of victory gardens, or even the creation of fallout shelters." However, it would require a commitment that lasted years after the red, white, and blue ribbons had faded and been removed from houses. To the Bush administration, terrorists with a global reach, whether part of the axis of evil or nonstate organizations, such as Al Qaeda, could win only if Americans lost heart or grew disinterested in the effort. In many ways World War IV would be more difficult to sustain than earlier conflicts. There would be few Normandy landings or Berlin airlifts to mobilize support. This would continue to be a frustrating, dirty, low-intensity conflict that might go on for years.

The Obama Doctrine on Terrorism

In his first months in office, President Obama has given the world what it wants to hear through his heady rhetoric. He has apologized to Europe, South America, and the United Nations for what many see as past American transgressions. Among other things, he has promised to end the torture of detainees, close Guantanamo Bay's prison, and suspend military tribunals.

His words, though well received abroad, masked many inconsistencies in fact. Military tribunals have been reestablished and Guantanamo's prison remains open. The talk of a realistic date for the actual removal of forces from Iraq and Afghanistan still remains a distant dream.

President Obama has increased U.S. involvement in Afghanistan and Pakistan. A new commander who is a specialist in unconventional warfare has taken over the more robust forces in Afghanistan. He has also continued and even increased the American attacks on suspected insurgent bases in Pakistan.

In short, President Obama may have used his "rock star" status to say what people in Europe and much of the rest of the world want to hear. In practice, his words may be different, but many of the Bush antiterrorism policies remain. The reality of global politics is forcing the Obama administration to adopt policies that it once criticized.

Admittedly, at this writing, it is still too early to forecast what the Obama government will do about terrorism. It may want to close Guantanamo, try detainees as criminals, and rehouse all detainees somewhere in the United States, but world events, domestic politics, and public opinion may prevent President Obama from achieving these goals.

Terrorism as a strategy cannot be ended. However, global terror organizations can! Other terrorist groups can be limited and, in time, contained at an acceptable level. The answer is for the established powers to actively engage the grievants in a way that will offer other opportunities for resolving conflict.

In the case of the Other World, the grievances that led to the use of terrorism as an option lie in the colonial past, the unresponsive governments, the festering Arab/Israeli dispute, the massive ignorance, the grueling poverty, and the total lack of hope among the masses. Many of these grievances are legitimate. They produce a frustration and a seething anger among willing recruits to terrorism. A solution may be found in the developed world's serious willingness to work to resolve the injustices that cause the anger expressed by the peoples of the Other World.

Summary

After nearly 600 years, Western colonialism has come to an end, and more than 100 new nations have gained their independence. Born out of the colonial struggle for independence, these new states are engaged in the uneven process of nation building. The traditional symbols of nationalism may not be universally present. Many countries have yet to meet the criteria necessary for a state as it is recognized in the West. Admittedly, these states have artificial and often illogical boundaries and are divided by political ideology and religion. They have, however, a common legacy of colonialism, which unites them. This unity is based on the development of a militant nationalism that is anticolonial, anti-neocolonial, and anti-Western.

If the hostility to the West is to be reduced, the Western policymakers must strive for a new fairness in dealing with the Other World. Fairness needs to be applied to policies on arms sales, trade, and banking. The present neo-colonial practices carried out by the West ensure that extreme poverty will be the fate for millions of Other World people. The poor will continue to pay high prices for what they purchase from the West while being paid low wages for what they produce. The perpetuation of this unfair relationship is simply a license for the West to "strip-mine" the Other World for anything that is of value. As long as this situation persists, the West should not be surprised at the hostility, social unrest, and ethnic rivalry coming from the Other World.

ISSUES FOR DISCUSSION

1. Should the Other World be held to the same labor standards advocated in the developed world? The case for hand-tied oriental carpets and the issue of child labor are considered.

For every person living in the United States, there are approximately 21 people living elsewhere. The majority of these people live at a subsistence level in the Other World. The circumstances of their existence dictate conditions of work that often seem harsh and immoral to Westerners. Is it possible or even fair to hold the Other World states to the same labor standards that have taken 200 years to evolve in the industrialized West?

There is a saying that the wealth of a society can be measured by the age at which the young must go to work. The International Labor Organization (ILO) has estimated that, "There are 250 million economically active children world wide."[34] Their jobs include debt bondage, armed conflict, drug trafficking, prostitution, and slavery. Child labor also includes the production of readily accepted commercial goods in the West, such as oriental carpets.

In oriental carpet factories stretching from Morocco across North Africa and South Asia to India and Nepal, the age of children working at the looms is young indeed. Ranging in age from four to midteens, thousands of young girls work up to 14 hours a day in the carpet factories. Fine, hand-tied oriental carpets are produced by children because their hands are considered to be faster, and they are more patient in their work than adults.

Oriental carpets are highly praised and find a ready market in the homes and offices of the United States and Europe. Almost all of these carpets are manufactured

Break Time: Child rug weavers taking a break in a North African carpet factory.

Source: Joe Weatherby

for export. Few Westerners understand or care to hear about the pain and suffering that is involved in the production of these beautiful, expensive works of art.

The defenders of child labor in the Other World point out that carpet factories and other industries are not unlike the nineteenth-century textile mills and mines that helped to create the wealth of modern Europe and the United States. To them, these harsh conditions are a temporary but necessary part of the development process. Other World businesspeople are outraged when they hear reformers in the West calling for boycotts of their goods simply because they were produced with the help of child labor. They are quick to point out that labor reform is simply another way for the West to restrict competition in a free-market economy. Other World states compete with the only advantage that they have: the willing backs of their young. To them, the old colonial metaphor still applies: After 200 years of playing industrial poker, the West has acquired enough of the economic chips to pronounce the game immoral and demand that the Other World join in a game of contract bridge.

The dilemma for the Other World is clear. The West is attempting to impose its own moral standards on a world that has very different values. In much of the Other World, a child who helps to support a poor family by working at the wheel or the loom is considered to be a good child. In places where the only advantage that industries have over the West is low labor costs, there is no alternative to child labor if the family is to live.

This same story can be repeated in industries that manufacture products destined for Western markets, including sporting goods, textiles, and shoes. Labor organizations in the West have asserted that as many as 100 million children must work in the factories of the Other World for their families to survive.

The developed world may have seen the elimination of the worst excesses of the nineteenth-century England of Charles Dickens. Cripplers may no longer haunt the slums of Cairo looking for children to turn into the beggars described in the stories of Naguib Mahfouz. Nevertheless, harsh working conditions for children remain throughout the Other World.

Under the circumstances, should the reader boycott the carpets, textiles, sporting equipment, and shoes manufactured in the Other World because of these labor excesses? To do so could deprive millions of poor people of their only hope for a livelihood. Or should the reader assume that, as has occurred with industrialization in the West, labor conditions will improve in Other World industries as manufacturing gradually improves the standard of living?

2. Can a Western democracy sustain a counterinsurgency effort over a long period of time?

Democracies, like the United States, are in a pre-election, election, or post-election period all the time. Politicians are forced to include the next election into any policy calculations that they make. At least until the end of World War II, American foreign policy was considered to be largely bipartisan. Even then presidents were free to consider public opinions if it went counter to what was believed to be American interest. During the Spanish Civil War (1936–1939), President Roosevelt denied aid to Republican Spain even though he was aware that this action would accelerate the rise of Fascism in Europe and possibly bring on a world war.[35]

Since the end of the "Cold War," the idea of a bipartisan foreign policy has all but disappeared. This situation has been accelerated by the rise of 24-hour news radio and television. Because they always need material, it is easier for these outlets to cover election politics than to analyze global events. Because of this election and media focus, every politician is more concerned about how actions will affect the next election. Under these circumstances, it is almost impossible for the American government to formulate any foreign policy that will be valued after the next election.

On the other hand, the insurgents have clear, long-term goals and all the time in the world to achieve their objectives. As was shown in both Korea and Vietnam, patience on their part can often triumph over firepower if the insurgents "hang on" long enough.

In Iraq, the Other World opposition has recognized that they can never militarily defeat the United States. They know that they cannot even inflict major damage on America. They also know, however, that if they can cause enough pain over a long period of time, the election process in democracies, like the United States, will, as the next election approaches, see that the low-intensity conflict is too politically costly to be continued.

In the long run, all the insurgents need to do is avoid losing to achieve the long-term goal of gaining their political objective. If you were an American policymaker, how would you overcome the inherent weaknesses of making a long-term, bipartisan foreign policy?

Review Questions

1. Describe the differences between colonialism and neocolonialism.
2. What were some of the motivations for traditional colonialism?
3. Were there benefits to the Other World gained from Western colonialism?
4. Define imperialism.
5. Define terrorism.

Key Terms

Artificial states—Former colonies whose borders provide no internal unity because they are the result of balance-of-power decisions made in Berlin, London, and Paris.

Colonialism—The relationship between a group of people in one country who are subject to the authority of the people in another country.

Neocolonialism—The process by which developed states use informal, indirect means to exert pressure on politically independent, less-developed states.

Other World nationalism—Nationalism that is nontraditional because it is anticolonial.

Population growth—Increase in the numbers of people living in an area caused by a combination of social practices geared to a more brutal age and modern health practices.

Prestige colonies—Colonies that are created to glorify the mother country.

Strategic colonies—Colonies used to support major colonies.

White man's burden—An expression glorifying colonialism taken from an 1899 poem by Rudyard Kipling.

Useful Web Sites

Asean: *www.aseansec.org*
Caricon: *www.caricom.org*
The Commonwealth: *www.thecommonwealth.org*
Unicef, USA: *www.unicef.org*

For Further Reading

Barnett, Thomas P. M. *The Pentagon's New Map: War and Peace in the Twenty-First Century.* New York: Berkley Books, 2004.
Berthon, Simon, and Robinson, Andrew. *The Shape of the World: The Mapping and Discovery of the Earth.* New York: Rand McNally, 1991.
Danzinger, James. "The Developing Countries in the Post-Cold War World." Chapter 17 in *Understanding the World: A Comparative Introduction to Political Science.* New York: Longman, 1996.
Gellner, Ernest. *Nations and Nationalism.* Ithaca, NY: Cornell University Press, 1983.
Ghaliand, Gerard, and Rageau, Jean-Pierre. *Strategic Atlas: A Comparative Geopolitics of the World's Powers.* New York: Harper & Row, 1990.
Lapping, Brian. *The End of Empire.* New York: St. Martin's Press, 1985.
Payne, Richard, and Nassar, Jamal. *The Politics and Culture in the Developing World: The Impact of Globalization.* New York: Longman, 2003.
Pettiford, Lloyd, and Harding, David. *Terrorism: The Undeclared War.* Wiltshire, UK: Selectbook Ltd., Devizes, 2004.
Porch, Douglas. *The Conquest of Morocco.* New York: Alfred A. Knopf, 1982.
Poulsen, Thomas. *Nations and States: A Geographic Background to World Affairs.* Englewood Cliffs, NJ: Prentice Hall, 1995.
Snow, Donald. *Cases in International Relations: Portraits of the Future.* New York: Longman, 2003.

Notes

1. For over 100 years, Argentina has claimed the Falkland Islands under the Spanish name Malvinas. In 1982, it fought a war with Britain for control of the island, which Britain won. Because most maps use the English name, that practice will be followed in this chapter.
2. Frederick Schuman, *International Politics: The Western State System and the World Community* (New York: McGraw-Hill, 1958), p. 307.
3. Brian Moynahan, *The British Century: A Photographic History of the Last Hundred Years* (London: Endeavor Group UK, 1997), p. 16.
4. Valerie Pakenham, *Out in the Noonday Sun: Edwardians in the Tropics* (New York: Random House, 1985), p. 10.
5. The expression "white man's burden" comes from the Rudyard Kipling poem of the same name. A sample verse is:

    Take up the white man's burden
    And reap his old reward:

The blame of those ye better
The hate of those ye guard.

From *Who Said What When: The Chronological Dictionary of Quotations* (London: Bloomsbury Publishing, 1988), p. 200.

6. William Tuohy, "Viet Nam, A Key Battle Reverberates: Diet Bien Phu Recalled," *Los Angeles Times*, 5 May, 1984, p. 18.

7. See W. M. Will, "Power, Dependency, and Misperceptions in the Caribbean Basin," chapt. 02 in *Crescents of Conflict,* ed. W. M. Will and R. Millett (New York: Praeger, 1985).

8. William Lyle Schurz, *This New World* (New York: Dutton, 1957), p. 112.

9. See Muammar al-Qaddafi, "Third Way," in *Islam in Transition: Muslim Perspectives*, ed. John Donohue and John Esposito (New York: Oxford University Press, 1982), p. 103.

10. Winston S. Churchill, *Their Finest Hour: The Second World War* (Boston: Houghton Mifflin, 1949), p. 519.

11. Lewis M. Alexander, ed., *World Political Patterns* (Chicago: Rand McNally, 1963), p. 262.

12. "Spain Must Be More Forceful on Gibraltar Issue." Spanish ABC Newspaper website, taken from BBC Monitoring Europe, Lexis-Nexis, the Academic Universe, February 11, 2009.

13. "Petitioners Tell Decolonization Committee Sovereignty Dispute Between Spain UK Should Not Displace the Right to Self-Determination." H. T. Media Ltd., June 7, 2005, accessed from Lexis-Nexis Academic Database.

14. "Spain Must Be More Forceful on Gibraltar Issue." Spanish ABCL Newspaper website, taken from BBC Monitoring Europe, Lexis-Nexis, the Academic Universe, February 11, 2009.

15. "Special Committee on Decolonization Calls on the United Nations to Expedite Puerto Rico's Self-Determination Process." States News Service, United Nations Release, Washington, D.C., taken from Lexis-Nexis, the Academic Universe, June 14, 2007.

16. "Her Last Hurrah; Puerto Rico," *The Economist* U.S. Edition, taken from Lexis-Nexis, the Academic Universe, June 7, 2008.

17. "U.N.: Freeze on Jerusalem Demolitions," BBC news, May 1, 2009, taken from Lexis-Nexis, the Academic Universe, May 1, 2009.

18. Katya Adler, "Demolitions Build Jerusalem Tensions." BBC News, London, May 1, 2009, taken from Lexis-Nexis, the Academic Universe, May 1, 2009.

19. Frank Sholdice, "Spain Keeps Firm Grip on Its Outpost in North Africa," *The Irish Times* (Ireland), 28 January 2003, p. 9.

20. Pakenham, p. 10.

21. Daniel Papp, *Contemporary International Relations* (New York: Macmillan, 1984), p. 112.

22. Merie David Kellerman, Jr., "World Bank: Developing Countries Facing Major Shortfalls; Global Growth Expected to Shrink in 2009." American.Gov – Engaging the World, May 25, 2009.

23. Taken from these Internet articles: "U.S. Almost Doubles Military Aid to Pakistan, Dawn Media Group, Pakistan, May 24, 2009 and Arshad Mohammad," U.S. May Boost Military Aid to Pakistan, Reuters News, May 24, 2009.

24. Jimmy Carter, *New Age Journal,* March/April 1990, pp. 52–54, 132–134.

25. Richard Norton Taylor, "International Arms Trade Up 20 percent in Five Years Says Peace Research Group." The Guardian online, London, May 1, 2009.

26. The Treaty of Westphalia (1648), which ended the Thirty Years' War in Europe, is the acknowledged beginning of the modern nation-state.

27. Clara Ferreira-Marques, "Putin Warns Against 'Double Standards on Terrorism," *Reuters Release* (Moscow), 6 November 2001.

28. Ibid.

29. Exective Order 13224: Blocking property with persons who commit, threaten to commit, or support terrorism. Issued by President George W. Bush on 24 September 2001.

30. "EU Gears Up to Fight Terrorism," BBC news release (U.K.). 20 September 2001.

31. Scott Wilson and Al Kamen, "Defense Department's Office of Security Review Reports Global War on Terror Is Given New Name," *The Washington Post,* Section A, Page A04, March 25, 2009.

32. Lloyd Pettiford and David Harding, *Terrorism: The Undeclared War* (Wiltshire, UK: Selectbook Ltd., Davizes, 2004), p. 13.

33. James Woolsey, "The War on Terrorism: The Pitcairn Trust Lecture on World Affairs," *Foreign Policy Research Institute,* Philadelphia, 1 October 2002.

34. Carina Roncevailles, "Weekender: Labor and Management; Campaign to Curb Child Labor," *Business World* (Manila: Business World Publishing), 7 February 2003, p. 27.

35. Peter Wyden, *The Passionate War, The Alternative History of the Spanish Civil War,* (New York: Simon and Schuster, 1983), p. 497.

3

Political Economy

Emmit B. Evans, Jr.

*We face a global economic slowdown and a food
security crisis, both of uncertain magnitude and
duration. Global warming has become more
apparent. These developments affect our efforts to
reduce poverty: the economic slowdown will
diminish the incomes of the poor; the food crisis
will raise the number of hungry people in the
world and push millions more into poverty;
climate change will have a disproportionate
impact on the poor.*

BAN KI-MOON[1]

The global systems of economic production and distribution that
determine the allocation of the earth's resources have created and
maintain a world of gross disparities. The 85 percent of the world's
population living in the Other World of the Global South possess only
20 percent of the planet's wealth, while 80 percent goes to the
15 percent living in the industrialized Global North; these disparities in
wealth translate into related inequities in food, health, shelter, and life
expectancy.[2] And current world trends are toward rapidly increasing
inequality: As United Nations Secretary-General Ban Ki-moon observes
above, the global economic crisis that began in 2008 is widening the
separation between the very rich and most of the world's peoples, while
climate change driven by global warming is unleashing devastating
environmental transformations being felt immediately and most severely
in the Other World.

Chapter 2 described how the global systems of production and distribution that have determined the contrasting lifestyles of the citizens of the industrialized West and the Other World were initiated 500 years ago. The first voyage of Columbus in 1492 marked the beginning of patterns of Western domination that have evolved through a series of stages to the globalization of today.

This chapter traces the evolution of the global political economy from mercantilism to capitalism to globalization, and explores the challenges and opportunities before us as we realize our common future with the peoples of the Other World in a rapidly evolving global society.

POLITICS, ECONOMICS, AND POLITICAL ECONOMY

Politics is commonly defined as the authoritative allocation of values, or who gets what, when, and how. The political process, in other words, determines how those things people value most (such as survival, material goods, wealth, and status) are distributed among a society's, or the world's, peoples. Analysts of the political process have long noted that *power* is the primary factor that determines who gets what and when; an even more concise definition of politics is that it is simply the exercise of power. Power, in turn, is defined as the capacity to control other people's behavior.

There are three types of power: violence, knowledge, and authority. In conflict over the allocation of those things people value, violence is the most fundamental type. Most people place a high premium on avoiding pain and on survival. As Thomas Hobbes observed, when nothing else is turned up, clubs are trumps; the only appeal to violence is violence itself. There are limits, however, on the use of violence to maintain political control: Coercion is expensive, violence tends to escalate, and people will not tolerate rule by violence indefinitely. To maintain their regimes over time, political elites must base their rule more on knowledge and authority.

Most political elites attempt to rule through authority, an institutionalized form of power based on the claim that government has the legitimate right to rule. The authority of government, however, ultimately derives from its ability to control the forces of violence in society. *Government* is defined as the institution that has the *enforceable* right to control people's behavior. In determining the allocation of scarce values, laws are actually a form of sublimated violence through which the decisions of government are backed by the ability to enforce dictates with a court system and police and military forces.

Governments that last over time also derive much of their power from the control of knowledge. Elites use knowledge power both to control what people know and to create and manipulate images and ideologies they want people to believe. As noted by Niccolò Machiavelli, with time, the rule of lions must give way to the rule of foxes.

Analysts of the political process have long noted that self-interest is the driving force, or the engine, of government. Those with political power strive to advance their personal interests, serving broader community interests only to the extent necessary to maintain their positions of control. Closely related is the observation that power corrupts, or compels those with the power to determine who gets what to use public resources for private benefit. And absolute power corrupts absolutely.

The logic of the preceding definitions and observations carries one directly to the conclusion that all governments are *oligarchies,* or political systems controlled by a few to further their self-interests. Governments serve political elites either directly, as in communism and fascism, or indirectly through payoffs derived from serving the interests of economic elites, as in socialism and capitalism. If power determines who gets what and if power corrupts, then there is a natural human tendency for those in control of government to use its institutions and processes for personal gain.

In analyzing political and economic affairs, it is useful to think of politics and *economics* as closely related, interconnected processes. Before the emergence of classical liberalism from the eighteenth-century writings of John Locke and Adam Smith, politics and economics were in fact studied under the single discipline of *political economy.* The artificial separation of that study into fields of political science and economics has been in large part driven by the assertion that there is no necessary connection between politics and economics. The position is that, under a free-market system, government need only be involved in economic affairs to the extent necessary to provide for defense, protect private property rights, and supply some of the infrastructure for the economy.

Wealth and political power are inseparably linked, however. Governments are integrally involved in the economic affairs of most countries, usually serving the interests of the dominant economic group in society. In Communist and Fascist systems, governmental and economic institutions are formally fused, and political and economic elites are one and the same. In Socialist and capitalist systems, nominal separations between governmental and economic institutions are bridged by informal networks of mutual interests between elites and by "revolving door" mechanisms through which individuals circulate back and forth between institutions. The role of political elites in free-market economies is to maintain conditions within which economic elites have the freedom to pursue their interests with a minimum of interference from other interests in society. Freedom here is the freedom to maximize profit through manipulating supply and demand and the psychology of consumer need and preference.

Pause and reflect for a moment on the fundamental connections between political and economic processes apparent in the following definitions:

POLITICS: Who gets what, when, and how
ECONOMICS: The production, distribution, and use of wealth

The perspective of political economy, which views politics and markets as "in a constant state of mutual interaction,"[3] therefore, provides a useful analytical tool.

STAGES OF GLOBAL POLITICAL ECONOMY

Mercantilism

Mercantilism was based on the belief that the power and glory of a government was a direct function of the wealth of its monarchy. The goal of a mercantilist political economy was the accumulation of as much wealth in precious metals as possible. The initial voyages of global exploration financed by Spain and Portugal were essentially quests to locate new sources of gold and silver, and the conquests of Other World territories that followed created colonies to implement and maintain the mercantilist system.

Mercantilist political economy was simple and direct. The colonial powers posted governors, military forces, and administrators in the colonies of the Other World to manage and enforce the mining and transfer of precious metals from the Other World to the monarchies of the West. The first global political economy incorporated the peoples of the Other World into a global order as forced labor to produce wealth allocated to the coffers of the royal families of Europe.[4]

Capitalism

The process of industrialization brought two fundamental changes in global political economy. First, it created a new economic elite of industrial capitalists and financiers whose wealth and power grew to outstrip that of monarchs. As a new economic class of capitalists emerged with increasing power, the control of Western governments shifted from royal families to new oligarchies controlled by those with industrial and financial wealth. Second, the economic value of the colonies shifted from precious metals to the raw materials of industrial production and capitalist trade. The colonial military and administrative structures established as a part of mercantilism now served to transfer industrial raw materials and trade goods to benefit a new capitalist Western elite.

FROM COLONIALISM TO NEOCOLONIALISM AND "DEVELOPMENT"

The exploitation of Other World peoples and resources under mercantilism in the initial stages of capitalism was explicit. The Western colonial powers wanted the wealth of the Other World and used the force of colonial control and administration to extract it. The transition from colonialism to *neocolonialism* described in Chapter 2 was accompanied by a seemingly new approach to Other World political economy that appeared to change an emphasis on exploitation to a new emphasis on the development of Other World countries. *Development* appeared on the international agenda with the winding down of the colonial era and the explosion of newly independent states in the late 1940s.

For many, economic development was part of the logic of political independence. Industrial economies were an integral feature of the Western states that formed the model for most of the new political entities. For the masses caught up in the torrent of rising expectations released by the promises of independence, a higher standard of living seemed a right that had been won through the struggle for political freedom. For others, building the economies of the new states presented opportunities to establish more effective forms of domination and control through new and more subtle forms of colonialism.

Development has been a dominant feature of Other World economic, political, and social affairs for the past 60 years. Disagreements over how it should

The Global Marketplace: Fried chicken in China, Burger King in Korea, and McDonald's in Saudi Arabia.   *Source: Joe Weatherby and Olga Carter*

be pursued and, indeed, how the concept should even be defined have been the source of ongoing conflicts that have ranged from discussion and debate to terrorism and war. Consequently, understanding the contemporary Other World without an understanding of development is difficult. Toward that end, in the following pages we consider various definitions based on competing systems of values and beliefs, survey the history of development efforts, evaluate the successes and failures of those efforts, and consider the prospects for development as we proceed in the twenty-first century.

Values, Ideologies, and Development

Attempts to define development in social, economic, or political terms begin on shaky conceptual grounds. Most people think of the concept as an unfolding of events through a succession of states or changes, each of which is preparatory for the next and all of which contribute to some final end. Such efforts are, thus, exercises in *teleology*, or attempts to explain natural phenomena as being directed toward some final cause or purpose. The assumptions that such ultimate purposes exist and, if they do, that we are intellectually capable of discerning them may be presumptuous from the start.

Human beings are, however, a precocious lot, and doubts about the limits and validity of our knowledge have seldom stopped us from designing grand theories that explain current events in terms of where we are headed. Karl Marx's Communist utopia and John Maynard Keynes's capitalist utopia were both built on teleological theories. What people usually do when defining "where we are headed" is describe that future state in terms of their personal values, or where they would *prefer* for us to go. At this point political values and ideologies (or belief systems) become important in defining development.

Development and Conservative Values   A fundamental element in conservative value systems is the belief that one of the keys to human development lies in providing those with special strengths and abilities the freedom to pursue their individual interests without constraint. In a dialogue with Socrates reported over 2,300 years ago by Plato in *The Republic*, a Greek sophist named Thrasymachus argued that it is the natural right of the strong to take more than their equal share of what the world has to offer. The strong are morally justified in designing and operating the institutions of government to pursue their interests; "might makes right." Over the intervening years, these ideas, which have become known as *the Doctrine of Thrasymachus*, have provided the rationale for a variety of conservative ideologies that often argue—in social Darwinist, survival-of-the-fittest terms— that protecting the special positions and abilities of those who have risen above the common masses is necessary for the evolution of the human species and the grandeur of humanity.

Capitalism is a contemporary version of the Doctrine of Thrasymachus. One of its basic tenets is that the most secure avenue to development is provided by supply-side economic strategies that encourage and facilitate the accumulation of capital by the able and adept. According to Keynes, to develop, societies must pass through a transnational phase in which human greed and avarice are unleashed by the drive for personal profit to propel us through the "tunnel of economic necessity," wherein a concentration of capital in the hands of a few will create an industrial system capable of producing material abundance.

In the Other World, capitalist ideas and ideals have taken the form of "takeoff"—or modernization—theories, which hold that the surest way to achieve development is to maximize the opportunities for investment by private firms, most of which are located in the industrialized world. The goal is to create a critical mass of concentrated capital that will support the takeoff of Other World economies into sustained economic growth. A more liberal interpretation of this theory adds that the investment of public funds in physical and human infrastructure is a necessary complement to the private market.

In capitalist economic systems, the primary measure of economic progress used throughout the world is the rate of increase in gross domestic product (GDP, formerly gross national product [GNP]), a quantitative measure that represents the total of all goods and services produced by an economy in a year. In Other World countries pursuing takeoff development strategies, increases in GDP indicate that economic output is expanding and economic development is taking place.

From a conservative perspective, substantial inequality in the distribution of the wealth created by expanding economic output is viewed as natural, necessary, and just. Human beings are viewed as unequal in essence: The poor are poor because of shortcomings *within themselves*, often considered to stem from race, gender, or class. Efforts to substantially improve their lot are not only futile but unjust in that they take from those at the top of society, who have earned their position through their special talents and virtues, and whose unencumbered progress is necessary for human evolution. Although life is unavoidably harsh for the poor, the capitalist utopia does promise eventual material abundance for all. In the short run, relative economic prosperity for the weaker members of society can best be achieved by the creation of jobs through the concentration of capital into large-scale industries.

Development and Liberal and Radical Values   Those who hold liberal and radical belief systems take a very different view of the nature and degree of differences among people, which lead to very different definitions of the goals of development and how those goals should be pursued. From this perspective, human beings are considered to be equal in essence: Although a certain level of inequality is natural in any society because of relatively minor differences in health, intelligence, and emotional balance, the tremendous inequalities that exist within societies and among countries are viewed as primarily the result of shortcomings *within political and economic processes and institutions*. Julius Nyerere, a former president of Tanzania, captures this idea when he writes

> [E]ven when you have an exceptionally intelligent and hard-working millionaire, the difference between his intelligence, his enterprise, his hard

work, and those of other members of society cannot possibly be proportionate to the difference between their "rewards." There must be *something wrong in a society* where one man, however hard-working or clever he may be, can acquire as great a "reward" as a thousand of his fellows can acquire between them.[5]

Whereas liberals and radicals agree on the essential equality of human beings, they differ in their solutions to inequality. Liberals advocate peaceful, step-by-step reforms, often based on programs to redistribute wealth from the rich to the poor and to create more equal opportunities for the poor to compete. Radicals believe that, given the resources commanded by world political and economic elites and the manner in which they control existing political and economic institutions, established powers will always be able to keep ahead of and nullify any reform efforts. They argue that justice and equality for all can be achieved only through the overthrow of established political and economic institutions and the rebuilding of individual societies and the international order.

Whether achieved through evolutionary or revolutionary means, definitions of development put forth by liberals and radicals consistently target egalitarian values as the end toward which development should be directed, emphasizing freedom from poverty and exploitation. Measures of progress include the degree to which nutrition, health, housing, education, and economic security are available equally to all. Here, *equally* is not defined in absolute terms, but as "free of extremes": Because of differences in abilities that are free of extremes, some have more than others, proportionate to differences in abilities. Such definitions often include the ideal that society should encourage and facilitate the self-fulfillment and self-realization of all. This ideal is central to the utopia envisioned by Marx, where all would share equally in the resources of society and be free to develop their full potential as human beings. More recent examples carry the same theme: A contemporary writer hopes that "development will become a means to serve people";[6] another argues that "development should be a *struggle* to create criteria, goals, and means for self-liberation from misery, inequity, and dependency of all forms."[7]

As the world is becoming increasingly aware of the devastating and threatening global effects of pollution and resource depletion, environmental goals have been merged with egalitarian values to create concepts such as *eco-development*, or balanced social and environmental development. *Sustainable development* is defined as living within the limits of natural systems while ensuring an adequate standard of living for all, meeting the needs of the present without compromising the ability of future generations to meet their own needs.[8]

Such definitions make a sharp distinction between growth and development. *Growth* is defined as things simply getting bigger, or quantitative increases in economic output. In contrast, *development* is defined as things getting better through qualitative changes, which result in improvements in life for all in harmony and balance with nature. Strategies proposed to pursue such change generally emphasize decentralized efforts controlled by local populations to improve life and habitats at the local level. Supporters are encouraged to "think globally and act locally." *Appropriate technology*, or technology suitable to particular applications and needs even when more sophisticated technologies are available, is often a part of such strategies.[9] An example would be the use of 10,000 workers with picks and shovels instead of 10 Caterpillar tractors to build a system of levees to control the flooding of small, family agricultural plots, thus supporting small farmers and workers who might otherwise be unemployed and preserving topsoil that would otherwise be washed away.

A History of Development Efforts

Competing conservative and liberal or radical value systems gave rise to two different approaches to development after World War II. Some countries, including Cuba, Algeria, Libya, Angola, North Korea, Vietnam, and Cambodia, broke out of the world political and economic order that had been established by the colonial powers and joined the states of the Soviet empire and China to establish development programs ostensibly designed to pursue egalitarian values. With assistance from the major Second World powers, they adopted the ideas and ideals of Marx, Lenin, and Mao to create centralized command economies in which property was communally owned and economic activities were closely orchestrated by Socialist and Communist party elites.

Most Other World countries remained within the orbit of the old colonial order. With assistance from the Western industrial nations, they adopted development programs grounded in takeoff theory to establish free-market economies guided by capitalist economic policies and practices.

Free-market approaches are now coming to dominate most of the world, including the former states of the Soviet bloc and China. To understand the history of development efforts, one must explore the ascendancy of the free-market system of international capitalism.

Immanuel Wallerstein employs the concept of political economy in his study of the system of international capitalism, which he terms the *capitalist world-economy*, that has expanded from its genesis in sixteenth-century Europe to drive much of the politics and economics of the globe today.[10] Tracing that expansion, Wallerstein describes how the pattern of international relations among great world powers ranges on a fluid continuum: At one end, there is an almost even balance among powers of roughly equal strength (a rare and unstable condition); in the middle the powers group into two or more camps, with no side being able to impose its will (the usual state of international affairs); at the other end, a single great power is able to dominate (also a rare and unstable condition). He defines the latter end of the continuum as *hegemony*, or a situation in which a single world power is so dominant that it "can largely impose its rules and its wishes . . . in the economic, political, military, diplomatic, and even cultural arenas."[11] Such a condition of hegemony existed when the United Kingdom dominated world affairs from roughly 1815 to 1873, when the United States came to occupy a similar position of world dominance from 1945 until the early 1970s, and with the end of the cold war and the emergence of the United States as the world's sole hyper-power.

U.S. Hegemony and a New Postwar World Order The establishment of hegemony by the United States at the very same time that programs to develop the Other World were launched had a profound effect on the nature of development efforts and the role and position of Other World states in the international political economy. The United States emerged from World War II as the unchallenged dominant power in the world. It was able to use its power to implement a new world order that was carefully designed to serve its interests and the interests of the other former colonial powers in the capitalist world economy. The foundation for this new order was laid through the Bretton Woods agreements, signed by the Allied powers in 1944.

The Bretton Woods system erected three pillars around which the new order was built. The International Monetary Fund (IMF) was established to further cooperation on monetary matters among the countries of the world. Under IMF guidance, the U.S. dollar became the standard against which the value of other currencies was set, and the United States became the banker for the world. The General Agreement on Tariffs and Trade (GATT) was designed to promote world trade. Periodic trade conferences were scheduled to facilitate negotiations among world trading partners with the goal of maintaining "free" trade through low tariffs on internationally traded goods and services. The International Bank for Reconstruction and Development—or World Bank—which was originally created to facilitate investment in Europe after World War II, turned toward stimulating investment in the Other World.

The United Nations (UN) was chartered in San Francisco in 1945 as an international governmental organization designed to resolve political and economic conflicts between and among countries and promote world peace and development (see Figure 3.1). Two quasilegislative bodies constitute the core of the UN: the General Assembly, to which most states (now about 192) belong, and the Security Council.

Only the Security Council can take direct military action to enforce its decisions. The Council is composed of 5 permanent members—the United States, Britain, France, Russia, and China (each of which has the power to veto any proposal of the Council)—and 10 temporary, rotating members (none of which has veto power). Lacking the power to enforce its decisions, the General Assembly serves basically as a forum for expressing the opinions of member states.

Early Development Efforts With the success of efforts to rebuild the economies of Europe and Japan fresh at hand, the Western industrial nations launched a flurry of bilateral and multilateral efforts in the 1960s, which was dubbed the "development decade." The stated intent was to propel Other World economies to a point from which they could take off and achieve self-sustaining growth. John Kenneth Galbraith, a Harvard economics professor who had served as U.S. ambassador to India, published a book in 1964 that aptly described these early development efforts as attempts to copy the institutions and processes of the modern industrial powers. "Development," he observed, "is the faithful imitation of the developed."[12] Galbraith noted three characteristics of these attempts: symbolic modernization, maximized economic growth, and selective growth.

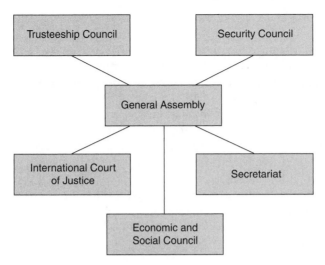

FIGURE 3.1 Core of the United Nations

Symbolic modernization gave a developing country the appearance of modernity. Airports and four-lane highways were built, tall buildings were erected, and impressive government offices were constructed. Efforts to maximize economic growth were directed at increasing economic output as measured by GNP. Growth strategies emphasized large initial capital investments from the World Bank, from private firms located primarily in the industrial nations, and from First World governments, with the goal of establishing industrial bases that could then be expanded. Domestic rates of taxation and savings were set to promote the fastest rate of growth possible.

Some efforts were targeted at building the infrastructure for an industrial society through the strategy of selective growth. A variety of foreign aid programs, many organized under the umbrella of the Development Assistance Committee of the Organization for Economic Cooperation and Development (OECD), were created to address this need. Electric, water, sewer, and communications systems were installed; loans were made to farmers and small businesspersons; and agricultural education and community development activities were initiated. The "green revolution" of the 1960s and 1970s is a good example of a selective growth strategy. Increases in agricultural production were sought to generate funds for industrial expansion through earnings from export crops and to increase the supply of food in Other World countries. Programs were undertaken to encourage the replacement of family-scale farms, which used native seeds, composting, traditional pest-control methods, and hand implements, with large-scale agribusinesses employing hybrid seed strains, fertilizers, pesticides, herbicides, irrigation, and mechanized farm machinery.

Those who conceived of and measured development in terms of increases in economic output were pleased with the results of these early efforts: With some exceptions, development programs were generating dramatic increases in

GNP. However, it did not take long for those who had hoped that the development decade would result in a better standard of living for the masses of Other World peoples to realize that the strategies described above were not contributing significantly to that goal. Benefits were accruing primarily to a few, while living conditions for most were not markedly improving; in fact, for some they were actually declining. Along with Galbraith's book, others with titles such as *False Start in Africa*[13] pointed out that the hollow imitation of Western symbols and an emphasis on supply-side economic policies, industrial development, and Western technologies would not result in the kind of economic and social change that would significantly benefit the many. The almost singular emphasis on building an industrial infrastructure and raising GNP meant that basic essentials such as food, housing, and health services were often neglected in favor of exporting minerals and cash crops to earn foreign exchange, much of which was sent back overseas in the form of profits for foreign corporations or spent on importing luxury goods for indigenous political and economic elites.

A Balance Sheet of Development   We are now in a position to evaluate the accomplishments of more than 50 years of sustained development efforts guided by takeoff theory. Advocates of this approach point with satisfaction to statistics that show that Other World GDP per capita has been growing at higher rates than were achieved by the industrial nations in comparable periods of their history, that life expectancy is increasing faster in decades than it did in an entire century in the industrialized world, and that substantial gains have been made in literacy and access to education. Critics point out that while these statistics accurately reflect the fact that conditions have improved in some ways for many and in many ways for some, they hide the true nature of economic processes that have resulted in tremendous disparities within Other World societies and among Other World countries: More than one-third are now so poor and economically underdeveloped that they are placed in a special "Fourth World" category in which development seems impossible.

Statistics compiled in the UN *Human Development Report* provide a useful balance sheet of the status of human development.[14] While the estimated share of the world's population living in extreme poverty fell from 28 percent in 1990 to 21 percent in 2000, some 2.5 billion people (roughly 40 percent of the world's population) survive on less than $2 per day, and some 15 percent survive on less than $1 per day. In the Other World, 1 billion people do not have safe water, 2.6 billion do not have adequate sanitation, 800 million suffer from malnutrition, and 11 million children die each year before reaching their fifth birthdays. While average income per household is growing worldwide, more than 1.3 billion people live in extreme poverty. Over the past decade, poverty rates have increased in sub-Saharan Africa; Latin America and the Middle East have registered no progress; and gains in South Asia have been negated by a growing population, creating an increase in the absolute number of people living in poverty.

After completing a similar evaluation in which he noted there were more people living in absolute poverty in 1987 than in 1960, Paul Harrison concluded

[T]his balance sheet can only be read as progress if one abstracts from the human realities. In terms of concrete individual experience, there is a greater absolute quantity of human suffering in the world today than ever before, and all the indications are that it will increase as we approach the millennium. For all the talk and all the action about development, *virtually no progress has been made in the task of eliminating absolute poverty; indeed, there has been gradual regress.*[15]

Harrison's comments parallel those of an Egyptian who once commented that the overall effect of development efforts in Egypt was that more people now lived longer in greater misery. Such is the state of human development throughout much of the Other World today as progress falters in reaching the Millennium Development Goals set by the UN General Assembly in 2000.

The links among poverty, security, and population growth are important in understanding this increase in absolute poverty. Poverty and fertility rates are directly related: The higher the degree of poverty in a society, the higher the rate of population increase. The instinct to survive dictates that poor families have more children than wealthier families for practical economic reasons: Children are a source of security for those living at the margins of survival. More children means more hands to help with the difficult tasks of eking a living out of a subsistence environment; a working child can contribute to household resources by age 6 and produce more than she or he consumes by age 12. More children increase the probability that one of them might be fortunate enough to secure an education, a rare job, and cash earnings to contribute to the family. More children means a greater likelihood that someone will be around to help when old age makes it impossible to survive on one's own. High infant and childhood mortality rates mean that the odds of accomplishing

Other World Shopping: "Supermarket Shopping" for prepackaged goods in Pasic, Peru. *Source: Craig Arceneaux*

all of these objectives are improved by having enough children to replace those who die young.

In transferring much of the wealth of the Other World to the industrialized nations, the forces of colonialism and neocolonialism have substantially contributed to the poverty that is fueling population increases in the Other World. These global shifts in wealth and family security have also contributed to declining fertility rates in the First World. Population policies that address fundamental issues of family security, rather than simply encouraging or enforcing birth control, are the surest way to reduce rates of population growth.

The manner in which the international political economy produces and distributes wealth is well illustrated by the production and distribution of world food resources. If the wheat, rice, and other grains produced throughout the world were distributed equally to all the world's peoples, each individual would receive 3,600 calories per day, well above the average U.S.-recommended daily allowances of 2,700 calories for adult males, 2,000 for adult females, and 1,300 to 3,000 for teenagers. Yet 9 million children die every year from starvation, and 4 billion people do not have enough to eat. The typical Western family of four consumes more grain (directly and indirectly in the form of meat) than a poor Indian family of 20.[16]

India, where more than one-third of the world's hungry people live, is one of the top cash-crop exporters in the Other World. The "green revolution" was instrumental in boosting India and a number of other countries to the status of agricultural exporters. The benefits of increased agricultural production in those countries, however, have often accrued to those wealthy farmers who could obtain bank loans to purchase the large irrigated farms; mechanized equipment; and expensive seeds, fertilizers, pesticides, and herbicides required for green revolution agriculture. Many poor farmers in these countries have in the process been displaced, driven to marginal dryland plots or the cities where they are unable to afford the food now produced through expensive farming methods on the lands they once tilled.

Brazil provides an especially illustrative example of the balance sheet generated by an economic development process driven by the singular pursuit of increased economic production. In 1964, a military coup established a new government that opened the country to foreign investment by providing an array of attractive incentives and freedoms. In the following 10 years, which became known as "the Brazilian economic miracle," the country's GNP tripled and Brazilian executives became for a time the highest paid in the world. Meanwhile, the real income of 80 percent of the population declined; the production of basic necessities such as food, clothing, and housing remained stagnant; and Brazil's infant mortality rate became the second highest in Latin America. Foreign-owned corporations gained control of 100 percent of Brazil's tire and rubber production, 95 percent of its automobile production, and 80 percent of its television and radio industry (while 60 Brazilian electronics firms were driven out of business or taken over by foreign firms). Foreign-owned companies, some with holdings in the millions of acres, displaced Brazilian farmers and shifted the emphasis from agricultural production to export products such as soybeans and beef for fast-food restaurants in the First World. These shifts created a shortage of black beans, the staple in the diet of Brazil's poor, with a resulting increase in malnutrition.[17] Surveying these statistics, a group of Catholic bishops and clerics issued a statement on the condition of the Brazilian people in 1975, concluding that

> [T]he Brazilian miracle has resulted in privileges for the wealthy. It has come as a curse upon those who have not asked for it. The rich become always richer and the poor always poorer in this process of economic concentration. Far from being the inevitable result of natural deficiencies, this tragedy is the consequence of international capitalism. Development came to be defined not in terms of the interests of Brazilian society, but in terms of the profits made by foreign corporations and their associates in our country.[18]

More recent "economic miracles" repeat the same pattern. In Mexico by the early 1990s, strong economic growth had resulted in a dramatic concentration of wealth and a widening gap between the rich and the poor: While 92.4 percent of the population earned less than $5,700 U.S. per year, the top of Mexico's socioeconomic hierarchy was occupied by seven Mexican billionaires, more than in Britain or Saudi Arabia. The Mexican government signed a free-trade agreement with the United States and Canada—the North American Free Trade Agreement (NAFTA)—that encouraged a flood of foreign investment and ownership in the country. Most recently, increasing growth and increasing inequality have characterized the political economies of the Asian Tigers of China, Taiwan, South Korea, Thailand, Indonesia, and Malaysia.

Understanding the Balance Sheet   The preceding balance sheet is not difficult to understand if one considers that the roots of capitalism lie in conservative value systems. Development based on takeoff theory has primarily benefited the strong because it is intended to; the accounting system of the capitalist world economy prioritizes individual gain, not egalitarian values. The history of Other World development is consistent with the 400-year trend of capitalism—an ever-increasing concentration of wealth in the hands of a few, much of which is spent on luxury consumption and speculation rather than being reinvested in any industrial infrastructure that might significantly benefit the many in either the short or the long run.

Through an analysis known as *dependency theory*, liberals and radicals in fact argue that, given the position of the Other World in the international political economy, development that would substantially improve the lives of a majority of the Other World's peoples is unlikely to occur at all. They point out that the designation "Third World" is an accurate description of that position: Although there is really only *one* world of political economy, with all the world's states linked in various fashions to the whole, most of the countries of Africa, Asia, and Latin America occupy tertiary positions on the periphery of the dominant political and economic order. Their primary function, as it was under formal colonialism, is to provide raw materials and cheap labor for the industrialized powers. Other World countries are now dominated by structures of neocolonialism that differ little in substance from the colonialism of the past.

From the perspective of dependency theorists, Other World political systems are particularly dependent on the Western industrial powers. Neocolonialism operates through the collusion of Other World political elites, who have been co-opted and coerced into serving foreign interests. International lending institutions often ensnare Other World elites in Mafia-like lending schemes that ensure allegiance to and control by Western interests.[19] Independence means only that political institutions originally established to facilitate and enforce the extraction of wealth from the Other World are now occupied by African, Asian, and Latin American politicians and bureaucrats instead of by expatriate colonial officials. These new elites serve as *brokers*, managing the flow of resources from their countries in return for brokerage fees (or commissions) in the form of foreign aid and other payoffs, which they use to maintain their positions of political control and to build their personal fortunes.

The rule of many Other World political elites in the neocolonial era constitutes a contemporary mercantilism in which national political economies are operated to increase the wealth of the rulers.[20] The widespread corruption, or the use of public office for private gain, that pervades Other World politics is a key factor in explaining why the development programs of many countries have done little to improve the lot of the masses. Much of the political instability endemic to Other World political systems stems from the fact that governments operated openly for private gain (or *kleptocracies*) have little legitimacy among, or acceptance by, a significant proportion of the population, in neocolonial times as in the past. The Al Qaeda movement of Osama bin Laden is one example of an attempt to free a country (in this case, Saudi Arabia) from a corrupt and repressive regime propped up by a neocolonial power (in this case, the United States).

Power vacuums resulting from the end of the cold war are contributing to spiraling levels of violence in many parts of the Other World. In the decades before the fall of the Soviet empire, both the United States and the Soviet Union delivered a substantial portion of their foreign aid in the form of military assistance. Other World dictators who were willing to wave one flag or another as clients in the ideological contest between capitalism and communism, sometimes adroitly playing one side off against the other, amassed enormous military capabilities. With the cold war balance of power now ended, stockpiles of weapons are fueling disastrous conflicts between and within Other World states. This factor played prominently in the rise of the Taliban in Afghanistan following the defeat of the Soviet Union in 1990, the 1990 invasion of Kuwait by Iraq, and in bloody civil wars and anarchy in Somalia in 1992, in Rwanda beginning in 1994,[21] and in Liberia in 2003.[22]

Perhaps more difficult to understand than the balance sheet of development is the fact that those countries that followed Communist and Socialist development strategies have been only a little more successful in accomplishing egalitarian goals and probably less successful in preserving the natural environment.

The inequalities that have developed in these states, although less dramatic than those in the capitalist world, indicate that the tendency of the powerful to serve their self-interests is not unique to capitalism. Economic growth and social inequality is a common pattern, with increases in economic output accompanied by increasing inequality throughout history.[23] The 400-year history of capitalism is an extension of a trend that began 6,000 years ago when humankind first established urban-based civilizations capable of creating wealth in surplus of the resources needed for human survival, a trend accelerated 2,000 years ago when Western civilization emerged in the Greek city-states and legitimized the value of individualistic materialism. While an appreciation of capitalist ideology helps one understand the particular details of the process through which development has come to benefit primarily a few in the capitalist world economy, one must go beyond the level of ideology to the underlying realities of politics, power, and self-interest to understand the universal links between increased economic output and greater inequality.

Increases in economic output, in Mesopotamia or ancient Greece or the Other World of the post–World War II era, go primarily to those groups within a society, and to those states within the international political economy, that are able to control the forces of violence and the institutions and policies that determine the distribution of that output. At this level of analysis, ideologies primarily represent efforts by political elites to use knowledge power to convince the public that the government is being operated in the public interest. While ideologies are useful in defining the goals and values that people of various persuasions believe *should* be served by development, they are relatively insignificant in determining political realities. The actual outputs of governments operating with "competing" ideologies are only marginally different; in this context, one can appreciate the observation that while under capitalism man exploits man, under communism it's the other way around.

GLOBALIZATION

The 1970s marked the emergence of globalization as the latest stage in the evolution of the global political economy. A worldwide recession in the 1970s followed in the 1980s by a crisis in the repayment of debts to international lenders by Other World governments provided the rationale for a shift away from a government-centered approach to development that emphasized Import Substitution policies to replace imported products with locally produced substitutes. *Neo-liberal economics* identified "too much government" as the cause of poor economic and financial performance, and offered a vision of development through cutting back the role of the state and privatizing public services and all aspects of the economy to allow unrestricted free-market "competition" and trade. Other World economies were viewed as insufficiently integrated into the global economy, and neo-liberal policies purportedly allowed them to size the opportunities of what came to be known in the 1990s as globalization.[24]

Globalization is an international regime in which the economic interests of multinational corporations and other nonstate actors (such as the International Monetary Fund and the World Trade Organization) are coming to supersede the interests and powers of individual states. Contemporary globalization is qualitatively different from the geographic and quantitative expansion of global economic activity that began with the first voyage of Columbus. While loyalty had previously gone toward serving the interests of national entities, from the sovereigns of the mercantilist era to the nationally based industries (and workforces) of global capitalism, loyalty is now toward the bottom line of transnational corporations and organizations. *Colonialism* was defined in the preceding chapter as a relationship in which a group of people located in one country is subject to the authority of people in another country. The logic and the drive of the capitalist world economy is now creating a fundamentally different global regime in which all the world's people are increasingly subject to the power of multinational institutions, and the workforces and resources of any country are valued as pieces to be integrated into serving private global economic interests.

National boundaries and loyalties are of little significance in a global economy driven by the exclusive and ceaseless pursuit of profit. In the evolving age of postindustrial production, the demand (and compensation) for labor is predicted to decline as a transnational elite seeks custom, designer goods made by specialized producers hired at the lowest wages possible from a global labor pool, rather than the standardized products of the mass assembly lines that have provided employment to many in the past.

Riccardo Petrella, a futurist for the European Union, describes how the forces of globalization are separating all the world's peoples into two classes that cut across national boundaries, divided into the "fast" and the "slow" on the basis of access to computer-based information and communications technologies. In this evolving structure, a global upper class of the affluent and privileged living in a high-tech archipelago of hyperdeveloped, walled, and gated city-regions and consisting of less than one-eighth of the world's population is emerging among a global underclass consisting of seven-eighths of the world's population left to fend for itself in a disintegrating social and environmental wasteland.[25]

Colin Leys defines this new international regime as a world

1. Dominated by multinational corporations
2. Regulated by the International Monetary Fund
3. Enforced by the military might of the United States[26]

In an era characterized by the privatization of government functions, private mercenary armies are also being formed to enforce this new global system. Private companies such as Xe Services (originally Blackwater USA) of Moyock, North Carolina; DynCorp of Reston, Virginia; and Executive Outcomes, a South African corporation formed by ex-members of the notorious apartheid-era 32nd Battalion of the South African special forces, offer states and corporations able to afford multimillion-dollar fees a full spectrum of military services and products.[27] Revenues from the private security market are expected to rise from $55 billion in 1990 to $202 billion by 2010. Private mercenary armies have been active over the past decade on every continent but Antarctica.[28] Every post–cold war U.S. military operation from the Persian Gulf to Somalia, Zaire, Haiti, Bosnia, Kosovo, Croatia, Afghanistan, and Iraq has involved significant involvement from private military corporations. Employees of private contractors working for the United States in Iraq as part of the war effort have outnumbered U.S. military personnel serving in the country.

The development programs that characterized much of the history of the Other World beginning in the 1940s are being rapidly abandoned under globalization. Since the 1970s, foreign aid programs have been steadily and significantly reduced as Other World countries are directed to pursue their economic development through integrating their economies into the global marketplace. As part of globalization, the functions of the GATT have been assumed by the World Trade Organization (WTO). Established in 1995 and headquartered in Geneva, Switzerland, the WTO has become a powerful multinational force working to set the rules of trade between and among the countries of the world.

The forces of globalization are driving down the standard of living of many in the Other World. The internal affairs of many Other World countries are coming increasingly under the direct control of IMF officials, who are imposing *structural adjustment programs* that change domestic spending patterns to make possible repayments on enormous debts owed to First World financial institutions. These changes often include cuts in health, education, and other social service programs. Much of this debt was incurred during oil shortages in the 1970s and grew with an increase in interest rates in the 1980s. In African countries, this debt typically amounts to five times annual export income.[29] Many Latin American countries now pay out one-fourth of their export receipts in debt payments on long-term loans, some of which do not even cover interest due. *Privatization programs*, which transfer the control of government services to private, for-profit firms, are further loosening the thin ties that link public resources to public needs. Globalized corporate agriculture is destroying jobs and small farms that have sustained Other World populations for millennia.[30]

The social, economic, and environmental costs of globalization have sparked backlashes in both the Other World and industrialized countries. The massive popular protest against the WTO in Seattle in 1999 brought together a coalition of trade unionists, environmentalists, farmers, students, religious activists, women, and indigenous peoples that now shadow meetings of the WTO, IMF, World Bank, and other multinational economic organizations around the planet.[31] The infusion of Western economic and cultural forms has sparked resistance throughout the world that Benjamin Barber aptly characterizes as driving a conflict between "jihad" (or reactionary fundamentalism) and the "McWorld" of global capitalism.[32]

The U.S.-led War on Terror following the September 11, 2001, attacks on the World Trade Center and the U.S. Pentagon, U.S. policies emphasizing unilateralism over multilateralism, and the U.S. invasion of Iraq in 2003 present additional challenges to globalization. Restrictions on immigration, foreign travel, and international trade stemming from heightened security measures, foreign policy disputes, rising worldwide anti-Americanism, and mounting violence against U.S. military forces, diplomatic offices, and commercial interests around the world are all working to severely restrict the openness required for a global economy.

CONCLUSIONS

The Politics of Change

Globalization and reactions against globalization both work to undermine the evolution of more democratic forms of government and society that could lead to more egalitarian and environmentally sustainable development processes. Globalization heralds a global class apartheid in which the strong are free to pursue their interests unencumbered by any sense of connection with or responsibility to the social commonwealth or the environmental commons. Fundamentalist reactions against globalization are driven by a parochial exclusiveness and hostility toward others at odds with the essence of democratic values and culture.

In contrast, those who prefer a different future face tremendous challenges. The qualitative changes in societies and in the international political economy necessary to achieve change that would serve egalitarian and environmental values are vast in range and scale. The range of change would have to include political, economic, and social processes and institutions, for all of these aspects of human organization are inseparably linked. Within this web of interconnections, it is impossible to separate economic development from political development or social development; improvements in the economic conditions of the less powerful could be achieved only through parallel improvements in political and social conditions. The scale of change would have to be fundamental, for the processes and institutions that currently determine the use and allocation of the world's resources are deeply and firmly entrenched. Changes of this extent would require radical transformations in the power relationships that hold these systems together. Changes in the technologies of development would have to be equally fundamental. It would require a 3,600 percent increase in the consumption of the earth's resources to bring Other World countries to the income levels of the developed countries using current technologies.

As we proceed into the second decade of the twenty-first century, however, there are signs that the centralized Western power structures that have long dominated our affairs are beginning to crumble under the pressure of converging crises of overpopulation, environmental destruction, resource scarcity, economic discontinuity, and sociopolitical decay. These crises may create opportunities for change in chaos not present in more stable times. As the Chinese have long noted, when there is great disorder under the heavens, the opportunities for change are excellent. Milton Friedman observes that "only a crisis . . . produces real change." And Abba Eban notes how "history teaches us that men and nations behave wisely once they have exhausted all other alternatives."

E. F. Schumacher observes that while some have challenged the ethic of materialism and argued for different priorities throughout history, "Today, however, this message reaches us not solely from the sages and saints but from the actual course of physical events. It speaks to us in the language of terrorism, genocide, breakdown, pollution, exhaustion."[33] Samuel Huntington hypothesizes a resurgence of Confucian, Japanese, Islamic, Hindu, Slavic-Orthodox, Latin American, and African civilizations against a Western civilization now at the peak of its power and global intrusiveness.[34] Benjamin Barber describes forces working to diminish the power of the nation-state.[35] Alvin Toffler argues that we are at one of the greatest turning points in history as breakdown and exhaustion in health, education, transportation, welfare, urban, and ecological systems converge to challenge the centralized power structures that control our societies.[36]

Support for these theses can be seen in mounting signs of institutional collapse and widespread public disenchantment in the Western industrial nations, and the recent rise of left-center governments as a reaction to the free-market policies of globalization in Brazil, Argentina, Uruguay, Venezuela, Bolivia, Honduras, Nicaragua, Guatemala, Paraguay, and El Salvador. Democratization and local autonomy movements erupting across the Other World, fueled by the irrepressible force of global mass communications, support these theses as well. A proliferation of globally based nongovernmental organizations (NGOs) is working to build a global civic culture and new global institutions working to control the excesses of globalization and directing the forces of global integration toward the common good.[37] Grassroots microcredit programs are spreading throughout the Other World to provide small businesspeople and producers with the capital needed to develop small-scale enterprises that employ and empower.

Changing power relations could provide those who envision development as a way to serve people and to create the means for self-liberation with opportunities in the coming years that seemed impossible in the past.[38] If the information technologies that are elevating knowledge to a position as the dominant source of power were dispersed among the world's masses, the resulting diffusion of power could result in the first true democracies the world has ever known. On the other hand, if the new technologies are controlled by a few, we could be plunged into a new Dark Age of Orwellian proportions. In the coming decades it is likely that those who control knowledge and the technologies of knowledge will also control wealth, violence, and the institutions of government.

As we proceed through a time of pivotal change in human affairs, the individual actions of each of us will count more than at any time in previous years, for we are all participants—whether as consumers, investors, or political activists—in the international political economy that we share with the peoples of the Other World. Our common future depends on our common efforts to build a more socially and ecologically sustainable world.

Summary

The first global political economy of mercantilism was created as part of the colonial era that began with the first voyage of Columbus in 1492. Mercantilism evolved into capitalism as industrial and financial elites came to control Western governments. Beginning in the 1940s, Other World international relations and domestic affairs were dominated by a concern with development. Driven primarily by the capitalist world economy, development programs guided by take-off theory resulted in significant increases in GNP/GDP and improvements in the lives of some Other World peoples; they also contributed to increasing inequality and growing numbers of people living in absolute poverty. While take-off theorists attribute these problems to the necessities of progress, dependency theorists view them as the result of the exploitation of the Other World by the industrial powers and Other World political elites through structures of neocolonialism. Advocates of both schools ground their positions in political ideologies that express fundamental beliefs and values about the way the world should be.

Globalization and fundamentalist reactions against globalization are now interacting to undermine the possibility of a more democratic future, with direct implications for increasing inequality, poverty, and environmental decline and increasing levels of political, economic, and social instability. Other trends indicate the possibility of changes in power relations that could make possible development designed to promote egalitarian and environmental values. We are living at a pivotal time of convergence in human affairs that will have fundamental consequences for the future of the global community we inhabit with the peoples of the Other World.

ISSUES FOR DISCUSSION
1. Can you refute the Doctrine of Thrasymachus?

The Doctrine of Thrasymachus consists of two reinforcing parts. Part I states that it is the natural right of the strong to take more than their equal share of what the world has to offer. This is a philosophical statement that addresses what is considered to be right and wrong, good and bad. Here, Thrasymachus asserts the unbridled right of the strong to take from the weak, drawing on their physical strength, intelligence, or any other attribute that would enable them to overpower others. Any means imaginable, including violence and fraud, is morally justified. Part II states that might makes right. Here, Thrasymachus addresses how the strong use government to serve their interests by writing and enforcing laws that work to their advantage. The idea that whatever the mighty say is right is right underlies the concept of relative justice—whatever the strong say is just is just, with some laws legitimately applied unequally to different citizens and some laws legitimately applied only to certain groups. For Thrasymachus, justice is whatever is in the interests of the strong.

Liberty, or the freedom to pursue one's interests without constraint, and equality, or freedom from relative poverty and exploitation, are conflicting values; a society cannot encourage one without sacrificing the other. On the one hand, if citizens are free to pursue private interests without constraint, some will invariably take advantage of others, creating greater inequality in society. On the other hand, efforts to build more egalitarian social orders can be pursued only by restraining personal liberty. The ideas expressed in the Doctrine of Thrasymachus are, thus, among the most significant in the history of political thinking in that they so unequivocally proclaim the value of liberty. They take us to the core of one of the central dilemmas of political organization:

Money, Sun, and Sand: Since the 1970s, Georgetown, capital of the Cayman Islands, has provided a tax-free refuge for the funds of the rich and famous from around the world. The branches of many foreign banks have been opened here to serve these customers. *Source: Joe Weatherby*

Government policies that restrain liberty stifle initiative, while policies that encourage liberty result in exploitation. As the basis for the conservative ideas and ideals that provide the foundations of capitalism, takeoff theory, and the ethic of globalization, they also take us to the heart of what development should be and can be about and to the inherent conflict between capitalism rooted in liberty and democracy rooted in equality.

If Thrasymachus is right, then all governments are oligarchies, or political systems operated by a few to serve their interests. While most governments claim to have been created by God to serve the people, such claims are part of the fraud perpetuated by elites to hide the fact that government is in fact designed to serve the interests of the strong. If the political institutions that control peoples' behavior to allocate societies' scarce values are operated by a few to serve their interests, then what we call "civilized" life rests on the exploitation of the weak.

Attempts to refute or support the ideas expressed by Thrasymachus are central to political philosophy. Can you refute the Doctrine of Thrasymachus? If so, how? If not, why not? Consider your response from both normative and empirical perspectives: Normative analysis is concerned with what should be, or with moral judgments of right and wrong; empirical analysis is concerned with what is, or the way things are in actual fact.

2. Internationally, how can you best protect yourself in an era of globalization and increasing inequality and conflict?

With 4.6 percent of the world's population, the United States presently consumes 40 percent of the world's resources. The citizens of the other industrialized countries consume another 40 percent. The 85 percent of the world's population living in the Other World are left to live from the remaining 20 percent of world resources.

These inequalities have been cited as one of the sources of the conflict resulting in the attacks on the World Trade Center on September 11, 2001. In his book *Blowback: The Costs and Consequences of American Empire*, Chalmers Johnson posits that in the decade following the end of the cold war, the United States used military force and financial manipulation to help maintain and increase the inequalities previously described, and that the twenty-first century may be a time of reckoning for the United States.[39] Specifically addressing the events of September 11 in a *Los Angeles Times* Opinion article titled, "The Lessons of Blowback," Johnson argues that in response to the attacks, the United States should

- Listen to the grievances of the Islamic peoples.
- Stop propping up repressive regimes in the area.
- Protect Israel's security but denounce its apartheid practices in Palestinian areas.
- Reform its "globalization" policies so that they no longer mean that the rich are getting richer and the poor poorer.

Johnson concludes that if the United States' only response to the September 11 attack is military reprisal, "the end result will not be 'victory' in a 'war on terrorism' but a further cycle of terrorist attacks, American casualties and escalation."[40] A 2006 National Intelligence Estimate (an analysis of U.S. security presenting the consensus view of all 16 U.S. intelligence agencies) titled "Trends in Global Terrorism: Implications for the United States," concluded that the war in Iraq has fueled global terrorism by fanning Islamic radicalism.[41] And a top military advisor to the U.S. Central Command cautions that the Obama administration's excalating military actions in Pakistan and Afghanistan ". . . are creating more enemies than they eliminate."[42]

Considering the implications of the preceding for your own safety and security, what do you feel you can do to most effectively address the increasing level of international violence characteristic of today's world?

3. Do you owe posterity and yourself a sustainable world?

The human species has been on the planet for an estimated 4.5 million years. For the bulk of that time, we had little effect on the natural environment, as our hunting and gathering activities caused only slight disturbances in the self-regulating natural ecologies we inhabited. We began concerted and determined efforts to dominate and control the environment to serve human ends 6,000 years ago with the first urban-based civilizations and have since been so successful that our technologies are now overwhelming the natural systems we evolved with and upon which we depend for our survival. Our impact has become so substantial that we have damaged many of the self-regulating and self-balancing mechanisms that controlled the natural world, creating disturbed ecosystems that can be kept from chaos and collapse only through constant human intervention and manipulation.

Many in the scientific community are now questioning our ability to maintain the necessary balances and equilibriums. The cumulative and long-term effects of pollution, resource depletion, and species and habitat losses seem to be so significantly altering the living world that doubts are being raised about our ability to sustain life as we know it. Unless we dramatically change our stewardship of the earth, our environment will probably become so irretrievably mutilated over the coming decades that future generations could suffer vast misery.

In response, some ask, "So what? Why should we care? What has posterity ever done for me?" At its extreme, the ethic of globalization in fact includes a nihilistic view that the planet is already so overburdened with population and pollution problems that it is beyond saving and that we should, therefore, live life to the hilt in the time we have remaining. This view provides another rationalization for the short-term greed that is driving the contemporary global economy.

Do you owe posterity a sustainable world? If not, why not? If so, on what is this obligation based? Exactly what are you willing to give up in your current lifestyle and levels of consumption to make life tolerable and possible for future generations? In your own future, how will you deal with the more frequent and intense hurricanes, flooding, drought, wildfires, and heat waves resulting from global climate change? In pursuit of these goals, are you willing to become more actively involved in the political process? How?

4. What are the challenges to and costs of attempting to maintain colonial rule in the twenty-first century?

While Iraq was not involved in the September 11, 2001, attacks on the World Trade Center and the U.S. Pentagon, it appears to many that a group known as the Neoconservatives in the White House used the event along with unsubstantiated claims that Iraq possessed weapons of mass destruction that posed an imminent threat to the world to justify the 2003 U.S. invasion and occupation of Iraq.

In an article titled "Beyond Regime Change," Sandy Tolan describes current U.S. policy in the Middle East as a neo-imperial vision to redraw the map of the Middle East as ambitious as the 1916 Sykes-Picot Agreement through which the British and the French carved up the Ottoman Empire.[43] Tolan documents a blueprint to

1. Control the flow of Middle Eastern oil
2. Ensure Israel's continued regional military superiority

Much of this "neo-imperial vision" is not in fact new, but a throwback to direct colonial rule. In the United States' role as the world's sole hyper-power, U.S. officials seem to believe they have the military might to reestablish the kind of direct rule exercised by the United States during the colonial era in the Philippines, Cuba, and Puerto Rico and by the British and French in their colonial empires. The initial administration of an occupied Iraq by U.S. officials and no-bid contracts to insider U.S. firms to "rebuild" the country met the basic criteria of colonial occupation defined in international law: territorial annexation, rule by foreign nationals, and control of natural resources.[44] Since the transfer of limited power and sovereignty to Iraqis with the disbanding of the Coalition Provisional Authority in 2004, the United States has worked to establish a neocolonial Iraqi government sympathetic to American interests. The Obama administration's troop drawdowns in 2009 do not include U.S. Special Forces, trainers, and advisors slated to remain in Iraq into the future on permanent "enduring bases" constructed around the country.

What are the challenges to and costs of attempting to maintain colonial and neocolonial rule in the twenty-first century? What forces help make such control possible? What forces are working against it? Will the U.S. government be able to successfully maintain a broker government that serves its interests? Why or why not?

Review Questions

1. Define *politics* and *economics*. How are politics and economics related? What is the role of government in the process of economic production and distribution?
2. Describe and explain the difference between *colonialism* and *neocolonialism*.
3. Explain the difference between *growth* and *development*. Describe and explain the results of more than five decades of programs to achieve development in the Other World.
4. Describe the links between poverty and population increase.
5. Define and describe the nature of globalization. What are the implications of current global trends for our natural environment and for social and political stability?

Key Terms

Brokers—Other World political leaders who act in the interest of First World countries and multinational interests.

Economics—The production, distribution, and use of wealth.

Globalization—Emerging international regime in which the economic interests of multinational corporations and other nonstate actors supersede the interests and power of nations.

Neocolonialism—Indirect control of Other World countries by First World countries and multinational interests.

Oligarchy—Government by the few, in the interest of the few.

Politics—Who gets what, when, and how; the authoritative allocation of scarce values.

Power—The use of violence, knowledge, and authority to control the behavior of others.

Structural adjustment programs—Domestic spending plans to make possible repayments on loans; often include cuts in health, education, and other social service programs.

Sustainable development—Living within the limits of natural systems while ensuring an adequate standard of living for all; meeting the needs of the present without compromising the ability of future generations to meet their own needs.

The Doctrine of Thrasymachus—(a) It is the natural right of the strong to take more than their equal share of what the world has to offer, and (b) might makes right.

Useful Web Sites

OneWorld.net: *www.oneworld.net*
Oxfam: *www.oxfam.org.uk*
Kiva (online microcredit loans): *http://www.kiva.org/*
Reshaping World Politics: NGOs, the Internet, and Global Civil Society: *www .oswego.edu/reshaping*
United Nations Development Programme: *www.undp.org*
World Trade Organization: *www.wto.org*

For Further Reading

Apter, David E., and Rosberg, Carl G., eds. *Political Development and the New Realism in Sub-Saharan Africa.* Charlottesville: University Press of Virginia, 1994.

Barber, Benjamin R. *Jihad vs. McWorld: Terrorism's Challenge to Democracy.* New York: Ballantine Books, 2001.

Barber, Benjamin R. *Fear's Empire: War, Terrorism, and Democracy.* New York: W.W. Norton, 2003.

Barfield, Claude E. *Free Trade, Sovereignty, Democracy: The Future of the World Trade Organization.* Washington, D.C.: The AEI Press, 2001.

Broad, Robin, ed. *Global Backlash: Citizen Initiatives for a Just World Economy.* Rowman & Littlefield Publishers, 2002.

Clapham, Christopher. *Third World Politics: An Introduction.* Madison: University of Wisconsin Press, 1985. *Foreign Policy* 107 (Summer 1997), Globalization: The Debate.

Croucher, Sheila L. *Globalization and Belonging: The Politics of Identity in a Changing World.* New York: Rowman & Littlefield Publishers, 2004.

Grieder, William. *One World Ready or Not: The Manic Logic of Global Capitalism.* New York: Simon & Schuster, 1997.

Harrison, Paul. *Inside the Third World: The Anatomy of Poverty.* London: Penguin Books, 1990.

Johnson, Chalmers. *Blowback: The Costs and Consequences of American Empire.* New York: Owl/Metropolitan Books, 2001.

Kiely, Ray. *The New Political Economy of Development: Globalization, Imperialism, Hegemony.* New York: Palgrave MacMillian, 2007.

Lenksi, Gerhard E. *Power and Privilege: A Theory of Social Stratification.* New York: McGraw-Hill, 1966.

Pachauri, R. K., and Reisinger, A., eds. *Climate Change 2007: Synthesis Report.* Geneva, Switzerland: Intergovernmental Panel on Climate Change, 2007.

Perkins, John. *Confessions of an Economic Hit Man.* San Francisco: Berrett-Koehler Publishers, 2004.

Rischard, J. F. *High Noon: Twenty Global Problems, Twenty Years to Solve Them.* New York: Basic Books, 2002.

Schumacher, E. F. *Small Is Beautiful: Economics as if People Mattered.* New York: Harper & Row, 1973.

Singer, P. W. *Corporate Warriors: The Rise of the Privatized Military Industry.* Ithaca, NY: Cornell University Press, 2003.

Soros, George. *Open Society: Reforming Global Capitalism.* New York: Public Affairs, 2000.

Tinder, Glenn. *Political Thinking: The Perennial Questions,* 6th ed. New York: HarperCollins, 1995.
Toffler, Alvin. *Powershift: Knowledge, Wealth, and Violence at the Edge of the 21st Century.* New York: Bantam Books, 1990.
Warkentin, Craig. *Reshaping World Politics: NGOs, the Internet, and Global Civil Society.* New York: Rowman & Littlefield Publishers, 2001.

Notes

1. Ban Ki-moon, "Forward," *The Millennium Development Goals Report 2008* (New York: United Nations, 2008), p. 3.
2. Charles W. Kegley, Jr., *World Politics: Trend and Transformation,* 12th Edition (Belmont, CA: Wadsworth Cengage Learning, 2009), pp. 127 and 138–140. For a detailed presentation of global inequalities, see Harold R. Kerbo, *World Poverty: Global Inequality and the Modern World System* (New York: McGraw Hill, 2006).
3. Jeffrey A. Freiden and David A. Lake, *International Political Economy: Perspectives on Global Power and Wealth* (New York: St. Martin's Press, 1987), p. 1.
4. Howard Zinn, *A People's History of the United States 1492—Present* (New York: HarperPerennial, 1995), pp. 1–8.
5. Julius K. Nyerere, *Ujamaa: Essays on Socialism* (Nairobi: Oxford University Press, 1968), pp. 2–3.
6. Charles K. Wilber, ed. *The Political Economy of Development and Underdevelopment* (New York: Random House, 1988), p. 25.
7. James J. Lamb, "The Third World and the Development Debate," *IDOC-North America* (January–February 1973): 20.
8. See "The Cocoyoc Declaration," adopted by participants in the UNEP/UNCTAD Symposium on Patterns of Resource Use, Environment and Development Strategies, Cocoyoc, Mexico, October 8–12, 1974. Reprinted in *International Organization 29,* no. 3 (summer 1975): 893–901; Lester Brown, et al., *State of the World 1991: A Worldwatch Institute Report on Progress toward a Sustainable Society* (New York: Norton, 1991); Jim MacNeill, Pieter Winsemius, and Taizo Yakushiji, *Beyond Interdependence: The Meshing of the World's Economy and the Earth's Ecology* (New York: Oxford University Press, 1991); and World Commission on Environment and Development, *Our Common Future* (New York: Oxford University Press, 1987).
9. See E. F. Schumacher, *Small Is Beautiful: Economics as if People Mattered* (New York: Harper & Row, 1973).
10. Immanuel Wallerstein, "The Three Instances of Hegemony in the History of the Capitalist World-Economy," in *International Political Economy: A Reader,* ed. Kendall W. Stiles and Tsuneo Akaha (New York: HarperCollins, 1991), pp. 427–435.
11. Ibid., p. 428.
12. John Kenneth Galbraith, *Economic Development* (New York: Houghton Mifflin, 1964), p. 3.
13. Rene Dumont, *False Start in Africa* (New York: Praeger, 1969).
14. *United Nations Development Programme, Human Development Report 2005* (United Nations Development Programme, 2005).
15. Paul Harrison, *Inside the Third World: The Anatomy of Poverty* (London: Penguin Books, 1990), pp. 465–466 (emphasis in the original).
16. Ibid., p. 276.
17. *Controlling Interest: The World of the Multinational Corporation* (San Francisco: California Newsreel, 1978).

18. Ibid.

19. John Perkins, *Confessions of an Economic Hit Man* (San Francisco: Berrett-Koehler Publishers, 2004).

20. Robert H. Jackson and Carl G. Rosberg, "The Political Economy of African Personal Rule," in *Political Development and the New Realism in Sub-Saharan Africa*, ed. David E. Apter and Carl G. Rosberg (Charlottesville: University Press of Virginia, 1994), p. 292.

21. See Robert D. Kaplan, "The Coming Anarchy," *This World* (13 March 1994), pp. 5–10.

22. Roger Morris, "Hurtful Hand on Liberia: U.S. Policy Bears Much of the Blame for That Nation's Calamity," *Los Angeles Times*, 31 August 2003, p. M5.

23. Gerhard E. Lenksi, *Power and Privilege: A Theory of Social Stratification* (New York: McGraw-Hill, 1966).

24. Ray Kiely, *The New Political Economy of Development: Globalization, Imperialism, Hegemony* (New York: Palgrave MacMillian, 2007), pp. 69–75.

25. Riccardo Petrella, "Techno-apartheid for a Global Underclass," *Los Angeles Times*, 6 August 1992, p. D6.

26. Colin Leys, "Learning from the Kenya Debate," in *Political Development and the New Realism in Sub-Saharan Africa*, ed. David E. Apter and Carl G. Rosberg (Charlottesville: University Press of Virginia, 1994), p. 227.

27. Elizabeth Rubin, "An Army of One's Own," *Harper's Magazine*, February 1997, pp. 44–55.

28. P. W. Singer, *Corporate Warriors: The Rise of the Privatized Military Industry* (Ithaca, NY: Cornell University Press, 2003), p. 9.

29. Debt relief to African countries totaling $40 billion in 2005 cancelled less than one-sixth of Africa's $295 billion debt and left out crucial countries such as Nigeria. The "relief" was more for image than for substance. See Abraham McLaughlin, "What Debt Relief Means for Africa," *The Christian Science Monitor*, 13 June 2005, p. 1.

30. See Vandana Shiva, *Stolen Harvest: The Hijacking of the Global Food Supply* (Cambridge, MA: South End Press, 2000).

31. See Robin Broad, ed., *Global Backlash: Citizen Initiatives for a Just World Economy* (Rowman & Littlefield Publishers, 2002).

32. Benjamin Barber, *Jihad vs. McWorld: Terrorism's Challenge to Democracy* (New York: Ballantine Books, 2001).

33. E. F. Schumacher, *Small Is Beautiful: Economics as if People Mattered* (New York: Harper & Row, 1973), pp. 293–294.

34. Samuel P. Huntington, "The Clash of Civilizations?" *Foreign Affairs* 72, no. 3 (Summer 1993): 22–49.

35. Benjamin R. Barber, *op. cit.*

36. Alvin Toffler, *Powershift: Knowledge, Wealth, and Violence at the Edge of the 21st Century* (New York: Bantam Books, 1990).

37. See George Soros, *Open Society: Reforming Global Capitalism* (New York: Public Affairs, 2000); and Craig Warkentin, *Reshaping World Politics: NGOs, the Internet, and Global Civil Society* (New York: Rowman & Littlefield Publishers, 2001).

38. See Sheila L. Croucher, *Globalization and Belonging: The Politics of Identity in a Changing World* (New York: Rowman & Littlefield Publishers, 2004).

39. Chalmers Johnson, *Blowback: The Costs and Consequences of American Empire* (New York: Owl/Metropolitan Books, 2001).

40. Chalmers Johnson, "The Lessons of Blowback," *Los Angeles Times*, 30 September 2001, p. M1.

41. Greg Miller, "Spy Agencies Say Iraq War Fuels Terror," *Los Angeles Times*, 24 September 2006, p. A1.

42. Doyle McManus, "U.S. Drone Attacks in Pakistan 'Backfiring,' Congress Told," *Los Angeles Times,* 3 May 2009, p. A1.

43. Sandy Tolan, "Beyond Regime Change," *Los Angeles Times* (December 1, 2002), p. M1. Tolan's sources include Richard Perle (Pentagon Defense Policy Board), David Wurmser (Special Assistant to the State Department), Donald Rumsfeld (Secretary of Defense), Paul Wolfowitz (Department of Defense), Elliot Abrams (Senior National Security Council Director), Dick Cheney (Vice President), Patrick Clawson (Institute for Near East Policy), Michael Ledeen (American Enterprise Institute), and Ariel Sharon (Prime Minister of Israel). See also Emmit B. Evans, Jr., "Iraq and the New American Colonialism," *Moebius* (Volume 1, Number 2, Spring 2003).

44. See Helena Cobban, "Military Occupations—The Good, Bad, and Ugly," *The Christian Science Monitor* (March 27, 2003), p. 11.

4

Women and Development

Dianne Long

Talking about man without talking about woman
is like clapping with one hand.

ANONYMOUS

Visual glimpses of the developing world in Western media often capture the faces, figures, and activities of women. Photos depict the tall Masai women of East Africa with their colorful garb, the Indian women in saris carrying children and water, the formless Afghan women veiled in blue burkas from head to toe scurrying through the marketplace. The developing world cannot truly be understood without discussing women. Yet these images and the stories accompanying them do not fully tell us about the lives of women in the Other World.

Women play a crucial role in development. Surprisingly little attention has been paid to their important involvement until very recently. The primary reason for this lack of attention is the fact that most attempts at development activities had been carried out by male-dominated institutions and reported from the perspective of international bureaucracies that did not recognize women's roles. However, women are an essential link to population control. They carry heavy responsibility for food production, not only for their own families but also for community marketplaces. They contribute significantly to wage labor, even though their wages tend to be very meager. Because they bear responsibility for family health and nutrition, they are aware of how pollution, desertification, and deforestation affect community health and prosperity. In the developing world, women face many obstacles—political, economic, and social. In various areas of the world, female children are less valued. This leads to high infanticide and child mortality rates. The United Nations' (UN's) *Millennium Development Goals (MDGs)* acknowledge the important role women play in development. The international community is rallying behind MDG targets for 2015 on improving literacy, reducing poverty, and enhancing the lives of women. Both the World Bank and the UN track progress with the expectation that significant development achievements can be reached. Women are now key actors in development.

Neglect, violence, multiple pregnancies, poor nutrition, and hard physical labor take their toll on women's well-being. In many areas of the developing world, school enrollments of females and literacy rates are lower than those for males. Individual and economic opportunities for females are diminished throughout life. Globalization, however, has produced significant changes in women's lives. Global communication networks and technology have helped women form global networks with Western women who identify with the plight of non-Western sisters and take up issues of gender equality. Globalization lessens gender differences and opens the door for educational and economic opportunity. However, the economic downturn globally pushes women out of the workforce since they are apt to be less educated and marginally employed primarily in agriculture and services.

This chapter takes note of four major factors that affect women in developing countries:

1. The legacy of colonialism
2. The push for modernization
3. The evolution of nationalism
4. The pervasiveness of globalization

Examining these factors as they affect women adds to our understanding of women's past, present, and future in the Other World.

WOMEN AND THE LEGACY OF COLONIALISM

Colonialism was not a new concept to either the European powers or to the colonies. It was the foundation of the Roman and Ottoman empires. What was new about colonialism in the eighteenth and nineteenth centuries was the scale of exploitation. This exploitation was largely fueled by the Industrial Revolution that arose in Britain. The period from 1750 to 1850 was one of rapid and profound social and economic change. Britain changed from a traditional agricultural society to a modern industrial one. The invention of the steam engine in 1769 and the development of steam for power resulted in the building of roads, railroads, and canals and started cotton textile manufacturing in England. By 1830, industry had been established in France, and soon thereafter, industry was a dominant factor in Germany and other countries of Europe. The United States and Russia entered the industrial age. Industrialization produced and required expanded markets, cheap labor, and raw materials, for which the industrial nations turned to the less-developed areas of the world, primarily Africa and Asia. *Imperialism,* the extension of rule of one society over another, was a natural consequence.

The precolonial world had a variety of cultural arrangements. Living in clans and extended families, women's lives had been shaped by centuries of local custom and necessary adaptation to change. There is no doubt that they shared power and responsibilities to survive. Certainly, their human experiences are reflected in every historical and geographic context. Western colonization, however, pushed aside the traditional patterns and introduced new concepts and requirements for gender both in private and in public, placing primary emphasis on the reproductive function of women and their role in the rearing and nurturing of children. Women's lives were considered to be limited to this "private" or internal sphere of home and children, while men were considered to operate in the "public" or external sphere, managing matters outside the home. Men were seen as having roles that included economic planning and building, settling conflicts, waging war, and bonding with other males for political and economic strength.[1]

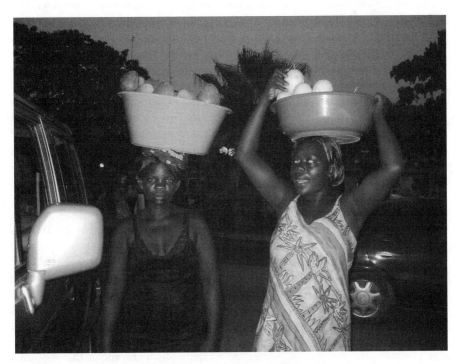

Capitalism: Women selling fruit in Angola.   *Source: Olga Carter*

European values shaped women's lives. In the sixteenth and seventeenth centuries, Spanish and Portuguese colonizing efforts brought Catholicism and "macho" attitudes that diminished the roles of indigenous women. In the nineteenth century, a pattern of patriarchy spread throughout industrialized Europe and was introduced into the developing world. In the new industrial world, both politics and economics were considered to be male concerns, and female power over any part of the sector declined. European cultures put decision making and property into the hands of male heads of household. Women were part of that property. A patriarchal pattern, therefore, replaced other customary patterns. England, especially, became a world power. During the rule of Queen Victoria (1837–1901), England was transformed from an island at the edge of Europe to an empire where the sun never set, and where the monarch was crowned the Empress of India and ruler of vast areas of Africa and the Pacific. Although the monarch was a woman, power was in the hands of political and industrial men.

Colonial administrators, taking charge of the developing world from a Victorian perspective, ignored the importance of women to community life and to local economies. The few female rulers like Queen Victoria ruled to maintain the elite family royal line. Men made decisions, held property, and restricted women to subservient roles. In Africa and Asia, women had been primarily agricultural workers. New developments introduced into these areas required that men be trained to work for wages on plantations and large-scale farms. The men often resisted and ignored the training, and colonial administrators often failed to comprehend the weakness of their agricultural programs. Nevertheless, development established ownership and dominance, men were forced to comply with new conditions, and women were shut out of their traditional subsistence farming. Even where women had strong political and economic roles—as they did in West Africa—their positions in traditional societies were eliminated. They could no longer hold any positions of importance, such as clan chiefs, judges, or managers of resources.[2]

Traditional societies usually held their land in common, not as individuals. Land reform was introduced with colonialism. European powers granted land titles to European entrepreneurs, government officials, and important "native" leaders. The government redefinition of ownership, and land grants, dispossessed women in the private economy and empowered male leaders in the public economy. Families were forced to abandon the subsistence farming that had always met family needs. Their land was taken for commercial agriculture. Women, who had always done at least half of the agricultural work, were deprived of their lands and were pushed into smaller and less fertile areas to continue their struggle to feed their families and neighbors. Food supply, distribution, nutrition, and health of women and children suffered. The land that had been community property, farmed for the common good, had become commercial and was used for the profit of others.[3]

Even today, women in the developing world face challenges as farmers and homemakers. Vandana Shiva, one of India's leading physicists and environmental activists, documents in *Stolen Harvest* the impact of corporate agriculture on small farmers, the majority of whom are women. Shiva chronicles the resistance movement of women organized to protest new commercial shrimp industries in India where 15 jobs are lost for every new job created. The shrimp industry competes for water, and small quantities of water are imported in tankers for household drinking and other needs. Contaminated water is often used for cattle, causing cattle to die. Milk and beef become scarce.[4] The intrusion of companies such as Monsanto, with its genetically engineered seed and its herbicides, destroys hundreds of weed species of plants that poor women depend on for food, fodder, and medicine.[5]

In the developing world, women continue to be deprived of educational opportunities. They are less likely to be chosen by families to attend school, and they are the first to be taken out of school to help at home and bring needed monies to families. School fees are a burden on poor families, and scarce funds mean fewer school opportunities for girls and young women. Literacy rates for women in many countries are low. In Niger, only 15.1 percent of women are literate;[6] most have completed less than three years of formal schooling.

In Guatemala and other Latin American countries, *machismo* dominates as an aggressive assertion of male dominance over women. Likewise, the idea of *marianismo* exists in some cultures where women are considered morally superior to men. These scripted roles are expected to hold families together. Such self-images contribute to political conservatism that is easily exploited by political parties and military regimes. In Saudi Arabia and Qatar, more women then men are attending universities, yet they are barred from many occupations. When women break traditional gender roles, governmental and religious leaders complain. Schools for girls add to community costs. The refusal to let women drive is inefficient as fathers work only part-time and must run errands part-time. In Saudi Arabia and in the Islamic world, therefore, companies prefer to hire foreigners and unemployment increases, especially for young family men. Productivity, too, suffers when women who represent half of the potential workforce cannot participate.

Today, women's work is largely unpaid. We can assume that the persons are fully engaged in the workplace. Although they work longer days in support of families and bring funds into the family, 70 percent of women's time is unpaid work. The remainder centers on market activities, including raising crops and animals for sale, home crafts, manufacturing and related assembly, and prostitution. Women work very long hours per week in developing areas. International organizations are continuing to work to get countries to report data related to work time and to indicate the statistics for men and women. With better data, the United Nations and nonprofit organizations can address women's work and equity issues by developing policies and programs to help women. Even today, women's work in developing countries is not valued in the marketplace, and it is not compensated in the home.

THE EVOLUTION OF NATIONALISM

The colonial era was disrupted by the two major economic and political events of the twentieth century: the Great Depression and World War II. Major realignments of power occurred, and many areas of the world experienced an explosion of newly independent states. The spirit of *nationalism*—a political philosophy that holds that the welfare of the nation-state is paramount—spread. Nationalism necessarily, however, treats individual rights and group rights within the society as secondary. Women, in particular, have had to take a back seat to nationalism.

In 1945, 51 nations formed the United Nations. Since then, many new nations have formed: 192 nations are now UN members—most are from the Other World. The original 51 nations of the UN had been in existence for many years and had long-standing political and economic structures, clear geographic boundaries, and an established national identity. In contrast, the new nations created after World War II were formed out of the colonial lands with arbitrary boundaries and a legacy of dependence on colonial powers. Nation building required citizens to take on a national identity to serve as an empowering ideology. This proved difficult in some places where governments attempted to oversee a coalition of various competing cultures. In other places, religious beliefs and cultural patterns initially helped to forge a new identity. In the North African nation of Algeria, for example, the nationalist effort was imbued with strong family values and Arab-Islamic codes prescribing women's roles. Women worked for independence there as they have done in Palestine and elsewhere, only to be asked to go back to the kitchen when independence was won. Women protested. Nevertheless, upon independence from France in 1962, the new rulers of Algeria committed themselves to socialist modernization while attempting to set aside gender concerns in deference to national development. In 1992, civil war caused further disruptions. Terrorists and extreme political groups harassed women and created a general uneasiness in the population. A successful union of Islam with culture helped create a national identity for other nations in the Middle East, notably Iran, Iraq, and Lebanon. Palestinians, even without a homeland, also forged a national identity out of a merger of religious and cultural values.

A nation-state comprises many power relations within its boundaries: economic, political, legal, and cultural. The creation of legitimacy is a prime consideration. New nations have reduced and simplified social codes to give them legal force. Modern African nations, for example, used the "rule of law" to gain legitimacy. By law, women gained legal rights to schooling, property, and divorce. In practice, applications of law were sometimes arbitrary, and women were denied rights. Many codes continued to emphasize the public-private divide. Modern legal processes emerged as a form of imperialist intervention. Although women worked with men in the struggle for independence, economic opportunity, basic human rights, and the right to vote, women's voices were ignored as new states worked to design new governing institutions. As nations evolved, the battle for human rights—including those of women—was viewed with the suspicion that champions for such causes were collaborating with an imperialist Western enemy.

The case of Afghanistan illustrates this point. The Taliban leadership dominated other tribes, establishing a very conservative religious policy that disallowed the education of women and relegated women to wearing the *burka*—the blue covering transforming a woman into a shapeless, faceless identity. Women teachers and professionals lost their jobs and were punished for appearing in public without a male protector. Women were confined to their homes. Before the fall of the Taliban regime, protest was regarded as treason and could be met with harassment or death. Women have returned to school and to market, and many women removed the burka following the fall of this Afghan government. Others have taken up government posts and organized campaigns for elected positions in legislatures and in executive offices in local governments.

In general, new nations have adopted bureaucratic forms of government. In these large formal organizations, decisions are made at the top of the organization and those below follow orders. These decision structures have served male interests. New governments pushed women aside and intruded in both private and public lives. Although patterns of opposition from women were different from one geographic space and one historical time to another, any resistance caused new social conflicts. In the end, women and the state viewed each other with suspicion.

The lack of a middle class necessary for running a democracy made governing difficult. Few, therefore, are surprised that, in some nations, only women from the upper classes have been able to represent women's issues. In China, India, Pakistan, and the Philippines, for example, women in politics came from the upper economic, educated stratum of society. They knew little of the struggle of poor women. Their individual successes were dependent on pragmatic male support in political parties and state government. Gender-specific issues, such as prenatal care, contraception, and women's property rights, were discouraged.

During the past two decades, women have begun to enter local politics and legal disputes to represent their interests. Beginning in the mid-1960s, women have entered politics in greater numbers, and a few women were even elected to the office of head of state. Sirimavo Bandaranaike of Sri Lanka held office from 1959 to 1970 after her husband's assassination, and again from 1970 to 1977. Her daughter Chandrika Bandaranaike Kumaratunga became prime minister in 1994 and president later in the year when she named her mother as prime minister. Indira Gandhi of India held power from 1966 to 1977 and again from 1980 to 1984. Her son Rajiv followed as prime minister. Likewise, Benazir Bhutto of Pakistan followed her father into the post of prime minister from 1988 to 1990. This pattern illustrates the dominance of ruling elites. Violeta Barrios de Chamorro rose to power in Nicaragua in 1990 after years of political campaigning following the death of her husband, a wealthy landowner who was politically active in opposing the ruling Somoza regime.

Until very recently, women historically had been left out of political leadership. In 1980, women held fewer than 10 percent of parliamentary seats in advanced democracies of Europe and the United States. By 2005, the seats women held increased to 15 percent, and now the number of seats held by women is over 20 percent in many countries. Thirty-six percent of Cuba's parliamentary seats are held by women; Costa Rica's lower house is 38.6 percent women. Argentina's lower house has 35 percent women, and its upper house has 41.7 percent. In comparison, the United States has 15 percent in the House of Representatives and 14 percent in the Senate; Niger, 12.4 percent; Ethiopia, 21.9 percent in the lower house and 18.8 percent in the upper house; and 6.5 percent of Chad's parliamentary seats are held by women.[7]

With democracy and multiple-party governments giving women the opportunity to run for elected office, they willingly take to the campaign trail. Dr. Massouda Jalal was forced to stop teaching in Kabul University in Afghanistan when the Taliban took power. She signed up to head a UN program and started bakeries in Kabal to allow war widows to feed their families. When the Taliban fell, she ran for president, getting 1 percent of the vote. She was later appointed to the president's cabinet. She hopes to run again. In Afghanistan, about 44 percent of all registered voters are women. In Iraq, more than 55 percent of the voters are female and represent a third of the delegates elected to design the constitution that was adopted in 2005. Despite obstacles, women want to be integrated in society. In 2006, women in Afghanistan held 27.3 percent of the seats in the lower house of parliament and 22.5 percent in the upper house. In Iraq, women held 25.5 percent of parliamentary seats in 2006.[8]

In November 2005, Ellen Johnson Sirleaf was the victor in Liberia's first presidential elections since the end of a 14-year civil war. Named the "Iron Lady" by supporters, she became the first elected female head of state in all of Africa. She has a political career spanning over 30 years, beginning with criticizing Liberia's military regime in the 1980s and later going into exile. Educated in the United States, she held a number of banking positions, including Africa director at the United Nations Development Programme. Many think her banking experience and her Harvard education will be beneficial in steering the Liberian economy.[9]

Political leaders, however, manipulate the traditional family concept to reinforce their own authority. Just as the father makes decisions in a family, in new states the leader makes decisions for "the children." As women make educational gains and move into work roles outside the home, there are big consequences. Families enjoy the added income and social status. Their children can compete for better marital partners. Women gain self-worth and can begin to negotiate power within the family and community. They can begin to challenge socially approved norms of dress and behavior. A case in point is female circumcision. Women worldwide continue to protest this practice of genital mutilation, a form of social control practiced in many areas of Africa and the Middle East, that has caused pain, infection, and death. Surveys indicate that 98 percent of Egyptian women have been circumcised.

In new nations, government corruption has often developed as the way of doing business. Legal and illegal uses of power operate with little public accountability. Even with clear laws, rulers are often above the law, and corruption is a part of everyday living. Some politicians, bureaucrats, and citizens give the law itself low status. The capacity to enforce law is overshadowed by other interests, and the rule of law is undermined. Protest then replaces petition. Although their visibility makes them open to punishment, women in many parts of the world have come to organize to confront the nation's rulers, its rules, and its pattern of corruption. They have come to address two main issues of our time: nationalism and the oppression of women.

WOMEN AND THE PUSH FOR MODERNIZATION

There is a widespread belief that modernization in the Other World, along with democratization, urbanization, and industrialization, will improve women's lives, offering opportunities and rising economic and social status. This belief has not always proved true. Modernization was introduced to agricultural communities to improve production of cash crops. Foreigners developed large-scale plantations and other agricultural businesses. Men—and some women and children—found that they could survive only by going to work for the new owners, usually for low wages and long hours to buy food and other necessities. Commercial agriculture created powerful new requirements: advanced technology and training, modern equipment, synthetic fertilizers and herbicides, and the money to buy them. Commercial agriculture provided colonial people with technical training in farming methods. Modernization did not trickle down to everyone. Women continued to have smaller garden areas to grow crops for the table. Soils and water supply were at times marginal, and harvests could be disappointing. In some countries, women also went to work on plantations for small wages, while still carrying the responsibilities for house, family, and garden. Caught up in both the deteriorating family economy and modernization requirements, their lives were not improved.[10]

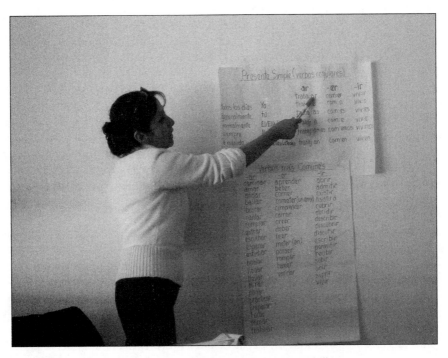

School Days: A teacher pointing out words during a grammar drill in Latin America. *Source: Craig Arceneaux*

New financing mechanisms were introduced along with changes in agricultural production, distribution, and consumption. Local farmers were required to adapt to the new agricultural industries introduced into the Other World, or they were displaced from the land. Trying to maintain themselves, they acquired debt. The World Bank, the UN, and nongovernmental organizations (NGOs) extended loans to farmers to buy seed, equipment, and fertilizer. Credit was not extended to women. Having no access either to economic resources or to technical training, they were marginalized and excluded. Even in North Africa and Asia, where women farmers first cultivated cotton and rice, women became irrelevant to commercial agriculture.

Forests, along with other natural resources, were placed under new ownership. Extracting timber became a commercial enterprise. Forests had traditionally been the source of firewood for heating and cooking; for fruits, plant products, clothing, and important herbs in medicinal preparations; and for small and large animals for food and other necessities. Now women were excluded from forestlands that had always been crucial to their way of life.

Like other natural resources, mines were claimed for commercial use. Minerals and ores were important materials for shaping farming and household implements. In the new system, tools could be purchased only with hard currency. Without currency, women did without. In many areas of the world, women had traditionally managed fisheries and brought home the catch to feed the family and sell at market. With colonialism and modernization, commercial companies took the place of women.

Urbanization (the rise of cities) developed from the economic needs of the Industrial Revolution. Factories for production, banks for finance, and offices for government and commercial operations were built. Industrialization required urbanization; urbanization brought with it modernization. Villages developed into cities with electricity, telephone and telegraph communications, water and sanitation systems, contemporary buildings, roads and railroads, and other essentials of modern life. Jobs were centered in cities, and both men and women migrated to them out of economic necessity. Men took jobs in industry and in low-waged building projects. Women worked in industry too, primarily in textiles and parts assembly for manufactured goods. Where women could not find jobs, they turned to earning wages by domestic labor or prostitution to survive. Apart from traditional families and clan protection, women became even more vulnerable to violence, disease, and isolation.

Gender equality is an important component of modernization. Colonialism set the values for inequity, and modernization must address this issue. Indeed, colonialism can be considered an obstacle to modernization today. If gender discrimination is a source of endemic poverty, then efforts are required to diminish the discrepancies between men and women. The two dominant approaches to achieving equity are *mainstreaming* and *empowerment*. The goal of mainstreaming is to bring women into the regular economic, political, and social life enjoyed by men. The goal of empowerment calls for the design of special opportunities for women to have choices in their lives. Progress is slow even though some gains have been made. UNIFEM is the women's fund at

Female Israeli Soldiers on Duty in Jerusalem: Almost all Jewish females are subject to doing some military service in Israel. *Source: Olga Carter*

the United Nations. It provides financial and technical assistance to innovative programs and strategies to foster women's empowerment and gender equity. UN General-Secretary Ban Ki-moon insists that gender equity is essential for development. In UNIFEM's 2008/2009 report *Who Answers to Women,* Ki-moon identifies two indispensable elements of gender-responsive accountability. "First, women must be legitimate members of any oversight or accountability process. Second, national commitments to gender equality and women's rights must be among the standards against which public decisions are assessed." He launched a UN global campaign Unite to End Violence Against Women believing that ". . . the primary litmus test of gender-responsive accountability will be the elimination of violence against women."[11]

The United Nations Development Programme (UNDP) has six practice areas for mainstreaming.[12] The first of these is full participation of women in democratic governance. In Pakistan, 30 percent of local government seats are reserved for women. The second is poverty reduction. Two-thirds of the one billion adults who cannot read are women. They are the first to leave school and the last to get medical care. Third is crisis prevention and recovery. More than 80 percent of refugees from war and internal crisis are women and children. Fourth, energy and environment programs are needed to bring access to modern energy services and to reduce pollution. Fifth, information and communication technologies are important to increasing women's skills and abilities to network for their own safety, welfare, and ability to engage in the society at large. Lastly is human immunodeficiency virus (HIV) and acquired immune deficiency syndrome (AIDS) prevention. The disease is pandemic, spreading quickly in Africa and other areas of the world. Teenage girls are five to six times more likely to be affected by HIV than boys their age. In Malawi, for example, infants die at a rate of 1 in 10, as opposed to 6 in 1,000 in the United States. The HIV rate in Malawi is at least 1 in 10 or 11.8 percent compared to a U.S. rate of 0.6 percent. The condition of women in the developing world is continuing to improve, yet the progress is slow.[13]

Although there are small improvements in the conditions of women, life is still harsh for them in the developing world. Where there once was plenty of food, now cash crops such as tobacco and sugar are grown to support imperialist economies. Commercial forests, mines, and fisheries pushed out independent farmers, crafts and trades workers, and herders. In many places, men travel to far-off plantations, mines, and cities for work, leaving women to tend to home. Family life is fragmented. Young people, male and female, travel to cities out of economic necessity. Scarcity of food and other necessities has increased. Health services are still primitive—especially in rural areas. Women and infants suffer unusually high death rates. Coping with scarcity and with survival is now almost solely a woman's concern.

WOMEN AND GLOBALISM

Political independence and economic development are intertwined. Industrial economies, an integral component of the Western nation-states, formed the model for most of the new political entities. For the masses caught up in rising expectations, independence and nation building held great promise. A higher standard of living seemed a right that had been won through the struggle for nationhood. These new independent nations, however, were vulnerable to external factors such as international economic and political ties; they were dependent on the outside world for trade, technology, economic aid, and military aid. They were weak in enforcing laws and regulating security. The governments often had little control over factors such as intimidation and corruption.

In many countries, national policies reflect a gender division of labor. Women are held to the low-paying jobs in the public economy or to the non-paying jobs in service of the family. Poor women are forced to migrate because of economic necessity, not by personal choice. The traffic in prostitutes, mail-order brides, and domestic services, and slavery conditions in clothing assembly bear this out. In national, legal, and political systems, women do not have the same legal remedies available to men, and they may be forced to deal with dangerous circumstances, ending in abuse and sometimes death. The news of such conditions travels across the Internet where many organizations continue to bring issues related to abuse of women to worldwide attention.

Furthermore, states have been helpless to control HIV and AIDS spread through sexual activity as part of sexual tourism, especially in Africa and Asia. The UN reports over 33 million cases of HIV/AIDS in the world. A disproportionate number of cases are reported in women. Half of all HIV/AIDS cases affect women aged 15 to 49 who live in the developing world. Children number 3 million of those with this disease. Many contracted HIV/AIDS from their mothers before birth or after through breast-feeding. According to a recent UNIFEM report, half of the women in the world have HIV/AIDS. In sub-Saharan Africa the numbers soared to 61 percent in 2007 and to 43 percent in the Caribbean. Rates in other parts of the world are as follows: 29 percent Asia, 26 percent Europe and Central Asia, and 26 percent in Latin America.[14]

Until recently, international organizations and development conferences have not concerned themselves with women's lives but have concentrated on those of men. The Fourth World Conference on Women was held in China's capital, Beijing, in September 1995. More than 50,000 members attended and declared that women's rights are human rights. The Beijing Declaration and Platform for Action resulted. This platform encourages 100 countries and UN organizations to make commitments to improve the status of women. They look for important changes in national policies that restrict women's rights, such as changes in inheritance laws and property rights. They ask countries to improve data gathering and set targets for increasing the enrollment of women in primary school and female literacy. They look for countries and organizations to participate in international development in a coordinated way. The conference messages underscore key concerns. The first concern is that women's rights are human rights. Second, discrimination and violence against women must end. Third, equality for women is an important goal politically, economically, and socially. Fourth, issues of population control and development that include women's voices are global concerns. The platform builds on progress made in previous UN conferences on women—in Mexico City in 1975, in Copenhagen in 1980, and in Nairobi in 1985. Each conference emphasized the role women have in development and the importance of protecting human rights. UNIFEM holds an annual meeting to bring attention to women's issues and to mobilize events to empower women. The 2009 conference in Chicago urged the international community to act to end violence against women. Walks to end violence are planned in response to the conference call.[15]

In response to these global discussions, UN organizations, the World Bank, and the U.S. Agency for International Development have focused more attention on women as appropriate recipients of development efforts. These organizations have echoed the concerns of the Beijing conference and its call to action. A key element for many projects is increased school enrollment and literacy for girls as well as boys. Females who are educated tend to marry as adults rather than as adolescents. They have fewer children, they have access to important information on health and nutrition, and they have greater opportunities for better wages in the marketplace. Other international conferences related to poverty have also begun to give prominence to those projects that address the status of women and the feminization of poverty. The 1994 International Conference on Population and Development stressed this point in its examination of health and reproductive rights: increasing female education is necessary for population control.

For organizations such as the UN and World Bank, ignoring the plight of women is increasingly difficult. International conferences demand that women's voices be heard and that human rights abuses be addressed. In response to pressure from women's networks, international organizations have directed themselves toward improving literacy of women and increasing female enroll- ments in school. They have also urged nations to dedicate themselves to the same goals. In addition, NGOs have begun to focus on women as being key to economic development. Programs are designed to help women become knowl- edgeable about contraception and family planning and to improve nutrition and prenatal care. Women's needs are considered, such as drilling new wells for drinkable water, designing improved cooking methods using little available fuel, and providing small loans to women for starting businesses that market their products and crafts. These early efforts offer much hope.[16]

Nevertheless, the data on women and development show a crisis looming. Life expectancy and literacy are dropping in some counties, with decreases being greater for women than for men. For some, economic growth is below zero, and opportunities for women are limited. A number of countries have increased child mortality, especially female children. People still live on less than $1 per day; women head many families. A deteriorating regional or global economy hurts women disproportionately as they have fewer job and income options.

More than 150 heads of state and world leaders at the historic Millennium Assembly of the UN in September 2000 promised to do their utmost to end pover- ty and to improve the lot of women. Poor countries are attempting to pursue good policies, tackle corruption, and raise domestic resources; however, rich countries need to support countries that demonstrate good policies. As gender equity im- proves, the status of women is expected to climb and poverty to diminish.

Summary

The Other World is a difficult place for women. The legacy of colonialism stressed patriarchy and ignored the important economic and social roles women played in developing societies. *Nationalization* concentrated power into the hands of a few political leaders who saw women as marginal to the goals of forming a new gov- ernment. Corruption also made women's lives difficult, as abuses against women often went unpunished. *Modernization* shifted populations to cities and shifted economic life from small farming plots to large agricultural businesses that pushed women into undesirable land. Sustaining human life became more difficult. *Globalization* brought international corporations into decision making on both so- cial and economic policy. Economic opportunities have been meager. Women have been required to perform low-wage jobs. Their contributions to family economies have been underestimated. Women also have been subjected to violence, abuse, and prostitute trafficking. The high incidence of HIV/AIDS in women and children are a consequence of the spread of disease across continents and seas. International conferences, like the one in Beijing, continue to press for change in women's status and to make women's rights an important issue in the human rights struggle.

ISSUES FOR DISCUSSION

1. Is development good news for women in the developing world?

Many think development will benefit all in a society. This is not always true. From the 1950s to the 1980s, women did not reach wage parity with men even in modern developing nations. Per capita income rose dramatically in many places in the Other World, but women continue to lag behind men. In some countries of Asia and Africa in particular, women have significantly less access to resources and to income opportunities. Primary school enrollment and literacy data continue to show a gender gap between women and men, even though many nations and international organizations stress gender equity. In some cultures, women provide the family's basic needs. Men in the family may decide to use earned income for business or personal gain. Women in much of sub-Saharan Africa must provide shelter, clothes, school fees, and medical care for themselves and for their children. Men may acquire radios, bicycles, and other objects for personal consumption. Children's nutrition and health actually have worsened in some countries even when per capita income increased. This pattern exists in Guatemala, Belize, Mexico, and India.

Women's work may not always provide economic opportunity. Where jobs are created for women, wages are low and women are forced to work two jobs: one at home and one in the formal economy. Working women in developing countries often put in 12 to 18 hours a day. The World Bank, the largest international aid agency in the world, now promotes economic opportunity for women in its development efforts. The Women in Development (WID) program was created in 1977 to ensure those women were part of a project design. The program operated in a male-dominated agency with top-down directives. Later, in 1993, a Gender and Development (GAD) division replaced WID. Feminist critiques were critical of the organization. Since then, the World Bank has tried to listen to women's voices in designing its programs.

2. Can women find the opportunity for increased literacy, despite their secondary status in Other World societies?

Almost every international meeting on human rights and the eradication of poverty has targeted increased literacy for women, but the reality is that in many societies, women are not valued. School fees are expensive, and young girls and women are needed at home to help with chores or to work in factories and plantations so the family can afford school and job opportunities for boys. Patriarchal attitudes persist and block potential benefits for women.

The UN Population Fund continues to track the close connection between education and fertility. The more education women have, the more likely they are to have small families. In the southern Indian state of Kerala, the fertility rate is low, 2.3 children per woman. Why is it so low when others may have three or four times as many children? Most claim it is because female literacy in Kerala is 66 percent—many times greater than in other areas of India. In addition, women of Kerala have social and legal status. They can inherit land, and families must make a money gift to the bride's family when a marriage takes place. In other areas of the developing world, the bride's family commonly gives money to the groom instead of receiving money. Many experts also believe that women with education appear to look for more equality in marital arrangements and for more economic opportunities for themselves and their children.

3. Can women in developing nations have a voice in government?

Today there are very few women running for political office and serving in legislatures in both the developed and developing worlds. Women's voices have been ignored, and women have been cast to the sidelines. Traditional society suggests that women restrict their efforts to the home rather than to public life. The burden of household management, childbirth, and care for children and the elderly remove women from having opportunities to learn about government offices and policy issues. Certainly, low levels of literacy for females in many areas of the developing world play a big part in denying women a voice in government. International organizations have taken up the banner of equality in government and encourage women to become informed and to run for local, regional, and national offices. Feminist voices have collectively made a difference. Participating in meetings and organizations, they pressure for changes in both national and international policies that restrict women.

Economic development and literacy are prerequisites to more political opportunities. Women face a number of obstacles in gaining equity with men. In Asia and Africa, laws are often ignored. Without the ability to have voice or to protect property, women's lives continue to be determined by other persons and by other forces.

Improving the status of women is key to gender equity and to political voice. In Bangladesh, for example, the Grameen Bank gives women small loans to develop businesses. Participants become important parts of a local economy, raising domestic animals, making handicrafts, and growing important agricultural products for the market. They also have begun to pressure for a decision-making role in the villages in which they live.

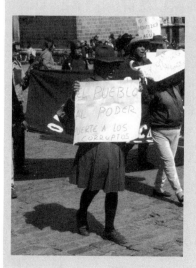

A Street Protest in Cusco, Peru: This woman is carrying a sign in the protest rally that translates, "Power to the People. Kill the Corrupt."   *Source: Craig Arceneaux*

4. How has globalization hurt women?

Globalization has brought more job opportunities, but many of these are low-tech and low-wage jobs. Manufacturing has moved from the industrialized world to the developing world because wages are low. Environmental and labor regulation often does not exist, and working conditions are unsafe and unhealthy. Because women are less valued, many women and children are hired to fill production jobs, and they are paid less than men for the same jobs. When there is a slowdown in production, women are the first to get fewer hours or to be laid off. Cuts in spending for education and health disproportionately affect women. Where cash crops are introduced into the agricultural economy, women lose their family plots and are forced to forage for food and walk great distances for essential drinking water and firewood.

5. Why is educating women so important to economic progress?

Women who are educated delay having children. They also have fewer children and are informed about family planning. As a result, they can invest more in the few children that they have. UN data indicate that there are fewer infant deaths, healthier children, and higher literacy rates for the offspring of educated women. They can contribute economically to the family, managing the crops and animals and developing crafts. Studies also suggest that women give more of the budget to education, health, and nutrition. School enrollment is increased for the children of educated women. These women get involved in family and community decisions to advance the well-being of others.

Review Questions

1. How has colonialism affected women in the Other World?
2. How has modernization affected women in the Other World?
3. How have nationalism and economic development affected women in the Other World?
4. What obstacles do women experience in the developing world?
5. What progress have women made in political life?

Key Terms

Empowerment—Providing women with choices in their lives.
Globalization—Expanding market activity across the globe.
Imperialism—The extension of rule of one society over another.
Machismo—Aggressive assertion of male dominance over women.
Mainstreaming—Bringing women into the regular economic, political, and social life enjoyed by men.
Marianismo—Assertion that women are considered morally superior to men.
Modernization—Replication conditions of industrialized nations.
Nationalism—Political philosophy that holds that the welfare of the nation-state is paramount.

Useful Web Sites

Feminist organization site with links: *www.feminist.org*
United Nations Development Programme site: *www.unifem.undp.org*
United Nations site: *www.un.org/womenwatch*
World Bank site: *www.worldbank.org*
World Neighbors site: *www.worldneighbors.org*

For Further Reading

Ahmed, Leila. *Women and Gender in Islam.* New Haven, CT: Yale University Press, 1992.
Bayes, Jane H., and Tohidi, Nayereh Esfahlani, eds. *Globalizations, Religion, and Gender: The Politics of Implementing Women's Rights in Catholic and Muslim Countries.* New York: Palgave Macmillan, 2001.
Datta, Rekha, and Kornberg, Judith, eds. *Women in Developing Countries: Assessing Strategies for Empowerment.* Boulder, CO: Lynne Rienner Publishers, 2002.
Edwards, Michael, and Gaventa, John, eds. *Global Citizen Action.* Boulder, CO: Lynne Rienner Publishers, 2001.
Jabri, Vivienne, and O'Gorman, Eleanor. *Women, Culture, and International Relations.* Boulder, CO: Lynne Rienner Publishers, 1999.
Kelley, Rita Mae, Bayes, Jane H., Hawkesworth, Mary E., and Young, Brigitte, eds. *Gender, Globalization, and Democratization.* New York: Rowman & Littlefield Publishers, 2001.
Kumar, Krishna, ed. *Women and Civil War: Impact, Organizations, and Action.* Boulder, CO: Lynne Rienner Publishers, 2001.
Narayan, Uma. *Dislocating Cultures: Identities, Traditions and Third World Feminism.* New York: Routledge, 1997.
Scott, Catherine V. *Gender and Development: Rethinking Modernization and Dependency Theory.* Boulder, CO: Lynne Rienner Publishers, 1996.
Tulchin, Joseph S. *Democratic Governance and Social Inequality.* Boulder, CO: Lynne Rienner Publishers, 2002.
Visvanathan, Nalini, Duggan, Lun, and Nisonoff, Laurie, eds. *The Women, Gender and Development Reader.* New York: St. Martin's Press, 1997.
Waylen, Georgina. *Gender in Third World Politics.* Boulder, CO: Lynne Rienner Publishers, 1996.

Notes

1. See the essays in Uma Narayan, *Dislocating Cultures: Identities, Traditions, and Third World Feminism* (New York: Routledge, 1997).
2. See Mary Poovay, Catherine R. Stimpson, eds., *Uneven Developments: The Ideological Work of Gender in Mid-Victorian England* (Chicago: University of Chicago Press, 1999).
3. Vandana Shiva, *Stolen Harvest: The Hijacking of the Global Food Supply* (South End Press, 2000), pp. 48–60.
4. Ibid., pp. 316–318.

5. Ibid.
6. United Nations, *Human Development Report, 2006. Beyond Scarcity: Power, Poverty, and the Growing Water Crisis.* (New York: United Nations Development Programme, 2006), p. 371.
7. Ibid., pp. 380–383.
8. Ibid., p. 383.
9. newsvote.bbc.co.uk.
10. A discussion of debt appears in the *World Development Report 2005*, pp. 268–271.
11. www.unifem.org, *Progress of the World's Women 2008/2009: Who Answers to Women? Gender and Accountability*, p. ii.
12. United Nations Development Programme, *Gender Equality: Executive Summary, November 2002*, www.undp.org.
13. UNDP Report, 2005, pp. 246–249, and *World Almanac 2009*, pp. 784 and 831. See also UNDP Report 2005, pp. 246–249.
14. *Progress of the World's Women 2008/2009*, p. 129.
15. www.unifem.org
16. www.un.org and www.worldbank.org have extensive data banks.

CHAPTER

5

Latin America

Craig Arceneaux

[Latin] America is ungovernable, the man who serves a revolution plows the sea; this nation will fall inevitably into the hands of the unruly mob and then will pass into the hands of almost indistinguishable petty tyrants of every color and race.

ATTRIBUTED TO SIMÓN BOLÍVAR BY GABRIEL GARCÍA MÁRQUEZ

IN HIS NOVEL *THE GENERAL IN HIS LABYRINTH*

The capital city of La Paz, Bolivia, sits in a bowl, surrounded by spectacular mountains whose efforts to reach the heavens often leave them veiled by passing clouds. The view is awesome, and easily lulls one into a state of deep reflection. A closer look, however, reveals the somber reality. Reaching out from the urban center and making their way up the mountain slopes on all sides of the bowl are the slums and shantytowns of La Paz. Here, plumbing and electricity are scarce or nonexistent, roads sit unpaved, and the escarpments that afford such distant photogenic vistas conspire to create an ideal setting for floods and landslides. The outlying slums are the first and often last stop for the unemployed, downtrodden, and desperate who have made their way from the countryside with hopes of a better life in the city.

El Alto is the epitome of these fringe localities. Nonexistent as a city 23 years ago, today the city burgeons with some 800,000 mostly indigenous people living in squalid conditions. Some of the first settlers were the thousands of tin miners left jobless when state industries were privatized in the 1980s. Sharecroppers and farmhands arrived soon after, as the dictates of globalization withdrew price supports and agricultural subsidies. As they sought refuge in El Alto, their situation worsened as neoliberal reforms, arguably implemented more vigorously in Bolivia than in any other Latin American country, mandated government cutbacks on basic services.

Seven miles from the capital, El Alto is perched atop a highland plateau within eyesight of La Paz. At an elevation of 13,320 feet, it tops La Paz's already incredible elevation of 11,913 feet. But just as the clouds may gather to shield the view from the capital below, the elites of La Paz, who champion their European origins, sought to ignore the poverty and peril of the highlands. Estranged from their fellow citizens, the elites look to the newfound opportunities opened by globalization—the low inflation rate, access to capital markets, and new technologies leading to the discovery of vast oil and gas reserves—opportunities not felt by those at lower economic rungs—and higher altitudes. El Alto, however, grew increasingly difficult to ignore. The city sits alongside the main road into La Paz and near the international airport. Why is this significant? Neglect allowed the population of El Alto to multiply, and it is in numbers that those in El Alto soon found their power. With sheer numbers, they were able to close down the international airport, block all main roads, and crowd city streets. The elites discovered that the masses could bring La Paz to a standstill. In fact, their actions generated policy changes and even presidential resignations in 2003 and 2005. Their support was critical to the election of the current president, Evo Morales, who hopes to give a voice to the previously unheard masses and reverse the neoliberal reforms of the past. These protests would have been unthinkable under the military governments that ruled the country from 1964 to 1982.

Such social activism is a hallmark of democracy and opens new channels of communication where young political institutions are found wanting; however, it can also overwhelm a fledgling democracy and derail vital long-term economic policies. The despondency that surrounds La Paz beckons immediate attention, but that same ambition for a swift and successful undertaking may have opened a fateful cycle of disorder as the mob moves to replace, one after another, politicians unable to ferry immediate socioeconomic gains. Where the impoverished see hope in the progressive policies of Evo Morales, communities in the eastern lowlands of the country see a threat. They sit on lucrative natural gas deposits and fear that the central government in distant La Paz will pilfer their newfound wealth for the short-term economic benefits of those in the highlands. It is they who now foment protest in Bolivia. They have even gone so far as to threaten secession as Morales remains firm in his commitments.

The story of Bolivia appears to corroborate the sentiments attributed to Simón Bolívar some 200 years ago. The account draws together a number of issues found throughout Latin American countries—poverty and inequality, foreign pressure to maintain neoliberal policies, governability, the politics of ethnicity, and social protest. Many of these issues can be linked to globalization. Nonetheless, Latin American countries have interacted with globalization differently, resulting in distinct social, economic, and political patterns. Bolivia's cycle of disorder, therefore, is countered to the south by Chile, which has embraced economic globalization with success and to the north by Costa Rica, which has celebrated stable, democratic rule for almost 50 years. This chapter outlines those common threads that distinguish Latin America as a region within the Other World as we look to the geography, demography, and the history of the region. Then, as we look to the current politics and economics of the region, we see that globalization has produced an assortment of experiences. These differences are illustrated most prominently in the individual case studies on Mexico, Brazil, and Cuba. Finally, in the "Flashpoints" section, we look to international efforts to support democracy in Venezuela and the guerrilla war in Colombia.

GEOGRAPHY

Latin America constitutes only 15 percent of the world's landmass, but the region stretches itself across nearly three-quarters of the globe in a north-south direction. It embraces an array of geographic contrasts that allow it not only to mimic many other areas of the world but also to flaunt some environments not found any-where else on earth. Those accustomed to the Mediterranean climate of Los Angeles, California, would feel somewhat at home in Santiago, Chile, which also sits in a mountain basin plagued by air pollution. The lush jungles of the Congo in Africa find a parallel in the Amazon region of South America. The arid heat and sterile plains of the Gobi Desert in Mongolia are matched by Chile's Atacama Desert. The highland cities of Nepal in the Himalayas have their counterparts in Bolivia. The tropical island settings of the South Pacific have their equals in the Caribbean. And, lest we forget the southern portion of South America rests just 600 miles from Antarctica, a trip to this region will bring the visitor in contact with chilly environs populated by penguins, whales, seals, and seabirds.

Latin America, however, also boasts many unique natural characteristics (see Figure 5.1). Soaring mountains and a location near the equator have com-bined to give Peru most of the world's tropical glaciers. Most famously, Charles Darwin did his landmark study on evolution in the Galapagos Islands, which offers a variety of exceptional creatures and plant life. Likewise, in the coastal deserts of Chile and Peru, one may easily find a Humboldt penguin nesting near a cactus. This biodiversity is not lost on the rest of the region. Of the 10 most biodiverse countries in the world recognized by the United Nations Environmental Programme, five sit in Latin America: Brazil, Colombia, Ecuador, Mexico, and Peru. Latin America is also not without its superlatives. At 22,841 feet, Mount Aconcagua in the Andes is the highest mountain in the Western Hemisphere. With its 3,212-foot descent, the Salto Angel waterfall in Venezuela cannot be bested. Meanwhile, Iguaza Falls on the border of Argentina and Brazil can lay claim to being the widest in the world. The Rio de la Plata, sepa-rating Argentina from Uruguay, is the widest river in the world, at 120 miles. The entire continental United States could be placed within the Amazon River

TABLE 5.1 Characteristics of Latin American Countries

Country	Population (millions)	Population Growth Rate (%)	Infant Mortality Rate (per 1000) Live Births	Population Under 15 Years of age (%)	Life Expectancy (in years)	Urban Population (%)	Literacy Rate (%)	Arable Land (%)	Per Capita GDP ($US)
Bahamas	0.309	0.536	23.17	25.9	65.78	84	95.6	4.58	28,600
Cuba	11.451	0.233	5.82	18.3	77.45	76	99.8	27.63	9,500
Dominican Republic	9.65	1.489	25.96	31.4	73.7	69	87	22.49	8,100
Grenada	0.0907	0.468	13.23	32	65.95	31	96	5.88	13,400
Haiti	9.035	1.838	59.69	38.1	60.78	47	52.9	28.11	1,300
Jamaica	2.825	0.755	15.22	31.4	73.53	53	87.9	15.83	7,400
Belize	0.307	2.154	23.07	37.9	68.2	52	76.9	3.05	8,600
Costa Rica	4.253	1.356	8.77	26.7	77.5	63	94.9	4.4	11,600
El Salvador	7.185	1.656	21.52	35.4	72.33	61	80.2	31.73	6,200
Guatemala	13.267	2.066	27.84	39.4	70.29	49	69.1	13.22	5,200
Honduras	7.792	1.956	24.03	38.1	69.4	48	80	9.53	4,400
Mexico	111.211	1.13	18.42	29.1	76.06	77	91	12.66	14,200
Nicaragua	5.891	1.784	25.02	33.8	71.5	57	67.5	14.81	2900
Panama	3.36	1.503	12.67	29.3	77.25	73	91.5	7.26	11,600
Argentina	40.913	1.053	11.44	25.6	76.56	92	97.2	10.03	14,200
Bolivia	9.775	1.772	44.66	35.5	66.89	66	86.7	2.78	4,500
Brazil	198.739	1.119	22.58	26.7	71.99	86	88.6	6.93	10,100
Chile	16.601	0.881	7.71	23.2	77.34	88	95.7	2.6	14,900
Colombia	44.644	1.377	18.9	28.9	72.81	74	92.8	2.01	8,900
Ecuador	14.573	1.497	20.9	31.1	75.3	66	91	5.71	7,500
Guyana	0.772	0.181	29.65	25.7	66.68	28	98.8	2.23	3,900

continued

TABLE 5.1 Continued

Country	Population (millions)	Population Growth Rate (%)	Infant Mortality Rate (per 1000) Live Births	Population Under 15 Years of age (%)	Life Expectancy (in years)	Urban Population (%)	Literacy Rate (%)	Arable Land (%)	Per Capita GDP ($US)
Paraguay	6.995	2.346	24.68	36.7	75.77	60	94	7.47	4,200
Peru	29.546	1.229	28.62	29.1	70.74	71	92.9	2.88	8,400
Suriname	0.481	1.103	18.81	27.1	73.73	75	89.6	0.36	8,900
Uruguay	3.494	0.466	11.32	22.4	76.35	92	98	7.77	12,200
Venezuela	26.814	1.508	21.54	30.5	73.61	93	93	2.85	13,500
Comparison states									
Austria	8.21	0.052	4.42	14.5	79.5	67	98	16.59	39,200
Hungary	9.905	−0.257	12.99	15	72.44	68	99.4	49.58	19,800
Ireland	4.203	1.12	7.77	20.9	78.24	61	99	16.82	46,200
USA	307.212	0.975	8.27	20.2	78.11	82	99	18.01	47,000

Source: CIA World Factbook, 2009.

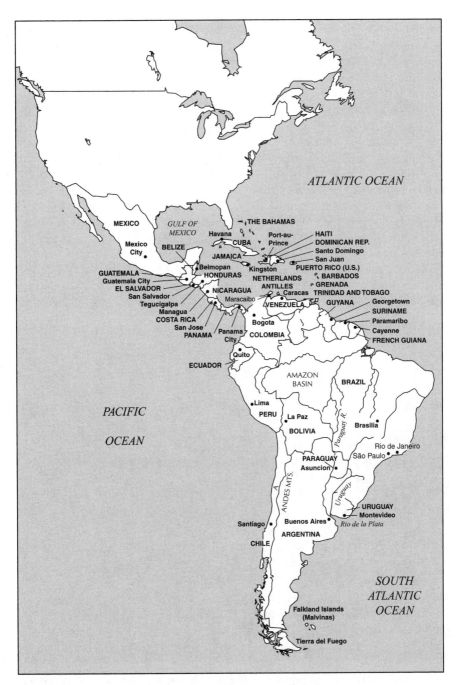

FIGURE 5.1 Political and Physical Characteristics of Latin America

basin, which hosts the largest rain forest in the world. The length of the mighty Amazon River may be surpassed by the Nile, but the Nile would need to be combined with the Mississippi and Yangtze rivers to match the water flow of the Amazon. No one would deny that California's Death Valley is parched, with its average annual rainfall of just 1.6 inches, but this cannot compete with the 0.03-inch average of Arica, Chile, the driest spot on earth. Mexico's Copper Canyon is deeper and vaster than the Grand Canyon in Arizona.

Looking south from the United States, the geology of Latin America begins with the Mexican Plateau. The plateau is couched by mountains to the east and west and comes to a rather abrupt end where it collides with a volcanic zone of mountains running east to west. Mexico City is located here and sits below the towering volcanoes of Popocatepetl and Ixtaccihuatl. A string of volcanoes continues south, more active ones along the highlands of Central America and less active ones capping the northern cone of South America from Colombia to Venezuela. Very active volcanoes also spring up at the furthermost reaches of the Caribbean in the Lesser Antilles and along the Andes mountain range, most prominently near Ecuador and throughout the Argentine–Chilean border.

South America is dominated by two natural features: the Andes and the Amazon River basin. The Andes form a well-defined range along the Argentine–Chilean border. But as they make their way up the backbone of

Slash and Burn: Slash and burn agriculture is a practice where a field is cleared by cutting and burning all vegetation. Farming after this process kills the land in only a short time. The Amazon farmer, whose field is in this photograph, has a hard choice. He can continue to farm in the old way and harm the environment or he can move his family to one of the "tin can" slums that surround most Latin American cities. *Source: Craig Arceneaux*

the continent, through Bolivia, Peru, Ecuador, and Colombia, before they wane along the coast of central Venezuela, they break into a number of ranges, creating isolated valleys that continue to separate settlement patterns and impede trade and communications to this day. Tropical highlands are found on the eastern side of the Andes in Colombia, Peru, Bolivia, and some parts of Ecuador. The climate and remote settings of these environs are ideal for the coca cultivation and cocaine processing that has plagued these countries. The vast rain forest of the Amazon River basin cuts into the northern half of the continent from the east. To its north sits the Guiana Highlands, and to its south lay the Brazilian massif and its highlands. Ranchers covet these savannah and scrublands and can easily expand their holdings into the rain forest through slash-and-burn techniques. Livestock pastures claim responsibility for 70 percent of the deforested land in the Amazon.[1] Below the Brazilian highlands, one finds the Paraná River system, which links the inland capital of Asunción, Paraguay, to the Atlantic through Argentina and serves as an important source of hydroelectric power. To the west of the Paraná, the fertile, dry lowlands of the Argentine Pampas begin their march southward. Patagonia, with its barren steppes butting up against the final reaches of the Andes, constitutes the southernmost area of the continent. This desolate area found its way into the lore of explorers in 1520 when Ferdinand Magellan claimed to have seen nine-foot giants he named "Patagons" (big feet). Hernán Cortés, Sir Francis Drake, and other explorers made the same claim, and labeled the land Patagonia, or "land of the big feet."

Natural disasters have been an unfortunate by-product of the expansive tropical areas, as well as the seismic activity in the volcanic regions. Impressive rainfalls often produce flooding in the Mexican highlands, through Central America, and in the northern cone of South America. In 1999, flooding killed 30,000 in Venezuela. Caribbean hurricanes develop regularly from July to October. Nicaragua and Honduras have yet to recover from Hurricane Mitch, whose path of destruction killed over 8,000 and left almost 3 million homeless in 1998. Over 1,000 perished in the earthquakes that rocked El Salvador in 2001, and in 1985, Mount Nevada del Ruiz erupted, killing some 21,000 in Colombia. In its 2008 annual report, the United Nations (UN) Office for the Coordination of Humanitarian Affairs noted that natural disasters in Latin America killed 1,400, affected 10 million, and produced over $60 million in damages.[2] Much of the death and destruction in the region results from the deforestation that results as the impoverished masses seek resources in their surroundings, the uncontrolled land use that leads those seeking shelter to build on precarious hillsides, the lack of effective early warning systems, and an infrastructure ill-suited for rapid evacuations—all aspects of the underdevelopment found throughout the Other World. As such, one can reasonably question the expression *natural disaster* and consider if "political" disaster might be more accurate. After all, hurricanes, flooding, earthquakes, and even volcanic eruptions of similar magnitudes afflict the United States, but the numbers of those left injured or dead are miniscule in comparison.

The political geography of Latin America has been more variable than many realize.[3] Poorly documented colonial boundaries set the stage for dispute, and unstable governments both invited and ignited war. The War of the North

American Invasion (1846–1848), as it is known in Mexico, deprived Mexico of half her landmass. Several of the Central American states emerged first as part of Mexico and then attempted confederacy before they went their own ways. Likewise, Colombia, Venezuela, and Ecuador united as Gran Colombia at independence but later separated. Guatemala claims large parts of Belize, disputing the borders enforced when the country was a British colony. Venezuela lays similar claims on neighboring Guyana. The United States engineered the separation of Panama from Colombia in 1903 to facilitate control over the planned canal. Ecuador was once double in size, but Peru gobbled up her interior in the early nineteenth century. Peru faced downsizing of her own, as defeat in the War of the Pacific (1879–1884) transferred land to Chile. This same war would hand Bolivia's Pacific outlet over to Chile as well. While Chile saw success in the north, Argentina asserted its control over the unclaimed lands of Patagonia, also coveted by Chile. Bolivia also lost land in the nineteenth century as corrupt leaders sold off large swaths to Brazil to line their own pockets and lost yet more to Paraguay in the 1930 Chaco War. That land grab hardly substituted for Paraguay's utter defeat in the 1864–1870 War of the Triple Alliance, which pitted Argentina, Brazil, and Uruguay against tiny Paraguay. The war is still identified as a source of Paraguayan underdevelopment. The country lost about one-third of its territory to Argentina and Brazil and saw roughly one-half of its population killed.

The emergence of U.S. hegemony in the twentieth century stifled many incipient interstate wars, but earlier territorial movements left bitter memories and stoked tensions that continue to this day. Changes in political geography are important for two reasons. First, war bred rivalry and nationalism, which aided nation building but also contributed to the rise of militaries that would later turn inward to overthrow their own governments. Second, though past unification efforts failed, they provide a historical sense of legitimacy for new integration schemes such as the Central American Parliament or the Union of South American Nations (UNASUR), as well as rhetorical calls for unity like Venezuela's Hugo Chavez and his appeal for solidarity in the face of North American exploitation and aggression.

PEOPLE AND CULTURE

In dealing with an area of hemispheric proportion, we should not be amazed by the cultural and physiological variation among the indigenous present when the first Europeans arrived. Three massive civilizations dominated the region at the time of conquest. The martial Aztec Empire in the lower portion of Mexico located its capital at Tenochtitlán (modern day Mexico City) and exacted tribute from the conquered peoples of its surroundings. The Mayan civilization, acclaimed for its architectural and scientific achievements, was a looser association of chiefdoms emanating from Mexico's Yucatán peninsula, southward through Guatemala. The Incan people were an archetypal empire, with a nobility and state that controlled all natural resources. From Cuzco, Peru, their leaders oversaw city-states in the peaks and valleys of the Andes in a territory that reached from Ecuador in the north to midway through Chile in the south.

The debate over the size of Latin America's population at the time of conquest rages on, with numbers that range from 12 million to upwards of 100 million.[4] Despite the disagreement, most studies place over 60 percent of the population within the Aztec, Mayan, or Incan Empires. The remaining were scattered chiefdoms or tribes, though other large settlements existed such as the Mapuche in northern Chile and Argentina, the Chibchas of the Colombian highlands, and the Yanomami of the Amazon. One indicator of the extent of cultural diversity is the number of languages found throughout the region. In Mexico alone there were more than 200 different linguistic groups. Another matter on which few scholars disagree is that pre-Colombian Latin America housed several very large cities. As many as 100,000 to 200,000 lived in Cuzco, while 150,000 to 300,000 settled in Tenochtitlán. Both rivaled and may have even surpassed the contemporaneous sizes of London and Paris. Tourists in Mexico City often visit the pyramids of Teotihuacán. These pyramids were recognized as mysterious, ancient ruins even by the Aztecs (who attempted to mimic the settlement in their own capital) and represented the centerpieces of one of the largest cities in the world at its peak in 400 A.D., when 200,000 lived there.

Today, the indigenous represent just 10 percent of the total population in the region, but their numbers are concentrated in Bolivia, Ecuador, Guatemala, Mexico, and Peru, where they constitute between 30 and 60 percent of the

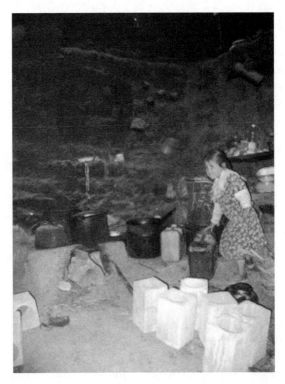

Dinner: In much of the Other World, children must start work at a young age. This girl is helping in the kitchen of a house in the Andes. Source: *Craig Arceneaux*

population. The indigenous population suffered an estimated mortality rate of 45 percent to 90 percent during the first century of contact with the Europeans, who brought with them previously unheard of diseases such as smallpox, measles, and yellow fever. The tropical highlands offered some refuge from disease and European subjugation, but the impact was especially brutal in the tropical lowlands of Mexico and Central America, as well as the Caribbean. Colonists imported African slaves, especially to the Caribbean region and Brazil, to work the newly established sugar plantations. Settlements in present-day Colombia and Venezuela served as slaving stations. The demographic legacy of the Spanish and Portuguese colonialism is clear in these countries.

Argentina sits on the other side of the demographic spectrum. Indigenous populations were historically lower here, as was European settlement due to the lack of mineral wealth. The need for labor did not come until the turn of the nineteenth century, under a light manufacturing boom, at just the same time that many Europeans were fleeing their economically depressed countries for new opportunities in the Americas. Some arrived at Ellis Island in New York and others at the port in Buenos Aires. In fact, today one in three Argentines traces his or her roots to Italy. Uruguay, where 90 percent of the population claims European heritage, is similar.

Today, however, individuals of mixed European and indigenous blood, or *mestizos*, make up most of Latin America's population. The African populations have also mixed to create large mulatto groups as well. The result is a medley of peoples in the region, one that struggles to create a Latin American identity and come to terms with issues of conquest and enslavement. Indigenous peoples can point to the majesty of their ancient civilizations, but colonization decimated not only their numbers, but their culture as well. The Spanish consolidated dispersed settlements into concentrated townships, known as *reducciones*, and they granted vast properties, or *encomiendas*, to settlers and included the labor of the resident indigenous population. Later, the *mita* system created a rotating, forced labor scheme that required indigenous communities to hand over one-seventh of their adult male population on an annual basis. The early Catholic clergy actually quarreled over whether Indians had souls or not in a debate that flowed from a much more fundamental question, "Are the indigenous human beings?" Even those who answered in the affirmative retained a disdainful, patronizing tone: The indigenous were savages in need of far-reaching acculturation if they were to become members of civilization. Such perspectives perpetuated the social, political, and economic exclusion of indigenous peoples far beyond independence.

But racial relations in Latin America have developed differently than in the United States. Much of this flows from different perspectives of how ethnic identity is defined. After abolition in the United States, states and localities scrambled to define "colored" on the basis of blood percentage, and similar benchmarks were placed on Native Americans. Today, no such legal definitions exist (the U.S. Census Bureau allows individuals to self-identify), but that history has contributed to a "biological" approach to ethnic identification, one that led many Americans during the 2008 presidential election to debate whether Barack Obama was "black enough." But in Latin America, the widespread mixing of European, African, and indigenous peoples has produced a "constructivist" approach that embraces a more fluid ethnic identity based on cultural customs. This approach occurred as *mestizo* intellectuals (especially in Mexico and Peru) in the early twentieth century sought to come to terms with questions of national identity and the large indigenous populations that surrounded them. For many, the "Indian," mired in squalid and exploitative conditions, represented the very flip side of modernity. How then, could indigenous identity serve as a vehicle for nationalism? The intellectual movement of *indigenismo* denied the biological basis of race, and in its place promoted culture and the arts as sources of identity. They argued that contemporary Indians, insofar as contact with Spanish settlers long ago changed their lifestyles and traditions, moved away from authentic indigenous identities. In a way the argument was that "we are all *mestizos* now." Indigenous identity did not exist in bloodlines, but rather in cultural celebrations, traditions, and the arts—activities that *mestizo* intellectuals took upon themselves to preserve and promote.

On the one hand, the fluid identity promoted by *indigenismo* aids social mobility and thus a more egalitarian society. But others counter that the movement "de-Indianized" indigenous peoples and allowed the *mestizo* elite to appropriate their identity.[5] Hence, in 1983, the Second Conference of Indian Nationals and Organizations of South America declared, "*Indigenismo* must be rejected because it corresponds to the ideology of oppression. Since its origin it has served the racist interests of governments, missionaries, and anthropologists."[6] A plaque near the ruins of Tlatelolco in Mexico City, where the Aztecs stood their last ground, reflects this struggle over identity. It reads: "On August 13th, 1521, Tlatelolco, heroically defended by Cuauhtemoc, fell to the power of Hernan Cortés. This was neither a triumph nor a defeat, but the painful birth of the mixed race that is Mexico today."

Today those of European heritage retain many elite positions, while those of native bloods continue to live in squalor. A 2005 World Bank study notes that extreme poverty in Mexico is 4.5 times higher in predominantly indigenous areas than nonindigenous areas and sets poverty among Ecuador's indigenous at 87 percent and upwards of 96 percent in the rural highlands. It also recognizes that the trend of poverty for the indigenous continues to worsen.[7] These destitute conditions fed the Zapatista guerrilla movement in Southern Mexico and spurred indigenous groups to play a central role in protests leading to presidential ousters in Ecuador and Bolivia.

Two in five Roman Catholics worldwide live in Latin America, so it should be no surprise that this religion predominates in the region. Because the Catholic Church so closely identified itself with the Spanish and Portuguese *conquistadores*, the colonial authorities, and later traditional and even modern elites, however, its link to many populations has been nonexistent, weak, or altered. At independence, to rebel against Spain also meant rebelling against the Church, and this created an uneasy relationship in many countries. As testimony, a visit to the gravesites of Chile's independence leaders requires a trip to the General Cemetery, located on the once-far outskirts of Santiago because the Catholic Church refused burial on their grounds. Likewise, though the remains of the Great Liberator, General José de San Martín, rest in the Metropolitan Cathedral of Buenos Aires, they are in a den, structurally separate from the hallowed interior of the church. Church affairs remained central to Latin American politics through the nineteenth century, as Conservative parties lobbied to protect religious privileges, while Liberal parties sought greater separations of church and state. Civil war often broke out between the two. More recently, the church hierarchy drew tremendous criticism as it turned its head, or even grew complicit, in the repression under the military dictatorships of the 1960s and 1970s. Hoping to strengthen relations with Latin America, in 2002 the Vatican canonized its first indigenous saint, Juan Diego. His vision of the Virgin of Guadalupe in 1531 and her miraculous impression on his cloak helped to convert indigenous peoples in the critical early years of colonization. But the twenty-first century celebration in Mexico stirred as much indignation as vindication. Official portraits of the Chichimeca Indian distributed by the Church revealed a pail-skinned, bearded figure. For many, the move only reaffirmed the inability of the Church to establish authentic relations with indigenous communities.[8]

The Catholic Church, however, has always had its progressive elements as well. Miguel Hidalgo and José Maria Morelos, heroes of Mexican independence who fought for the indigenous and social justice, were both priests. Colombian

Most Latin American States have had their Share of Violence: This outline of a human body on the Plaza of Three Cultures at Tlatelolco in Mexico is a grim reminder of the massacre that took place here when the government brutally repressed a large student protest on October 2, 1968. *Source: Craig Arceneaux*

priest Camilo Torres blended Christianity with Marxist thought to create Liberation Theology and helped found the ELN guerrilla group in Colombia. Much of the progressive movement comes from the lower ranks of the Church hierarchy, whose upper level is typically quick to distance itself or historically excommunicate dissidents of traditional doctrine. Nonetheless, there are important exceptions such as El Salvador's Archbishop Oscar Romero, assassinated for his criticism of military repression in the 1980s; Guatemala's Bishop Juan José Gerardi, killed in 1998 after publishing a document on military abuse; and Bishop Samuel Ruiz, who defended the claims of the Zapatistas in Chiapas, Mexico.

Because of the mixed background of the Catholic Church, other faiths have moved to attract the disaffected. Many traditional African religions had an important impact on the region's religious culture. Blending African gods with Christian saints and local tradition, Latin Americans have produced such exotic rites as *Candomblé* in Brazil and *voodoo* in Haiti and Cuba. More recently, evangelical Pentecostal Protestant churches have gained a tremendous following, especially among the poorest classes in Central America and Brazil. With their focus on individual responsibility and a personal relationship with God, critics argue that they push an inherently conservative agenda that devalues questions of social justice and collective action. Though the evangelicals have not translated their growing numbers into political influence, their connection to General Efraín Ríos Montt of Guatemala (a member of the Pentecostal *El Verbo* Church) is an important exception. Christian fundamentalists from the United States sent millions of dollars to support his military government from 1982 to 1983, when he presided over a brutal counterinsurgency campaign that killed tens of thousands of indigenous persons in the name of anticommunism. Ríos Montt's stigma continues to haunt Guatemalan politics. Human rights activists celebrated in 2006 when a Spanish judge indicted him for crimes against humanity and called for his extradition but were left dismayed after his election to congress in late 2007. The position affords the ex-dictator immunity privileges that would require lengthy legal processes to undo.

HISTORY

The Colonial Experience

The *reconquista*, the 700-year battle to expel Islamic Moors from the Iberian peninsula, set the stage for Spain's colonial exertion.[9] Eager to consolidate political control, the monarchy looked to secure overseas resources through mercantilism. In the Americas mining was aggressively promoted, agriculture was geared toward exports (not foodstuffs for the local population, but spices and dyes), and manufacturing was actively discouraged. This economic formula would have far-reaching repercussions on development in the region. Back at home, regional nobles threatened the monarchy because they had grown accustomed to local autonomy under the *reconquista*, and fighting had gained them affluence and glory. Would they now turn against royal authority? To avert such risks, the monarchy tended to send the avaricious, self-seeking, "up and coming" nobility to the New World. So individuals such as Hernan Cortés, who conquered the Aztecs in 1521, Francisco Pizzaro, who followed suit against the Incas in 1535, and other *conquistadores* were very enthusiastic about war, and set a militaristic tone as government emerged in colonial Latin America. Finally, Spain was an empire emboldened with a conquest spirit. They had militarily conquered the Moors; the Spanish Inquisition was in full swing to combat Jews, Muslims, various infidels, and later Protestants; and in the Western Hemisphere, they would Christianize the Indians.

The Spanish Empire slowly crumbled as the Netherlands broke away, and constant warfare developed between Spain and France and England (between 1650 and 1770, Spain would experience only 18 years of peace). With war, shipping grew more difficult. In the mid-seventeenth century, one large fleet a year would leave Latin America for Spain. Galleons flush with bullion from Peru and Mexico would converge in Havana, Cuba, and then sail together for protection to Spain. By the end of the seventeenth century, these trips became so dangerous that fleets would sail, or only make it, every four or five years. Mercantilism itself proved to be a curse as gold and silver flooded the Spanish economy, raising inflationary pressures and undercutting Spanish producers in international markets. Mercantilism also raised tension with colonists who would have rather purchased cheaper goods from the British or French. The mercantile wall wrought round the Americas soon fell to incursions by Dutch, British, and others seeking trade with the burgeoning populations and compelled the Spanish to expend more on defense. Hence, as economic malaise in Spain intensified the need for precious metals, defensive requirements abroad led more to remain in Latin America.

Spain's gradual deterioration would have long-lasting effects on the politics of Latin America. Financial difficulties meant that Spain would have to build an empire on the cheap.[10] The sale of administrative offices in the colonies provided some revenue. To address the minimal pay, Spain conceded widespread profit-making policy authority to colonial officials. They could manipulate land-use laws, sell commercial licenses and skim port fees, and collect extra taxes on land transfers. Many also used their positions to take bribes from local merchants, violating rules against intercolonial trade. The fusion between public service and private gain would breed a culture of corruption and impunity that continues to beleaguer Latin American politics today. Another enduring political impact emerged from Spanish military concerns. To advance the war effort, governmental and military roles were often united. This would ease the entry of the military into politics, a problem that would later plague Latin America.

The Wars for National Independence

Spain had a natural reaction to its imperial decline. Seeking to safeguard what it could, it allowed only the *peninsulares*, or those born in Spain but sent to America, to hold the highest colonial offices. *Criollos*, of European blood but born in the New World, were deemed less trustworthy. The move raised tensions between the two groups. The anxiety deepened as Spain responded to continued military setbacks with calls for more military units. This meant expanding the officer corps, which traditionally had been reserved for *peninsulares*. By necessity, more and more *criollos* were allowed to enter the higher ranks. Consider what was happening. Latin Americans increasingly viewed government as something foreign, while the military began to emerge as the only truly national institution.

Still, the *criollos* were not prepared to confront the privileged status of the *peninsulares*. In the general scope of society, they too were privileged. Together with the *peninsulares*, they sat atop a social hierarchy that placed the vast majority of the population—the *mestizos*, mulattos, and indigenous—far below. Desiring reform but fearing revolution, the *criollos* balked and accepted the status quo. Only a colossal blow to the Spanish Empire would shake their reticence.

That blow came in the form of the French Revolution. Napoleon's political vision rejected monarchy and led him to invade Spain, depose King Ferdinand VII, and place his brother, Joseph Bonaparte, in control in 1808. *Criollos* largely rejected the new ruler and argued that since Spain no longer had a government, sovereignty reverted to colonies, and independence was theirs. Several local rebellions began in Buenos Aires, Caracas, and Mexico. The end of the Napoleonic Wars, however, reestablished the Spanish crown, and many *criollos* withdrew their support for rebellion. Spanish forces quelled the remaining rebellions, and by 1815 all seemed to have returned to normal. But more shocks were to come from Europe.

First, Great Britain, eager to speed the fall of Spanish control in Latin America, sent troops to aid the independence movement in Caracas and furnished significant naval support in Peru. This gave time for the independence leaders to combine and coordinate their forces. It especially reignited the forces in the north of South America led by Simón Bolívar, who attained control of the region by 1819. Second, while Ferdinand VII did regain his position, he succumbed to reformist pressures in Spain. A liberal constitution with an anticlerical tenor appalled the conservative *peninsular* class and led many to reinvigorate the rebellion. Their impact was felt immediately. For instance, though the Great Liberator, José de San Martín, found military success across Argentina and north from Chile, *peninsulares* and *criollos* supportive of the monarchy initially forced him to stop in Peru. When word of the reforms arrived, however, these same groups joined the revolt. A similar story unfolded in Mexico. Spanish General Agustín de Iturbide originally fought to put down the independence movement but then switched sides after hearing of the reformist moves by the monarch. Mexico achieved independence in 1821, and Iturbide declared himself emperor. The Central American states, with landed elites attracted to the conservative independence movement, annexed themselves to Mexico for a time.

The clashing motives behind independence denied Latin America the *founding myths* that are so important to the growth of nationalism. By "myths," we do not mean fabricated stories of the past, but rather shared historical narratives that express deep-seated, common values and thereby bind a people as a nation. Was independence a fight for liberty much like the French and American Revolutions? Was it a move to safeguard conservative traditions and the status of privileged groups such as the large landowning hacienda elites,

Catholic Church, and the armed forces? Or, in the eyes of the indigenous masses, was it a revolution denied?

Postcolonial History and the Beginnings of U.S. Involvement

The wars for independence wrought a heavy toll. They decimated the civilian labor force, reduced livestock populations, and diverted machinery from industry to military uses. Trade virtually stood still from 1810 to 1826. Thereafter, separatist groups and lawless bands in the hinterlands hindered commerce. The public debt mushroomed under the burden of military spending. Tax collection was difficult, so governments had to pull loans, especially from Britain, that would burden them well after independence.

War also undermined traditional lines of authority as the demand for military leadership opened new opportunities for the *mestizo* class. *Peninsulares* and *criollos*, concerned first with military victory, did not mind supporting a *mestizo* if he could get the job done. At independence, however, this left *mestizos* with no alternative careers in charge of large, disparate military forces. Many became *caudillos*, or military strongmen known for their avaricious ways. The *peninsulares* and *criollos* withdrew to their haciendas, where they could essentially act as self-sufficient units far off in the countryside and leave government to a *caudillo*. *Caudillo* rule, however, typically fed the following vicious circle: A *caudillo* would assume the presidency with fanfare from his troops—they had achieved the ultimate power quest—taking the capital. Then the *caudillo* would find little money in the treasury, and his troops, accustomed to war booty and expecting reward, would withdraw support. Another *caudillo* would then come forward and topple the president, and the process would begin anew. This describes the politics of much of Latin America from 1820 to 1870.

The United States had little influence during these times. On December 2, 1823, in a message to Congress, President Monroe declared what has come to be known as the Monroe Doctrine, which expressed three themes: a prohibition on the establishment of new colonies or the transfer of existing colonies in the Americas, U.S. abstention from European involvements, and the exclusion of Europe from the Western Hemisphere. In retrospect, the doctrine appears bold and is often presented as such in U.S. school textbooks. In reality, however, the Monroe Doctrine largely fell on deaf ears. The document actually grew out of a British suggestion that the United States issue a joint statement with Britain. Britain wished to restrain France from taking advantage of the Spanish retreat in the region and desired independent states. With the world's largest navy and burgeoning commercial interests, Britain had more interest in trading than territorial conquest.

Indeed, throughout the nineteenth century, European intervention in the Americas was common. A street in Buenos Aires is named *Defensa* to acknowledge the battle against British troops, who attempted to take the city twice in 1806 to 1807. French troops marched across Mexico in the 1860s in support of an Austrian duke welcomed as an emperor by Mexican conservatives. Spanish warships shelled the coasts of Chile, Peru, and Ecuador from 1865 to 1866 in a move partly spurred by postindependence animosity. British expeditionary forces landed in Nicaragua and Venezuela for long periods to enforce debt payments. U.S. intervention and influence in the nineteenth century competed with Europe and was largely confined to Mexico and Central America. Of course, Mexico felt the full brunt of the U.S. forces, losing half its territory in the aftermath of the U.S.–Mexico War (1846–1848).

The Spanish-American War (1898) marked the true beginnings of U.S. influence throughout the region. The acquisition of Puerto Rico and Cuba symbolized a southward shift in U.S. foreign policy, as the United States sought to consolidate its hold on the hemisphere. The Roosevelt Corollary (1904) to the Monroe Doctrine declared that the United States would prohibit incursions by foreign creditor nations into the hemisphere by undertaking preemptive invasions and occupations of insolvent Latin American countries. Using this inflated view of its self-appointed role, the United States justified military intervention in many of the states of the Caribbean and Central America. In response to the animosity produced by these actions, Franklin Roosevelt promulgated the "Good Neighbor Policy" to profess U.S. respect for Latin American sovereignty. Global politics, however, soon overshadowed the expression.

With the development of the Cold War in the late 1940s and the accompanying goal to contain Communism, there was once again a tendency to justify intervention. In 1948, the United States declared Communist groups, even if entirely homegrown, to be foreign threats. The Johnson Doctrine, pronounced in 1964, called for the destabilization and overthrow of Marxist governments even if they had been popularly elected. In the view of Latin Americans, the arrogance reached its apex in the 1960s and 1980s, when the United States supported brutally repressive military dictatorships as bulwarks in the struggle against Communism—presumably in the name of freedom and democracy.

ECONOMICS

Mercantilism stifled early economic growth in Latin America. Then the long wars for independence and periods of *caudillo* rule interrupted economic opportunities in the nineteenth century. The region fell increasingly behind as industrialism expanded in Western Europe and the United States, but the economies of those countries would reach back and reinsert Latin America into the world economy in a subsidiary role during the late 1800s. Growing urban classes and manufacturing in the industrialized countries created demands for Latin American foodstuffs and raw materials. The demands pressured Latin American governments to cast aside *caudillo* rule so that they could stabilize and centralize. Though the new economic formula boosted national incomes, it brought with it inequality. Those with access to export markets or able to find jobs in the export sector thrived, but those without these advantages lost ground.

The newfound wealth also opened new vulnerabilities. The lack of a diverse entrepreneurial class or developed capital markets tended to push investment in a single direction and led countries to concentrate exports within just a few, or even one, commodity. Historical data show that by 1938 coffee constituted

92 percent of Salvadoran exports, sugar amounted to 78 percent of Cuban exports, tin made for 68 percent of Bolivian exports, and coffee was 45 percent of Brazilian exports.[11] Other examples abound: copper from Chile, bananas from throughout Central America, oil from Venezuela, and *guano* from Peru to fertilize the agricultural fields of Europe. Later, Uruguay would see its economy boom simply because the clothing of U.S. soldiers in the Korean War required wool from its vast sheep ranches. Such concentrated export markets placed Latin America on a roller coaster of economic swings. A 20 percent drop in the price of coffee could spark a recession in Guatemala or Colombia. An unusually poor rainy season could do the same.

Latin America would be forced to confront its export dependency when global economic demand fell during World War I. The global recession of the 1930s intensified the economic malaise and brought with it instability that saw militaries intervene in governments throughout the region. World War II also interrupted global demands for commodities. Latin America responded with *import substitution industrialization* (ISI) to create more diverse economies. This economic policy called on the government to shut out imports of manufactured goods with tariffs so that domestic infant industries could develop behind a protective trade wall. Government also stimulated manufacturing with subsidies or public ownership of industries. To ensure a market for their goods, governments supported wage increases and labor rights. ISI, thus, engendered a populist political alliance of the working class, middle class groups finding jobs in the burgeoning bureaucracy, and national industries. The primary products sector was squeezed to fund the program. Populist leaders, such as Juan Perón in Argentina and Getúlio Vargas in Brazil, presided over growing economies in the 1940s and 1950s.

By the 1960s, however, the ISI model had been exhausted. The primary products sector degenerated as it was pressed to bankroll the program and could no longer act as the cash cow it once was. The manufacturing sector did indeed develop and diversify, but protectionism allowed it to grow fat. Government found that it was subsidizing businesses that could not compete in global markets. Economic decline ensued, followed by political turmoil as business subsidies were withdrawn and wages could no longer be supported. Militaries intervened throughout the region and attempted to dismantle the ISI system from the 1960s to 1980s, but they proved incompetent—unable to devise an alternative economic formula. The military governments did have one advantage the populist governments did not: their impeccable anticommunist credentials. Prompted by U.S. foreign policy, foreign banks saw in them trustworthy, stable allies in the effort to protect free enterprise and readily showered them with loans. With ISI policies still anchored in place in most countries, however, the loans not only delayed the inevitable, but made things worse as debt accumulated. Mexico defaulted on its debt in 1982, and much of the region soon followed suit, initiating a crisis so intense that the 1980s would be tagged "the lost decade."

If there was any silver lining to the economic devastation of the 1980s, it was that it exposed the ineffectiveness of military government. The experience was so traumatic that it initiated a sea change in Latin America. Democracy, not military dictatorship, would guide government. Many thought that similarly dramatic reversals in economic policy would make economic malaise a thing of the past. State-led ISI programs were tossed aside in favor of neoliberal policies that encouraged economic openness in trade and investment. Soon, cooperation began to undermine old geopolitical rivalries. The nations of the southern cone (Brazil, Argentina, Paraguay, and Uruguay—Venezuela would apply for full membership in 2006) signed the Treaty of Asunción in 1991 to create MERCOSUR (The Common Market of the South). Modeled on the European Union, MERCOSUR has reduced restrictions on trade and investment and has served as a forum for broader integration efforts. Roads, gas pipelines, and electricity grids are being integrated, and the countries are looking to unify immigration policies and even educational systems. Bolivia, Chile, Colombia, Ecuador, and Peru are associate members of MERCOSUR. At the other end of the hemisphere, Canada, Mexico, and the United States launched the *North American Free Trade Agreement (NAFTA)* on January 1, 1994, which focuses more narrowly on trade and investment. The countries of the isthmus created the Central American Integration System (SICA) to aid cooperation in a number of policy areas, but the new Central American Free Trade Agreement (CAFTA) with the United States may overshadow economic collaboration within SICA. Other regional groupings include the 13 English-speaking countries that make up the Caribbean Commonwealth (CARICOM), and the Andean Community, which hopes to combine with MERCOSUR and create the Union of South American Nations (UNASUR).

The economic opening of the 1990s put Latin America on another rollercoaster, reminiscent of the commodity export economy at the preceding turn of the century. Though the extreme examples have passed, many countries remain highly dependent on a few commodities. In 2007, aluminum made up 48 percent of Jamaica's exports, natural gas constituted 40 percent of Bolivia's, and fish represented 24 percent of Panama's.[12] But investment flows are the new vulnerability of this economic opening. Countries throughout the region sold off vast government industries created under ISI and privatized many services previously allocated by the state. Governments relaxed controls on capital markets so that foreign investors could move money across borders more easily and with less taxation than in the past. Stock markets in Mexico, Brazil, Argentina, and Chile emerged as new sources of interest for investors throughout the world. Total private capital flows to the region increased from $13 billion in 1990 to $41 billion in 2003. As an indicator of growing confidence in governments now viewed as beholden to neoliberal economic policies, purchases of bonds increased from $101 million in 1990 to a staggering $12.8 billion in 2003.[13] The new investment flows powered economic growth in the early 1990s. The problem, however, was that many of those same investments could be withdrawn as easily and quickly as they came. Investors target a country when they grow confident in it. But bad news can easily erode that confidence. Moreover, a herd effect may develop as skittish investors lead others to rethink their portfolios. The withdrawal of investments dampens demand for national currencies, decreasing their value, and creating currency crises as speculators unload their currency holdings before they lose more value. This is what happened in Mexico in 1995, Brazil in 1999, and Argentina in 2001 to 2002.

The economic downturn in the latter 1990s undermined U.S. efforts to create a Free Trade Area of the Americas (FTAA). In the early 2000s, the uncompromising policies of the Bush administration and the unpopular war in Iraq tore at U.S. credibility and opened its leadership position to sweeping criticisms. In his address at the opening of the 2005 Summit of the Americas in Argentina, presidential host Nestor Kircher declared that the United States had the "inescapable and inexcusable responsibility" for policies that not only provoke poverty and misery but also destabilize democratic governments. Venezuelan President Hugo Chávez proclaimed, "The FTAA is dead and we are attending a funeral here." In its place, he proposed the "Bolivarian Alliance for the Americas" (ALBA, in its Spanish acronym) to promote socially conscious economic policies, sustainable development, and international programs that redistributed resources to poor communities and countries. In an apparent acknowledgment, the United States has since concentrated its economic efforts on bilateral free trade agreements, most recently with Colombia, Panama, and Peru. Meanwhile, ALBA has grown to include nine member states: Antigua and Barbuda, Bolivia, Cuba, Dominica, Ecuador, Honduras, Nicaragua, and Saint Vincent and the Grenadines, and Venezuela (Paraguay is an observer).

In Latin America, economic crisis seems to be an endemic feature that simply changes its stripes through time—from the commodity price fluctuations of the nineteenth century to the debt crises of the 1980s and the currency crises of today. The vulnerabilities of dependency are a common thread during these crises. Most recently, in 2008 the collapse of housing prices in the United States and elsewhere and the strain this placed on the financial sector created a global financial crisis. According to the April 2009 *World Economic Outlook*, published by the International Monetary Fund (IMF), this has generated a "trifecta of shocks" in Latin America: The banking crisis has boosted borrowing costs and trimmed capital inflows; a drop in commodity prices has undercut the region's most prominent comparative advantage in trade; and the recessions in advanced economies (especially the United States) have reduced revenues from exports, tourism, and remittances from migrant laborers. Following negative growth through 2009, the report predicts only a modest recovery through 2010.[14] Ultimately, however, distribution, not growth, determines the political importance of economic matters in the region. In the United States (which holds higher levels of inequality than most developed countries), the wealthiest 10 percent receive 31 percent of all income, while in the majority of Latin American countries, the wealthiest 10 percent receive 40 percent to 47 percent of all income. Inequality remains higher than in any region of the Other World, and things are not getting better. Every country saw growing inequality since the 1990s except for, ironically, Brazil, whose improvement was still not enough to remove its listing among the most unequal societies on earth.[15]

GOVERNMENT

In the 1970s, one could count the "free" governments of Latin America on one hand: Costa Rica, Colombia, and Venezuela. The major countries of South America had military-installed, bureaucratic-authoritarian regimes, while those in Central America retained a more personal and unstable rule by the armed forces. The bureaucratic-authoritarian regime was a phenomenon of the 1970s and 1980s and is distinguished from the tradition of authoritarian governments in Latin America by several characteristics. Military officers cooperated with career bureaucrats to staff government agencies. The working class was eliminated from directly influencing policy because political parties and labor organizations were curtailed or prohibited altogether. The government favored the establishment and, to some degree, the middle class because groups from these sectors were in the best position to define policy and protect their interests as the influential bureaucrats came from their ranks. This condition resulted in an acute case of bureaucratic or military myopia, which interpreted all problems as technical in nature and reducible to an administrative solution rather than negotiation. This kind of government provided the appearance of stability so satisfying to foreign investors and often succeeded in attracting business from abroad. In time, however, it aggravated and finally alienated the members of the domestic middle class. They may have originally welcomed the military "solution" to the rising social chaos, but in time they felt threatened by the growing entry of foreign investment challenging their economic status.

The military regimes of the 1960s and 1980s left a traumatic legacy of human rights abuses. In some cases, the abuse was carried out within civil wars. From 1978 to 1985 the Guatemalan military implemented a "scorched-earth policy" to root out suspected insurgents from countryside villages. The campaign left some 75,000 dead and produced more than one million refugees. Few, if any, were immune from persecution in Latin America. In 1980, the rape and murder of three U.S. Catholic nuns in El Salvador brought international attention, as did the assassination of Archbishop Oscar Romero that same year. In Argentina, labor was induced in expectant female political opponents. After delivery, the mother would be murdered and the child handed over to a military family for adoption. Sometimes fathers would be forced to witness the atrocity. In 1995 the prominent Argentine journalist Horacio Verbitsky published "El Vuelo" ("The Flight"), which documented how naval authorities would drug suspects and then take them by helicopter to be dumped over the Atlantic Ocean. In the hope they would sink quickly and never be found, the officers would slit their stomachs. A widespread tactic had officers "disappear" political opponents. In the past, detention, torture, and killing would leave a paper trail as the official records of police stations and courts documented movements. To avoid blame, military governments kidnapped individuals and disposed of their bodies in undisclosed locations. Those seeking information of their whereabouts would typically receive the same answers at police stations or wherever they inquired: "They must have joined the subversives," or "Perhaps they left the country." The most systematic disappearances took place in Argentina. Estimates range from 10,000 to 20,000. Beyond those killed, many more tens of thousands survived their torture, and yet more were detained and often deprived of their possessions or employment.

Many of the militaries received amnesties or other guarantees to coax them from government. The struggle to revoke these coerced concessions and pursue justice continues to agitate Latin American politics. That struggle has elicited ingenious legal strategies. In Chile, an amnesty prohibits prosecutions of human rights abuses committed before 1978. The courts ruled that disappearances were "permanent kidnappings," and as crimes in progress they could in fact be processed. On another front, Chilean jurists have successfully argued that an amnesty cannot take effect without knowledge of the crime itself. Hence, though prosecution remains proscribed, investigation does not. Justice remains curtailed, but at least those responsible can be identified and perhaps shamed into remorse. In Argentina, amnesty covered murder and torture, but it did not address the kidnapping of babies that took place so systematically. This allowed the courts to process generals as leaders of a criminal kidnapping network. More dramatic changes took place in June 2005, when the Argentine Supreme Court declared the military amnesties unconstitutional.

For many, military impunity is but a symptom of more pervasive accountability issues in government. Democracy is indeed the norm in Latin America, but the lack of some basic ingredients hounds democratic consolidation. Political parties remain weak and often fail to bridge societal concerns and government. Without such access to policymaking, social movements feel compelled to take more direct action through disruptive protests, labor strikes, and demonstrations. Congresses are underfunded and poorly staffed; hence, though constitutions design them to balance the presidential power, they often lack the resources to do so. This allows power to concentrate in the executive office, and provokes charges of imperial presidencies. A lack of faith in the courts has spawned a vigilante culture. A UN study found 482 reported lynchings (the actual number is certainly much higher) in Guatemala from 1996 to 2002.[16] Protestors developed the *escrache* (from *escrachar*, slang for "to uncover") in Argentina in response to the denial of justice after military rule. An *escrache* develops as the whereabouts of a perpetrator is learned. Citizens surround his house, distribute flyers and inform neighbors, write graffiti, and give speeches to publicize past iniquities. Today, protestors use *escraches* in reaction to all sorts of misdeeds. In 2004, a nightclub fire killed 190 in Buenos Aires. As the public learned of code violations and blocked emergency exits, an *escrache* developed outside the owner's home, forcing the police to take him into protective custody. Could he receive a fair trial now? The *escrache*, increasingly in use throughout Latin America, emerged because of ineffective judicial systems, and there is no doubt that many deserve its wrath; but there is also no doubt that it further undermines those same ineffective judicial systems.

Today, many speak of a *New Left* in Latin America—a resurgence of populist, progressive politics keenly oriented toward criticisms of U.S. imperialism. In reality, there are both radical and moderate New Left camps. As Fidel Castro passes from the limelight, Venezuela under Hugo Chávez is certainly the champion of the radical New Left. With regional efforts such as the ALBA and a proposed Banco del Sur to counter the loaning activities of the IMF and World Bank, Chávez has sought to solidify ties to like-minded governments. Recently elected leaders in Argentina (Cristina Kirchner), Bolivia (Evo Morales), Ecuador (Rafael Correa), and Nicaragua (Daniel Ortega) side closely with Chávez. But Chávez's attempts to wield influence abroad have sometimes backfired. His comments on presidential elections in Mexico and Peru were interpreted as meddling by electorates in these countries and inadvertently rallied electoral turnout on the right. A more moderate New Left finds its leadership in Luís Inácio "Lula" da Silva of Brazil and Michelle Bachelet of Chile. Tabaré Vázquez of Uruguay echoes their more pragmatic critiques of neoliberalism. He often rails against U.S. imperialism but has also endorsed free trade agreements with the United States.

Throughout Latin America, the United States receives the most strident support from Colombia, which draws almost one-third of all U.S. aid in the region. After Ecuador's Rafael Correa shut down the United States' only air base in South America in 2009, Colombia promptly opened negotiations with the United States for use of its air bases. Leaders throughout the region, whether squarely in the New Left or not, largely welcomed the transition from the Bush to the Obama administration. Many leaders expressed confidence that President Obama would not only embrace a more multilateral approach in the region, but that he would revise the U.S. foreign policy fixation on terrorism and security, which views Latin America as relevant only insofar as migration and drug trafficking burden the United States. Their hope is that the United States will engage Latin America on a variety of fronts that instead underscore opportunity, such as trade and investment, cultural exchange, democratic strengthening, cooperative research on alternative energy, poverty alleviation, education, and environmental sustainability. At the 2009 Summit of the Americas in Trinidad, President Obama embraced these hopes, remarking in his opening statements: "There is no senior partner and junior partner in our relations; there is simply engagement based on mutual respect and common interests and shared values. So I'm here to launch a new chapter of engagement that will be sustained throughout my administration." Energetic applause followed his words, but suspicions remained. Nicaraguan President Daniel Ortega used his remarks to launch a 50-minute denunciation of U.S. imperialism. Bolivia's Evo Morales met privately with President Obama to disclose his firm belief of a CIA plot to assasinate him. And Hugo Chávez greeted Obama with Eduardo Galeano's *Open Veins of Latin America* to spotlight the theme of exploitation in U.S.-Latin American relations. As his foreign policy agenda develops, President Obama may find the change he believes U.S.-Latin American relations need to be quite different from the change Latin American leaders want.

CASE STUDIES

1. Mexico

The drawn-out war for independence, *caudillo* politics, and the U.S. invasion all took their toll on the political and economic stability of Mexico for much of the nineteenth century. Things would change under the *Porfiriato* (1877–1911), named after José de la Cruz Porfirio Díaz who occupied the presidency for much of this time. He ruled with an iron fist and thumbed his nose at constitutional restrictions on reelection. Under the *Porfiriato*, the country underwent its first round of economic development. The dictator opened the country to thorough exploitation by foreigners. In four years, railroad track increased fivefold as soon as Díaz granted the concession to external interests in 1880, foreign trade increased by a factor of nine, and the United States became Mexico's chief trading partner. The costs of progress, however, were excruciating for the majority of the population. Indigenous peoples were chased from lands coveted by foreign corporations or large domestic businesses, and Díaz did his best to ensure that the cheap labor that attracted foreign investment remained cheap.

The economic squalor of the lower classes and political exclusion of the middle classes set the stage for the Mexican Revolution (1911–1920). The Revolution propelled several figures into the national spotlight: Emiliano Zapata, head of the peasant movement, who demanded land and the restoration of traditional communal holdings; Venustiano Carranza, who represented the landed oligarchy and was favored by the administration of President Woodrow Wilson; and Francisco ("Pancho") Villa, in command of countryside militias that comprised cowboys, small ranchers, and agricultural workers from the northern state of Chihuahua. The effort to legitimize the Revolution found its expression in the formation of an official political party, the National Revolutionary Party, which would later be renamed the Institutional Revolutionary Party (PRI). The revolutionary elite initiated this creation and imposed it from the top down. It provided a structure through which the major social, political, and economic forces in the state could seek expression. It also provided a means by which they could be controlled by the establishment.

Elected in 1934, Lázaro Cárdenas is the most admired president in the hearts of the Mexican people and is seen as the embodiment of the Revolution. He stoked Mexican nationalism by expropriating the foreign-owned oil industry and won over the dispossessed with an agrarian reform that distributed 44 million acres of land. Not all this land was turned over to individuals; much of it favored indigenous groups and went into communal holdings called *ejidos*. The economic turn from the *Porforiato* was obvious, but in the political realm, the PRI stunted change with both the carrot and the stick. The PRI embraced populist policies but made it clear that it would control implementation and expect electoral support in return for economic benefits. The PRI would dole out public works projects, subsidized foodstuffs, or employment opportunities in the local bureaucracy to curry favor. Those communities that failed to support the PRI in the next elections would see those benefits withdrawn. To guarantee its position, the party would often resort to electoral fraud. For those individuals and groups that protested too vociferously, the PRI always retained the option to repress. A 2006 official inquiry into the 1964 to 1982 "dirty war" period documented human rights abuses, including 797 disappearances and 2,141 cases of torture, and traced responsibility to the presidential office.[17]

Patronage politics allowed the PRI to retain rule during the "Mexican Miracle," when the economy charted steady growth that averaged upwards of 4 percent per year. The 1980s debt crisis, however, laid a terminal blow to this formula. The economic strain tempted the party leadership to opt for a solution reminiscent of the Porfirio Díaz days— a reopening to foreign economic interests. Carlos Salinas de Gortari, elected in 1988, continued the process begun by his predecessor of moving the country's industry out of public control and into the private sector. His efforts culminated with the signing of NAFTA in 1993, which created a free-trade area with Canada and the United States. As in the days of Díaz, growth has followed, but so too has inequality. The pride of Mexico's rural indigenous—the *ejido* system—fell victim to government cuts in 1991. The move spurred migration to the already-swelling cities, placing extreme pressure on urban services, and helped to feed rural rebellion, as in Chiapas in 1994. Likewise, NAFTA reforms opening Mexico to greater foreign investment undermined the nationalized oil industry crafted by Cárdenas. Mexico now boasts the highest per capita income in Latin America, but the greatest gains from NAFTA have gone to the northern and central regions of Mexico, the more educated workforce engaged in international trade, and those irrigated, more productive farms able to compete against U.S. and Canadian producers. Those unable to gain have been doubly disadvantaged, as the reduction in state subsidies and social welfare dictated by neoliberal reform hit them hardest.[18]

Economic reform under NAFTA, however, would be one-half of a package that also included political reform. With democracy spreading across Latin America in the 1980s, international attention focused on Mexico. Electoral fraud and corruption by PRI came under greater scrutiny and grew increasingly difficult. Opposition parties, especially the right-wing PAN (National Action Party) and the left-wing PRD (Party for a Democratic Revolution), began to win more congressional seats and governorships. Events came to a head in the July 2000 presidential election, which saw the end of the PRI's 70-year lock on the presidency. PAN candidate, and former Coca-Cola executive, Vicente Fox, took the presidential sash and committed himself to further economic and political reform. Nonetheless, Fox would have to deal with the new Mexican reality—democracy. Mexico was now officially a competitive multiparty state. The absence of a majority in congress compelled Fox to compromise and bargain with the PRI and PRD.

Early on, Fox gave great priority to migration and had high hopes for some sort of amnesty program for undocumented workers, as well as a more liberal migration program. The culture of migration is something initiated and sustained by the United States, first under the *Bracero* programs beginning in the 1940s, which invited millions across three decades, and today under immigration policies that ineffectively chase migrants through deadly desert border regions but do virtually nothing to exact punishment on U.S. businesses that hire illegals. For the reality is that the United States depends on cheap labor as much as Mexico depends on worker remittances, and though U.S. communities may be upended by the influx, U.S. businesses exert tremendous pressure to ensure political lethargy toward their cheap labor. Moreover, the U.S. fixation on terrorism after September 11, 2001, essentially wiped immigration reform from the political agenda of the Bush administration.

The inaction on migration policy was a severe blow for the Fox administration. A second blow came after the United States fell into recession in 2001 to 2002. With migration reform gone and a sluggish economy, Fox's PAN party began to lose steam. The 2003 U.S. invasion of Iraq led many Mexicans to rethink the new relationship with the United States that had grown over the past decade. All this fueled support for the left-wing PRD, and their candidate in the 2006 presidential election—the populist mayor of Mexico City, Andrés Manuel López Obrador. The bitingly close election ultimately saw PAN candidate Felipe Calderón win by just 0.56 percent of the vote (233,831 out of 41,557,430 votes). López Obrador, assured he had been denied victory through foul play, protested and called on his supporters to march on the capital. Nearly one million did. Calderón was sworn in as president in December 2006 but in a rushed ceremony marred by the vociferous protests of his congressional opponents.

Was the election tainted? An observation team from the European Union deemed the elections clean. Similarly, thousands of citizens deployed by various Mexican civic organizations found no systemic evidence of fraud, although some irregularities were uncovered. The congressional electoral results largely echoed the presidential vote (with PAN gaining a plurality). Should we assume that they too were manipulated? That would have required a much more comprehensive effort, making detection by observers all the more likely. Finally, Mexico's electoral watchdog (Instituto Federal Electoral, IFE) and its electoral court (Tribunal Electoral del Poder Judicial de la Federacion, TEPJF), which hears complaints, are well respected both nationally and internationally due to their track record of diligent observation during the transition to democracy in the 1990s. Few were surprised that, when López Obrador filed his official complaint, the vast majority of investigations focused not on the election itself, but on (legitimate) criticisms of the campaign such as the use of public funds for Calderón, negative campaigning, partisan actions on the part of the Catholic Church (illegal in Mexico), and campaigning abroad and by foreign citizens on behalf of Calderón.

Still, the electoral controversy tells us much about the state of democracy in Mexico. It is a country with democratic political institutions, but that does not necessarily mean a consolidated democracy. The response to the election made it clear that the Mexican populace still lacks confidence in government. Trust is a requisite for democracy, and in Mexico it is lacking—and for good reason. Seventy years of patronage politics under the PRI produced an instrumental approach to electoral politics. Though democratic politics have become a reality since the late 1990s, the inactivity of politicians to address the growing socioeconomic disparities under neoliberalism tears at the legitimacy of government and. ultimately, democratic politics.

Things have not grown easier for the Calderón government. Drug-related violence, responsible for 2,477 deaths in 2007, took 5,400 lives in 2008. Meanwhile, economic growth fell from the meager rate of just 3 percent in 2007 to just 1 percent in 2008, and into negative territory in 2009. As if this were not enough, a swine flu epidemic hit the country in 2009. The country came to a near standstill for several weeks as individuals took shelter from the contagion. International visitors rethought their vacations, wreaking havoc on the tourist industry—once considered the country's only hope for economic growth during the recession. Mexico is no doubt a country in crisis, but these problems are hardly "Mexican" crises. The raging appetites of U.S. drug addicts instigate the violence, and the easy smuggling of high-powered small arms (illegal in Mexico) from north of the border helps to sustain it. The economic crisis was almost inevitable given the close connections with the flailing U.S. economy that have intensified since NAFTA. And the swine flu, although initially a Mexican event, soon emerged as a global pandemic. While the weak rule of law, a dependent economy, and substandard health codes set the stage in Mexico, the forces of globalization open the door to other causes and allow consequences to be felt far beyond national borders.

These events have buffeted Mexican politics. In the aftermatch of the electoral controversy, the PRD fell victim to infighting and saw its stature fall in the public eye. The PAN, having presided over a period of unmet expectations and deepening crises, also saw its prominence ebb. Mexican activists called on voters to express their displeasure in the 2009 congressional elections by defacing their ballot with a large "X." Over 1.3 million—almost 6 percent of voters—complied. The remainder saw little choice other than to cast their lot with the dominant parties. But this time, many shunned the PAN and PRD in favor of the PRI, which secured a plurality of seats. The former authoritarian bulwark now claims a majority in the lower house when paired with its coalition partner (The Green Party). The PRI points to its victory as vindication for its sordid past. But with the PRI in a leadership position, others look at the violence, corruption, and growing squalor and fittingly ask, "How much has changed?"

2. Brazil

Brazil holds a titanic presence in Latin America. About one in three Latin Americans lives in Brazil. Its economy accounts for approximately 35 percent of all economic activity in the region. Its territory covers just over 41 percent of Latin America's geography. Conscious of its role as steward of one-third of the world's rain forests, the country hosted the first-ever Earth Summit in 1992 to address problems of environmental degradation and consider issues of sustainable development. For Brazil, size means everything. The country's modest per capita income of $10,100—just above half the countries of the world—hardly stands out. But its GDP of over $1.6 trillion, which places Brazil just inside the top 10 economies of the world, captivates the attention of investors, financiers, and business worldwide. The country's huge population means that even in the midst of dire poverty in which about 45 million live on less than $2 per day, a middle class of over 60 million strong provides an abounding market for the production, distribution, and sales of economic goods and services. Brazil boasts modern cities, with all the amenities one would expect in New York, London, or Paris. In the outlying communities, or *favelas*, as they are known in Brazil, however, one sees a different world—one dramatically captured in the film *City of God*—where wanton violence blends with indigence to create a Hobbesian world of survival. Desperation is more intense in the countryside, where the 37 largest landowners hold as much as the 2.5 million smallest landowners, and an estimated 4 to 5 million persons remain landless.

The politics of size and distribution distinguish Brazil, and globalization links the two. Brazil's alluring economy affords it advantages uncommon in the Other World. Investors make concessions that they would never accept in Bolivia or Haiti to gain access to Brazil's ample resources and lucrative markets, and international banks still loan even as the country veers from the strict neoliberal guidelines of IMF conditionality. This leeway gives the country more opportunity to address distributive issues, but whether or not that opportunity is taken is a political question, one that is only now being tested under the presidency of Luís Inácio "Lula" da Silva, from the progressive Worker's Party (*Partido dos Trabalhadores,* or PT). But even Lula, as he is commonly known, has been accused of holding back on promises to address economic inequality. Part of this has to do with the magnitude of the problem: Inequality in Brazil is so vast, economists tirelessly debate how best to attack it and even whether it is possible. Another part of the answer, however, comes from the other opportunities afforded by globalization. Brazil is indeed a player on the economic stage, and with this role comes the pressure of lucrative incentives to further integrate into the world economy. Often, the pursuit of these international economic goals comes at the cost of domestic matters, such as reducing economic inequality.

Brazil held on to the ISI model through its military dictatorship from 1964 to 1985 and afterward, even as the economy began to tumble. With a seemingly endless queue of interested investors, it could not be so easily pressured into accepting the dictates of neoliberalism. The debt crisis, however, forced a rethinking of economic policy. Per capita gross domestic product (GDP) in 1990 was what it was in 1980, the last year of the "economic miracle," and triple-digit inflation became commonplace. Still, Brazil would move toward "heterodox" policies (mixtures of ISI and neoliberal economics) rather than embrace orthodox neoliberal economics. The economy began its turnaround under President Fernando Henrique Cardoso (1995–2003). He installed the *Real Plan* and inflation declined from 50 percent per month to around 3 percent. The purpose of the plan was to cut inflation by revaluing the currency (known as the *real*), tightening the supply of money and credit, and stabilizing prices by instituting wage and price freezes. Even as Brazil's economy stabilized, however, other problems persisted.

Cardoso's second term (1999–2003) was not a pleasant one. From the start, he faced a yawning fiscal deficit. The man who preceded him as president, Itamar Franco, was the governor of Minas Gerais and started the year by declaring a 90-day moratorium on the payment of his state's debt to the federal government. With the economy beginning to tilt, currency speculators bet against the Brazilian *real*. To defend the currency, the government raised interest rates as high as 50 percent, thereby contributing to the recession. Cardoso was on the horns of a dilemma. Should he go back on his campaign promise to control inflation, or should he let the *real* float and hope that the resulting devaluation would encourage exports and arrest the decline in foreign exchange?

His economic problems were compounded by the fact that he had previously secured a $41.5 billion loan from the IMF on the commitment to reduce the fiscal deficit. This was to be accomplished by raising taxes and charging taxes on pensions. If the government were to arrange more favorable interest terms for Minas Gerais, it would have to do the same for all 27 states, and that would endanger the budget deficit and create difficulties with the IMF. President Cardoso governed with a legislative coalition that included, as one of the three most important members, Governor Franco's party, the Brazilian Democratic Movement party (PMDB). Cardoso could not afford to alienate such an ally if he hoped to institute fiscal and social reforms.

The Cardoso administration reneged on its IMF commitments. In January 1999, barely two weeks into its second term, the currency was devalued. Overnight the *real* lost 20 percent of its previous value. The hope was that now-cheapened Brazilian goods would raise exports and the increase in foreign exchange would allow a decline in interest rates to further stimulate the economy. The short-term jolt pushed growth toward 5 percent, but the economy soon stagnated. Midway through 2002, despite the backpedaling of early 1999, the International Monetary Fund agreed to loan Brazil another $30 billion. This was done not only to address economic difficulties but also to shore up investor confidence in light of the rising prospects of leftist presidential candidate Luís Inácio "Lula" da Silva.

Lula himself, however, appeared increasingly aware of the pressures of globalization and the attendant concerns of the Brazilian electorate. The one-time lathe operator, labor leader, grade-school dropout son of a family of sharecroppers, and political prisoner changed his attire and his message. Retaining his core messages—pledges to improve schools, fight corruption, create new jobs, end hunger, and restore international respect for Brazil—he pledged to honor Brazil's foreign debts and abide by the IMF agreements that Brazil's previous president, Fernando Henrique Cardoso, signed. Lula, whose lengthy alliance with trade unionists, community activists nurtured by Catholic "liberation theology," and leftist academics still instilled skepticism in the business community, won the presidency in a runoff election on October 27, 2002, defeating Cardoso's successor, José Serra, 61.2 percent to 38.7 percent of the vote.

Lula has remained popular, winning reelection in October 2006 with about 60 percent of the vote in the second round. Though the vote received equals his first victory, important changes may have occurred in the composure of that vote. Lula first came to office with high hopes of social, economic, and political change and promised to address, not just simply cater to, the needs of Brazil's destitute. He promised land for 400,000 families (and title deeds for 500,000 squatters), but fell short of the target, reaching just 245,000 by the end of his first term.[19] The landless movement MST (*Movimento dos Trabalhadores Rurais Sem Terra*) had mobilized its 1.5 million members for Lula's first election but was dissatisfied with the results. The distribution was slow, those that did receive land lacked more supportive agricultural extension programs, forced evictions by large landowners cut into the gains, and violence against activists continued unabated. In one of the few cases of countryside violence that made U.S. headlines, in 2005 a rancher in the state of Pará hired men to kill U.S. nun and activist

Dorothy Stang. Stang angered the rancher after she informed local authorities of his illegal burning to open new pastureland in the jungle, leading to a fine.

More recently, Lula's energy initiatives have raised tensions with would-be supporters in the countryside. In planned synchronicity with George Bush's January 2007 State of the Union Address, in which he proposed a shift away from petroleum and toward biofuels to sustain consumption habits in the United States, Lula announced a massive increase in government support for Brazil's sugar-based ethanol industry. By March, the two leaders had begun negotiations on programs to share biofuel research and development expertise and to promote ethanol throughout the hemisphere. Lula could not turn down the opportunity: The ethanol industry already employed some 500,000, Brazil tops the world as a producer and exporter of ethanol, and the country saves tens of billions of dollars per year using biofuels rather than petroleum. The country is well established to take advantage of growing international biofuel markets. Critics, however, see several costs associated with expanding biofuel production.[20] Experimentation in the use of soybean, sunflower, palm, castor bean, and corn oil continue, but in Brazil, sugar remains the primary product for ethanol, and an increase in biofuel production means more sugar cane production. This places pressure on local governments to reduce land use provisions that protect sensitive habitats, intensifies the concentration of land ownership as those with greater resources gobble up more land, and feeds nationalist tensions as multinational corporations seek their own profits. Though sugar producers claim that the business does not infringe on the precious ecosystems of the Amazon because sugar grows best in the grassland savanna regions, farming in these regions collides with ranching enterprises, that in turn look to the Amazon, which is easily burned to open new pastures. Finally, consumer groups raise questions of food security. The growing demand for sugar raises its price, and the multitude of food products that use sugar. Mexico fell into similar circumstances in early 2007 when corn farmers directed their sales to the corn-based ethanol industry, and Mexicans saw tortilla prices increase 40 percent to 50 percent. Frustrated by the lack of progress in land reform and growing links between Lula and agro-business, the MST officially withdrew its support for Lula at its Fifth National Congress in June 2007.

Lula's problems in the urban areas are no less daunting. Violence has long plagued the *favelas*, and the fear that this bloodshed will make its way into the middle- and upper-class areas has instigated an equally disconcerting level of violence. Gun violence kills some 45,000 per year in Brazil; Rio de Janiero alone has a yearly homicide rate of over 6,000. The violence surpasses many states embroiled in war. Often, the police are just as much part of the problem. Summary executions of suspects are commonplace, and torture by local authorities is well documented. Police often "occupy" neighborhoods, much like in a war zone, for weeks at a time. The violence includes "guns-for-hire" that carry out murders for loan sharks or even for legitimate businesses embittered by the throngs of street children whose presence dampens sales. Many of these death squads hire active and retired police officers. In April 2007, authorities in the state of Pernambuco announced that they had broken up one such death squad, known as Murder Incorporated, responsible for some 1,000 murders from 2003 to 2007. The organization charged $500 to $2,500 per killing.[21] Other violent groups include the *milícias*, para-policing groups staffed by off-duty police officers, prison guards, or firemen, that originally developed in the 1970s as community self-defense leagues seeking to rid neighborhoods of criminal circuits and drug traffickers. As the *milícias* gained control, however, they acquired interests of their own and began to charge residents for "protection" and even many local services such as gas, electricity, and transportation.

Local politicians are wont to prosecute the *milicias* because, as noted, many employ public security officers, and political leaders see their shakedowns and service monopolies as the price to pay to keep out criminal organizations. For the local residents, however, this is simply victimization by a group with a different name, and, to make matters worse, they are often caught in the cross fire as the ousted criminal organizations fight to resume control of the neighborhood. An Amnesty Internal report documented the violence, which exploded in mid-2006, and laid blame on unreformed public security systems, political negligence, and socioeconomic inequality.[22]

The Lula Administration has not stood idle in the face of urban violence. In 2004, the government pushed through a constitutional amendment that made human rights abuses federal offenses, thereby allowing many cases involving police abuse to be addressed at the federal level (and assumedly beyond the more corruptible local governments). Lula prominently referenced public security in his second inaugural address and followed his commitment with a $3.3 billion, five-year plan that views crime not simply as a police issue but as a social problem with solutions geared toward social programs and the education and the rehabilitation of offenders. But the immensity of the problem, so obviously connected to Brazil's disquieting inequality, may be too much. Globalization also makes it all too easy for Brazil's elites, in comfortable quarters with their attention riveted on the economic opportunity from abroad, their interests directed to international cultural offerings, or their time devoted to entertaining prominent foreign guests, to separate themselves from outrages in their own society. Lula's pedigree set him in opposition to such lifestyles, but the pressures of governance have forced compromises that in the view of many have gone too far. Looking back on his first term, Maria Luiza Mendonca (director of the Human Rights and Social Justice Network—a Brazilian umbrella group) declared, "This was a government that didn't face up to the powerful rural and economic oligarchies . . . He hasn't attacked the structural problems that cause things like hunger, illiteracy, and poverty. Lula has lacked courage and he has lacked daring."[23]

3. Cuba

Cuba, the largest of the Caribbean Islands, was late in severing colonial ties with Spain. Although the Cubans had initiated several independence movements throughout the nineteenth century, the final attempt came on the eve of the twentieth. A mysterious explosion that sent the American battleship *Maine* to the bottom of the Havana harbor in 1898 provoked an uninvited North American intrusion into Cuba's war of independence. As a result of the North American intervention and the Spanish defeat, Cuba became a U.S. protectorate for the next 35 years.

Cuban pride was trampled when Cubans were forced to accept the provisions of the Platt Amendment in exchange for nominal independence. The amendment stipulated, among other things, that Cuba could not enter into substantial foreign agreements without approval by the United States. It ceded to the United States the right to intervene to maintain a "stable government" and the right to "acquire and hold the title to land for naval stations." Cuba was forced to incorporate the amendment into its constitution before the United States would agree to remove occupying troops. This passage provided the justification for intervention in Cuban affairs by the United States from 1906 to 1920. In 1934, the treaty was abandoned as part of President Franklin D. Roosevelt's "good neighbor policy"; however, the naval base at *Guantánamo Bay* is still under U.S. control.

Until the revolution of 1959, Cuba was seen as an extension of the United States. Its economy was so integrated with that of its northern neighbor that it was treated as another of the 50 states. In 1903, Cuba and the United States worked out a reciprocal trade agreement that gave sugar a 20 percent reduction from existing U.S. tariffs in exchange for a 20 to 40 percent tariff reduction for Cuban imports from the United States. Because sugar was to become the source of 80 percent of Cuba's foreign exchange, this relationship increased dependence on the United States. The relationship also propelled U.S. investment. By 1928, Americans owned more than two-thirds of the island's sugar production,[24] a situation that contributed greatly to the growing anti-Americanism of Cuban nationalism.

U.S. meddling came again in 1933, when Washington intervened to support the rise of Sergeant Fulgencio Batista after a popular rebellion displaced the dictator Gerardo Machado. Batista, however, would soon evolve into a dictator of his own right and dominate Cuban politics for the next 26 years. It was an era of rampant corruption and abuse of power that would soon give rise to protest and rebellion.

After seeing his election to a representative office nullified in the 1952 elections, Fidel Castro decided to turn to armed rebellion. He and a group of 165 youths staged a romantic and vain attack on the Moncada Barracks on July 26, 1953. The attack was a disaster. More than half of the party was killed or captured. Fidel and his brother Raúl avoided harm but were sentenced to 15 years in prison.

Good luck always followed Fidel Castro. In an attempt to appease the opposition, Batista declared an amnesty and the Castro brothers were released in 1956. They were exiled to Mexico, where others joined the future revolutionaries in training for the overthrow of Batista. Later that year a band of 82 revolutionaries sailed for the island. The landing was another disaster. The popular uprising that was to erupt on their arrival never materialized. After several days of mishaps, all that survived from the invasionary expedition were 12 guerrilla fighters who managed to slip into the Sierra Maestra Mountains, where they would remain pretty much unnoticed until their interview by Herbert Matthews of the *New York Times* the following year.

The interview gave "the bearded ones" the exposure they needed to mobilize the latent anti-Batista sentiment throughout the island. Every revolutionary act would elicit a repressive countermove by Batista, which in turn only stimulated further disobedience and subversion, until his support dissolved, and he fled from Cuba on New Year's Eve, 1959.

What accounts for Castro's subsequent rise to power? Unlike other revolutions in Mexico or China, the Cuban revolution emerged after a relatively brief period of conflict. The corrupt politics of the previous half century had thoroughly discredited the establishment. There was no one to compare in stature with the popular and charismatic revolutionary hero. The *Partido Socialista Popular* (PSP), which was the name under which the Cuban Communist party operated, had been slow to back the guerrillas in the Sierra Maestra, joining in the revolutionary movement only at the last minute. The PSP was also suspect because of its long alliance with Batista and its contribution to the organization and maintenance of workers' support during his regimes. So why did Castro become a Communist?

Any authentic reform of the Cuban political and economic structure would have to break the U.S. control of the sugar economy. That act would also entail a thoroughgoing agrarian reform because sugar production was the foundation of the system. The alternative would have to be a Socialist or some other economic system with strong central direction from the state. Castro sought to consolidate the revolution, and to do so, he availed himself of the only anticapitalist apparatus in existence at the time, the PSP. Washington's policies also contributed to Castro's Communist turn. A boycott and sabotage during the Eisenhower administration were followed by the unsuccessful Bay of Pigs invasion in 1961 and assassination plots against Castro sanctioned by the Kennedy administration. With the U.S. threat a reality, the Soviet Union stood as a ready ally. Castro drew on the Communist party and Soviet advisers to replace the fleeing technicians and professionals dissatisfied with the increasing Socialist direction of the revolution.

The Soviet Union supported Cuba with $5 to $6 billion in annual assistance as late as 1989. But with the fall of Communism in the Soviet Union, and a move by newly independent Russia to embrace Western-style market reforms, Cuba would be forced to do without Soviet aid. Ironically, despite all its efforts at agrarian reform, Cuba found itself as dependent on sugar as before the revolution. From one of the bright spots in the Other World in terms of quality of life for the worker, Cuba has taken a plunge. The move to reinvigorate the economy with mild economic reforms and a tourist industry has brought on new social and economic divisions. A many-layered economy has emerged with the top level reserved for those who have access to foreign currency. The consequence is that many who are employed in menial occupations, such as hotel workers and cab drivers, who frequently come in contact with foreigners, or those who are lucky enough to have friends and family on the outside who can send them dollars, enjoy a better economic status than others, such as doctors or teachers, who make substantial contributions to society through their labor but lack external contact. This latter status engenders a degree of racial tension because whites are more likely to have access to foreign remittances than blacks. As Andrew Zimbalist comments, "Cuba has become a class society, defined by access to hard currency through work, politics, or family abroad."[25] Prostitution is rampant once again as both men and women attempt to procure the hard currency from visiting tourists.

The U.S. embargo, in place but expanded since 1960, has contributed to the post–cold war economic decline. In addition, the United States has taken measures in hopes that Cuban Communism is nearing its end and needs only one small push. In 1992, the Cuban Democracy Act (also known as the Torricelli Bill) took effect. The statute had the effect of increasing the costs of goods transported into Cuba by prohibiting foreign-based subsidiaries of U.S. companies from trading with the island. It allows private groups to send food and medicines but forbids ships entering Cuban ports for the purposes of trade from accessing U.S. port facilities for 180 days. This restriction annoys U.S. allies by extending the influence of the United States beyond its territory. It authorizes the president to declare any country providing assistance to Cuba ineligible for aid under the Foreign Assistance Act of 1961, ineligible for assistance or sales under the Arms Export Control Act, and ineligible under any program providing for the forgiveness or reduction of debt owed to the U.S. government. It stipulates other restrictions as well, but these were enough to cause Castro to make some economic accommodations to attract foreign capital.

There have been some tenuous experiments with capitalism. The administration allowed the use of farmers' markets where farm products could be sold directly to the public. Another example would be the permission of *paladares,* or small private in-house restaurants with a maximum capacity of 12 seats to be served exclusively by members of the household. In an effort to accumulate foreign investment, Cuba has modified its economic doctrine to encourage the development of tourism. In an attempt to accumulate foreign exchange, the government requires that investors hire

Cuban labor and pay the Cuban government in foreign currency. The government then pays the Cuban workers in *pesos* at the Cuban rate. This maneuver allows the government to make a profit on the exchange rate between what the government is paid in foreign currency and what it pays its citizens.

Economic development in Cuba has been stymied further by the United States' Cuban Liberty and Democratic Solidarity (*Libertad*) Act of 1996. Also known as the Helms-Burton Bill, the statute, in part, codifies the different embargoes on trade and financial relations in effect since the Kennedy administration. It requires the president to produce a plan for providing economic assistance to a transitional or democratic government in Cuba as well as authorizing U.S. nationals with claims to property confiscated in Cuba (including those who were Cuban citizens at the time of the confiscation) to file suit in U.S. courts against persons who may be "trafficking" in that property (Title III). This latter provision can be suspended by the president for periods of six months at a time if he considers it necessary to the national interest of the United States and if it will expedite the transition to democracy in Cuba. The fourth title of the statute requires the denial of visas to, and exclusion from the United States of, persons who, after March 12, 1996 (when the legislation was passed), confiscate or "traffic" in confiscated property in Cuba claimed by U.S. proprietors.

Regime change would not come from above. These people have too much to lose. Those below would have an extremely difficult time. Intelligence channels permeate the society in large part because of the need to maintain readiness against the omnipresent threat of an external invasion. The more the United States threatens Cuba, the easier it is for the government to rally mass support for the defense of the revolution. The very security precautions that must be instituted against the

Street performers entertain tourists on a Havana plaza in Cuba.   *Source: Craig Arceneaux*

eventuality of a U.S. invasion are the same ones that prevent the success of any domestic uprising.

In July 2006, a surgical procedure forced Fidel Castro to hand government over to his brother, Raúl, who had been serving as Defense Minister. It will be interesting to see how many of the social programs launched by the Cuban revolution will survive his passing. Life in Cuba, however, is unlikely to return to what it was before the revolution. From a U.S. policy perspective, the question is whether the normalization of relations will be conducive to a less-disruptive transition. The Obama administration has relaxed some of the restrictions on travel and remittances for Cuban-Americans with family members in Cuba, and acceded to demands by Latin American leaders to consider the resumption of Cuban participation in the *Organization of American States (OAS)*. Nonetheless, U.S. policy still insists on regime change before we relax the embargoes. That does not seem realistic. We do not have to like a government to deal with it. There are too many examples where we do that already, and the Cuban case by itself shows how isolation and pressure embolden dictatorial rulers.

FLASHPOINTS

The Organization of American States (OAS) and Venezuela

The Organization of American States was created in 1948 to serve as a forum for the promotion of cooperation in social, economic, and political affairs. It has always served as a medium for conflict resolution in the Western hemisphere as it promoted dialogue to dissuade suspicions, as well as collaborative efforts toward a variety of common threats, from Communism to environmental disasters to international terrorism. Increasingly, the OAS has directed its energy toward conflict resolution in the domestic politics of countries through the promotion and strengthening of democratic institutions. In 1991, the OAS adopted Resolution 1080, which obligated an official response in case of the "sudden or irregular interruption" of democracy in any OAS member state. The Protocol of Washington, signed the following year, strengthened that response by calling for the suspension of an implicated member state. In 2001, the OAS passed the *Inter-American Democratic Charter* to spell out what constituted democratic rule and stipulate regional responses to and penalties for *alterations*—not just *interruptions*—of democracy.

What difference have these developments made? Democratic promotion is a complex assignment, especially for an organization that has traditionally championed sovereignty—the insulation of domestic political affairs from outside influences. Indeed, sovereignty has proved a resilient force for democratic promotion. It has both blocked and, more importantly, distorted the regional drive to maintain democracy. How? As the value of democratic promotion butts heads with the value of sovereignty, the OAS finds that it can address some democratic threats with ease, whereas others are deemed too sensitive—too deep within the realm of domestic politics. Hence, the OAS will show great resolve against coups. The member will be suspended and sanctions enforced. These actions helped reverse democratic threats in Guatemala (1993) and Paraguay (1996), such that today coups seem very unlikely in the region. Another threat, that of electoral fraud, is also firmly monitored, and current elections in the region are typically free and fair. When the more problematic concerns of democratic growth crop up, however—strengthening legislatures, expanding accountability, ensuring equal access to the justice—all those long-term factors so important to democratic consolidation, the OAS treads much more carefully. OAS members will condemn and/or sanction electoral mischief or coups, but mere criticisms of executive power or unresponsive judiciaries are viewed as incursions into domestic politics. That means that these problems tend to fester and grow as threats to democracy. More importantly, by protecting democracy only when risk is at its greatest, the OAS may actually shore up "low-quality" democracies and, thus, undermine its own efforts. This can be seen in the case of Venezuela.

In his 1998 presidential bid, Lieutenant Colonel Hugo Chávez campaigned on a platform of wholesale political change, christening his cause the Fifth Republic Movement (MVR) to signal the opening of a new political order. True to his word, President Chávez oversaw the adoption of a new constitution but has pushed the delicate machinery of democracy to its limits. His critics find ample fodder in the concentration of executive authority, violations of judicial autonomy, the corrosion of federal institutions, mass-level groups that threaten the independence of civil society, pilfering of the state treasury for populist policies designed to curry favor, and a fiery rhetoric that all too often equates opposition with sedition.[26] But these actions do not appear on the OAS radar screen, with its concentration on coups and electoral mischief.

Chávez moved quickly to reshape Venezuelan politics. In the midst of his electoral honeymoon, he presided over a referendum to call a constitutional assembly on April 25, 1999, and, upon its success, elections for a constituent assembly on July 25. The opposition squabbled and ran far more candidates than seats, thereby splitting its vote, while government officials aided Chávez by distributing lists of favored candidates so that supporters could decipher the extended ballot. With representation from *Chavistas* at over 90 percent, the assembly took office on August 3, 1999, completed a draft by late October, scurried through debate, and presented the proposed constitution to the public on November 19. The December 15 referendum date left only 28 days for public debate on the historic change.[27]

Allegations that state funds were used to stimulate favor and a year-end congressional investigation into fraud in the July election were quickly overshadowed by the news of torrential flooding that would eventually kill some 30,000 people and leave hundreds of thousands homeless. The crisis became politicized as it justified greater public spending and led to more intense redevelopment efforts by the armed forces.[28] With Venezuelan society still in shock and under the influence of massive public spending, Chávez went ahead with mega-elections for 6,000 public posts in the country in July 2000 (further local elections would be held in October). The elections also included the presidency and allowed Chávez to refresh his six-year tenure when he garnered 59 percent of the vote, an outcome aided by the still-fractionalized opposition and all-time-high 42 percent abstention rate.

International observers from the OAS were not absent during these developments, but they only monitored the elections, which they consistently found to be largely clean. Every assessment from the OAS endorsed the electoral outcome and in doing so added to the legitimacy of Venezuelan democracy. If elections are the benchmark of democracy, and Venezuela consistently received a passing grade, this was a reality that certainly did not resonate with a significant sector of Venezuelan society, whose confidence in governing institutions was suffering a swift decline.

The disjuncture between Venezuelan politics and the assessments of international observers became increasingly apparent through 2001. In November, the decree of 49 "enabling laws" that significantly affected property rights with little consultation from business provided a signaling event. Middle-class groups agitated by populist policies were joined by labor unions critical of recent government interventions in their elections, and together they initiated a massive December strike that would last over a month. A February 2002 call for Chávez to resign by several high-ranking military officers spiked the opposition's mettle. But in April 2002, the Venezuelan crisis would become clear to all—those inside and outside the country. Violent street protests led to some 20 deaths and 60 serious injuries, providing the spark for a coup led by business leader Pedro Carmona and some military units. The Bush administration, long unabashedly critical of Chávez and supportive of the opposition, proved reluctant to condemn the action.[29] With democratic survival clearly in the balance, however, other OAS members felt compelled to act. The 19-member Rio Group (a caucus within the OAS) happened to be holding its annual meeting in Costa Rica at the time and called for a special session of the OAS General Assembly. Ultimately, though, the coup fell apart because of internal pressures as Carmona quickly alienated his early supporters.

Nonetheless, the antagonisms and schisms that brought about the coup remained; indeed, they were deepened by the violence surrounding the three-day coup. The OAS responded with a resolution "to encourage Government of Venezuela to explore the opportunities the OAS affords for promoting the national dialogue."[30] After five months of negotiation, in October 2002, Chávez and the opposition agreed to accept a "Tripartite Working Mission" comprising the OAS and the Carter Center with technical support from the UN Development Program.

Still, "dialogue" was conditioned and decided just as much, if not more, in the streets of Venezuela than in the negotiating efforts of the Tripartite Mission.[31] It was as if the opposition and government required a learning period of confrontation. That period, initiated by sporadic midyear strikes, intensified in October, when 14 military officers marched to Plaza Altamira in Caracas to pronounce their "legitimate disobedience" and lead a protest that continued for months and swelled to the tens of thousands. Finally, a general strike beginning in December and affecting much of the oil industry, crippled the economy.

Only after these efforts failed did the opposition take the negotiations more seriously.[32] In May 2003, the government and opposition accepted a proposal to hold a referendum on the presidency. But even with the pressure to hold another vote, both sides wavered. Opposition elements in the National Assembly held up appointments to the National Electoral Council (CNE, the official electoral board), and negotiations delayed its activation until September.[33] At that time, the body, now holding a majority of members identified with the government, refused a referendum petition from the opposition on procedural grounds. Violent protests again rocked Caracas, and more followed in February 2004, when the CNE delayed its decision on a subsequent petition with some 3.4 million signatures—almost 1 million above the required 2.54 million. When, in the following month, the CNE declared only 1.8 million of the signatures to be valid, the protestors found little reason to back off—despite the fact that the OAS and Carter Center officially supported the CNE decision.[34] The Tripartite Mission did play an important role as it offered to oversee a *reparo* (repair) period, in which signatories would verify their signatures. Though the *reparo* was marred by verified accusations of intimidation toward signatories, the process ended successfully in early June and opened the door to an August 15 referendum.

Foreign observation of the referendum created the same trap as had previous assessments of Venezuelan elections. By focusing so squarely on the cleanliness of electoral procedures, outsiders again missed the democratic forest for the electoral trees. In the lead-up to the election, the Chávez government engaged in massive spending, fueled by an opportune increase in oil prices. Other suspect strategies included naturalizing some 300,000 immigrants in the hopes of creating a new voting bloc of Chávez supporters and an attempt to stir national security concerns by coloring the arrest of alleged Colombian paramilitaries as a coup plot.[35] Meanwhile in the year leading up to the referendum, two critical reports pointed to the real problems in Venezuela: One by Human Rights Watch surveyed attacks on judicial autonomy, and another by the Inter-American Commission on Human Rights took note of "a clear weakness in the fundamental pillars of the rule of law within a democratic society," placing emphasis on the impunity with which armed civilian groups act to stifle political debate.[36] These reports exposed just some of the failures of democratic deepening in Venezuela—failures to which the OAS member states paid less attention. And in this environment, the referendum was an ill-suited mechanism for reconciliation.

The official results gave Chávez a clear victory, with 59 percent of voters rejecting his recall. Opponents were furious and questioned the outcome. The Tripartite Mission conducted an additional audit to assuage the opposition, to little avail.[37] Venezuelan politics, then, remained insecure as issues of democratic quality continued to fester. No amount of evidence could convince the opposition that Chávez won the referendum; the political atmosphere had grown too bitter. What means nothing to the opposition, however, could not be more important to the OAS and its members. A clear signal of "mission accomplished" has been emitted. Even the United States has acquiesced, portraying the vote as a chance for reconciliation. Has the OAS done a service for Venezuelan politics? Without OAS pressure, elections could have been tainted, and a successful coup would probably be much more likely. But the piecemeal approach to democratic protection also allows Chávez to use the OAS stamp of approval to further the legitimacy of the Venezuelan political system, when clearly large portions of the population feel otherwise. Is this a case in which no OAS action would be better than just some?

Violence in Colombia

The long history of violence in Colombia starts with Simón Bolívar's victory over the Spanish loyalists. Frustration with the area's incapacity to achieve civic harmony prompted the quotation attributed to the liberator with which we start the chapter. Bolívar wanted to see a strong executive elected for life. His comrade in arms, General Francisco de Paula Santander, became the first president of what is today Colombia. He championed a decentralized federal system with a reduced role for the Roman Catholic Church. This became the basis for the Liberal party doctrine. Opposition to this view characterized the Conservative party, and the two forces fought each other for the remainder of the nineteenth century, most notoriously in the Thousand Days War (1899–1902).

A split within the Liberals led by Gabriel Turbay on the right and the nationalist-populist Jorge Eliecer Gaitán on the left allowed the Conservative Mariano Ospina Pérez to win with fewer votes than those amassed by the two Liberals in 1946. Gabriel Turbay died the following year, and Ospina Pérez began attacks against the Liberals. This started the bloody period in Colombia known as *la violencia*. In 1947 the *gaitanistas* (the followers of Gaitán) swept the congressional elections and left no doubt that Eliecer Gaitán would win the presidential election in 1948. On April 9, 1948, however, Gaitán was assassinated. The assassin was mobbed, beaten to death, and his corpse was dragged to the presidential palace. Bogotá erupted into riot, burning, and looting, and the convulsion became known as *el bogotazo*.

The strife between the rival parties continued in earnest, and, in a desperation move reminiscent of Hobbes's "state of nature," members from both sides asked for deliverance at the hands of the military dictator Gustavo Rojas Pinilla. He ruled from 1953 to 1957 but alienated both Liberals and Conservatives over time. In response, the Liberal leader Lleras Camargo met with his counterpart Laureano Gómez and agreed on a constitutional reform known as the National Front, allowing the Liberals and Conservatives to alternate in office at all levels of government for the next 16 years. The elites thereby had concluded an understanding; unfortunately, even though women were given the right to vote, too many of the concerns of the majority of the population were not addressed.

The 1960s were a time of uprisings in Latin America, and the United States was anxious that other Cubas not arise; so it countered with a carrot—the Alliance for Progress—and a stick—the School for the Americas, in which the U.S. military gave instruction on countersubversion. Attempts by the Alliance to institute agrarian reform in Colombia floundered on the political maneuvering of the large landowners. Thwarted in their attempts to bring about their vision of a more equitable society and motivated by the examples of Fidel Castro and Ernesto "Che" Guevara in Cuba, young students and a sympathetic priest named Camilo Torres took up arms. The official candidate of the National Front in the April 19, 1970, election was Misael Pastrana. The excluded groups united in the Popular National Alliance to oppose his candidacy by nominating former president Rojas Pinilla, who lost by two points. The cry of fraud rent the air, and dissatisfaction with the traditional political process engendered the organization of two rebel groups, the *Fuerzas Armadas Revolucionarias de Colombia* (FARC) and the April 19 Movement (M-19).

As a result of a subsequent peace initiative, both of these groups suspended their armed conflict with the government and sponsored legal political parties. The M-19 garnered brief success, capturing 28 percent of the vote for the special constitutional election in 1990. The Patriotic Union (UP) sponsored by the FARC in 1985 achieved limited influence by winning 14 seats in Congress in 1986. Their numbers were soon diminished by the assassination of more than 3,000 of their leaders and supporters, including two of their presidential candidates. The only UP senator winning an election was killed the day he took office, and his successor was forced into exile under threat of death. The experience discouraged further legal political participation by the reform movement.

It is easy to see why Colombia is presently considered the most violent country in the hemisphere. The guerrillas prosper because they have the support of the peasantry. Most commentators would agree that the peasants' situation has deteriorated in the past three decades. The opening up of the markets associated with the implementation of neoliberal economic policies has had a severe effect on the economics of the small landholder. The 2,299,804 small farms represent a mere 15.6 percent of the total arable land. Of these, over four-fifths are considered minifarms. The trend in Colombia is toward ever-larger farms. The world coffee price has declined; high production costs resulting from the overvaluation of the *peso* and a parasitic infestation of the crop has made it very tempting to switch to growing coca and poppies. Official statistics indicate that the FARC operates in over half the territory. Yet, it would be inaccurate to characterize them as narcoguerrillas, as some have tried to do. The Colombian military and government of Álvaro Uribe Vélez has used that ploy with success in extracting military assistance from the United States. Initially, the FARC supported themselves by robbery and kidnapping for ransom; now they raise revenue by taxing the narcotics operations in the areas they control. They, however, are not the narcotraffickers. The guerrillas merely supervise the commerce and are preferred by the *cocaleros* to the *narcotraficantes* because they maintain order and protect them from the murderous agents of the organized drug cartels.

The large landowners have always resorted to violent methods in resolving their disputes with the peasants. In control of the political apparatus, they traditionally have had access to the military and police in helping them settle disputes or, should these not be available, their own paramilitary forces. These paramilitary forces united their operations under the United Self-Defense Forces of Colombia (AUC) in 1997. They quickly became Colombia's leading human rights abuser, accounting for the vast majority of all atrocities. Originally designed as hired guns, their leaders grew wealthy over time and developed their own interests in narcotrafficking and agrarian estates.

The violence is self-sustaining because, as Nazih Richani has elaborated, it has reached a "positive-sum, economy of scale."[38] A military impasse has been achieved by the belligerent factions, and a "symbiotic" balance of sorts has resulted. The violent arena reduces the price of land, which is then purchased by the newly rich narcotraffickers looking for a means to launder their money. The military, in turn, is able to receive growing proportions of the national budget. The FARC collects a "war tax" from the corporations, landowners, and ranchers in the area. The military, in the areas in which they set up their drug extermination operations, extract a "tax" in the form of multiple bribes, which the *cocaleros* find more onerous than that paid to the FARC. Narcowealth has gone into the purchase of four to six million *hectares* (a *hectare* is approximately 2.5 acres) used primarily for cattle grazing. The new ranchers naturally join with the established ones in opposing the agrarian reform espoused by the FARC and look to the AUC for protection. The military benefits by receiving salary supplements for hazardous duty in the "red zones." Retired military personnel can secure lucrative consulting fees by training the AUC paramilitary forces—often composed of former soldiers. The

A Coca Plantation: Once processed, elements of the coca plant can be made into cocaine.

Source: Craig Arceneaux

military and paramilitary are allies, and, hence, there is no control over the latter, who have engaged in grisly massacres of suspected guerrilla sympathizers. Groups with such names as *Monchecabezas* (decapitators) have terrorized the population in an attempt to isolate the FARC from its supporters.

The violence in Colombia holds international significance. Neighboring countries, such as Panama, Venezuela, and Ecuador, feel the effects of instability as guerrillas often make their way across borders for sanctuary. The drug production fueled by the conflict spurs crime in the region through narcotrafficking and the laundering of drug profits. The United States, the world's largest market for cocaine and heroin, also feels the impact of Colombian violence. The traditional approach used by the United States to combat narcotrafficking is to address the production of drugs—their cultivation and processing. U.S. officials point to the success of the approach during the 1980s in Peru and Bolivia, where coca cultivation declined dramatically. But critics note that the supply-side focus of the United States easily falls victim to what is called "the balloon effect." Production declined in Peru and Bolivia only because it moved to Colombia. An alternative would be a stronger demand-side focus—attacking drug trafficking by concentrating on consumption in the United States. Latin Americans, noting that drug trafficking would nearly disappear without the U.S. addiction, view the focus on destroying cultivation and processing as typical U.S. arrogance because it defines drug trafficking as a problem created and sustained by Latin America.

The demand-side focus was intensified in the 2000 Andean Counterdrug Initiative, also known as *Plan Colombia* because nearly all the funding goes to this country. The program has channeled some $6 billion to combat drug production, with 80 percent of the monies devoted to military assistance. The Obama administration has expressed a commitment to shift more funds to social and economic development, and more generally to "Colombianize" the program (i.e., gradually transfer budgetary responsibility for the different programs to Colombia). Nonetheless, his administration allocated $513 million to the program for 2010, not far off the mark of $547 million authorized for 2009 by the Bush administration. Change is difficult here; no politician wants to be accused of being soft on drugs. But has the program shown any success? In 2006, over 200,000 hectares were eradicated, most through the aerial spraying of chemicals (and its attendant environmental effects). Replanting and movement by *cocaleros*, however, meant that this hardly put a dent in the overall amount of coca grown—a net reduction of only 8,000 hectares (from 86,000 to 78,000). Likewise, studies of coca harvests show that their yields have increased some 40 percent, such that reductions in acreage are being made up for by increases in productivity.[39] This point is important because proponents of the supply-side focus initially argued that the focus on cultivation would decrease supply, drive up prices, and then lead to a decrease in usage. What this logic ignores is the impact of the balloon effect within Colombia (growers simply move about the country, cluster plants on smaller, less detectable plots, and/or cultivate strains of more potent coca to allow more cocaine in smaller plots). Also, should prices be affected, we should not expect addicts to react like rational consumers and decrease their use.

The politics of violence in Colombia have taken a more scandalous turn of late. President Álvaro Uribe Vélez (elected in 2002 and to a second four-year term in 2006) won popular appeal by running on a security platform and instituting a tough approach to the FARC, one that emphasized military action over negotiation. His approach to the AUC, however, was more compromising. For them, he negotiated a rather lenient amnesty in 2004 that required testimony on involvement in abuses, the return of stolen property and assets (though this has not been strictly enforced), and no more than a charge of sedition (an easily pardonable conviction in Colombia) for the most egregious of abusers. However, revelations of close government contacts with the AUC and related drug traffickers raised suspicions of ulterior motives on the part of the Uribe government. Casualties of the scandal include the imprisonment of 40 congressional allies and Uribe's security chief and the resignation of Uribe's foreign minister. Congressional investigations have even looked into ties between the Uribe family, narcotraffickers, and the paramilitaries going back over 25 years. A newly invigorated Supreme Court, intent on protecting the integrity of the law, ruled in early 2007 that demobilized paramilitaries could be charged with an array of crimes, leading many to resume arms. The continuing divisiveness of Colombian politics gives one little hope that the pattern of violence found throughout the country's history will abate any time soon.

Review Questions

1. What are some causes of underdevelopment that are particular to Latin America?
2. How can the United States best address drug trafficking?
3. Account for the historically strong role of the military in Latin America.
4. Why are the United States and Cuba finding it so difficult to overcome their differences?
5. Employing examples from your reading, account for the endurance of violence as a way of pursuing political, social, and economic ends in Latin America.

Key Terms

indigenismo—A prominent intellectual movement in Latin America that identifies ethnicity with cultural attributes rather than biological differences.

caudillo—Literally, the "man on horseback." The history of Latin America is littered with what amounts to "war lords" who seize political power through extralegal means and govern by force of their personalities, inhibiting the institutionalization of the political process.

founding myth—A historical account of the origins of a country. Though certain details of the story may be embellished or overly romanticized, the importance of founding myths is not so much their accuracy as their embodiment of common values and ideas to serve as a source of nationalism.

ejido—Communal landholdings in Mexico. A traditional source of pride for the lower classes in the peasantry, today they are viewed as an impediment to further neoliberal economic reforms.

escrache—A form of protest meant to draw attention to individuals considered guilty of egregious crimes against society.

Guantánamo Bay—A United States naval installation on Cuba's southern Caribbean coast, which the United States obtained from Cuba as a condition for removing American troops after the Spanish-American War. This base, which is currently housing prisoners taken in the battle against the Taliban and Al Qaeda terrorists, has been a source of irritation to Cuban nationalists.

Inter-American Democratic Charter—Signed on September 11, 2001, this document commits the OAS to the protection and promotion of democracy in the Western Hemisphere.

ISI—Import substitution industrialization is an economic doctrine that promotes the notion of a self-sufficient national economy. The disruption of trade during two world wars and the inter-war global depression helped to establish the policy. Since then it has become apparent that the policy would have a difficult time succeeding in the face of the limited markets associated with most of the Latin American economies and the external competition from the more advanced nations. The policy has been eclipsed in recent times by the notions of "free trade," promoted by the United States and the International Monetary Fund (IMF).

NAFTA—The North American Free Trade Agreement is a treaty initiated in 1994 establishing a free-trade area among Canada, Mexico, and the United States. It represents an attempt to promote the economic policy of free trade in contrast with the protectionism, tariffs, and quotas associated with import substitution industrialization. Other countries of the hemisphere are experimenting with regional free-trade areas, such as that among Brazil, Uruguay, and Argentina (MERCOSUR) in the southern cone. The current talk, led by the United States, is to establish a hemisphere-wide, free-trade area known as the Free Trade Area of the Americas.

New Left—Newly risen political leaders in Latin America who reject neoliberal policies and criticize U.S. hegemony in the region. Though they commonly embrace progressive, populist policies, there are in fact significant differences between the more extreme and more moderate factions.

Organization of American States (OAS)—The OAS emerged after World War II with the establishment of the Rio Treaty in 1947 and the 1948 Treaties of Bogotá. It took the nations of Latin America over a century after their independence to trust the United States to the point of joining it in an alliance to protect the security of the hemisphere as well as promote democratic institutions. With the waning of the cold war, the emphasis of the organization has changed from security to advancing democracy and human rights. These issues are now threatened with the problem of narcotrafficking.

Useful Web Sites

The Inter-American Development Bank: *www.iadb.org*
The InterAmerican Dialogue: *www.iadialog.org*
UTLANIC at the University of Texas: *www.lanic.utexas.edu*
The Washington Office on Latin America: *wola.org*
The Political Database of the Americas: *www.pdba.georgetown.edu*
Organization of American States: *www.oas.org*

For Further Reading

Arceneaux, Craig. *Bounded Missions: Military Regimes and Democratization in the Southern Cone and Brazil.* University Park, PA: Penn State University Press, 2001.

Arceneaux, Craig, and Pion-Berlin, David. *Transforming Latin America: The International and Domestic Origins of Change.* Pittsburgh, PA: University of Pittsburgh Press, 2005.

Atkins, G. Pope. *Latin America in the International Political System,* 3rd ed. rev. Boulder, CO: Westview Press, 1995.

Blouet, Brian W., and Blouet, Olwyn M. *Latin America and the Caribbean: A Systematic and Regional Survey.* Hoboken, NJ: John Wiley, 2005.

Camp, Roderic Ai. *Politics in Mexico: The Democratic Transformation.* New York: Oxford University Press, 2003.

Crandall, Russell, Paz, Guadalupe, and Roett, Riordan. *The Andes in Focus: Security, Democracy, and Economic Reform.* Boulder, CO: Lynne Reinner, 2005.

Franko, Patrice. *The Puzzle of Latin American Economic Development.* Lanham, MD.: Rowman and Littlefield, 2007.

MacDonald, Gordon J., Nielson, Daniel L., and Stern, Marc A. *Latin American Environmental Policy in International Perspective.* Boulder, CO: Westview Press, 1997.

Mainwaring, Scott, and Valenzuela, Arturo, eds. *Politics, Society, and Democracy: Latin America.* Boulder, CO: Westview Press, 1998.

Molineu, Harold. *U.S. Policy Toward Latin America: From Regionalism to Globalism,* 2nd ed. Boulder, CO: Westview Press, 1990.

O'Donnell, Guillermo. *Modernization and Bureaucratic-Authoritarianism: Studies in South American Politics.* Berkeley: Institute of International Studies, University of California, 1973.

Oppenheim, Lois Hecht. *Politics in Chile: Socialism, Authoritarianism, and Market Democracy.* Boulder, CO: Westview Press, 2007.

Purcell, Susan Kaufman, and Rothkopf, David. *Cuba: The Contours of Change.* Boulder, CO: Lynne Rienner Publishers, 2000.

Roniger, Luis, and Sznajder, Mario. *The Legacy of Human Rights Violations in the Southern Cone: Argentina, Chile, and Uruguay.* New York: Oxford University Press, 1999.

Rouquié, Alain. Translated by Paul E. Sigmund. *The Military and the State in Latin America.* Berkeley: University of California Press, 1987.

Skidmore, Thomas E., and Smith, Peter H. *Modern Latin America,* 6th ed. New York: Oxford University Press, 2005.

Smith, Peter H. *Democracy in Latin America.* New York: Oxford University Press, 2005.

Notes

1. Henning Steinfeld et al. *Livestock's Long Shadow: Environmental Issues and Options* (Rome: Food and Agricultural Organization of the United Nations, 2006), p. xxi.
2. United Nations Office for the Coordination of Humanitarian Affairs. *OCHA Annual Report 2008* (New York: United Nations), p. 69.
3. Brian Loveman, *For La Patria: Politics and the Armed Forces in Latin America* (Wilmington, DE: Scholarly Resources, 1999), pp. 27–62.

4. David L. Clawson, *Latin America and the Caribbean: Lands and Peoples* (Boston: McGraw-Hill, 2004), pp. 141–143.

5. Marisol de la Cadena, *Indigenous Mestizos: The Politics of Race and Culture in Cuzco, Peru, 1919–1991* (Durham: Duke University Press, 2000).

6. South American Indian Information Center, *Working Commission Reports: Second Conference of Indian Nations and Organizations of South America, Tiwanaku, Bolivia, March 6–13, 1983* (Berkeley: South American Indian Information Center, 1984).

7. *Indigenous Peoples, Poverty and Human Development in Latin America: 1994–2004* (Washington, D.C.: World Bank, 2005).

8. "Latin America's Indigenous Saint Stirs Anger, Pride." *Los Angeles Times*, July 30, 2002.

9. Loveman, 1999, pp. 1–26.

10. Robert W. Patch, "Imperial Politics and Local Economy in Colonial Central America: 1670–1770," pp. 77–107, *Past and Present* (May 1994).

11. Simon Hanson, *Economic Development in Latin America* (Washington, D.C.: Inter-American Affairs Press, 1951), p. 107.

12. Economic Commission for Latin America and the Caribbean. *Statistical Yearbook for Latin America and the Carribean* (New York: ECLAC, 2008).

13. *World Development Indicators* (Washington, D.C.: World Bank Group, 2005).

14. *Regional Economic Outlook: Western Hemisphere April 2009* (Washington, D.C.: IMF, 2009), p. 87.

15. David de Ferranti et al., *Inequality in Latin America and the Caribbean: Breaking with History?* (Washington, D.C., 2003).

16. Angelina Snodgrass Godoy. *Popular Injustice: Violence, Community, and Law in Latin America* (Palo Alto: Stanford University Press, 2006).

17. Por la Fiscalía Especial para Movimientos Sociales y Políticas del Pasado (FEMO-SPP). *Informe Histórico a la Sociedad Mexicana—2006.* (Mexico City: Procuraduría General de la República, 2006).

18. *NACLA Report on the Americas.* "Mexico's Haves and Have-Nots: NAFTA Sharpens the Divide." (January 2002) 35, 4: 32–35.

19. "Brazilians Wonder: Where's the Reform?" *Christian Science Monitor,* March 22, 2006, p. 7.

20. Isabella Kenfield, "Brazil's Ethanol Plan Breeds Rural Poverty, Environmental Degradation," *Americas Program Discussion Paper,* International Relations Center, March 6, 2007. Available online at www.americas.irc-online.org.

21. "Brazil Breaks Up 'Killing Firm,'" BBC News Online, April 13, 2007. www.news .bbc.co.uk.

22. "Brazil: From Burning Buses to Caveirões: The Search for Human Security," *Amnesty International Report,* May 2, 2007. Available at www.amnesty.org.

23. "Brazilians Wonder: Where's the Reform?" p. 7

24. Hugh Thomas, *Cuba: The Pursuit of Freedom* (New York: Harper & Row, 1971), p. 557.

25. Susan Kaufman Purcell and David Rothkopf, eds., *Cuba: The Contours of Change* (Boulder, CO: Lynne Rienner Publishers, 2000), p. 13.

26. Ronald Sylvia and Constantine Danopoulos, "The Chavez Phenomenon: Political Change in Venezuela," *Third World Quarterly* 24:1 (February 2003): 63–76. Steve Ellner and Daniel Hellinger, eds. *Venezuelan Politics in the Chavez Era: Class, Polarization and Conflict.* Boulder, CO: Lynne Rienner Publishers, 2003.

27. Jennifer L. McCoy, "Demystifying Venezuela's Hugo Chavez," *Current History,*: February 2000: 66–72.

28. Ibid., 69–70.

29. "Chavez Ouster Draws U.S. Backing, Then Opposition," *Associated Press Worldstream*, April 17, 2002, Lexis-Nexis Online.
30. "Declaration on Democracy in Venezuela," AG/DEC. 28 (XXXII-O/02), 2002.
31. Margarita López Maya, "Las insurrecciones de la oposición en el 2002 en Venezuela: Causas e implicaciones," XXIV Congress of the Latin American Studies Association, March 27–29, 2003, Dallas, TX.
32. Ibid., xxx.
33. "Opposition Squabbles, Deadline Passes," *Latin American Weekly Report*, May 20, 2003; "Deal May Break 'Fifth Man' Impasse," *Latin American Weekly Report*, July 8, 2003.
34. "Venezuela: Opposition Shuns CNE and Takes to the Streets," *Latin American Weekly Report*, March 2, 2004, Lexis-Nexis Online; "Venezuela: Opposition May Scuttle the Referendum," *Latin American Weekly Report*, April 20, 2004, Lexis-Nexis Online.
35. "Regime Change or Bust: Venezuela," *The Economist*, March 13, 2004. Lexis-Nexis Online; Venezuela: Opposition Denounces 'Fraud by Naturalisation'," *Latin American Weekly Report*, July 13, 2004, Lexis-Nexis Online.
36. "Rigging the Rule of Law: Judicial Independence Under Siege in Venezuela," Human Rights Watch, June 2004 (New York: Human Rights Watch); "Report in the Situation of Human Rights in Venezuela," Inter-American Commission on Human Rights, December 2003. Available online at www.oas.org.
37. These assessments can be found in "Auditoria de los resultados del procesos del referindum revocatorio presidencial Venezuela," OAS and Carter Center, August 26, 2004. Available online at www.oas.org; "Last Phase of the Venezuelan Recall Referendum: Carter Center Report," Carter Center, August 21, 2004, available online at www.cartercenter.org; also see "U.S. Firm Defends Exit Poll," *Associated Press Online*, August 20, 2004, Lexis-Nexis Online.
38. Nazih Richani, "The Political Economy of Violence: The War-System in Colombia," *Journal of Inter-American Studies and World Affairs* 39, no. 2 (1997): 37–81.
39. United Nations Office on Drugs and Crime—Colombia Office. *Colombia: Coca Cultivation Survey 2006*. Bogotá, Colombia.

CHAPTER

6

Sub-Saharan Africa

Ira Reed

Seek ye first the political kingdom and all other things will be added unto you.

KWAME NKRUMAH

Viewed nearly a decade into the new millennium, these words from one of Africa's liberation leaders in the post–World War II generation seem quaint or naive. Independence from colonial rule did not bring "all other things." As emphasized in this chapter, Africa's problems have multiplied in the past few decades. In addition, foreign interests often either focused elsewhere in the world or did more harm than good. The political instability, economic decline, social unrest, environmental degradation, and debilitating disease that became commonplace in most of the states of the region will not quickly improve, despite some hopeful developments.

From 1957 to 1993, more than three dozen African colonies achieved independence, some peacefully and others violently. Despite the different roads taken, a common theme ran through these new states in their early years: hope, excitement, deliverance.

This early enthusiasm struck a responsive chord in the West. Some leaders were genuinely supportive of the new order. British Prime Minister Harold Macmillan declared that "the winds of change" were blowing through Africa and would have to be accommodated. Youthful President John F. Kennedy embraced the notion of a Peace Corps, with Africa a major recipient of hundreds and then thousands of practical idealists. Furthermore, many believed that the East-West conflict would be fought in the Other World, and the battle for the hearts and minds of the people of Africa was seen as an important objective.

If this earlier period was one of optimism and gains in Africa, then the 1980s was one of pessimism and losses. In fact, the period has been described as "the lost decade." Although there are success stories and some recent encouraging signs, the overall situation is disheartening. While it is true that the 1990s witnessed a modest increase in participatory political systems, these changes yielded mixed results at best. As we will see in the "Case Studies" and "Flashpoint" sections of this chapter, several of the wars in Africa have abated or ended, but other violent conflicts continue to fester, and many African nations remain unstable. In a number of African countries, either military rule or strict civilian governments persist, in which democracy, at least as we understand it in the West (e.g., freedom of speech and press, fair and competitive elections, and an independent judiciary), is significantly restricted or nonexistent. In a few states or areas within states, warlords or rebels have taken over, and real governments of any sort have ceased to exist.

By virtually any index, the economic situation has worsened. Per capita income, already the lowest in the Other World, actually declined during the 1980s and gained little in the 1990s. (For recent figures, see Table 6.1.) The international monetary debt of most African states soared. Unemployment or underemployment continued its upward climb. Most agricultural products and minerals are fetching lower world prices than 20 years ago, causing even those states rich in resources to face periods of declining prices. Many millions simply do not get enough to eat.

The picture is not any brighter in other areas. The population explosion continues with a few significant exceptions and is again far higher than in the rest of the Other World. Food production has not kept pace with population growth, and despite rising food imports, the average African has less to eat now than in 1980. Environmental degradation increases yearly, and the underlying support systems sag under the onslaught. More and more species are endangered as impoverished humans encroach on their habitat, sometimes killing the animals for profit. Similarly, the quality of education is in serious straits, and new health problems such as acquired immune deficiency syndrome (AIDS) dwarf older ones, some of which have been curbed or eliminated, whereas others, such as malaria, ebola, polio, and tuberculosis, have burst anew among the population.

History and geography provide some clues to the causes of this unhappy situation. A discussion of the political, social, and economic realities within and beyond Africa today provides additional explanations. The case studies illustrate the dilemmas the peoples of Africa are facing. The chapter concludes with "Flashpoints" on current trouble spots and issues. (Discussion of the five North African states bordering the Mediterranean is included in Chapter 8.)

TABLE 6.1 Characteristics of Sub-Saharan African Countries (by region)

Country	Population (Millions)	Population Growth Rate (%)	Infant Mortality Rate (per 1000 Live Births)	Population Under 15 Years of Age (%)	Life Expectancy (in Years)	Urban Population (%)	Literacy Rate (%)	Arable Land (%)	Per Capita GDP ($US)
Benin	7.863	2.67	79.6	44.1	53.44	44.6	34.7	13	1,100
Burkina Faso	13.903	3	91.3	46.8	49.21	17.8	21.8	13	1,300
Cape Verde	0.421	.61	46.5	37.9	71.02	55.9	76.6	11	6,200
Côte d'Ivoire	17.655	2	89.1	40.8	49	44.9	48.7	8	1,600
Gambia	1.642	2.78	71.6	44.3	54.54	26.1	40.1	18	1,900
Ghana	22.479	1.97	54.9	38.7	59.12	45.4	57.9	12	2,500
Guinea	9.690	2.62	90	44.4	49.65	34.9	29.5	2	2,000
Guinea-Bissau	1.442	2.05	105.2	41.4	47.18	34	42.4	11	800
Liberia	3.042	4.84	155.8	43.1	40.39	46.7	57.5	1	1,000
Mali	11.681	2.68	107.5	48.1	49.51	32.3	19	2	1,200
Mauritania	3.177	2.87	69.5	45.6	53.51	61.8	51.2	0	2,200
Niger	12.525	2.9	118.2	46.9	44.03	22.2	28.7	3	900
Nigeria	131.86	2.38	97.1	42.3	47.44	46.7	68	33	1,400
Senegal	12.191	2.65	61.4	42.2	56.69	49.6	39.3	12	1,800
Sierra Leone	6.005	2.29	160.4	44.8	40.58	38.8	35.1	7	800
Togo	5.549	2.72	60.6	42.3	57.86	35.1	53.2	38	1,700
Burundi	8.09	3.59	63.1	46.3	51.29	9.9	59.3	44	700
Comoros	.752	2.76	66.6	42.2	63.47	28	56.5	36	1,000
Djibouti	0.516	1.90	97.51	43.3	43.37	87	67.9	0	3,700
Eritrea	5.65	2.58	43.3	42.8	61.78	21	58.6	5	700
Ethiopia	85.237	3.21	80.8	46.1	55.41	17	42.7	10	800
Kenya	39.002	2.69	54.7	42.3	57.87	22	85.1	8	1,600
Madagascar	20.653	3.00	54.2	43.5	62.89	29	68.9	5	1,000
Malawi	14.268	2.38	89.05	45.8	43.82	19	62.7	21	800
Mauritius	1.284	0.78	12.2	22.5	74	42	84.4	4	12,100

Mozambique	20.53	1.8	112.1	44.8	40.9	35.6	47.8	4	1,300
Rwanda	9.638	2.77	87.2	41.9	48.99	18.3	64.9	35	1,500
Seychelles	0.082	0.43	15.1	25.9	72.34	49.9	91.8	2	7,800
Somalia	8.863	2.83	114.9	44.4	48.84	34.8	37.8	2	600
Sudan	41.236	2.08	61	42.7	49.11	38.9	60.9	5	2,100
Tanzania	37.445	2.09	96.5	43.7	50.71	35.4	69.4	3	700
Uganda	29.207	3.57	68.5	50.3	51.75	12.2	66.8	25	1,800
Zambia	11.288	1.66	100.5	46	38.44	35.7	68	7	900
Zimbabwe	12.237	0.6	51.7	37.4	39.5	34.9	90.7	7	2,300
Angola	11.993	2.18	186.6	43.8	37.63	35.7	67.4	2	3,200
Cameroon	17.658	2.24	67.2	41.5	52.86	51.4	67.9	13	2,400
Central African Republic	4.303	1.51	85.6	41.9	43.74	42.7	48.6	3	1,100
Chad	9.944	2.32	91.5	47.9	47.2	24.9	25.7	3	1,500
Congo Republic	3.702	2.64	85.3	46.4	53.29	31.6	83.8	0	1,300
Democratic Republic of Congo	62.661	3.39	88.6	47.4	57.2	53.5	67.2	3	700
Republic of Equatorial Gabon	.540	2.02	89.2	41.7	51	48.1	87	5	2,000
Guinea	1.425	2.04	54.5	42.1	53.99	83.8	63.2	1	6,800
Sao Tome and Principe	0.193	3.13	41.8	47.5	67.64	37.8	79.3	2	1,200
Botswana	1.64	1.5	53.7	38.3	50.58	51.6	81.2	1	10,500
Lesotho	2.022	0.14	87.2	36.8	39.97	17.9	82.2	11	2,500
Namibia	2.044	0.48	48.1	38.2	43.11	32.4	85	1	7,000
South Africa	44.188	−0.46	60.7	29.7	42.45	56.9	82.4	10	12,000
Swaziland	1.136	−0.34	71.8	40.7	32.23	23.5	79.6	11	5,000

Sources: CIA World Factbook, 2009.

GEOGRAPHY

Africa, second in size only to Asia, has some of the world's mightiest rivers and abundant mineral resources. Nevertheless, the region has more than its share of natural impediments to development, including its relative isolation from other areas of the world. The Atlantic Ocean is located to the west of the continent and the Indian Ocean to the east. Prevailing wind patterns on the west coast minimized maritime contacts between Africans and Europeans until the fifteenth or sixteenth century. With the Sahara (the Arabic word for *desert*) in the north, it is easy to understand why overland transportation from Europe and North Africa was and is spotty. The Kalahari Desert in the southern part of the continent is an additional obstacle.

Africa's great rivers—Nile, Zaire (Congo), Niger, Zambezi, and Orange—all have cataracts, sand bars, or other obstructions, which also undermine rather than enhance commerce and communications. The continent's smooth coastline and, thus, its lack of natural harbors, has been another problem, although today coastal cities such as Dakar, Lagos, Luanda, and Dar es Salaam are highly important.

Most of the region's interior is flat or gently undulating. The major exception is the Great Rift Valley system in eastern Africa, which runs north to south for hundreds of miles and features deep trenches, 20 to 50 miles wide, carved into the earth. Inactive volcanoes, frequent earth tremors, and occasional earthquakes occur in the area. Lake Victoria is the largest lake in Africa, and Mount Kilimanjaro is the continent's highest mountain, 19,340 feet above sea level.

Whatever the focus, African geography runs the gamut from scarcity to abundance. Although temperatures are generally high, rainfall, when abundant, gives rise to lush vegetation; more often, the absence of rainfall contributes to a parched landscape. Varying soil quality also helps produce rainforests, savannas, or deserts. Mineral resources follow the same oscillating pattern. Some areas in central and southern Africa are uniquely blessed, whereas other locales are virtually void of substances valued in the modern world (see Figure 6.1).

The complex interaction of temperature, rainfall, population growth and distribution, and soils is of crucial significance in Africa today, and the consequences of global warming threaten to disrupt reliable, traditional sources of livelihood and food. The human habitat was formerly more hospitable. Thirty-five hundred years ago what is now the Sahara was green. Just 40 years ago, the Sahel, which includes the area lying just south of the Sahara, was able to sustain a population of perhaps 20 million. Today, famine is an ever-present danger. Millions of nomadic herders, traders, and small farmers have become refugees trying to eke out a living in an increasingly unforgiving environment.

As a result, both the farmers, whose land becomes more difficult to till, and the herders are forced to move to overcrowded cities. Nouakchott, for instance, the capital of Mauritania and on the edge of the Sahel, has grown from 20,000 people in 1960 to more than 673,000 today. Many of its people barely survive; some starve. The same might be said of Khartoum, the capital of Sudan, some 3,000 miles away. In the past few years, eastern and southern Africa has been affected in a similar way. In fact, the encroaching desert, aided by drought, has affected some two dozen African states. In 1998, the flooding Nile meant that

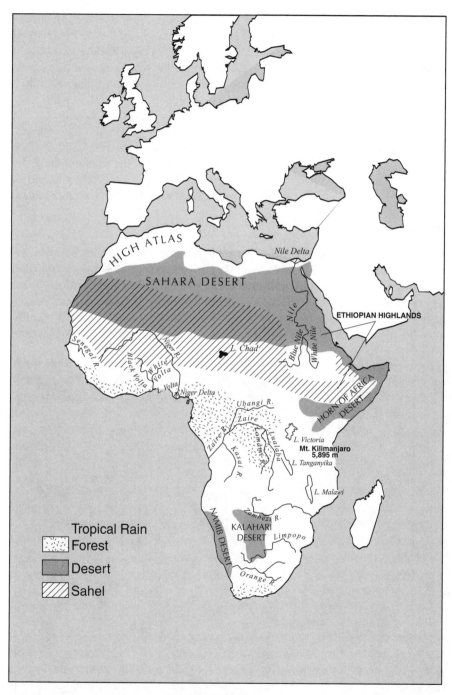

FIGURE 6.1 The Physical Geography of Africa

hundreds of thousands of people near Khartoum were victimized both by an absence of rain and a deluge of water. In 2004, the problems of the northern desert areas were compounded by hordes of devastating locusts, leading to a severe famine and humanitarian crisis in Niger the following year. A severe drought in 2005 brought famine to Malawi, a nation also mired in partisan political turmoil.

In the past, Africa's strategic importance rested on its mineral wealth in the central and southern parts of the continent and its geographic "chokepoints" on the perimeter of the region. High-tech industries of the West relied on platinum, chrome, and vanadium, which are found almost exclusively in Africa. Gibraltar, the Suez Canal, Bab el Mandeb, and the Cape of Good Hope at the southern tip of the continent were strategic areas of interest to both East and West. With the end of the cold war, both the economic and geopolitical standing of the region declined.

PEOPLE

Africa's people have been divided by many factors, including race, ethnicity, language, religion, country, and class. The importance of race was established as early as the fifteenth century. Later, it was tied to class when positions in society became dominated by Europeans. Because of the colonial legacy, the belief that one race is superior or inferior to another still has considerable significance in Africa. The emphasis on race was clearest in South Africa, where

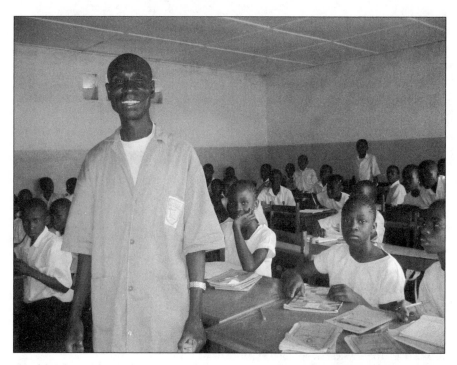

Proud Teacher with His Class in Lubumbashi, Democratic Republic of Congo: This beaming teacher must manage two separate shifts with 50 students in each class every day. Many see universal education as the key to a brighter future for Africa, but adequate access and resources remain limited in most sub-Saharan African nations. *Source: Olga Carter*

apartheid, a form of separate development based on race, was officially proclaimed by whites in 1948 and rescinded only in 1990.

Race remains important in many other African countries. In several former French colonies, there are almost as many Europeans now as there were at independence more than four decades ago. There, as elsewhere, Europeans have many of the most prestigious and best-paying jobs. Often, being white gets one a better seat in a van or truck or allows one to be waved through a checkpoint while others with a darker skin must wait. For the present then, Europeans, a name often given to all whites, still enjoy a high social status and lifestyle far above that of most of the indigenous population.

Between the Europeans and the Africans on the ladder of success are the Indians of East and South Africa and the Lebanese of West Africa. Both groups are major forces in retail and wholesale merchandising and in the economy generally. Because of their positions, both are also targets of protest from those below them on the ladder.

In a discussion of language, ethnic groups, cultures (and subcultures), and religions, the key concepts are diversity and complexity. There are, conservatively, many hundreds of different ethnic groups. (Because of the negative connotations of the words *tribe* and *tribalism*, terms such as *ethnic group*, *subnational community,* and *micro-nation* have replaced them.) There are, therefore, many hundreds of distinct languages and cultures. Although some groups number in the millions of members, others have only hundreds. The sheer number of such groups throughout Africa makes this dimension unique to the continent. Ethnic divisions are a powerful force today. Struggles in such diverse states as Angola, Burundi, Congo, Ethiopia, Kenya, Liberia, Mauritania, Nigeria, Rwanda, Sierra Leone, Sudan, and Uganda may be explained, in part, by deep-seated ethnic divisions.

African religions, again diverse and complex, have generally accommodated external religions, accepting some aspects and modifying others. Christian missionaries, who preceded colonial officials, remained after their government's departure. Although numbers are hard to confirm, there is a consensus that the number of people embracing either the monotheism of Christianity or Islam in some form is growing rapidly. The Roman Catholic population, for instance, has grown considerably in the past decade to more than 120 million, and the late Pope John Paul II visited the continent no fewer than 12 times. Some church experts thought that an African Pope, specifically a respected Nigerian Cardinal, might be elected this time, but the College of Cardinals elected a German instead. Local customs and beliefs have challenged Rome's pronouncements; indigenous churches, therefore, abound. Islam has been an important political factor in many countries in the Sahel, the *Horn of Africa*, spreading deeper into Central and West Africa, and militant fundamentalist movements have made inroads in nations such as Somalia.

Most people in the West give their primary support to the nation-state, but such a commitment is rare in Africa. Race, ethnicity, and religion have historical and deep-seated appeals that compete with the nation-state. With a large majority of Africans still continuing to live in the rural areas, developing support for the nation-state is a challenge. Only rarely do state and ethnic boundaries coincide. Nationalism is further hampered by the small size and population of many of the countries, as well as their lack of resources.

A belief in a shared past or shared future, in myths or traditions, in joint economic or social institutions, or in a common culture is in short supply on the national level. Rarely is there a common indigenous language. In fact, in most African states, the official language is a European tongue. In conflicts between personal, family, village, or ethnic ties on the one hand, and a national perspective on the other, the larger focus usually loses. National leaders and others in the intelligentsia have the media at their disposal in their call for increased support for the state, and expanding education for children and adults helps. Nevertheless, developing a broadly based nationalism is proceeding slowly.

As in the former Soviet Union (including the Other World nations treated in Chapter 9) and Eastern Europe, class formation is expanding and perhaps sharpening. With few exceptions, the emergence of a small elite class, often tied to one ethnic group, has become the norm. For the time being, a comfortable lifestyle is beyond even the aspirations of the great majority. With the move to privatization described in the section on economics, some will improve their lot dramatically, but many others will become more embittered as the good life passes them by.

At the beginning of the twentieth century, the continent of Africa had fewer than 100 million people. Its population now is more than 973 million (nearly 800 million of whom live in the sub-Saharan region). During the 1970s and 1980s, the population growth rate increased to more than 3 percent a year. Different sources say that the region's annual population increase has moderated to around 2.5 percent. That means well over a billion people on the continent by 2025, but some factors, including population control policies and the ravages of AIDS in southern Africa, might curb this rate in certain areas. Despite the regional differences, sub-Saharan Africa maintains the dubious distinction of the highest population growth rate in the world.

The birthrate in sub-Saharan Africa declined slightly in the last generation, but the death rate had declined more. By 1995, the gap had become immense, with an annual birthrate per thousand of 43.1 and a death rate of 14, but by 2007, these figures had changed to 40 and 15, respectively. Because the infant mortality rate has declined dramatically, there is one less reason for parents to want more children, lessening the traditional preference for large families. Botswana, Kenya, Côte d'Ivoire, Tanzania, Djibouti, Guinea, and Zimbabwe have achieved varying degrees of success at population control. Kenya, which a decade ago was averaging close to 4 percent growth per year, then the world's highest, is now just above 1 percent, and average family size there declined from 8 in the 1970s to 5.4 in 1998. Only a small percentage of married African women use modern contraceptive methods, even in the midst of the AIDS crisis. In most countries, the status of women is low and their sex education lags behind that of men. The religious admonition calling for large families is another factor driving population growth and hindering condom use.[1] Many fear that the continent's life-support systems will be overwhelmed and the mortality rate will increase. Over the past 40 years, economic growth has barely kept pace with population growth. Life expectancy at birth in sub-Saharan Africa in 2008 stood at only 50 years, by far the lowest in the Other World. Of the 26 nations categorized as having "low human development" in the 2008 United Nations (UN) Human Development Index, a widely recognized measure of the quality of life that combines life expectancy and educational statistics, all but one (East Timor) are sub-Saharan African, including the lowest-ranked 21 nations. (Strife-torn Somalia is not ranked.) Of the sub-Saharan nations on the African continent, Gabon holds the highest ranking on this index at 107. The UN has established the Millennium Development Goals, eight ambitious targets for positive human change by 2015; despite some limited progress, sub-Saharan Africa faces the greatest hurdles of all the Other World regions to reach them.[2]

HISTORY

Africa's history before the arrival of the Europeans was rich, varied, and complex. It encompassed many types of political systems, social structures, and economic patterns. It also involved considerable interaction with the peoples of North Africa, the Arabian Peninsula, and even China. Africa has been called "the cradle of human history," "the cradle of mankind," and "the first habitat of man." These phrases apply because the oldest human remains, dating back at least 3 million years, were found in eastern Africa. Nevertheless, many people did not think Africa had a history because, to them, history was based on written language. This bias has now been corrected. In certain areas south of the Sahara, written Arabic was in use 1,000 years ago. More importantly, we now realize that oral traditions, archaeological exploration, comparative linguistics, art styles, ethnography, radiocarbon dating, and a host of other tools can provide evidence of a rich history, predating the written word.

The domestication of cattle is 6,000 to 7,000 years old in Africa. Working with metal and iron, planting crops, and engaging in long-distance trade are occupations that go back millennia as well. In fact, there is much discussion today about how much Egypt, often referred to as the cradle of civilization, was influenced by areas further south. The Khoikhoi (Hottentots), San (Bushmen), and Twa (Pygmies) had long inhabited much of central and southern Africa until incursions from West Africa around the eleventh century began to reduce their spheres.

African kingdoms of great size and wealth predate the European colonial presence by many hundreds of years. Some of the best-known empires—Ghana, Mali, and Songhai—which together lasted over 1,000 years, were in the western Sudan, south of the Sahara. Here, Islam made its presence felt, especially among the rulers of Mali and Songhai. Great Zimbabwe in southern Africa, with its imposing stone structures, reached its apex in the fifteenth century. New archaeological research is uncovering more evidence of other sophisticated, well-organized, sub-Saharan African civilizations.

By the eighth century, Arab traders had brought Islam to the Horn of Africa, from which it gradually spread south and west. The Arab presence, however, went back much further, especially along the east coast. In succeeding centuries, traders pushed into the interior, although African culture remained dominant throughout. The Arab influence was great, however, from the formation of towns along the Indian Ocean to the rise of Swahili as the most important language in the region. The arrival of the Portuguese, with their superior military power, at the end of the fifteenth century signaled the rapid decline of Arab culture in the area.

Until the latter half of the nineteenth century, there were few Europeans in sub-Saharan Africa, especially in the vast interior. Despite their small numbers, they had a profound and lasting impact on African life. The institution of Western-style slavery cost the continent anywhere from 12 to 50 million men, women, and children (see the "Flashpoints" section.) In the seventeenth and eighteenth centuries, slaves were the major export from the west coast of Africa.

By 1850, the European presence in Africa had existed along narrow coastal strips for over 350 years. The Portuguese in the fifteenth and sixteenth centuries, the Dutch in the seventeenth century, and the British in the eighteenth and first part of the nineteenth centuries had been dominant because of sea power. By about 1850, newfound European attention to the "Dark Continent" coincided with turbulence in several parts of Africa and resulted in greater penetration of the interior than ever before. The European objectives in Africa included raw materials to feed the Industrial Revolution, new markets, promising investments, naval bases, the renewed drive to "save souls," and a multifaceted quest for new knowledge.

THE COLONIAL EXPERIENCE

Despite the increasing presence of the Europeans, 90 percent of the continent was ruled by Africans until the last two decades of the nineteenth century. The European powers had not thought the benefits of occupation were worth the costs. As the foreigners jockeyed for power and prestige on the continent and around the globe, the situation quickly changed. The European states moved to establish a series of colonies in the region, and the possibility that the new competition would result in war was seen as a real danger. From October 1884 to February 1885, a conference to discuss the future boundaries of Africa was held in Berlin, at which almost all the important European powers (but, tellingly, no Africans) were represented. The decisions reached at the *Berlin Conference*—and elsewhere in Europe in the remaining 15 years of the nineteenth century—established the basic political map of the continent to this day.

Africa was artificially divided to suit the objectives of the colonial governments. Preexisting ethnic, linguistic, and cultural units were ignored. Figure 6.2 depicts a striking contrast with the boundaries of only 11 years earlier. Throughout Africa, closely knit people speaking the same language were suddenly separated. It was from these diversions that future generations' secessionist movements and border claims, known as *irredentism*, would spring.

The heyday of European colonial rule in Africa lasted for only 50 or 60 years; however, those few decades changed the face of the continent forever.[3] The impact of colonialism depended on the type of rule instituted, the presence

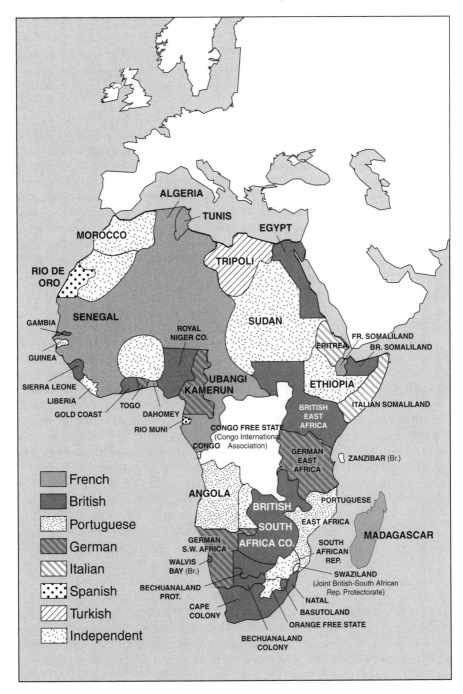

FIGURE 6.2 European Colonization in Africa, 1895

or absence of white settlers, and the particulars of the African elite. Most importantly, each African ethnic group had its own political and social system. Each responded to colonial rule in a different way, ranging from willing acceptance to bloody resistance of the outside powers. The Baganda people of East Africa welcomed the European presence. In contrast, the Ndebele-Shona Rebellion (1896–1897) against English-speaking settlers in what is now Zimbabwe, the Ashanti and Fulani resistance against the British in West Africa (1900–1901), and the Maji Maji Rebellion contesting harsh German rule in East Africa (1905–1907) all resulted in a strong European show of force followed by occupation.

The British generally practiced indirect rule, a system in which they were removed from day-to-day activities; instead, they used the traditional authorities, who were now responsible to them. The other colonial systems employed direct rule, in which the European administrators played a much more extensive role in everyday African life. The British, concerned about costs, emphasized the economic dimension and were more aloof; the French, the leading practitioners of direct rule, were more intimately involved, held out the slight possibility that their subjects might become French citizens, and had a more lasting effect on their colonies.

Whatever the differences, the similarities were more important. The colonial powers' dominance occurred everywhere. Different peoples were divided or united by fiat, and long-time trading patterns were subject to fundamental change as the societies themselves were transformed in a hundred different ways. The indigenous populations suffered altered political arrangements, alien tax structures, forced labor, and directed changes in individual wants and societal norms. By shifting the roles and selection processes for traditional political leaders, the colonial authorities unintentionally sowed the seeds for far greater political changes in years to come. Much of the economy fell under the influence, if not control, of the Europeans, who wished to substitute one or two cash crops or minerals for subsistence farming. Foreign goods and the widespread use of colonial currencies were also introduced. Cities, roads, and railroads were constructed for the benefit of the colonial rulers' administrative and economic interests. This colonial infrastructure tended to divide Africa rather than link it together; even today, the African map reflects the extractive goals of the imperial powers (see Figure 6.3). In addition, the missionary and soldier added their particular persuasions to that of the administrator and merchant. By 1920, only Ethiopia, Liberia, and the Union of South Africa were free from formal European control, and the last was run by a white minority.

The new order scarcely touched the lives of the masses in many of the colonies. The people had little contact with Europeans, except when it was necessary to pay some new tax, live under some new law, or adopt a new plan for local land use. For the majority living in the rural areas, change or adaptation was to be a very gradual thing.

In the Portuguese, German, and Belgian colonies, the rule was far more harsh and the impact was often far more devastating. Villagers were routinely taken, with or without their leaders' approval, to work on roads or other projects. Impressment, however, was the least of it. The Congo Free State, for instance,

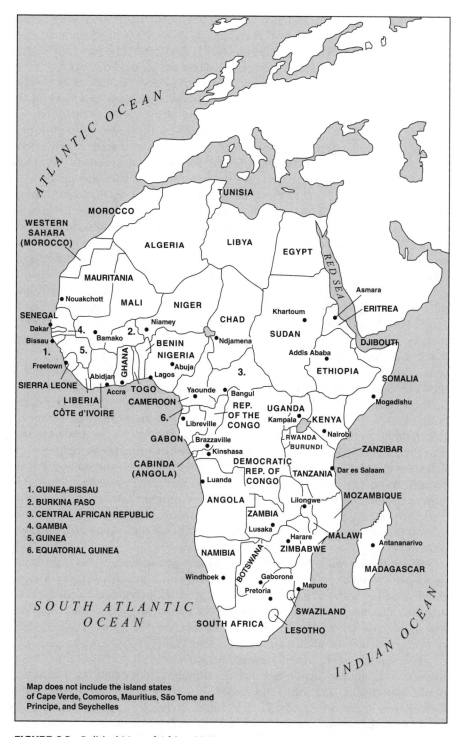

FIGURE 6.3   Political Map of Africa, 2010

was the private preserve of the Belgian king, whose control was so inhumane that after about 20 years he was forced to cede his 900,000-square-mile playground to the government of Belgium, which then established an only slightly more benevolent rule over this mammoth colony in the middle of Africa.

The movement to independence can be described in one of two ways: structurally or chronologically. Among the most important structures in the movement, especially to the generation coming of age in the early 1900s, was the church. This institution was part of the white establishment, with its distinction between superior and inferior values, but it was also a source for Western-style education and a breeding ground for future nationalists. Although Christianity first undermined local cultures and traditions, later, independent, indigenous Christian churches came to question colonial government policies. Other institutions of change were located in the fast-growing cities. These included the tribal unions and associations; trade unions or workers' solidarity organizations; the rudimentary mass media; the soldiers and ex-servicemen, who had traveled beyond the colony; and finally, overt political movements. All contributed to the requests for greater responsibility by the local, African elite; to calls for autonomy or power sharing by the growing nationalist movement; and, ultimately, to demands for independence, now backed by the masses.

In both World Wars, African troops participated on behalf of their European masters, gaining valuable training and combat experience. They also observed that the Europeans were not invincible. Chronologically, the trickle of restrained nationalism before 1885 became a torrent of calls for independence in the years after World War II. West Africa moved ahead more quickly than East Africa, which in turn led the southern part of the continent. Overall, the British colonies were in advance of the French, who led the Portuguese. Even the British were cautious, however, expecting at most a slow devolution of power. The British anticipated that black parliamentary governments would be established by local leaders, who would be "properly" educated and trained. For the French, those few Africans who gained political power would do so not in African political structures, but as overseas representatives in the French National Assembly in Paris. The other European powers believed that any growth of political consciousness would change the status quo and, thus, was unthinkable.

When World War II began in 1939, no one would have guessed that independence for most of the African colonies was only a generation away. Despite the depression of the 1930s, colonial rule appeared immutable. Certainly, there were the firebrands who agitated for greater rights for Africans, but they were few in number and cautious in method, despite an occasional protest or even riot at a particular location.

The war, however, had a tremendous effect on all parties. Tens of thousands of soldiers saw action beyond the continent. They returned home with newly honed skills and ideas and settled in the cities rather than returning to their homes in the rural areas. They became a part of the mass independence movements that were destined to sweep the continent. The new militancy was fueled by large numbers of students returning to Africa from overseas, the demands of an increasingly urbanized population, and a new generation of political leaders. The battered European powers, meanwhile, were simply hoping to hang on at home and had little interest and few resources for the colonies, thousands of miles away.

Africans under French rule were ready for a new day. Early in the war, General Charles de Gaulle had promised greater local autonomy (but not self-government) and increased rights for the peoples of French West Africa (FWA) and French Equatorial Africa (FEA) if they supported him in his battle against Vichy France and Nazi Germany. Similarly, in 1941, U.S. President Franklin Roosevelt and British Prime Minister Winston Churchill promised in the Atlantic Charter "to respect the right of all peoples to choose the form of government under which they will live." At the end of the war, the newly founded UN called for self-determination, and the two emerging superpowers—the United States and the Soviet Union—both supported changes in the existing colonial order.

The beginning of the end for colonial rule came with a railway workers' strike in FWA in 1946, followed by disturbances over economic issues in the Gold Coast, a presumed model British colony in West Africa, in early 1948. This latter protest, in which ex-servicemen played a major role, spread to the other British colonies in the area. In those postwar years, a new law and a new constitution in Paris also accelerated change throughout FWA and FEA. In the years that followed, Africans who lived thousands of miles apart, spoke hundreds of different languages, and were subjects of several colonial powers took up the unifying cry of self-government.

Independence came first to the Gold Coast (renamed Ghana) in 1957. The next year, President de Gaulle angrily accepted Guinea's vote to follow suit.[4] At the same time, the other colonies that had been carved out of FWA and FEA chose federation with France, allowing Paris continuing control of foreign affairs, internal security, and defense. In 1960, the logjam broke as the remaining 11 French-speaking colonies became independent. The same year, Nigeria ended its colonial relationship with Britain to become a regional magnet. For the next 20 years, the march to independence continued, and by the end of 1980, only Namibia, on the southwest coast of Africa, remained in a dependent status; South Africa, despite UN resolutions, refused to give up its controlling interest over the former German colony it had inherited as a mandate after World War I. Finally, in 1990, even this dependency ended, as a general agreement on regional relations in southern Africa was reached.

Independence throughout the region had been achieved. But if this were a time for celebration, it was also a time of great concern because a consensus on future directions within each state, let alone within regions or the continent as a whole, never existed. Older animosities that sometimes had been kept under wraps by the colonial power burst forth. Opposing local, national, and supranational forces threatened the stability of the fragile new states. Furthermore, the economic dimension was no more secure than the political, as local economies remained vulnerable to both domestic and international interests. The former colonial states were independent, but their governments lacked the sustained support of the people or, in some cases, the international community. Without such support, unity and economic well-being were unlikely.

GOVERNMENT

To understand African government in the early 2000s, one must realize that there has been an incredible compression of major political events. The older Africans of today grew up in the heyday of colonial rule, lived through World War II and the nationalist rush to independence, and finally, have experienced the disappointments and instabilities of the post-independence years. The scholar Ali Mazrui quoted former Tanzanian President Julius Nyerere as saying that while some countries are trying to reach the moon and beyond, many Africans are still trying to get to town.[5] Such traditional institutions and values as the extended family and communal ownership of property are under attack while a new set of institutions and beliefs is not yet fully in place.

Instead of rule by the people, African independence has usually resulted in the continued rule of the few, though the new elites are indigenous, not foreign. The urban community, not the majority in the countryside, gets the bulk of state-run programs. In the cities, it is the small middle and upper classes that benefit from government. Despite a long history of group participation in decision making in many societies, pronouncements in the decades after independence were usually made by and for the few. The result was too often an elite driven by self-interest and even greed, while the many were disregarded. A view of politics as a means of extraction and personal enrichment, fostered under the experience of colonial rule, continued into independence, often with devastating results, as corruption among elected and appointed officials became commonplace.

Political solutions tried elsewhere in the Other World have faced opposition and indifference from societies in Africa. A major problem for the social elites is that the people have little faith in them. Although a few traditional authorities such as Chief Mangosuthu Gatsha Buthelezi of the Zulu people in South Africa exercise considerable political influence, such examples are rare. Almost all African states comprise many ethnic groups, and traditional authorities may be unsuccessful in reaching out to those who owe them no special allegiance. Moreover, few of these authorities have real political power. They may also carry the baggage of colonial days, when their functions were usually altered by their European overlords, thus leading to the loss of respect from their subjects.

By the early 1980s, competitive political party systems in Africa were a rarity. This fact would have surprised earlier generations because, in many cases, the political party was in the forefront of the march to independence, and in doing so, gained mass support. Some parties managed to gain the grudging blessing of the colonial rulers, who looked fondly to their own political parties as models.

As the twentieth century ended, there were two schools of thought regarding African political systems. One was stated by Susan Rice, then Assistant Secretary of

State for African Affairs and now the U.S. Representative to the UN in the Obama administration, in an address to the African Affairs Association in late 1997:

> Africa stands at a crossroads. . . . There is now more reason for optimism about Africa's future than at any time since the wave of independence over 30 years ago. . . . Democracy is ascendant. . . . Economic growth is also increasing. . . . Regions of stability are . . . emerging throughout the continent . . . [I]n many countries . . . reconciliation is supplanting confrontations as the means of bridging differences rooted in the past.[6]

The other was summarized by Judith Matloff, reporter for the *Christian Science Monitor*, as she wrapped up almost six years in the region in early 1998:

> I'd like to leave Africa saying that it had turned a corner into peace and prosperity and that most of the countries were on the right track. But that would be myopic and downright dishonest. The poverty and lack of education are so endemic, the access to arms so easy, and the democratic institutions so fragile that it's unlikely that the world's poorest continent will change overnight.[7]

These two seemingly contrasting positions, stated over a decade ago, remain valid today, and both are grounded in realities. Analysts come up with very different assessments of perceived democratic trends in the region, and Westerners often see Africa as cut from one piece of cloth, not as distinct states. Through the media, it is usually the wars, the poverty, the human rights abuses, the diseases and, thus, the resignation that stand out. As far-removed states back off, the international lending institutions and nongovernmental aid agencies have become more prominent. Such institutions and agencies, however, have a long way to go. Then-UN Secretary General Kofi Annan, from Ghana, elected to a second term and awarded the Nobel Peace Prize in 2001 for the UN's peacekeeping efforts, bemoaned both divisive and draining colonial systems and more recent African leaders who had too often resorted to "heavy centralization of political and economic power and the suppression of political pluralism."[8] Centralized and personalized forms of government, patterns of corruption, ethnically based decisions, and human rights abuses, asserted Annan, were all too common. Coups and other extra-legal power transitions still occur, including the assassination of the elected president of Guinea-Bissau in 2009. Even in the emerging African democracies, elections are often viewed as tainted and the winners as lacking legitimacy. Recent elections in Ethiopia, Madagascar, Mauritania, Nigeria, Togo, Zimbabwe, and Kenya have been disputed or come under suspicion. Rarely has a recent African election gone unchallenged, often through violent protests, and many elections fall far short of generally accepted norms of free, fair, and competitive. Beyond the need for free and fair elections, emphasis for democratic reform in Africa centers increasingly on rule of law, good governance practices, and rooting out corruption.

WANGARI MAATHAI

Wangari Maathai

Source: AFP Getty Images

Originally trained as a biologist, Kenyan Wangari Maathai became active in women's rights and founded the innovative environmental organization, The Greenbelt Movement (GBM), in 1977. Through GBM, women plant trees to restore damaged ecosystems, empowering the women and giving them purpose and self-esteem in the process. Despite strong opposition from the Kenyan government under Daniel arap Moi, Maathai's GBM grew in popularity and stature. With a change in administrations in the 2002 elections, Maathai was elected to parliament and served as Assistant Minister of the Environment, Natural Resources and Wildlife from 2003–2007, and, in 2005, she was appointed Presiding Officer of the African Union's Economic, Social, and Cultural Council (ECOSOCC). Her work with GBM emphasized the connections between human rights, environmentalism, democratization, and peace, leading to the award of the prestigious Nobel Peace Prize in 2004. In citing her for the award, the Nobel Committee wrote:

> She has taken a holistic approach to sustainable development that embraces democracy, human rights and women's rights in particular. Her efforts have been adopted by other countries as well. We believe that Maathai is a strong voice speaking for the best forces in Africa to promote peace and good living conditions on that continent.[9]

As an African woman holding a high position in government, Maathai is a rarity.

Most commentators agree that any long-term strategy for the future of Africa that does not consider women prominently is doomed to failure. Women figure strongly as victims in nearly all of Africa's most serious dilemmas; they must now be brought to the forefront in the decision-making processes that will lead to solutions. As Chipo Lungu, executive director of the Zambia National Women's Lobby Group, put it, "The men haven't done a good job of running our countries, so maybe now we are looking for a Big Woman, not a Big Man, to do the job. The list of corrupt, incompetent and just foolish male leaders is a long one."[10]

Despite the fact that GBM has planted 30 million trees in Kenya alone and accomplished much good, environmentalists in sub-Saharan Africa face enormous challenges. Civil wars and careless profiteers exact terrible tolls on the environment, threatening, for example, the famed mountain gorilla population in Congo and invaluable rainforests in much of Central and West Africa. Life-support systems throughout the continent are at risk.

Still, as some African writers have noted, all environmental problems do not rest with the Other World; for example, Africa has contributed little to the emissions resulting in greenhouse gases and global warming, but its resources suffer from the effects of climate change and other consequences of pollution produced elsewhere. Africa faces human issues that cannot yield to simple admonitions from the developed nations to protect nature and end pollution. Africa's capabilities to protect its own environment, given the pressures of conflicts, health issues, and the debt crisis, among other factors, are limited without understanding and substantive assistance from those in the developed world with the means and technology to make a difference. (To learn more about Wangari Maathai's work, visit her official Web site, www.wangarimaathai. com. Her memoir, *Unbowed*, was published in 2006, and her prescriptions for Africa's ills, *The Challenge for Africa*, appeared in spring 2009.)

Pan-Africanism and Regional Cooperation

In July 2003, the recently formed *African Union (AU)* held its second annual summit meeting in Maputo, Mozambique. African heads of states and other political representatives came together to continue to chart a new path for African integration roughly along the lines of the European Union. Few ordinary Africans seemed to be paying close attention, however, to these potentially momentous deliberations. Tens of millions of Africans were simply too busy trying to make their daily way or, worse, survive the threats of famine, disease, or civil war. (Even President Bush, visiting the continent during these sessions, did not bother to attend.) An estimated 30 million Africans, on the other hand, were preoccupied that summer with a new reality TV show, *Big Brother Africa*, which brought together 12 young adult Africans, each from a different country, for several months, living under the constant glare of cameras in a TV format popularized in the United States and Western Europe.[11] To many African fans, the show represented hope for the future, breaking down national stereotypes and pointing to the possibility of positive cooperation across borders. To its critics, though, the program negatively reflected on African values with its casual relationships in the midst of the AIDS pandemic; its voyeurism; and its depiction of an upscale, urban lifestyle out of reach of most Africans. Which (if either) of these events better represents the future and promise of *pan-Africanism*—the solemn gathering of men in suits issuing declarations and decisions on new integrative directions for Africa or the Western-style reality TV show with a distinctively African twist?

This chapter highlights some, but by no means all, of the many conflicts in sub-Saharan Africa in the early 2000s. Guinea-Bissau, Chad, Congo (Brazzaville), Namibia, Lesotho, Zambia, Burundi, Kenya, and Uganda are among the states not prominently mentioned in these pages that have been beset by instability and violence. In several cases where opposing forces initially have been unwilling to seek solutions except through the gun, there have been attempts by outside individuals, countries, or organizations to stop the fighting. The notion of a common heritage, common values, and a common future kindles interest among those grown weary by the upheavals. After all, pan-African congresses had been held during early decades of the last century.

Back in the early 1960s, there was a struggle between more militant governments who wanted to work for continental fusion and Mother Africa and those who, having just gained independence, did not wish to be swallowed up by some larger entity. Antagonistic blocs of countries formed. Trying to stem the hostilities, 30 African states met in the Ethiopian capital of Addis Ababa in May

1963. The result was the creation of the Organization of African Unity (OAU), the principles of which included

1. National independence over continental unity,
2. Nonintervention in the affairs of another state,
3. The sanctity of national boundaries,
4. The responsibility of Africans for peacefully solving their own problems,
5. The adoption of a nonaligned or neutralist stance, and
6. Equality of all sovereign states.

Support for liberation movements was agreed to in a resolution, but it was not a principle on which the organization was founded.

In the ensuing years, OAU membership swelled as more colonies became independent. Annual meetings of heads of state and foreign ministers were held, often amid great pomp and ceremony, to promote political, economic, and cultural cooperation. As in the UN, however, hard decisions involving action were in short supply.

In the last decade, financial problems and coming to grips with the traditional unwillingness to intervene "in the affairs of another state" were stumbling blocks. In any case, as we know from the Balkan region in East Europe, regional intervention is difficult and perilous. The OAU was all but invisible in the civil wars in Somalia and Rwanda in the first half of the 1990s and played a peripheral role in other trouble spots since then, preferring rather to cede responsibility to smaller entities. Equivocation on the "noninterference issue" remained, despite support for collective action by national leaders at a 1993 OAU conference.[12]

Given its mixed and often disappointing record, the OAU undertook in 1999 an ambitious and far-reaching program of reform. Beginning in 2002, the body changed its name to the African Union and initiated steps over a number of years that, if successful, will lead to much closer cooperation and eventual integration among the member states.[13] One factor inhibiting progress in the old OAU was the requirement that all major decisions be unanimous; reaching agreement on matters of substance among dozens of disparate states is notoriously difficult. The reforms are to introduce some majority voting, a permanent legislative body, and, eventually, a common currency similar to the European Union's euro. Although there has been progress in institutional development and holding conferences on important issues, whether the new reforms can stay on track and make a real difference in the continent's ongoing political and economic problems remains to be seen. Critics contend that early results have not been encouraging given the limited role the AU has played in its formative years in resolving the crises Africa has faced. Its substantive, peacekeeping efforts in the continuing Darfur, Sudan, conflict were augmented by a larger UN force beginning in fall 2007, but problems there persist (see the "Flashpoints" sections). Current AU chairman Muammar al-Qaddafi, the "Brother Leader" of Libya, has called for a rapid move to fuller continental unity, but his sweeping, ambitious plan has met a mixed reception.

Smaller geographical organizations have been somewhat more active, albeit not always successful, in political-military matters. The Economic Community of

West African States (ECOWAS) played an important role in the long-festering conflict in Liberia in the early 1990s, in Sierra Leone later, and more recently in Liberia again. In most of these cases, Nigerian soldiers were instrumental in curbing the fighting. Similarly, the Southern African Development Community (SADC), under its Chair, South African President Nelson Mandela, tried to broker a cease fire in the 1998 Congo war (see Central Africa and the *Great Lakes Region* in the "Flashpoints" section), but achieved minimal results.

Especially in economic matters, SADC has been the most important and successful of the regional entities, with numerous linkages established. South Africa and its former President Mandela, however, by their very prominence, have produced a wariness or even hostility from some of the other members. The economic clout of South Africa is both a hope and a concern for other member states. There is still much SADC can do to help the region's southern tier of countries, but national sensitivities and personalities loom large. Otherwise, the effectiveness of the more than 200 additional organizations for regional cooperation has been mixed at best.

African Relations with Outside Powers

Over the last century, Africa's relations with outside powers have gone through several stages and may now be entering a new one. As the earlier discussion in this chapter suggested, the colonial powers consolidated their control over most of the continent in the 1890s. At least through World War II, the United States, the Soviet Union, and China did not challenge the domination of the existing order. Even the advent and pursuit of the cold war did not at first change this order. The Other World, and especially Africa, was not seen as a major theater of competition. Conflicts might flare around the perimeter of the Soviet Union and even to a limited degree in Latin America, but Africa was a backwater.

As African states began to achieve independence in the late 1950s, however, this situation began to change. The U.S.-Soviet rivalry became global, and soon the Chinese entered the maneuvering. In addition, the French continued their strong economic and military presence in the region. For 20 years the jousting continued unabated.

By the 1980s, this foreign competition began to ebb. The superpowers and China became more selective in their involvements. The ideological orientation of any one state was not viewed as very important. The Soviet Union was the largest supplier of military aid to the region, but then, under Mikhail Gorbachev, it reduced military material bound for Mozambique, helped broker the Cuban pullout from Angola, played a supportive role in achieving Namibia's independence, and withdrew its commitment to what had been its closest ally in the region, Ethiopia.

The Western influence had been much in evidence economically. France was the country that had long had close relations with its former colonies. By the mid-1990s, this had changed. Almost all the first generation of African post-independence leaders who embraced France passed from the scene. More importantly, in late 1993, France greatly reduced its support for the common currency used in almost all of French-speaking Africa. These former colonies, thus, became more vulnerable to the shifts in world markets. Furthermore, France later decided to withdraw its garrisons from the continent, but in 2003, it sent thousands of troops in a perilous and controversial mission to end a civil war in the Côte d'Ivoire and led a special UN mission to curb ethnic violence in the Democratic Republic of Congo. Under then–Prime Minister Tony Blair, Britain strongly advocated increased aid to Africa from the developed world, at the 2005 Gleneagles, Scotland, Summit of the G-8 nations. Both France, under highly visible President Sarkozy, and China, with growing economic ties and ambitious projects, appear to be increasing their interest and activism in sub-Saharan Africa. Both India and Brazil have recently stepped up their political and trade contacts with Africa to bolster their own growing economies.

SUB-SAHARAN AFRICA AND THE UNITED STATES   The United States enjoys enduring, deep, and rich connections of culture and heritage with sub-Saharan Africa. With the election of President Barack Obama, whose late father hailed from the small Kenyan village of Kogelo, these connections have been greatly enhanced in the eyes of Africans, many of whom view President Obama as virtually one of their own. Most Africans would probably agree that maintaining close and friendly ties with the United States is crucial to a positive future for Africa. However, most Americans are not well informed about African affairs, and the American media rarely covers Africa except in times of political or economic crisis, natural disaster, or a visit by the U.S. president. Normally, it is difficult to find hopeful or positive images of Africa in our mainstream media outlets. This contributes to a sense that Africa is a lost cause teeming with corrupt, greedy politicians, endless civil wars, pirates, and horrible epidemics and famines, deserving perhaps of humanitarian attention, but a futile case for more foreign aid or direct intervention.

After the cold war, the United States abandoned anticommunism as the linchpin of its African policies and with it went its support for corrupt leaders. Longtime ally Mobutu Sese Seko, president of Zaire (now the Democratic Republic of Congo), was rebuked for activities that made him one of the richest men on the continent, if not the world, while silencing any potential opposition. There is an African proverb that says "When the elephants fight, it is the grass that gets trampled." This proverb was often applied to the cold war, with the two superpowers in the role of elephants and Africa the grass. As some African commentators pointed out, things also do not improve for the grass when elephants "make love"; things have improved little, if any, for Africa since the end of the cold war. On a more positive note, Washington played key diplomatic roles in long-festering civil wars in Angola, Ethiopia, Liberia, and ultimately, perhaps, in the Darfur region of Sudan.

While the Clinton administration paid considerable attention to Africa, arguably with mixed results, many African advocates feared that a Bush administration would neglect the continent. The former Texas governor's remarks during the 2000 presidential campaign were not encouraging; he seemed much more interested in relations with Mexico and the rest of Latin America than with

Africa and argued against U.S. intervention and involvement in Africa. However, the Bush administration, with the leadership of Secretaries of State Colin Powell and Condoleezza Rice, perhaps the two most influential African Americans in any U.S. administration to that point, did not ignore Africa. Emphasis was placed on coping with the AIDS crisis, the threats of international terrorism, development of free markets, and democratization, all likely to remain key components of U.S. policy for Africa during the Obama administration. Secretary Powell visited Africa in the spring of 2001 and later that year made these remarks at the annual dinner of Africare, a prominent U.S. nongovernmental organization (NGO) that raises funds and promotes humanitarian causes in Africa: "AIDS could kill a continent. It is a catastrophe. It is a disaster. It is a pandemic of the worst kind."[14] (The Bush administration's $15 billion package to combat AIDS is discussed in a "Flashpoint" section.) Powell also gave assurance that U.S. focus on international terrorism, the subject of another "Flashpoint," would not distract it from paying attention to Africa's other problems.

During his July 2003 whirlwind trip to Africa, when he visited five nations in as many days, President Bush repeatedly emphasized that Africans "are not alone" in facing their problems. Despite the words, Africa still ranks low in America's priorities, with U.S. exports to and imports from the region constituting 1 percent of total U.S. foreign commerce. With the global economic downturn, U.S. trade with Africa declined 15 percent from 2001 to 2002, and 90 percent of that trade rested with only four nations: mineral-rich and industrial South Africa and oil-producing Nigeria, Angola, and Gabon. New initiatives are being shaped, however, including the New Partnership for Africa's Development (NEPAD), that involve a commitment from AU nations' leaders to promote good governance, peace, and economic reform with assistance from G-8 nations. These conditions are similar to those contained in President Bush's Millennium Challenge Account, which would provide additional development aid only to those needy Other World nations that practice good governance and embrace free enterprise. Perhaps nothing dominated President Clinton's Africa policy as much as working "to accelerate Africa's full integration into the global economy."[15] The Bush administration pursued similar goals. For countries embracing Washington's prescription for development, special trade preferences in modest amounts of public funds have been available through the much-vaunted African Growth and Opportunity Act, passed in 2000 (its provisions and developments can be monitored at www.AGOA.gov). Funds to strengthen democratic institutions also are being made available. Since 1996, the United States also has sponsored the Africa Crisis Response Initiative, which trains and advises indigenous troops in peacekeeping activities.[16] In a related program, Operation Focus Relief provided training and equipment for Nigerian and other forces assigned to peacekeeping duties in Sierra Leone (see also the "Flashpoint" on international terrorism). The Bush administration's 2007 decision to centralize U.S. Security policies toward Africa in one command, AFRICOM, met with some controversy in Africa, especially over the initial desire to find an African-based headquarters for U.S. military operations there. Washington also focuses on the African dimension of such global issues as weapons proliferation, drugs, infectious diseases, terrorism, air navigation, education, and the environment. In the early days of the Obama administration, there has been little to suggest any major shifts away from these priorities and basic policy directions, although there are likely to be differences in specific policy implementations and tone.[17]

The United States, after encountering serious problems while intervening in Somalia in 1993, curbed its interest in Africa. Getting bogged down in quagmires that involve revamping police and security forces, reestablishing basic services, rebuilding infrastructure, and creating jobs did not have support in Washington. The Republican Congress was intent on slashing foreign aid, especially to most African states, where no vital American interests were seen to be at stake.

The presidential trips, such as President Clinton's lengthy 12-day tour in 1998 and President Bush's shorter 5-day 2003 sojourn (and those of the First Ladies, including several by Laura Bush) to Africa, carry major symbolic importance, a statement that Africa matters to the United States today and would matter more tomorrow. Although President Obama's first brief visit to Africa while in office included only one model nation, Ghana, and came at the end of a longer journey to Russia and Italy, it significantly took place early in his administration and included a major policy speech that centered on self-reliance for Africans in solving their own problems. As with his immediate predecessors, President Obama's visit included a pilgrimage to a somber debarkation point for the West African slave trade, and he acknowledged the historic burdens, including colonialism and exploitation, that have contributed to Africa's relative lack of progress. He praised Ghana's notable achievements in democratization, holding up its efforts as a model for other nations. Secretary of State Hillary Clinton followed up President Obama's brief visit with a substantial seven-nation tour several weeks later. Still, Africans seek concrete results beyond the rhetorical goodwill.

ECONOMICS AND NATURAL RESOURCES

Despite the euphoria and optimism generated by the election of Barack Obama, Africans soon had to face the somber realities of the global economic crisis. In some respects, sub-Saharan African economies have not suffered all the ill effects visited on Western and Asian nations by the global financial crisis of 2008–2009. African banks and financial markets had not been a part of the risky loans and exotic investment instruments that caused the severe recession in much of the developed world. Still, African economies, heavily dependent on healthy and prosperous markets elsewhere for their exports, are hardly immune to the fallout of the global financial crisis and face the loss of much of their hard-earned progress and growth of recent years. In a pattern familiar from the bitter experiences of colonial and post-independence years, Africans are again threatened with hardships and setbacks in the wake of a crisis not of their making that originated thousands of miles from their homes for reasons far removed from their own struggles for a decent standard of living. Further, the massive foreign aid from the international financial institutions, donor nations, and NGOs on which so many African nations depend is at risk from the global financial crisis even as harsh critics of foreign aid point to the harmful impacts of aid dependency on African economic development. How has sub-Saharan Africa, so rich in natural and human resources, found itself in such a vulnerable economic position? This chapter has already suggested that African physical geography, including temperature, rainfall, coastlines, rivers, soils, and the like, created difficult conditions for its peoples. Moreover, foreigners exploited the natural habitat in many parts of the region. For instance, the colonial powers instituted cash crops and the export of livestock, which in turn meant widespread clearing of the land and, sometimes, depletion of the soil. Similarly, Europeans carving up the continent created or heightened local rivalries, which resulted in conflicts that also affected the landscape. The decline of large areas of present-day Africa has been caused more by human than natural factors. Exploding populations, the movement from countrysides to cities, the devastating civil wars, and the shift from a nomadic to a sedentary way of life have major ramifications.

Economic patterns established in Africa a century ago continue to have great relevance today. The search for legitimate trade in the decades after the abolition of slavery resulted in the introduction of cash crops such as cocoa, coffee, tea, cotton, ground nuts, and palm oil, and in renewed exploration for minerals. Gradually, a shift from subsistence farming to exports took place. In almost all cases, the colonies depended on no more than three crops or minerals for almost all their earnings. Thus was Africa gradually drawn into the global capitalist system, albeit as a minor player. This pattern remains true today.

After independence, the future at first looked promising. Some countries followed the Western model of letting free enterprise dominate the economy; others chose to have the state play the major role. In either case, the 1960s and early 1970s was a period of growth throughout the continent. Unlike Asia, most of the countries were feeding themselves, and unlike Latin America, most of the land was either communally owned or run by small farmers. Foreign investment was forthcoming and commodity prices were high.[18]

With the first oil price shock in 1973, this rosy picture began to change. Only a few African states had appreciable amounts of oil; others were forced to spend more of their precious capital and then to borrow money at high rates of interest to secure oil for industry. By the late 1970s, prices had peaked and were beginning to fall for both agricultural products and minerals. Deindustrialization resulted from declining domestic demand brought on by reduced income and shortages of foreign exchange. Poor maintenance and lack of spare parts, the protection of inefficient basic industries, and political considerations accelerated the economic decline. Drought became more pronounced in the Sahel region south of the Sahara. Sub-Saharan Africa's total debt, which had been $6 billion in 1970, rose to $125 billion by 1987.

By the early or mid-1980s, stagnation had been replaced by economic decline. Governments were living way beyond their means. African per capita income began to decline. Millions who had only barely been eking out a living now fell deeply into poverty and, in some cases, faced starvation.

A

B

Night and Day: (A) This little girl in the Democratic Republic of the Congo is afraid of the camera. (B) Elites in the Democratic Republic of the Congo enjoy the evening at their club.

These problems give a sense of the enormity of the economic disaster Africa is weathering. By 1990, 325 million people, or 62 percent of the region's population at the time, minus South Africa, were living in absolute poverty.[19]

Per capita income hovered in the $300-a-year range (U.S. dollars). Seventeen years later, only the population figure had substantially changed for this large cohort.

How can this situation be altered? For more than a decade, the answer most often given by foreign governments and international lending agencies is privatization bolstered by foreign aid and debt forgiveness. That is, outside help, including additional loans and the restructuring or even writing off of outstanding loans, will be made available to African countries only if they agree to major policy reforms that substitute market forces for state-directed economies with additional calls for good, transparent governance that curbs corruption.

Reforms focusing on currency devaluations, reductions in government expenditures, and limits in domestic credit were begun by the International Monetary Fund (IMF) in the early 1980s. The World Bank, noting that little had been accomplished, added other "structural adjustments." It sought to increase producer prices, reduce or eliminate subsidies and trade restrictions, improve education and health systems, pay far more attention to the environment, encourage foreign investment, and champion small producers. A domestic bicycle industry or low-cost local roads for nonmotorized vehicles were looked on favorably. Above all, it emphasized private enterprise.

By the mid-1990s, more than two dozen countries in Africa adopted major economic policy reforms. These states embraced the reforms or capitulated to Western prescriptions. Outside criticisms of these programs included the reduction in the quality and quantity of government services; the introduction of user fees, which disproportionately hurt the poor; and the increased cost of basic foodstuffs and transportation.

Structural adjustment at the national level may be inadequate unless the Western countries open their markets by ending their own subsidies and protectionist policies, pay decent prices for African goods, and curtail or suspend debt repayments. Any benefits for African states are likely to take years, if not decades, whereas adverse effects of reform are instantaneous. If discontent rises, government instability and repression will be the likely results. The IMF and World Bank argue that states taking the plunge have done better than those that have not. That is small consolation to millions of individuals who have experienced worsened conditions.

On balance, sub-Saharan African economies early in the new century improved over the beginning of the 1990s, if not over 10 or 20 years earlier than that, and some growth rates and poverty-reduction figures showed promise. "Better fiscal policies, greater trade liberalization, and more-realistic foreign exchange rates in sub-Saharan Africa have helped lead to the rising per capita income—an average of 1 to 1.5 percent a year the past two years."[20] The World Bank estimates that a 6 percent economic growth rate is necessary for real improvement. Although Botswana was the only African nation in some recent years to attain that figure, 2005 to 2006 saw growth rates for the whole region in the 5.6 percent to 5.7 percent range, according to World Bank statistics.[21] However, with the global economic crisis adversely affecting demand and prices for Africa's exports, estimates for economic growth in 2009–2010 are much lower.[22] For example, the demand and prices for the critical Zambian copper industry have fallen sharply.

There are major problems, specific and general, and the economic turnaround is sputtering. Foreign aid, long a controversial if major source of finance for some African nations, has come under more fervent attack of late. Such divergent voices as the noted American travel writer and novelist Paul Theroux, Nobel Peace Prize winner and environmentalist Wangari Maathai (see Box 6.1 earlier in the chapter), Ghanaian economist George Ayittey, and Zambian economist and former World Bank official Dambisa Moyo have mounted strong criticisms on the various shortcomings of aid. Theroux, who had served as a Peace Corps volunteer in Malawi and college teacher in Uganda, undertook an arduous journey through Africa in the earlier part of this decade and found the aid community particularly aloof and unhelpful.[23] Maathai bemoans the "syndrome of dependency" and dispiriting images of stark need which she contends that foreign aid has engendered, and Ayittey argues, "That foreign aid has failed to accelerate economic development . . . is no longer in dispute."[24] The strongest indictment of foreign aid comes from Moyo, who believes that the impact of aid from the major international lenders and wealthy nations has been so negative for Africa that it should be phased out completely over a 10-year period, an unlikely prospect given how entrenched aid programs have become.[25] While her major criticisms center on institutional aid from large multinational organizations and governments rather than short-term emergency and charitable relief, she also takes on celebrity donors such as Irish rock star Bono because she believes they inadvertently promote African helplessness and hurt indigenous entrepreneurs. All feel that aid policies have undermined African initiative and contributed to rampant corruption. In light of the global financial crisis, when some strapped donors are looking for excuses to reduce or even eliminate aid while some recipients are urging increases or at least a steady flow, the debate over foreign aid for Africa is likely to continue. Proponents of aid, while admitting many missteps in earlier years, argue that aid is simply morally necessary and right. They further contend that, with hard lessons learned from experience, aid has been reformed to avoid corrupt officials and instead reach the people who need it while also becoming increasingly environmentally friendly and sustainable. For example, Ellen Johnson Sirleaf, the president of Liberia, counters, "Critics say that African economies are shrinking, that poverty is rising and that failing aid is the culprit. But this argument is at least a decade out of date. Africa's turnaround is real, the evidence indisputable. Africans themselves have been the key to this reversal, but more effective aid has played an important role."[26] Aid is likely to remain a part of the development picture in Africa despite the critics and the current crisis, but it must be used with better purpose and results than has been the case in the past if it is to contribute to the lasting, positive economic development in Africa that people so desperately need.

Government debt has hindered many states in the region. There is a concerted movement, particularly on the part of the creditor G-8 nations, to provide debt relief without stringent conditions, such as the preparation of detailed Poverty Reduction Strategy Papers, to the Heavily Indebted Poor Countries

(HIPC) and, thus, better tend to their social needs. Critics contend that debt relief and aid alone are not panaceas for the economic ills of those countries because they do not alleviate the plight of all the poor and must be accompanied by sound sustainable development programs, fairer trade terms, and direct investment in African businesses.

There is good news: Although public monies are declining, they are more than offset by private funds. There is also bad news: The flows go to only a few countries, including South Africa. Furthermore, global economic instabilities, insufficient market shares by small countries to attract major investors, skill deficiencies, inadequate infrastructure, downbeat coverage of Africa by the media, and chance events such as natural or manmade disasters, are detrimental. Arms purchases, often with kickbacks, "crony companies" that lack competence, payments to security forces or the military, "white elephant" projects, and ruling elites engaging in capital flight continue to exacerbate the financial drain.

Much of the modern global economy is driven by high technology, but Africa is the least-wired continent with the fewest Internet subscribers. In the UN Human Development Report of 2001, which focused on high technology and telecommunications, Africa ranked last on virtually every indicator of all the regions of the Other World, and despite much progress, these rankings have not changed. Africa's Internet users are made up of the region's elite and foreigners. Africa has by far the lowest number of phone lines per capita in the world, computer usage is minimal, and online users number in the low millions, a majority of whom live in South Africa.

World Wide Web access, however, is growing, cell phones, now estimated to be used by 1 in 12 Africans, are commonplace except in remote areas. Numerous Western government agencies, foundations, universities, and corporations are supplying financial, material, and training aid to speed Africa's entry into the high-technology information age. There is growing optimism that "Africa in cyberspace" will dramatically increase as technology costs become cheaper and more congruent with the continent's needs, making the region far more competitive in the tough global market and facilitating exciting new connections within and outside Africa. Mike Jensen, a South African widely acknowledged as a leading authority on Africa's entry into the "wired" world, noted in 2000,

> The development of the Internet is at a critical point in Africa. Web-based services could help accelerate the continent's economic growth and poverty alleviation, but these tools place large demands on an underlying infrastructure that is currently incapable of servicing them. . . . It will require greater commitment by African leadership to open up the telecommunication sector to ensure that the potential of the Internet is fully exploited.[27]

Progress in Africa's online activities is evident, but much work remains to be done in closing the "digital divide."

Globalization Comes to Africa? This busy port scene in Luanda, Angola, a nation until recently ravaged by a long civil war, belies the fact that sub-Saharan Africa ranks last of all the major regions of the world in international trade, despite its vast resources. *Source: Olga Carter*

Sub-Saharan Africa has great natural resources, much of them untapped. The United States gets almost as much of its foreign oil from the region as it does from the Middle East. In addition to the major petroleum sources along the coast of West Africa, there are also promising prospects in Chad and Sudan. Similarly, natural gas in commercial amounts appears to exist in Angola, Congo, Equatorial Guinea, Gabon, Ghana, and Cameroon. New resources used in the Western high-technology industry are being exploited in Africa but not always for the benefit of the people as a whole. The risks of investing in natural resource extraction are great, but so are the potential profits. Corruption, weak environmental protection (which permits groundwater contamination and unknowing populations coming into contact with uranium waste), and lax miner safety are some of the hazards to be overcome. Overfishing by European and Asian fleets is another reality. Although foreign access fishing agreements bring in hundreds of millions of dollars, which help service the debt, the payments come at the price of depriving millions of local inhabitants of a vital food source. On balance, one may fairly say that globalization, with the accompanying influence of multinational corporations based far from the continent, has not been kind to sub-Saharan African resources and economies. Sub-Saharan Africa has simply not been positioned to reap all the rewards of globalization while suffering many of its downsides; in some respects, the region still plays the traditional colonial role of a supplier of nonrenewable resources to richer nations.

CASE STUDIES

1. South Africa

South Africa, the dominant economic powerhouse of sub-Saharan Africa, has made relatively little progress in recent years toward its promise of lifting the vast majority of its population out of their substandard living conditions. With the largest involvement in the global economy of any state in the region, South Africa has the most to lose in the current economic crisis. Further, the nation has experienced two presidential turnovers in recent years, one through a loss in confidence in the sitting president by his dominant African National Congress (ANC) party and the other through the election of a popular party leader who had labored under the cloud of alleged corruption and abuse charges. On the other hand, South Africa has taken much pride in hosting the prestigious Soccer World Cup in 2010, a sporting event rivaling the Olympics in the eyes of much of the world. Still, even this source of justifiable national pride is tinged with racial overtones, since soccer is seen as the "black" sport, while the white minority tends to favor rugby.

The key point about South Africa's political history is that although blacks outnumbered whites by five to one, political power remained with the minority until 1994. Over the generations, white domination wore many faces. At the turn of the twentieth century, the British defeated the Afrikaners in a bloody civil war. The Afrikaners were a people whose ancestors came mainly from the Netherlands beginning in the seventeenth century. After the Boer War there were four separate states, with Great Britain in charge of them all; then in 1910, the four fused into one Union of South Africa, and London became all but invisible. Fearing for the future of blacks in the country, a forerunner to the ANC arose two years later. However, it could do nothing to prevent the Land Act of 1913, which prohibited blacks from owning land in most areas and from owning quality land in all parts of the country. Another important date is 1948, the year that the Afrikaner-backed National party won the whites-only national elections. The newly elected party formally instituted a policy of apartheid, or separate racial development. From then on, blacks (and to a lesser extent, Indians) and those of mixed race, called coloreds, were treated as inferior beings. Brute force, including the arrest of the leaders, legislation, and custom enshrined the new order. For the next 36 years, despite nonviolent protests and occasional acts of sabotage, the status quo of white domination and black subordination prevailed.

Significant resistance to apartheid increased through the 1960s and 1970s. Beginning in late 1984, disturbances became more widespread, and violence by both the state and opponents of apartheid intensified. Arrests numbered in the thousands. A year later, the government declared a state of emergency in much of the country. Authorities tried to keep order by imposing controls on dissidents, including the media. The economy began a downward spiral, helped along by damaging strikes. Limited sanctions imposed by several governments, including the United States, and the loss of many foreign companies were also detrimental. Nevertheless, the white ruling class held firm.

In the late 1980s, the South African government tried both the carrot and the stick to impose its will. The authorities offered minor reforms, and relations improved with some surrounding black-run states; however, several thousand people died because of political unrest, and a second emergency decree resulted in tens of thousands of additional arrests. A change of direction seemed impossible.

Change did come, however, and it came rapidly. There are several explanations for the shift. First, Frederik W. de Klerk, succeeding P. W. Botha as president and head of the National party in 1989, gradually moved his forces in a different direction, including calls to prepare a new constitution and share power.

At the same time, the situation fundamentally improved in neighboring Namibia and Angola. South African leaders perceived that the abating U.S.-Soviet confrontation would lessen the threat of Communism within their own borders. Many in the country also noticed democratization in other parts of the world. Both the South African government and the ANC saw a military solution to the internal unrest as unlikely. In addition, the economy continued to sag, and Western powers warned that tougher sanctions were a possibility. Demands for change came from all directions.

The winds struck with gale force. Nelson Mandela, jailed in the early 1960s for promoting the violent overthrow of the government, was dramatically released by Prime Minister de Klerk in 1990, along with other dissidents. The government also lifted the 30-year ban against the ANC, the Pan-African Congress, the South African Communist party, and many other organizations. Over the next few months the government rescinded the state of emergency throughout the country, curbed the secretive state security system, reduced the military budget, and ended political censorship. It also repealed the Separate Amenities Act, thus opening public hospitals, restaurants, libraries, buses, and parks to all.

The first half of 1991 shook apartheid to its roots. Its pillars—the Lands Acts, Group Areas Act, and Population Registration Act—were repealed, and the Internal Security Act was severely amended. It took three more years of maneuvering, however, before the ultimate goal of one person, one vote was achieved. The ANC and the rival Zulu-based Inkatha movement, led by Chief Gatsha Buthelezi, clashed, resulting in thousands of deaths. There were divisions among the whites as well, with a small minority refusing to consider any changes. But in late April 1994, the people of South Africa, including millions of black citizens, went to the polls for the first time in the country's history.

As expected, the ANC was the big winner, receiving 63 percent of the vote as Nelson Mandela became president. Because they did not receive two-thirds of the vote, the victorious party had to work with non-ANC members in Parliament in the writing of a new constitution. The National party finished second and became the official opposition. In addition, de Klerk became one of two vice presidents. The Inkatha Freedom party finished third. In a bid to form a government of unity and reconciliation, Mandela offered a number of cabinet positions to members of the other two parties. Buthelezi became the Home Affairs minister.

Many people predicted that given the struggle that preceded the election, the following months would be ones of upheaval. It did not work out that way. There were growing pains, yes, but both in political circles and throughout the country there was relative tranquility based on a foundation of gradual change. The move from international outcast to liberal democracy in one year was phenomenal. Although some complained that Mandela was moving too slowly to institute reforms, most were supportive of the pace and direction of change. Racial strife gradually eased. Economic growth caught up with population growth for the first time in a decade. Of course, South Africa still faces very serious problems. Gaining political power is a lot different than gaining economic power. Major economic disparities along racial lines continued as poverty cuts deeply across the black majority while a majority of the wealth remains in white hands.

> For many the situation has not yet changed much—the landless; the homeless; the black African majority, more than 40 percent of whom live in absolute poverty; women and children, who are the majority of those living in deprivation, especially in rural areas; and the growing numbers of those who are unemployed, underemployed or living on less than $1 a day.[28]

Land reform or redistribution is a deeply felt issue by many landless farmers. The government promulgated its land restitution program in 1995, but was hesitant to promote widespread change for fears of alienating white farmers and undermining the agricultural sector. The 1 million homes that the government, with private-sector backing, committed itself to building by 1999 were not completed. There are also disagreements with traditional authorities over what to do with tribal lands.

Economic growth is not keeping up with population growth, and formal unemployment is running close to 25 percent. The national currency has been in rapid decline, while foreign investments have been only a fraction of the amounts expected, lowered more by the current recession. University tuition has climbed, and many who looked to the new government to set things right have been acutely disappointed. Credit, especially for the poor, has been hard to come by, and global competition for foreign assistance is intense.

Another major problem is dealing with South Africa's past. The Truth and Reconciliation Commission, headed by Archbishop Desmond Tutu, was created by a parliamentary act in 1995. It delved into the dark corners of the apartheid years. The Commission's goal was to bring the past to closure by inviting those who had transgressed to testify in public. Toward that end, the Commission had the power to grant amnesty to those who gave an account of their crimes and who could show that the struggle over apartheid was behind their acts. It was not necessary for the perpetrator to show remorse. There were confessions of terrible acts on both sides. Although some refused to testify and many South Africans were not reconciled, the attempt to put the past in the past was remarkable.

Since the end of apartheid, political violence has abated, but criminal violence has increased. The crime wave transcends race, ethnicity, and class. The murder rate is several times that of the United States, and rape has been an especially severe problem. Lawlessness, though, is nothing new in South Africa. How can the country "restore an ethic of lawfulness" after the ANC encouraged people to long defy the white authorities? (There are also disgruntled white farmers and white police officers, disaffected ANC members, and long-standing ethnic conflicts.) Police corruption and low rates of arrests and convictions have caused many to lose faith in their criminal justice system. A statistic indicates that "two-thirds of Johannesburg's citizens and half of Cape Town's were victims of crime between 1993 and 1997 alone."[29] In 2008, rampant violence aimed at resented foreign guest workers left scores dead.

After six years of work, a new constitution was inaugurated in 1997. A balance was struck between a strong central government and devolving considerable powers to the states. There are strong statements protecting individual rights. Private property rights are balanced by the need to redress past discrimination. The 1999 election results showed that the ANC had lost none of its popularity, receiving over 66 percent of the vote, just a sliver away from the two-thirds mark that would have allowed it to make certain changes in the constitution if it so wished. Thabo Mbeki succeeded Mandela as president. President Mbeki was widely regarded as a very able, experienced administrator, even though he obviously lacked Mandela's international stature and charisma. Mbeki was unable, however, to control South Africa's mounting economic, social, and health problems, and many were disturbed with his idiosyncratic views on human immunodeficiency syndrome (HIV) and AIDS, which have hit his nation especially hard. Mbeki's August 2007 firing of a deputy health minister popular with South African AIDS activists and respected in the international AIDS community refueled the controversy. (See "Africa and AIDS" in the "Flashpoints.") Concerns were also raised over Mbeki's adherence to external and historical reasons to explain his administration's lack of economic progress for his nation. The corruption that has long plagued the politics of much of the continent has now also reached South Africa. Still, the ANC won an overwhelming majority of 70 percent of the votes in the nation's 2004 parliamentary elections, returning Mbeki for his second five-year presidential term. Then-Deputy President Jacob Zuma was fired in June of 2004 under suspicion of corruption and accepting bribes from a French arms supplier, a scandal that rocked the ANC political establishment at the very top. Zuma was acquitted of that charge in a lengthy trial that remains under dispute, and he subsequently survived a serious rape charge and heated trial that split the nation and revealed disturbing attitudes toward sexual inequality. Zuma emerged from these trials as a serious contender for president in the elections of 2009, enjoying wide support in his Zulu base and endorsed in September 2007 by the nation's leading trade union organization. He was selected to lead the ANC in late 2007, but the clouds of renewed corruption investigations hung over him and over top officials. Mbeki's divisive and sometimes abrasive leadership style led to his dismissal as president by the ruling ANC in 2008; Kgalema Motlanthe was chosen by the ANC as interim president. In the 2009 election, widely watched in part because of splintering within the ANC, the ANC and its presidential candidate, Jacob Zuma, nonetheless won a decisive victory, although they fell barely short of the "magical" two-thirds majority in the parliament.

What of South Africa's image beyond its borders? Mandela himself remains a much revered senior statesman, though he had clashed with the United States over his kind words for Cuba, Iran, Libya, and Syria—countries that gave support to the antiapartheid struggle at a time when the cold war made the United States timid. Mbeki was a more controversial president, and the populist and somewhat flamboyant Zuma's accomplishments remain to be seen. In southern Africa, there is disquiet over one country so obviously more powerful than the others. The South African military's intervention in neighboring Lesotho in 1998 to deal with unrest there underscored this concern. Although South Africa has been a champion of a regional common market, some of the other countries are concerned about being in that country's orbit.

2. Nigeria

Next to South Africa, Nigeria is viewed as the country in sub-Saharan Africa with the greatest potential. Recurring political instability, corruption, ethnic and religious strife, and economic mismanagement for the past 50 years, however, have taken their toll. For example, a deadly army assault against troublesome Islamic militants in summer 2009 increased already-strained tensions between the largely Christian and Islamic segments of the country.

Nigeria's population of 146 million people is the largest on the African continent. Thirty years ago, the country was an economic powerhouse as well. In 1977, per capita gross domestic product (GDP) was $1,000. Ten years later, the figure had dropped to $370; in 1992 it was $320. For the period 1980 to 1992, Nigeria's economic growth rate was negative 20.4 percent. In that period, the country slipped from the Other World's middle-income to low-income group. By 2005, per capita GDP had climbed to $14,800, finally above the figures of a quarter century before.

A major factor in the decline was the precipitous drop in oil prices. The government and many upwardly mobile people lived way beyond their means during the oil boom. Yet the masses saw little of the new wealth; current higher oil prices are not expected to improve the situation. As the last decade drew to a close, the international debt soared to $35 billion, and the government agreed to begin a very stiff structural adjustment program (see Economics and Natural Resources above). In this environment, ongoing social unrest further undermined foreign investment.

The military government that came to power in a 1985 coup (there have been seven coups since independence in 1960, and many more attempted coups) promised elections and the return to civil rule at the beginning of 1993. Indeed, elections were held, but when the military rulers, who had run the country for all but 12 years since independence, did not like the results, they simply annulled them. After that, strikes, riots, additional instability in the military, rule by decree, summary executions of the regime's opponents, and a seemingly never-ending economic downdraft occurred. The election victor, billionaire Moshood Abiola, went to jail, was placed in solitary confinement, sentenced to death, and finally had that sentence commuted. The military, then under the control of General Sani Abacha, ushered in five years of brutal rule while defying global condemnations. General Abacha, who rapidly became a billionaire, also attempted to head off further criticism by belatedly promising a return to civilian rule by late 1998.

Before 1995 ended, nine dissidents, including Ken Saro-Wiwa, a prominent author and playwright, were executed. The government charged that they had fomented strife that led to the murder of several rivals in a major oil-producing area. Saro-Wiwa had protested that the production had resulted in serious pollution in the area. He also railed against the refusal of the corrupt government to give even a fraction of the riches to his poor Ogoni people living in the oil-rich coastal sector. Worldwide condemnation followed the hangings, with none other than South African President Nelson Mandela calling for an embargo on Nigerian oil. Under the best circumstances, however, getting approval for such a global action is difficult and even more difficult enforcing it. Nigeria, for instance, is the fifth-largest foreign supplier of oil to the United States and owed over $30 billion to Europe and Japan. Serious insurgency over oil resource distribution inequities and environmental neglect in the Niger Delta region continues to plague the nation. In a 2009 attempt at reconciliation, the government has offered amnesty to militants there in exchange for disarmament, but the principal guerilla group is leery of government promises, and the violence could escalate if the plan fails.[30]

In June 1998, Abacha died of a heart attack. A month later, Abiola, still in prison, also died. With the despised head-of-state and his main nemesis gone, the question simply was "What now for Nigeria?" Abacha's replacement, General Abdulsalami Abubakar, gradually moved in a new direction. Many political prisoners were released from jail, and the officers' sentences were commuted. A start was made to face up to the omnipresent corruption, with several leading figures, including Abacha's security advisor, arrested. Most important, national assembly and then presidential elections were held in February 1999. Olusegun Obasanjo was chosen to lead the new civilian government that formally took power three months later. Obasanjo had headed a military regime in the late 1970s before voluntarily yielding power to an elected civilian government. More recently, he had been jailed from 1995 to 1998 on a dubious claim that he was plotting to overthrow Abacha. Although some felt that the newly elected Obasanjo was too close to the military leaders he was replacing, others thought he was the right man for the challenges facing the troubled country.

Sweeping poverty and ethnic and regional tensions are deeply rooted. British colonial rulers favored Muslim northerners because they were seen as more obedient and conservative than southerners. After independence, northerners continued to rule at the national level, whether the country was under civilian or military rule. Yet the oil and the major financial, commercial, and industrial centers are in the south. The hope was that President Obasanjo would be able to quell the country's long-time divisions. Despite good intentions and promising pronouncements, this goal proved elusive. Deadly ethnic clashes continued, some involving government troops and most pitting northern Muslims against southern Christians. For example, more than 200 died in rioting resulting from a controversy over the staging of the Miss World pageant in Lagos in November 2002 when a newspaper reporter suggested that Mohammed himself would have wanted to marry a contestant. Frightened pageant officials hurriedly moved the contest to London. Sparked in part because of the adoption of Islamic Sharia law in many of Nigeria's northern states, more than 10,000 people have died in ethnic/religious violence since the return of democracy in 1999.

Nigeria has vast oil reserves; it is the world's sixth largest producer of oil, with revenues of $30 billion a year. The country also has many minerals, fertile land, and more than 30 universities. Nigeria, however, also has a run-down infrastructure (the nickname for the National Electric Power Authority, or NEPA, is Never Expect Power Again). Chronic unemployment plagues the nation's young people. The nation has not come to terms with the abuses committed by some members of the military during its troubled past. In December 2001, Nigeria's Minister of Justice was assassinated by gunmen invading his home, another indication of Nigeria's ongoing instability.[31] International observers cited widespread irregularities in the nation's April 2003 state, national assembly, and presidential elections, but these questionable electoral practices might not have changed the ultimate outcome of the vote that returned Obasanjo and his ruling People's Democratic Party to power. His party prevailed again in disputed April 2007 elections that brought the relatively unknown Umaru Musa Yar'Adua, a governor of a state in the largely Muslim north, to the presidency with an overwhelming majority of votes. With Yar'Adua's questionable health and lack of concrete progress in office, leading political families and business interests in Nigeria are already jockeying for a possible succession in the 2011 elections. Nigeria, which survived the deadly Biafra secession war in the late 1960s and has seen a succession of corrupt military and civilian governments, is trying to get back on track and approach its vast potential. It will not be an easy task.

3. Zimbabwe

Zimbabwe became independent in 1980 after a lengthy struggle to end white-minority rule. In the 1997 edition of *The Other World*, the country was considered a relative success story because economic growth had more than kept pace with population growth, family planning programs had made great strides, and ethnic disputes between the majority Shona and minority Ndebele had faded. Literacy rates were among the highest on the continent; racism had been contained; there was a good health care system, a thriving tourism industry, a police force that no longer generated fear, a functioning infrastructure; and environmental issues were being successfully met. Finally, there was a reasonable level of political stability.

The downside, always present, has worsened over the past decade. The economy has continued to slump, with inflation and interest rates rising. Many foreign investors left because of what they believed were ruinous government policies; unstable or even collapsed banks; a declining stock market; falling prices for such domestic commodities as gold, other minerals, and tobacco; a high debt load; and tax increases that many claim lined the pockets of President Robert Mugabe's supporters or favorites. Unions have risen up in opposition, as have students who claim government corruption. The press, one of the few institutions willing to speak out against the ruling elite, has suffered threats, arrests, and torture, and the president threatened journalists who criticized the violent, lawless actions of his supporters. Minorities, especially gays, are chastised by the president himself. In 2005, the International Monetary Fund threatened to suspend Zimbabwe's membership because of its irresponsible economic and fiscal policies, a move unprecedented since Communist Czechoslovakia suffered that fate in 1954, but the IMF gave the Mugabe government a six-month reprieve to initiate reforms. The country's membership in the British Commonwealth of Nations was suspended indefinitely in 2003. Mugabe remains defiant in the face of widespread condemnation of his policies, which have resulted in enormous unemployment, chronic shortages, and hyperinflation as high as 9,000 percent in 2007, from the United States and other Western powers, claiming neocolonialism and racism on their parts.

Charges of favoritism, luxurious living for the few, and crony capitalism are widespread. *The London Times* reported that "after a relatively slow start from independence in 1980, the Nigerian model has been adopted with alacrity; senior politicians take control of state contracts and licensing, violate all procedures, and pass on the right to politically well-connected businessmen."[32] There are bitter feuds between Mugabe's dominant Zimbabwe African National Union and the opposition party, the Movement for Democratic Change. Public and international support has plummeted. The country continues to have one of the highest HIV-positive rates in Africa.

As in South Africa, probably the most volatile issue is land ownership. Until recently, 4,500 white farmers owned more than 70 percent of the country's most fertile land, leaving the 7 million black farmers to engage in mainly subsistence farming. In the midst of rising discontent, President Mugabe announced that he intended to seize millions of acres of white-owned land and undertake a radical land reform program; he further stated the government would not compensate those who stood to lose their property and livelihood. The land grab, begun in 1997, ended in 2002 with over 35 million acres of white-owned farms seized. Damage to the economy from this policy has been catastrophic; the main beneficiaries are Mugabe supporters. In 2005, the Mugabe government undertook a disastrous policy of "urban renewal," termed "Operation Drive Out the Rubbish," which bulldozed poor neighborhoods of mostly anti-Mugabe residents and resulted in hundreds of thousands of displaced, jobless, and homeless city dwellers.

By mid-2009, the earlier promise of a stable, tolerant democratic regime in Zimbabwe seems again possible but yet unrealized; instead, political repression, famine, disease, and chaos have not disappeared. Mugabe's supporters continued intimidation and attacks against his political opponents, the press, white settlers, and blacks who worked on their farms. New measures designed to suppress opposition groups and the press were introduced before the 2002 presidential election. In March 2002, President Mugabe won reelection in a vote widely denounced by outside observers as unfair; he promptly had his major opponent arrested on charges of treason. Such tactics, along with other human rights violations, continued unabated through the following years. Many analysts now agree that the aging Mugabe, eager to cling to power, had become one of the despotic "Big Men" who litter the history of Africa's post-independence leadership. Doubts persisted that the spring 2008 parliamentary and presidential elections would be free and fair, given the recent history of Zimbabwean elections to the contrary, and both Mugabe's ruling ZANU-PF party and the opposition under union leader Morgan Tsvangirai claimed victory in an election widely denounced by the international community. Ultimately, the political impasse was solved by negotiating a power-sharing agreement somewhat similar to that forged in Kenya before, which left the now 85-year-old Mugabe in the presidency with control over the nation's security apparatus but gave the office of prime minister to Tsvangirai with several key ministries, including Finance, for his opposition party. In this uneven arrangement, Tsvangirai has sought to assert some authority and convince the world that Zimbabwe is turning away from the failed policies that cost the nation so dearly in goodwill, aid, and investment. It has been an uphill struggle; and by late 2009, the fragile coalition seemed in danger of complete breakdown, a prospect Zimbabwe's regional neighbors attempted to avoid through mediation. In a meeting with President Obama in 2009, Tsvangirai was able to secure promises of direct aid to the Zimbabwean people, but none for the government, which is still viewed wearily while Mugabe is in office. Observers now await the inevitable transition from the Mugabe era for further chance of positive change in this beleaguered nation.

FLASHPOINTS

Africa and AIDS

Recent estimates indicate that approximately 66 percent of the world's total HIV/AIDS cases afflict sub-Saharan Africans who comprise only 10 percent of the world's population, according to 2008 UNAIDS data.[33] In other words, approximately 20 million of the people suffering from HIV/AIDS are African, with several million new cases reported in the region each year and an estimated 1.5 million deaths in 2007 alone. Because 9 of the 10 countries with the highest infection rates are in Africa, these grim statistics will not improve on a regional basis any time soon.[34] Besides the terrible toll in human life, the epidemic will inevitably have a drastic effect on economic productivity in heavily affected areas for many years to come, reducing the chances to achieve critical development goals.

Unlike in other parts of the world, over 50 percent of HIV-positive adults in sub-Saharan Africa are women, and the infection rates are especially high for women in the critical child-bearing years. UNAIDS officials, thus, reluctantly decided that women infected with HIV should consider feeding formula instead of breast milk to their babies, a measure that has resulted in high infant mortality in some areas because of unsanitary conditions for administering the formula. Throughout the region, more than 12 million children are orphans because of AIDS. In Swaziland, the most highly infected nation in the world, nearly a third of the population has HIV.

Although statistics from different sources are not always congruent, the numbers are overwhelming. Dealing effectively with the epidemic is also overwhelming. There is too little money for tests, drugs, or directed support networks. Even in South Africa, health services are totally inadequate to provide treatment for AIDS. The costly combinations of antiretroviral drugs that help keep the virus in check among infected people in the North had been, until recently, largely out of reach in the South, where other problems press the population every day. Former President Thabo Mbeki of South Africa, where one in four women in their twenties is infected with HIV, caused much controversy with his challenges of accepted scientific studies on the relationship of HIV and AIDS, claiming instead that poverty and imperialism were causes of the disease. His administration's policies hindered modern treatment of AIDS in his country.

Can anything be done to combat the disease? Many major international organizations, such as the UN and World Bank, have rallied to address just this issue through special programs, conferences, and the Global AIDS Fund. Despite a lack of financial resources, the African Union has been active on this front, as have many private-sector and nongovernmental organizations. On the positive side, access to the expensive drug treatments is improving, and a fall 2001 ruling from the World Trade Organization

(WTO) relieved desperate nations of patent infringements in making or acquiring generic substitute drugs. UNAIDS has emphasized two recent programs. The first, "The Three Ones," intends to coordinate and integrate three national anti-AIDS efforts: (1) actions and policies, (2) authority and responsibility, and (3) monitoring and evaluation to avoid wasteful overlap and fragmentation, goals reached by many more target nations by 2007. The second program, called "3 by 5," was a concerted effort to extend antiretroviral treatment to 3 million worldwide by the end of 2005. Unfortunately, the 2006 UNAIDS Report concluded that the ambitious 3-by-5 goal fell far short of expectations despite accelerated treatment programs in the first six months of 2005 that doubled (to 500,000) the number of sub-Saharan African AIDS victims with access to the drugs. By 2007, however, nearly a third of the people who needed the treatments had access to them, and Botswana, through a dedicated and united national effort, achieved the highest treatment access rate in the world, at over 90 percent. Still, the agency credited the effort with greatly expanding treatment access and quality in affected developing nations.

Education is the one word most often offered in proposed strategies, and in Uganda the education is broad and multisectoral. The nation has been widely acclaimed for the success of its ABC policy—emphasizing *abstinence, being* faithful to one's partner, and condom use whenever appropriate. Even with its success in curbing the spread of the virus, however, Uganda has insufficient funds to treat those already afflicted. President Bush lauded Uganda's strong public programs in his 2003 trip to Africa, where he also promoted his five-year, $15-billion assistance program to combat the disease, to be directed primarily at afflicted African nations. Funding for the fight against HIV/AIDS in the region has increased markedly through this decade despite the current global economic crisis. Many nations and NGOs, recognizing the need to communicate relevant information to vulnerable groups in the most effective manner, use street theater and contemporary music groups to entertain while informing on AIDS. The most encouraging recent news involves the beginnings of decreases in infection, death, and HIV/AIDS-related orphan rates. As the Executive Summary of the 2008 UNAIDS Report states, "In sub-Saharan Africa, most national epidemics have stabilized or begun to decline." There is no magic bullet, but a multifaceted approach can produce encouraging results. Finally, the global community has mobilized resources to cope with this urgent epidemic, but the many generous international commitments of support and money must be realized. Care must be taken also not to lose momentum in combating Africa's other major health scourges, such as malaria, tuberculosis, and polio ($2.3 billion of the original Bush five-year, $15-billion package targeted such diseases), in confronting the enormity of the AIDS crisis.

Slavery and Human Trafficking

Slavery, both historical and modern, remains one of the most controversial, sensitive, and compelling subjects in sub-Saharan Africa. Questions about the impact of the historical slave trade on present-day Africa continue under hot debate. Was the European and American slave trade, which robbed West and Central Africa of millions of its young, able inhabitants over the course of several centuries, so devastating economically and psychologically that it has contributed materially to Africa's current state of underdevelopment? Should those areas in Europe and the Americas that benefited from slave labor hundreds of years ago, now all relatively rich, pay reparations to the victimized nations today? Many argue that the former slave-holding nations should not only apologize for these abominations against humanity but also pay substantial sums to try to set things right. Others contend that the historical slave trade was a regrettable but distant chapter of the past, perpetrated by ancestors long since gone, which has little relevance to the pressing issues of a new millennium. Questions also arise around the Arab-based slave trade in East Africa.

These issues arose in proposals and debates at the UN conference on racism and xenophobia held at Durban, South Africa, in 2001. The United States boycotted the conference, not only because of the controversial slavery reparations proposal but also because of a proposal from the Arab delegation equating Zionism, the movement for the state of Israel as a Jewish homeland, with racism. Ultimately, the conference proceeded with much acrimony and little resolution of the slavery issue. Condemnations of slavery were adopted that fell far short of a call for direct reparations, a redistributive cause whose time is not likely to come.

Aside from the debate over historical slavery, a few regions of Africa suffer from various forms of *modern slavery* and human trafficking. In Sudan and Mauritania, the two nations most often cited, traditional forms of chattel, or ownership, slavery persist into the twenty-first century. Usually, this slavery takes the form of wealthier Arab owners holding poorer black Africans in bondage, sometimes through generations and sometimes as a result of capture in war. Both governments deny the existence of such slavery and deem it formally illegal, but human rights activists insist that tens of thousands of slaves are held in the two nations. Furthermore, testimonials of escaped and liberated slaves confirm the practice. International awareness and outrage against the practice, perhaps less brutal than historical slavery but nonetheless invidious, are on the rise. In a hopeful development related to this international advocacy, Mauritania passed much tougher antislavery legislation in August 2007, but rigorous enforcement must follow to make a real difference. Organizations such as the American Anti-Slavery Group in Boston are agitating and taking action against modern African slavery; other groups and concerned individuals, using a controversial approach, are raising funds to buy slaves' freedom directly from their masters.

Another form of modern African slavery exists in West Africa, in which youths, usually boys from the more deprived nations such as Benin or Togo, sign fraudulent work contracts and become indentured or bonded laborers, usually with no pay, in large agricultural enterprises in the better-off West African nations such as Ghana. The good news about modern slavery in Africa is the heightened publicity, exemplified in the extensive coverage of the decrepit slave ship turned away from several West African ports in the summer of 2001, and the resultant calls for action from many quarters across the globe to abolish these anachronistic, inhumane practices once and for all.

Civil Wars and Communal Violence

This "Flashpoint" section surveys the causes and circumstances of significant cases of war and violence in various African regions. These conflicts include not only some now apparently settled but also others, notably the wars in Sudan, Somalia, Uganda, and the Democratic Republic of Congo, ongoing into 2009 despite international efforts at pacification. Arguably, persistent violence has been one of the greatest manmade obstacles to Africa's growth and progress.

Pessimistic observers of Africa's conflicts might simply designate the whole region as a flashpoint candidate. For example, the cover of a May 2000 issue of the influential weekly newsmagazine *The Economist* portrayed a photo, filling an outline African map, of a man with a rocket launcher on his shoulder. The issue is titled "The Hopeless Continent." This represents a gross exaggeration of the real situation. Several African countries, such as Mauritius, have suffered relatively little if any recent violent conflict; others have seen long- or short-term violent conflicts resolved without new outbreaks, as in Mozambique and, more recently, Angola, Liberia, and Sierra Leone. Still, few sub-Saharan African nations have avoided some form of civil, ethnic, or religious violence, coups, riots, or wars at some point in their postcolonial histories.

Generalizing about the root causes of violent conflict in sub-Saharan Africa is notoriously difficult. In earlier days, cold war rivalries played a prominent role, and the apartheid regime in South Africa destabilized much of the region beyond its borders. Some analysts point to the colonial heritage of violent conquest and coercive power. Greed and personal ambition have often been evident. Many of the more recent civil wars seem to arise from disputes over a volatile mixture of control and exploitation of valuable resources combined with ethnic animosities rather than differing political ideologies or approaches to national development.

Child Soldiers

A disturbing development in African civil wars over the past decade has been the increasing use of very young combatants, usually boys (but sometimes girls as well) in their early teens or even younger, fighting for rebel forces and, in some nations, government militias. For example, recent civil wars in Liberia, Sierra Leone, the Democratic Republic of Congo, Burundi, Uganda, Sudan, and now Somalia have seen widespread use of child soldiers. This is a departure from the practices of earlier African civil wars, where professional soldiers, adult insurgents and guerrillas, and hired mercenaries were the usual participants. Some African nations have yet to sign or ratify the international protocol on children in armed conflicts, which, among other provisions, forbids the military conscription of children under the age of 18.

While some of these underage, naïve troops appear to join the fights willingly for reasons of self, family, or village protection, ethnic or religious motivations, financial gain, or perhaps adventure, many more are coerced into enlisting through threats against themselves or family members if they do not cooperate. Child soldiers are also recruited as orphans after their parents have been slaughtered. Drugs and alcohol are widely employed as further means of control and as incentives to fight viciously without regard to their personal safety. Under fear for their own lives and the lives of their families, child soldiers have been forced to participate in horrible atrocities against civilian victims. Field commanders frequently prefer child soldiers in Africa's civil wars because they are easier to manipulate and discipline, cost little to maintain, and are often fearless in battle, lacking a mature understanding of the value of life.

Children who have been swept up as participants in Africa's civil wars have, if they survived, lost their childhood, the opportunity for an education, and a productive life. Instead, they have learned how to kill wantonly and brutally. In nations with settled conflicts, such as Sierra Leone, efforts to rescue the former child combatants and teach them to rejoin a peaceful society have been difficult but often borne fruit. The successful methods used for this slow process are similar to those in psychological deprogramming of individuals who have fallen under the sway of cults; they require patience, resources, and skill. Fortunately, the UN and many NGO human rights groups are attuned to the issues of the child soldier and are taking aggressive steps to educate the public and bring an end to this objectionable practice. Public awareness of the issue was heightened by the 2006 action movie *Blood Diamond*, starring Leonardo DiCaprio, set in the Sierra Leonean civil war and dramatizing the abuse of child soldiers in that brutal conflict, and Ishmael Beah's 2007 book, *A Long Way Gone: Memoirs of a Boy Soldier*, a gripping and chilling account of the author's experiences as a 13-year-old impressed as a solider for the government in that war.[35]

One factor that has facilitated the use of child soldiers is the ready availability of inexpensive, simple, lightweight firearms, such as the AK-47, that can be carried by a child as young as 8.

Weapons in Africa's Wars

The cold war is over, ending U.S.–Soviet competition in Africa. Americans are no longer backing one side in Somalia while the Soviets back neighboring Ethiopia. The United States no longer supports one side in the Angolan civil war while the Soviet Union embraces a competing group. Has there been an end to the bloodletting in Africa with the end of the U.S.–Soviet conflict? The answer is a stark no, as peace has failed to follow the demise of the superpower rivalry. Many of the weapons introduced into the continent during the cold war era remain, only to menace new generations of Africans. Additionally, many industrialized nations, including the United States, Russia, and others, continue to produce and sell weapons to Africa for profit, and arms brokers, particularly from the former Soviet Union and the Middle East, find markets in Africa for the massive surpluses of arms readily available in their regions.[36]

Today, civil wars in some African nations are waged more for control of valuable resources, such as diamonds in Sierra Leone or coltan, a mineral found only in the Congo used in computer chip production, than for the political or ideological reasons of the past. Control of the resources provides power and funding for continuing armed struggles.

There is money to be made in African conflicts. Countries as diverse as France, Romania, Egypt, Russia, and South Africa supplied arms to the warring parties in Rwanda during the post–cold war 1990s. In Angola, a cease-fire led to a partial demobilization of soldiers, causing small arms to fall into the hands of civilians. In southern Africa generally, "there is no doubt that the region is flooded with weapons [as] decades of warfare and violent political struggle have given rise to a pervasive gun culture."[37] South Africa, without a civil war, has the highest rate of civilian deaths from firearms in the world.

In Sierra Leone and Liberia, local warlords have traded diamonds, timber, iron ore, and agricultural products for small arms. In Rwanda, it was tea for weapons. In Zimbabwe, the commodities were ivory and rhino horns, and the commodity of choice in Angola was diamonds.[38] As the Somali government disintegrated in the early 1990s, some half-million weapons were spirited to competing factions. Land mines, a focus of much international concern, are present in abundance in Africa, particularly in war-torn nations such as Somalia and Angola. Cheap small arms have also upset traditional balances between ethnic groups on more local levels, as in western Kenya, where traditional raids between the Pokot and Marakwet peoples became much bloodier with the infusion of AK-47s.

Weapons sometimes jump from one country to another. Foreign mercenaries brought their own arms to Sierra Leone, Angola, and Zaire (now Congo), and attempts have been made to disarm combatants with gun-buyback programs. Cross-border police cooperation between the South African and Mozambican police has had some effect. In 2001, delegates from nearly 180 nations worldwide began negotiating the first international treaty aimed at curbing the illicit trade in small arms, but this process will take time to bear fruit. In the meantime, the bottom line is that light weapons are easily available in great abundance, and innocent civilians are the main casualties in the continuing carnage. This "Flashpoint" now turns to examples of several settled (at least for the present) and active national and regional African conflicts, beginning with Angola.

Angola

Angola's history has been highlighted by first, a very harsh colonial government, then a bitter struggle for independence, which was attained in 1975, and then an almost constant civil war that finally came to an official end in April 2002. Abundant resources include diamonds, oil, rich soil, and fish off the coast. The resources, however, especially the diamonds and oil, only exacerbated the tensions and the stakes in the protracted battle for control of the government and of the country's riches.

In the late sixteenth century, the Portuguese were the first European power to come to sub-Saharan Africa and the last to leave, and then only when opposition became too strong, both on the battlefield and back in Lisbon. The ensuing battles from 1975 to 1991 between the Popular Movement for the Liberation of Angola (MPLA) and National Union for the Total Independence of Angola (UNITA) took some 300,000 lives. In addition, starvation afflicted more than a half million people; one-half of the country's export earnings went for the war; the economy, even with oil revenue and considerable outside assistance, remained in tatters; and refugees numbered in the hundreds of thousands. With the cold war still going strong, 50,000 Cuban fighters entered on the MPLA side and a lesser number of South Africans supported UNITA. The Soviet Union and the United States lent their support in important but less overt roles as they supplied intelligence and weapons to the warring parties.

In 1991, a peace treaty was signed in Angola, officially ending the 16-year-old civil war. The agreement called for the former enemies to build a unified armed force, promote a multiparty political system and market economy, and plan for elections monitored by a UN observer force. When the votes were counted a year later and the MPLA claimed victory, UNITA refused to recognize the results, claiming it had lost because of fraud and ballot stuffing.

In the succeeding two years, thousands more were killed in renewed fighting. Another treaty was signed in November 1994. This time 7,000 UN peacekeepers monitored the cease-fire, and the opposition force was to have a share of the power. Again there were hopes that the contestants would be able to come together in a grand coalition, but again it was not to be.

The on-again, off-again war continued to wreak havoc on the country, drain the economy, and cause tens of thousands of people to flee to refugee camps in neighboring Congo and Zambia. Although the MPLA was not blameless, it was UNITA that had been hit by international sanctions for routinely violating the 1994 agreement, including not fully carrying out the demobilization of its forces. The number and intensity of the clashes increased and intensified between 1998 and 2001 as the Angolan government of national conciliation collapsed. Generally, the MPLA forces through this period were able to gain the upper hand over UNITA, but the civil war looked to be far from resolution. The UN finally pulled its peacekeeping mission, acknowledging there was no more peace to keep. Even in the Congo war (see the "Central Africa" subsection later), MPLA and UNITA backed different sides. With the death of long-time UNITA leader Jonas Savimbi in a government ambush in February 2002, negotiations led to the end of this decades-old civil war less than two months later. The people's hopes turned to rebuilding this ravaged nation, where, besides the awful loss and displacement of lives, the great mineral wealth had been squandered for over 25 years. Democratic and economic progress since the end of the civil war has been steady, but the sad legacies of the wasted years of conflict remain.

Wars in the Horn of Africa: Sudan and Darfur and Somalia

Ethiopia, Eritrea, Djibouti, Somalia, and Sudan—five different countries, all poor, with five different histories that affect one another—constitute the Horn of Africa. All have known war recently, and in two the fighting continues. Drought, soaring populations, and depleted natural resources are endemic to the Horn of Africa. Ethiopia is one of the oldest countries in the world, and Eritrea is among the newest; both are carving out new directions. After decades of unrest, Djibouti appears relatively stable in the early 2000s; Somalia struggles to rebuild a fractured, decimated state while enduring an Islamic insurgency; and Sudan, having resolved one of Africa's longest and ugliest civil wars, faces new challenges in Darfur.

From the 1890s until independence in 1956, Sudan was formally under joint Anglo-French control. In 1958, a coup brought a change of regime and ushered in an era of unrest and military uprisings, the most recent of which occurred in 1989. The sporadic civil war raged for over 35 years. The opposing forces comprised 30 million people in the mainly Muslim north and 8 million in the non-Muslim south. The northern-based government, dominated by Islamic fundamentalists, imposed itself on an evermore hostile south. Both sides used food as a weapon. To make things more complicated and more terrible, those opposing the government split into two groups and spent as much time fighting each other as the common enemy; there were divisions in the north, also. In 1993, the United States added Sudan to its list of countries that aided terrorism, claiming that the government helped individuals and groups bent on destabilizing other states in Africa and beyond, but the regime, once the home of Osama bin Laden, has provided some intelligence to the United States in the war on terrorism. The tragedy in Sudan rivaled that in Central Africa, but, until recently, received even less attention by the media or the nation-states of the world.

In 2002, the government and the two contending rebel groups signed a protocol calling for a six-year interim period followed by an internationally supervised referendum on self-determination for the south, but hostilities continued nonetheless. Hopes for a brighter tomorrow, fueled by dramatic accords signed by government and southern rebel negotiators in January 2005, were tempered, first by brutal attacks from government militias ("Janjaweed") on the inhabitants of the remote Darfur region of western Sudan, the site of another insurgency, and then by the death, in a mysterious helicopter crash in July 2005, of the popular, former rebel leader John Garang, recently installed as vice president under the terms of the peace agreement. The Darfur attacks, formally labeled as genocide by the U.S. government, resulted in thousands of deaths, tens of thousands of rapes, and hundreds of thousands displaced in spartan refugee camps, creating a humanitarian crisis. The complex situation is intertwined with ethnic identities rooted in colonial designations and resource conflicts between nomadic herders and settled farmers in the region, although the local antagonists involved are Islamic. The African Union, the UN, and the international community generally have focused much attention on the disaster, but not before a terrible human toll was extracted with further deterioration possible. One U.S. official admitted that attacks on villages finally abated largely because "there were no villages left to attack." Seven thousand AU peacekeepers, supported with financial and logistical aid from the West, are in place, but much of the damage has been done, with rough estimates in the range of 300,000 dead and over 2 million displaced in camps. The AU peacekeeping troops have become targets, with one rebel assault in September 2007 destroying a base and killing dozens of African peacekeepers. UN Secretary General Ban Ki-moon, after a week-long fact-finding mission, reported a complex situation of multiple conflicts spilling across borders of neighboring nations and calling for a comprehensive approach to the regional issues.[39] Hopes for relief in this terrible conflict, which has gathered momentum as an international cause, now rest with the completion of the deployment of 26,000 UN peacekeeping troops (UNAMID), which was to take place in fall 2007 in cooperation with the existing futile AU efforts, and a resulting political settlement that might be facilitated by their presence. Because of various delaying factors, less than 70 percent of the anticipated UN troops were deployed by mid 2009. Darfur returned to international headlines when the prosecutor of the International Criminal Court (ICC) brought war crimes and genocide charges against the Sudanese president, Omar Hassan Ahmad al-Bashir, in July 2008, resulting in an indictment by the Court on the war crimes charges in March 2009. (The ICC dropped the genocide charge for lack of evidence.) Al-Bashir dismissed the charges and warrant for his arrest as unfounded and racist, flaunting them with high-profile trips to friendly Islamic nations.[40] Finally, there is the politics of oil. More than 3.5 billion barrels of high-quality crude has been discovered in the southern part of the country, and a $1.2 billion pipeline has been built over nearly 1,000 miles of extremely harsh terrain to get the product moving toward global markets. The oil is in production, but there is little evidence that its proceeds will be used to improve the lives of all Sudanese citizens as agreed.

Because of inhospitable terrain and no obvious exportable economic resources, Ethiopia was able to keep its independence and its monarchy until conquered by Italy in 1935. Six years later, the British drove the Italians out and restored Emperor Haile Selassie to power. In seeking to enlarge his diverse state and alter the country's landlocked status, the emperor, with British approval, in 1952 claimed the former Italian colony of Eritrea without asking the Eritreans. A military coup in 1974 swept away the old Ethiopian order. Ethiopia then endured a brutal period of Marxist rule under President Mengistu Haile Mariam before his regime collapsed under pressures from nationalist guerrilla fighting units and the end of Soviet sponsorship.

By the time Mengistu fled in the spring of 1991, 2 million people had died under his 17-year reign. In the following months, representatives of 27 ethnic and political groups, including the Ethiopian People's Revolutionary Democratic Front (EPDRF) and the Eritrean People's Liberation Front (EPLF), met to work out the future of the country. Meles Zenawi of the EPDRF headed a transition government. Despite new programs, food shortages and severe rural poverty continued as population growth outstripped grain production by ever-widening amounts. The promised democracy under a 1994 constitution has made limited progress, and in a pattern repeated in many African elections, the fairness of the 2005 Ethiopian national elections were hotly disputed. The government arrested more than 30,000 protesters in the ensuing turbulent protests that resulted in nearly 200 deaths. A questionable 14-month trial of opposition leaders accused of inciting the demonstrations resulted in 30 life sentences and other convictions.[41] Still, most observers agree that internal political conditions are much improved over the pre-1991 era.

The region of the Horn has suffered from droughts and famines exacerbated by civil violence. Ethiopia experienced a severe episode in 1984 to 1985 that cost an estimated 1 million lives as starving villagers futilely migrated to poorly supplied feeding stations. Massive international aid eventually arrived, but too late for many victims. Threats of a similar tragedy loomed in the summer of 2003 but this time, it is hoped, tempered with lessons learned from past bitter experience.

With Ethiopia's consent, Eritrea invoked its right to self-determination in 1993. Following almost 30 years of war in which 250,000 people were killed, it became the first territory in Africa to secede successfully from another African country. In a referendum, 99.8 percent of the voters opted for independence, and the new nation embarked on a democratic transition, earning high marks for its political sensitivity and self-reliant economic programs.

In mid-1998, again in early 1999, and in May 2000, the two states waged a border war, complete with planes, tanks, and considerable casualties, belying the stated friendship between the two countries' leaders, Meles Zenawi and Issaias Aferweki. Rebellions by Eritrea had gone on since the early 1960s, when the actual annexation by Ethiopia had taken place. For the next 30 years there was minimal cooperation between the national government and its embittered province. Nevertheless, the leadership of both entities worked together to overthrow the hated Mengistu government. But the fraternal relations could not survive the peace.

On one level, this conflict was simply a disagreement over who owned a border area that had been drawn by Italy in 1885, but there were serious economic disputes as well. After the renewed fighting in May of 2000, the two nations agreed to a cease-fire, including UN peacekeepers in a buffer zone. The UN mediated a final demarcation of the disputed border in 2002, but tensions remain nonetheless.

Southern Italian Somaliland and northern British Somaliland were fused at independence in 1960. Nine years later, Mohammed Siad Barre seized power and became a ruthless president for the next 22 years. Even though the overwhelming majority of the people are from the same ethnic group, competing clans and subclans formed the basis for challenges to Barre and each other.

During the time of U.S.-Soviet rivalry, the United States first backed Ethiopia, while the U.S.S.R. supported Barre's version of Socialism. When Marxist Mengistu took power in Ethiopia, the two superpowers switched sides, both supplying their new beneficiaries with more weapons. Despite Barre's deplorable human rights record, the United States continued to funnel military and economic aid to Somalia until the late 1980s.

In 1991, Barre was finally ousted and a struggle for power between subclans began, bringing with it hardship and famine. As pictures of starving children filled television screens following initial UN hesitation, the world body began to supply food to hundreds of thousands of people. With provisions being hijacked or blocked at the capital of Mogadishu, UN observers, and then U.S. troops, arrived to assist. Gradually, the mission's objective changed (so-called "mission creep") from ending starvation to establishing a measure of peace and security to the country by ending the struggle for power. Later, the UN hoped it could rebuild the infrastructure, the economy, and finally the government itself. This change in objective involved the UN as a participant in the conflict.

By 1993, there were 25,000 American military personnel, thousands of other UN peacemakers, and countless private parties, all attempting to provide assistance. In October of that year, 18 U.S. Army Rangers lost their lives in a futile attempt to capture a Somali leader who was accused of fomenting strife. This incident has become fixed in popular memory through graphic video and in global popular culture through the 2001 movie *Black Hawk Down*. The international community beat a measured retreat, and within two years all military personnel were gone, though a few relief agencies braved the dangers and stayed. Some saw the operation as saving great numbers of lives and offering hope during a time of misery; others believed that UN members came too late and became too enmeshed in local politics and in "nation building."

Since then, there was no operating government in Somalia until fall 2000, when negotiations led to the beginnings of a return to law and order. Success is far from assured, however, as rival warlords and break-away groups maintain their armed militias outside government control, which seems to center in the capital of Mogadishu, where danger and instability forced the prime minister and his cabinet to spend seven months in virtual exile in Kenya from late 2004 to mid-2005. Floods and drought have taken their toll as the world became donor-fatigued and turned its attention elsewhere, but new concerns over international piracy and over Islamic fundamentalist insurgency have refocused attention on struggling Somalia. Rebel forces under the auspices of the Council of

Islamic Courts seized control in much of the nation, only to be repelled by the intervention of Ethiopian troops supporting the Somali government. When the Ethiopian forces departed in early 2009, the fighting intensified and the Islamic rebels made gains against the beleaguered government, supported with material aid from the United States and other nations and an inadequate contingent of AU peacekeepers. Al-Shabab, the major Islamic group involved in the fighting, has killed AU peacekeepers and several government minists and has fired mortar rounds at the plane of U.S. Congressman Donald M. Payne (D-NJ), who had been on a fact-finding mission. Deteriorating conditions forced moderate President Sharif Ahmed to declare a state of emergency and plea for international intervention. With break-away provinces, malnutrition, an overwhelmed and harried AU peacekeeping force, and international conflict-resolution efforts turned elsewhere, such as Darfur, the immediate prospects for Somalia are not bright.

The rise of international piracy off the Somali coast has alarmed the maritime community, leading to naval and air patrols by the United States, France, and other powers in attempts to protect the vital commercial and tourist shipping lanes in the region. Given the poverty and turmoil in Somalia, the lure of large ransoms paid for the safe return of kidnapped crews and passengers and for hijacked ships and cargo has led hundreds of young Somali men, some formerly peaceful fishermen, to turn to violent piracy on the high seas. Their brazen, well-armed attacks in small, high-speed boats against slower, unarmed merchant and cruise ships and private yachts have proved effective, lucrative, and hard to prevent. A dramatic rescue by U.S. Navy Seals of an American cargo ship captain who had given himself up as a hostage to save his ship and crew from capture by Somali pirates gained international attention in spring 2009. Despite the shooting deaths of three of the young captors in this rescue, piracy acts continued unabated. Several months later, an attempt by pirates to seize the same ship was repelled by private armed security guards aboard, a controversial practice adopted by some desperate shipping lines. With the flashy wealth displayed by successful Somali pirates, there is growing fear that similar forms of piracy might spread to other impoverished African countries, especially in the already unstable waters off West Africa.[42]

Central Africa and the Great Lakes Region

Without a doubt, events in Central Africa at the new century's onset were the most tumultuous, the most complicated, and the most dangerous in all of sub-Saharan Africa. Personal rivalries, ethnic antagonisms, cross-border conflicts, and precolonial and colonial currents mix in unpredictable ways. In the Democratic Republic of Congo (formerly Zaire), the third largest country on the continent, the past decade has witnessed the overthrow of a president who had ignominiously ruled since the 1960s; a successor who barely clung to power amidst charges of incompetence; an assassination leading to a young, untried president; and a war in which troops from several surrounding countries joined local forces. One humanitarian NGO, the International Rescue Committee, estimated that 3.8 million people died as a result of the civil war in rebel-held Eastern Congo through 2004.[43] In Rwanda, a terrible 1994 civil war that took hundreds of thousands of lives has been followed by continuing bitter ethnic hostilities across borders, with no final end to the killings. The mass killings in tiny Rwanda, stemming in part from long-standing ethnic rivalry between the dominant Tutsis and the majority, lower-status Hutus, led to refugee disasters, reprisals, and second-guessing of UN and Western power inaction. Prosecutions of alleged war criminals from this horror continue to this day, and the world witnessed moving 10-year memorials of the massacre in 2004, which also saw the release of the popular and moving film *Hotel Rwanda*, which depicted an aspect of heroic humanity amidst the carnage. Many neighboring countries, especially Angola, Burundi, Uganda, and Zimbabwe, already struggling with major political and economic problems, were pushed to the limit by convulsions emanating from Congo (then Zaire) and Rwanda. Burundi, which has been plagued by ongoing ethnic clashes similar in some respects to those of Rwanda, experienced outbreaks of civil war in 2003 that have now subsided. The international community rushed to avoid the mistakes that led to the awful massacres in its northern neighbor nearly a decade ago.

In the mid- and late-1990s, events in Rwanda became ever more closely entwined with those of neighboring Congo (both were under Belgian colonial rule). The huge state in the middle of the continent was a prize, with its lush forests, fertile croplands, and prodigious mineral deposits; however, its painful colonial experience as the Belgian Congo made it totally unprepared for independence in 1960. Not surprisingly, chaos resulted, in which racial, ethnic, and ideological conflicts brought the country close to disintegration. Outside states threatened to intervene, but a UN peacekeeping operation, despite many problems, provided the glue that kept the country together. After the UN departure in 1964, however, instability grew again. A year later, General Joseph Mobutu staged a coup and began to put his mark on the country, a mark that has become all-pervasive.

Thirty years later, Congo was going back in time. It was a country where political and economic conditions had gotten about as bad as they could get. In a change Mobutu dubbed African "authentication," the nation had been renamed Zaire and the general had become President Sese Seko Mobutu, but he ran a "kleptocracy," government by theft. Although Mobutu was a billionaire who maintained several residences in Europe, the World Bank declared Congo bankrupt in 1994. Massive corruption, including diamond smuggling, hyperinflation, and hunger were among the symptoms of his sick regime. Promoting tensions and divisions among the country's 250 ethnic groups to ensure his own longevity in office was another. Because of the disintegration of the government infrastructure, civil servants and soldiers were not paid and staged mutinies.

Because of the cold war, Congo for many years was the largest recipient of U.S. aid in sub-Saharan Africa. Indeed, Mobutu came to power with the help of the Central Intelligence Agency (CIA), which used the country as a staging area for activities throughout the continent while turning a blind eye to the endemic decay and corruption. Several attempts at democratic reform during the 1990s came to naught, and in the end the malaise was so advanced that a Tutsi-supported revolt, which started along the border with Rwanda in October 1996, swept the country in just seven months. The OAU principle of nonintervention in the affairs of another state had been ignored during the overthrow of Mobutu in which several neighboring nations collaborated.

The president, already terminally ill with prostate cancer, fled the country in May 1997 and died in exile four months later. Laurent Kabila, who was from southern Congo and had been a longtime opponent of the regime, was anointed to lead the rebellion and become the new president. Expectations ran high for a better tomorrow, but it was not to be, as his corrupt, chaotic, and war-torn term ended abruptly with his assassination by a disloyal bodyguard in January 2001.

His son Joseph Kabila, a 31-year-old army officer with little political or administrative experience, assumed the presidency. Many observers feared that the awful situation would deteriorate even further. On the contrary, the young and untried president showed stability and competence, and he spoke of building a peaceful, democratic future for his country. A failed 1999 cease-fire accord regained momentum. In the wake of several negotiated cease-fires, peace initiatives, and conferences, sometimes boycotted by one or more of the key parties, the efforts of international mediators such as Nelson Mandela, and the presence of UN peacekeeping forces, the civil war moved to an interim, transitional settlement in the summer of 2003. While Joseph Kabila kept the presidency, he accepted four vice presidents from the contending factions, and the long-suffering nation was poised to move toward reconciliatory measures, culminating in parliamentary and presidential elections in 2006. Kabila retained the presidency in a runoff, and despite charges of fraud, the electoral process did not spark extensive civil violence.

Even with these hopeful developments and the presence of a large UN peacekeeping force (itself the subject of criticism for inappropriate conduct), ethnic strife, rebel guerilla and militia attacks, and cross-border incursions continued. Often these actions targeted civilians for ruthless slaughter; child combatants were still prevalent. Women have been raped in large numbers by insurgents, government forces, and even some of the peacekeepers in what an appalled UN humanitarian official termed "almost a cultural phenomenon."[44] President Kabila's vow to push all foreign militias (including the dreaded Interahamwe, the Hutu extremists responsible for much of the killing in the 1994 Rwandan massacre) out of the country by the end of September 2005 was not a complete success, and in the troubled eastern sections of the nation, warlords and militias still cause trouble. Yet another peace accord between the government and warring militias was signed in 2008, but the people of the eastern Congo suffered renewed conflicts nonetheless. Congo's neighbor to the north, Uganda, has its own troubles with the brutal insurgency of the Lord's Resistance Army and charges of manipulated elections and repression of political opposition. The border region between these two nations remains tense, with violence often reported. Is this region's troubled past destined to follow it into the near future, or has it truly turned a new page? Time will tell.

West Africa

Long one of the most politically unstable regions of Africa, littered with civil wars and coups, conditions in West Africa at the turn of the last century were relatively calm. For example, Nigeria, Senegal, and Ghana were showing signs of participatory democracy, while civil wars and coups in Côte d'Ivoire, Liberia, and Sierra Leone were in various stages of abatement. Much of this superficial calm, however, preceded more gathering storms. Deteriorating ethnic relations in Nigeria are noted in the case study, and the rebel insurgencies in Côte d'Ivoire and Liberia reignited. Free elections in Senegal and Ghana, on the other hand, resulted in peaceful transfers of power, and a long, brutal civil war in Sierra Leone was settled with ECOWAS and UN peacekeeper intervention so that reconstruction could begin, leading to a successful election and power transfer in 2007.

During Francophile President Félix Houphouët-Boigny's 23-year term, Côte d'Ivoire, with a large French presence, enjoyed considerable stability and prosperity, if limited freedom and democracy. With his death in 1993, things began to unravel, and in September 2002, the nation experienced a renewed military rebellion that divided it along religious and sectarian lines, particularly the more Muslim north and Christian south. French military intervention and a brokered truce in Paris in the spring of 2003 failed to resolve the conflict. Despite other peacemaking attempts, new violence ensued. In April 2005, though, the civil war was officially settled through a power-sharing and disarmament agreement, but slow implementation forced cancellation of the planned 2005 and 2006 elections. Disputes continued until a March 2007 accord brokered by President Blaise Campoare of neighboring Burkina Faso finally called for reconciliation of the divided nation. Voter registration lists were finally completed for an oft-delayed election scheduled for late February 2010, but further delays are possible, and it remains to be seen when Côte d'Ivoire will return to the political stability and economic success enjoyed in earlier years.

Sierra Leone suffered a particularly vicious, decade-long, civil war that centered in part over control of the nation's lucrative diamond trade and was fomented by Liberian rebel intervention. The main Sierra Leonean rebel force, the Revolutionary

United Front (RUF) under its leader Foday Sankoh, appeared to have little political plan for the nation beyond exploiting resources; brutally intimidating and recruiting civilians, often children, as combatants; and seizing power. Attempts by neighbors through ECOWAS and various international actors, including the United States, to broker cease-fires and arrange a power-sharing settlement in the late 1990s failed. Renewed efforts by the UN, British, and ECOWAS forces (termed ECOMOG and consisting mostly of Nigerian troops) bore fruit in later years with the capture of Sankoh and the surrender and disarmament of most of the rebel fighters. Sierra Leone established a Truth and Reconciliation Commission based partially on the South African model to deal with the horrors of its past and try to rebuild for the future; trials of alleged war criminals began in 2004. Sankoh himself died of natural causes while in prison awaiting trial. With the war-ravaged nation ranking last (179th) in the world on the latest UN Human Development Index, much work remains to be done, but many see the recent elections as a promising development.

While the capital of Sierra Leone, Freetown, was established in 1787 by freed African slaves from Britain and its colonies, neighboring Liberia was founded early in the nineteenth century as a home for freed slaves repatriated from the United States. This group of "Americo-Liberians" constituting no more than 5 percent of the total population, nonetheless controlled Liberian politics and wealth through their True Whig Party and related Masonic Temple. The behavior and conduct of the True Whigs mirrored in many ways the society of the plantation masters they had left. Their aloof, arrogant rule came to a decisive and bloody end in 1980 in the form of a coup led by Sergeant Samuel Doe. Sadly, this regime change heralded the beginning of more problems for Liberia because the next two decades would be marked by civil wars that killed hundreds of thousands, left many more refugees and internally displaced persons, and ruined the faltering economy.

A ruthless rebel force led by Charles Taylor, now on trial in The Hague for war crimes in connection with illicit diamond trading in Sierra Leone's civil war, emerged to power in the later 1990s. His regime was soon challenged by other rebels, such as the Liberians United for Reconciliation and Democracy (LURD), whose brutal battlefield tactics against civilians belied their high-sounding name. By midsummer 2003, with a beleaguered Taylor holding only the capital city of Monrovia, desperate Liberians cried out for international peacemaking assistance, especially from the United States, whose forces had just toppled a dictatorial regime in Iraq. Liberians, with so many ties of heritage and economy to the United States, felt this special relationship should prompt U.S. forces to the rescue. Angry Liberians displayed the bodies of their slain relatives in front of the U.S. embassy after the Americans hesitated to make a quick response and the killing escalated. Taylor finally left the country to reluctant exile in Nigeria, as the United States and others had demanded, but evidence mounted that he still tried to run Liberia, including army and business interests, from abroad. Meanwhile, some 3,000 multinational ECOWAS troops, mainly Nigerians based in Sierra Leone, intervened to stop the fighting in the capital. The U.S. administration promised assistance to end the slaughter, sending over 2,000 Marines to the Liberian coast to support the coming ECOWAS and UN peacekeepers, but only a couple hundred actually landed. Calm finally prevailed under the ECOWAS troops, and the beleaguered nation held presidential elections in October 2005 that resulted in Ellen Johnson Sirleaf, a former World Bank official, besting renowned former soccer star George Weah in a runoff. (Interestingly, some of the campaigning among the 22 candidates took place in the U.S. Liberian community; although these citizens would not be allowed to cast absentee ballots, they had ample and needed funds for campaign contributions.)[45] Johnson Sirleaf is Africa's first female president (resurgent Mozambique has had a female prime minister, Luisa Diogo, since 2004), and reconciliation and rebuilding have begun under her rule. More than 40 years after independence, many nations of Africa continue to experience ethnic and religious violence and civil wars and insurgencies. A recent case in point is Guinea (Conakry), where a military coup by junior officers followed the death (from natural causes) of the long-term president in 2008. Ensuing human rights violations under the military regime, including killings of unarmed civilian demonstrators, have been widely condemned by the international community. The coup leader, army Captain Moussa Dadis Camara, narrowly survived an assassination attempt by an aide from a minority ethnic group in December 2009. All the news is not grim. On the contrary, many clashes of the past have been settled, and reconstructive efforts are ongoing in numerous nations, such as Angola, Burundi, Liberia, Mozambique, Uganda, Rwanda, Sierra Leone, and to some extent, the Democratic Republic of Congo, all previously afflicted by awful violence and unspeakable atrocities. The use of poor West African nations as transit points in the international drug trade is a disturbing development that could spark further violence. As the examples in this "Flashpoint" prove, though, declaring these African conflicts resolved for good is risky, and all African and international actors need to learn hard lessons from the mistakes of the past.

Sub-Saharan Africa and International Terrorism

After the striking events of September 11, 2001, the attention of the United States and much of the rest of the world was riveted by the vexing phenomenon of international terrorism, but Africa had already seen its awful impact in two related attacks. In early August 1998, powerful bombs exploded adjacent to U.S. embassies in Kenya and Tanzania, and resulted in the deaths of more than 260 people, including 12 American citizens. More than 5,000 were injured.

In this case, the terrorist acts apparently had their origin in the Middle East or Afghanistan. The perpetrators were taking vengeance against the United States for its pro-Israel policies and its support for what were seen as despotic governments in the Arab world. More generally, there was a backlash against the intrusion of American and Western culture and values into Islamic countries.

For Kenyans and Tanzanians the price was high. First were the many killed or injured and the ripple effect on their families. Many of the deceased or those seriously hurt were breadwinners. Thousands, therefore, had their lives uprooted. There were the economic impacts such as tourists staying away in droves and many shops and buildings destroyed, which could only be slowly reconstructed, if at all. To add to the bitterness, there was criticism that U.S. servicemen who were deployed in the hours and days after the bombings were indifferent to the plight of the Africans who were injured, focusing only on American casualties.

Two weeks later the United States struck back, launching surprise missile strikes on terrorist bases in Afghanistan and a factory in Sudan, which allegedly produced chemical weapons, although that evidence remains in question. In the meantime, Kenyans and Tanzanians tried to get on with their lives while Africans in other countries wondered if they would be next. An attempt by Kenyan citizens to sue in U.S. courts for compensation for damages from the embassy attack did not succeed. In November 2002, Kenya suffered a related terrorist attack, on a resort hotel in Mombassa frequented by Israeli tourists. This suicide car bomb attack, linked to Al Qaeda, claimed the lives of 10 Kenyans and 3 Israelis. On the same day, two "stinger" type missiles narrowly missed an Israeli airliner bound home with 271 aboard.

Sub-Saharan Africa's ties to the crisis of international terrorism are many and appear to be growing. Virtually every African government expressed sympathy and offers of aid to the United States following the September 11 attacks, and several African nations, such as Sudan, once a headquarters for Al Qaeda operations, were able to provide important intelligence assistance. Some critics fear, though, that closer ties with authoritarian regimes for help in the war on terrorism could have negative consequences later, as they did with anticommunism in the cold war.

Because Africa has many nations with large Islamic populations, it should not be surprising that there are also substantial followings for militant, fundamentalist, Islamist groups among the discontented and disaffected, especially youth. Susan E. Rice, Assistant Secretary for African Affairs in the second Clinton administration and now U.S. Representative to the UN, wrote in the *Washington Post*:

> What has Africa got to do with Osama bin Laden or terrorist finance networks? This: Africa is the world's soft underbelly for global terrorism. If we intend to win—and not just fight—the war on terror, we cannot view Africa as separate from our comprehensive, global war. . . . Al Qaeda and other terrorist cells are active throughout East, southern and West Africa, as well as North Africa. These organizations plan, finance, train and execute terrorist operations in many parts of Africa, not just Sudan and Somalia.[46]

Al Qaeda presence in Sudan and Somalia is widely acknowledged in intelligence circles. The Khartoum government, which has had difficult relations with Washington over the past decade because of alleged sponsorship of terrorism, previously hosting Osama bin Laden; the long, civil war with the black, partially Christian south; the more recent violence in Darfur; and allegations of modern human slavery, chose to avoid confrontation with the United States in the war on terrorism and instead became a source of intelligence. Somalia, still highly unstable with little central governmental authority, is reputedly a safe haven for Al Qaeda operations and might even provide some sanctuary for terrorist fighters escaping from the United States in Afghanistan. With help from Ethiopian authorities on the border, U.S. officials conducted scouting missions in Somalia late in 2001 for possible later actions against terrorist activities there. The United States maintains a contingent of Special Forces in Djibouti to deal with terrorist activity in the region. A Trans-Sahara Counter Terrorism Initiative, begun in 2005 and funded at $100 million annually beginning in 2007, provides U.S. Special Forces trainers on counter-terrorist tactics for troops from Chad, Mali, Mauritania, Niger, Nigeria, Senegal, and three North African states.[47] A new Africa Command (AFRICOM), established by the U.S. Department of Defense to help stabilize governments and promote regional security, has raised concerns in diplomatic and development communities over increased militarization of U.S. policy in Africa.[48] Several other Defense Department programs, most well funded, provide training, small arms, and border security in African nations, clearly with the goals of the war on terror in mind.

In an article titled "Blood on the Diamonds," *Washington Post* reporter Holly Burkhalter examined the illicit trade links of Al Qaeda terrorists, some of whom are linked to the 1998 embassy bombings, in securing diamonds at wholesale prices from Sierra Leonean rebels by way of contacts in neighboring Liberia, and then trafficking the diamonds at great profits to the world markets in Belgium. Legislative and other efforts to intercept and close down such lucrative terrorist financial dealings are underway.[49] Nigeria experienced deadly riots by extremist Muslims against Christians in northern cities such as Kano following the U.S. bombing of Taliban and Al Qaeda positions in

Afghanistan. Clearly, official positions in African countries are supportive of U.S. efforts to combat international terrorism, but opinions of the people "on the street" in African Islamic nations may not be so favorable to U.S. positions. Whether the attention on Africa resulting from concerns over international terrorism will be good for African interests in the long term remains to be seen, but short-term disruptions are likely.

Summary

> Don't worry. It's Africa. Nobody cares about Africa.
>
> From the movie Sahara, Paramount Pictures, 2005

The preceding line above spoken by a villainous warlord character in an action-adventure, "Indiana Jones"–genre film set in the deserts of Mali and in Lagos, Nigeria. Like most Hollywood movies, *Sahara* was intended to entertain rather than to inform, but it is replete with stereotypes, including the ruthless, greedy warlord intent on victimizing innocent indigenous peoples who oppose him (in this case with the slight variation that the warlord is black and the victims are Islamic "Tuareg" tribesmen). The warlord believed he could get away with his schemes because no one in the "outside world" would pay any attention. The truth, it is hoped, is that many in the United States and the world at large do care a great deal about Africa, but it is too easy to remain uninformed, underinformed, or misinformed about the realities of sub-Saharan Africa. The entire issue of the September 2005 *National Geographic* magazine was devoted to Africa, with thoughtful articles that concentrate on resources, the environment, and changing patterns of human life. Instead of the characteristic photograph, the front cover simply states, in large letters, "Africa," and beneath, "Whatever you thought, think again." This is sound advice both for the student new to the study of Africa and for those who consider themselves to be "old hands" because the region is in flux, and the outcomes should matter to all of us.

Natural geography and history impede positive change in Africa. Population, health, education, food, energy, and environmental concerns are troubling problems. Politically, the continuing quest for legitimacy, the social diversity and conflict, embedded corruption, the uncertain effectiveness of regional and pan-African cooperation, and varying international interest in Africa do not bode well for the years ahead. Finally, by many indicators, economic well-being is very tenuous for most Africans, especially with the loss of trade and capital because of the global economic crisis, while dependency on external agencies that prescribe privatization has increased. An interesting side effect of the economic crisis has been the reverse migration of many professional Africans away from Western nations hard-hit by the recession back to their homelands, countering the "brain drain" pattern prevalent for decades.[50] This is a two-edged sword for Africa; it brings home much-needed talent but results in the loss of vital remittances from higher professional incomes abroad.

As Africa moves into the twenty-first century, there has been no dramatic turnaround for the region; however, politically and economically there are glimmers of hope. Throughout the 1990s into the early 2000s, particularly gruesome civil wars, with many atrocities against civilians, raged in Congo, Liberia, Rwanda, Sierra Leone, Angola, and Sudan. Côte d'Ivoire, long one of the most stable governments in former French West Africa, suffered a violent military coup, and corrupt dictatorships held sway in several other West African nations. In addition to the shift to civilian rule in the important nation of Nigeria described previously in the "Case Studies," the civil wars have abated in Angola, Liberia, Sierra Leone, Rwanda, and part of Sudan, and in Burundi, where elections were held in 2005 and disarmament and rebuilding are ongoing. Congo, Côte d'Ivoire, Kenya, and Zimbabwe have implemented agreements for power sharing, albeit with mixed results; and Ghana, Senegal, and Kenya experienced relatively peaceful and significant transfers of power to opposition leaders through free and fair elections. However, optimism over Kenya's historic 2002 electoral success, where "big man" Daniel arap Moi had held authoritarian sway for nearly 25 years, has been reversed by the allegations of electoral fraud from the December 2007 presidential election and the ensuing severe communal violence. Incumbent Mwai Kibaki, of the dominant Kikuyu people, claimed victory over Raila Odinga of the rival Luo in the highly disputed voting that left over 1,000 dead in its wake by early 2008. A long-simmering civil war in Chad intensified in early 2008.

The AIDS crisis continues to rage and take an awful toll, but international donor attention is mobilized, and some national programs, notably those of Botswana and Uganda, have shown notable success. Fears that the Bush administration would put Africa on the backburner proved unfounded. Africans greeted the coming of the Obama administration with celebrations reminiscent of their euphoria over national independence, but they await concrete results from promised new programs and financial help amidst other U.S. priorities, such as dealing with the severe recession.

Among African leaders and scholars, there is a major debate about whether the causes and, thus, the implied cures of Africa's current ills are largely external (such as slavery, colonialism, imperialism, and globalization) or internal (such as poor leadership, corruption, and ethnic conflict). President Mbeki of South Africa is considered a strong proponent of the *externalist* position, while former President Obasanjo of Nigeria has made statements along the *internalist* lines. The long-simmering debate over the effectiveness of foreign aid has heated up of late, with some critics pointing to aid as a major source of Africa's underdevelopment despite good intentions, whereas others fear a loss of external capital in the wake of the global economic crisis. Although these are useful distinctions for analysis, many would agree that action for Africa is needed on all fronts, both outside and inside the continent. All must work together to cure Africa's ills.

People in many cases still fear their own governments, but they are also no longer suffering in silence. With many nations abolishing fees for public schools, attendance is up (although the UN estimates that nearly half of the school-age population—some 46 million children—have never set foot in a classroom), so literacy is rising. Modern technology is making inroads in the most distant villages, and, from Senegal to Nigeria to Kenya to Zimbabwe, the people, including women, "will be heard." Environmental protection and green policies are now given more than lip service even as much of Africa's rich natural heritage is under threat in the rush for progress and sheer survival. More people are standing up to mismanagement and corruption, and reformed business practices, lower risks of instability, and more capable governance are helping to attract increased foreign capital investment. Appropriate and relatively inexpensive "low" technology solutions, such as treated bed netting to stop mosquitoes and thwart the spread of malaria or "merry-go-round" manual well pumps ("play pumps") to allow children to play as they pump potable water to bring back to their villages, are making an appreciable difference in the quality of life.[51] Some see promise in the development of the African Union. Western powers, including the United States, seem to be paying increased attention to the region. Writing of the dangers for Africa in the global economic crisis, Liberian President Ellen Johnson Sirleaf concludes, "[I]t would be a cruel irony if, just as Africa began to succeed, its prospects were cut short by a crisis beyond its control. Strong action by African governments and robust support from the international community can keep Africa's recovery on track. Both should continue to do their part."[52]

Review Questions

1. What are the effects of the European Colonial Period, including the earlier slave trade on the current political and economic situation in sub-Saharan Africa? Why do some see foreign aid as harmful and even an extension of the patronizing attitudes of the colonial period, whereas others view aid as a vital component of Africa's development?

2. Why do many Africans believe that their own governments and leaders have not served them well? Are there exceptions to this pattern? Why has there been so much emphasis placed on good governance and curbing corruption?

3. Why has regional cooperation and integration in Africa proved so elusive, and what are the goals and prospects of the African Union?

4. What parts of Africa continue to suffer episodes of civil war and ethnic violence? Why? What previous civil wars have been resolved in recent years?

5. Why is there a special relationship between the United States and Africa? Why do some Africans fear that their interests have at times been marginalized in U.S. foreign policy? What roles do European nations and more recent powers such as China play in Africa?

6. What contributions has Wangari Maathai made to African development? Do you believe that she is a good role model for other Africans? Why is the political and economic participation of women vital for Africa's future success?

Key Terms

African Union (AU)—Founded in 2002, the association of all independent African nations that succeeded the Organization of African Unity (1963) to build new institutions and agreements leading to African integration and solutions to Africa's problems.

apartheid—The policy of racial discrimination and separation practiced by the white Afrikaner regime in South Africa until the coming of majority rule in the 1990s.

Berlin Conference—The notorious meeting of European imperial powers to divide Africa for colonial exploitation without the participation of Africans. This division is still reflected in today's political map of Africa; see Figures 6.2 and 6.3.

"The Elephants and the Grass"—From a Swahili proverb which claims that grass is trampled when elephants fight, with Africa cast in the role of the grass and the Western powers (and the former Soviet Union) and financial institutions in the role of elephants.

externalists and internalists—Those who explain Africa's problems and possible solutions on the basis of factors outside Africa (external), such as historical slavery, colonialism, the cold war and globalization, as opposed to factors within Africa (internal) such as corrupt leadership, ethnic conflict, and civil war.

Great Lakes Region—The volatile area that includes much of Central Africa comprising the northeastern part of the Democratic Republic of Congo, western Kenya, northern Tanzania, southern Uganda, and all of Rwanda and Burundi that has witnessed much ethnic violence, civil war, resource exploitation, and refugee problems.

Horn of Africa—The region of Northwest Africa consisting of Djibouti, Ethiopia, Eritrea, Somalia, and Sudan that has seen much instability, war, modern piracy, and disaster, both natural and human-made.

modern slavery—The practices of indentured servitude of youths and of chattel (ownership) slavery of black Africans in Sudan and Mauritania.

pan-Africanism—The idea, often associated with Kwame Nkrumah, the charismatic first president of Ghana, that African nations and peoples need to unite for their common good and survival; an ideal not yet realized in practice.

politics of extraction—A concept closely associated with corruption which holds that political power is intended for acquiring material well-being rather than serving the people, as practiced by the colonial powers and allegedly learned by some of Africa's own leaders, such as Mobutu of Zaire, after independence.

Useful Web Sites

Africare (United States–based charitable organization promoting aid to Africa): *www.africare.org*

Africa Action (United States–based advocacy organization for Africa): *www.africaaction.org*

All Africa Global Media (consortium for African news media): *allafrica.com*

The African Union: *www.africa-union.org*

The University of Pennsylvania's African Studies Program: *www.sas.upenn.edu/African_Studies/AS.html*

For Further Reading

"Africa in the 21ˢᵗ Century." *Journal of International Affairs*. 62, 2 (Spring/Summer 2009). [This issue is devoted to contemporary affairs in sub-Saharan Africa with 12 feature articles, an interview and several review essays.]

Ali, Taisier, and Matthews, Robert. *Civil Wars in Africa*. Toronto: McGill-Queen's University Press, 1999.

Ayittey, George B. N. *Africa Betrayed*. New York: St. Martin's Press, 1992.

—*Africa in Chaos*. New York: St. Martin's Press, 1999.

—*Africa Unchained*. New York: Palgrave Macmillan, 2005.

Bayart, Jean-Francois. *The State in Africa: The Politics of the Belly*. London and New York: Longman, 1993.

Beah, Ishmael. *A Long Way Gone: Memoirs of a Boy Soldier*. New York: Sarah Crichton Books, Farrar, Straus and Giroux, 2007.

Davidson, Basil. *The Black Man's Burden: Africa and the Curse of the Nation State*. New York: Times Books, 1992.

Gourevitch, Philip. *We Wish to Inform You That Tomorrow We Will Be Killed with Our Families: Stories from Rwanda*. New York: Farrar, Straus and Giroux, 1998.

Hochschild, Adam. *King Leopold's Ghost*. New York: Houghton Mifflin, 1998.

Kapuscinski, Ryzard. *The Shadow of the Sun*. Translated by Klara Glowczweka. New York: Alfred A. Knopf, 2001.

Leach, Melissa, and Mearns, Robin, eds. *The Lie of the Land: Challenging Received Wisdom on the African Environment*. Westport, CT: Heinemann, 1996.

Maathai, Wangari. *Unbowed: A Memoir*. New York: Alfred A. Knopf (paperback by Vintage Books), 2006.

—*The Challenge for Africa*. New York: Pantheon Books, 2009.

Mazrui, Ali. *The African Condition*. New York: Cambridge University Press, 1980.

Meredith, Martin. *The Fate of Africa: From the Hopes of Freedom to the Heart of Despair: A History of Fifty Years of Independence*. New York: Public Affairs, 2005.

Moyo, Dambisa. *Dead Aid: Why Aid Is Not Working and How There Is a Better Way for Africa*. New York: Farrar, Straus and Giroux, 2009.

The National Geographic Society. *National Geographic*. "Africa" Special Issue, September, 2005.

Nugent, Paul. *Africa Since Independence: A Comparative History*. New York: Palgrave-Macmillan, 2004.

Soyinka, Wole. *The Open Sore of a Continent*. Oxford and New York: Oxford University Press, 1996.

—*The Burden of Memory, The Muse of Forgiveness*. Oxford and New York: Oxford University Press, 1999.

Theroux, Paul. *Dark Star Safari: Overland from Cairo to Cape Town*. New York: Mariner Books, Houghton Mifflin, 2004.

Young, Crawford. *The African Colonial State in Comparative Perspective*. New Haven and London: Yale University Press, 1994.

Notes

1. Statistics in the last two paragraphs come from the World Watch Institute and Population Action International, *Human Development Report 1997* and *2008* (New York: New York University Press, 1997, 2005); the *2008 World Population Data*

Sheet published by the Population Reference Bureau (www.prb.org); and *The World Almanac and Book of Facts 2009*, (New York: World Almanac Books, 2009).

2. For details of the UN Millenium Development Goals, see www.un.org/millenniumgoals/. For the recent UN Human Development Reports (or for earlier years for comparison,) visit http://hdr.undp.org/en/reports/.

3. For example, A. N. Wilson writes of the British in the nineteenth century colonial era in *The Victorians* (New York: W. W. Norton, 2003): "Theirs was the period of the most radical transformation ever seen by the world. . . . Large tracts of the world, especially in Africa, were unmapped. After them, the 'Dark Continent' had been penetrated by European powers; the destiny of Africa had changed . . .," p. 1.

4. "Angrily" is an understatement. With independence, France cut all ties with Guinea and withdrew, taking with them everything from government vehicles to telephones.

5. Mazrui related the anecdote in the 1986 television series, *The Africans.*

6. Susan Rice, "A New Partnership for the 21st Century," address to the African Studies Association, November 14, 1997.

7. Judith Matloff, "African Anthem: Where Life Goes on, No Matter What," *Christian Science Monitor,* January 6, 1998, p. 9.

8. Robert Reid, "Annan: Africans Must Share Blame," *Associated Press,* April 16, 1998.

9. Quoted from the Nobel Peace Prize Award Citation, Norwegian Nobel Committee, November 27, 2004.

10. Quoted in Emily Wax, "Africa's Women Beginning to See Progress in Politics," *The Washington Post,* June 6, 2003, p. A6.

11. Emily Wax, "An African 'Big Brother' Unites and Delights," *The Washington Post,* July 14, 2003, p. A1. Despite many criticisms of the show, it made highly popular comebacks in the 2007 and 2008 seasons.

12. For a fuller discussion on this subject, see Herman J. Cohen, "Conflict Management in Africa," *CSIS Africa Notes,* February 1998, pp. 1–7.

13. The official progress of the AU, including joint actions, programs established, and annual summit meetings, can be followed through its Web site, www.Africa-Union.org.

14. Peter Carlson, "Powell, on Another Front," *The Washington Post,* November 7, 2001, p. C1.

15. Susan Rice, Assistant Secretary of State for African Affairs, "U.S.-Africa Policy," address to the National Association for the Advancement of Colored People, July 14, 1998.

16. In 1998, U.S. soldiers joined their Kenyan, Tanzanian, and Ugandan counterparts in Kenya to show that their hypothetical country of Sumang could be returned to calm after upheaval. Small-scale training and exercises involving U.S. troops and African peacekeeping forces continued into the early 2000s.

17. For one insightful perspective on likely issues facing Obama's policy toward sub-Sarahan Africa, see Princeton N. Lyman and Katherine Robineette, "Obama and Africa," *Journal of International Affairs,* 62, 2, Spring/Summer 2009, pp. 1–18.

18. Jennifer Seymour Whitaker, *How Can Africa Survive?* (New York: Council on Foreign Relations, 1988), pp. 30–31.

19. Alan B. Durning, "Ending Poverty," in Lester R. Brown et al., *State of the World, 1990* (New York: Norton, 1990), p. 139.

20. David Francis, "World Reaps Benefits of Economic Reform," *Christian Science Monitor,* February 10, 1998.

21. John Koppisch, "Lessons from the Fastest Growing Nation: Botswana?" *Business Week,* August 26, 2002, pp. 116, 118.

22. Ethan Kapstein, "Africa's Capitalist Revolution; Preserving Growth in a Time of Crisis," *Foreign Affairs*, 88, 4 (July/August 2009), p. 119.
23. Paul Theroux, *Dark Star Safari; Overland from Cairo to Capetown*. (New York:. Mariner Books, 2004). Theroux, citing many observations and anecdotal examples of the dysfunction of aid in the African nations he visited, also took umbrage at personal snubs and discourtesies from aid workers, some fellow Americans.
24. Wangari Maathai, *The Challenge for Africa* (New York: Pantheon Books, 2009), Chapter 4, "Aid and the Dependency Syndrome"; and George Ayittey, *Africa Unchained* (New York: Palgrave Macmillan, 2005), p. 155.
25. Dambisa Moyo, *Dead Aid; Why Aid Is Not Working and How There Is a Better Way for Africa* (New York: Farrar, Straus and Giroux, 2009). See also Gemma Ware, "Aid in Crisis; Who is Helping Whom?" *The Africa Report*, April–May 2009, pp. 24–27. This article includes a brief interview with Ms. Moyo.
26. "Keeping Africa's Turnaround on Track," *The Washington Post*, April 9, 2009, p. A 17.
27. Mike Jensen, "Making the Connection: Africa and the Internet," *Current History*; reprinted in ed. E. Jeffress Ramsey, *Global Studies: Africa* (Guilford, CT: Dushkin, 2001), p. 196.
28. World Watch Institute and Population Action International, *Human Development Report 1997* (New York: New York University Press, 1997), p. 103. The situation is little changed more than a decade later.
29. R. W. Johnson, "A Brutal Brush with Gun Law in South Africa," *The Sunday Times* (London), September 6, 1998.
30. Karin Bruillard, "In Niger Delta, Uneasy Peace as Rebel Disarmament Date Nears," *The Washington Post*, July 27, 2009, p. A13.
31. "Nigerian Justice Minister Shot Dead at Home," *The Washington Post*, December 25, 2001.
32. Jan Raath, "Mugabe's Grace and Favours," *The Times* (London), July 18, 1998.
33. These grim statistics and many others on the ravages of the epidemic and the effort to combat it in Africa can be found at UNAID's Web site, www.unaids.org. UNAIDS is a joint UN program created to fight the global epidemic.
34. In Zimbabwe, for example, where as much as 25 percent of all adults may be infected with HIV, average life expectancy, which was 62 in 1993, plummeted to less than 34 years by 2002. Of course, other factors besides AIDS, such as famine, contributed to this disturbing decline.
35. *Blood Diamond*, Warner Brothers Pictures, an Edward Zwick film, 2006. Although a Hollywood fictional dramatization, this film partnered with Amnesty International and other NGOs to inform and provide a channel for action through its Web site. Ishmael Beah, *A Long Way Gone: Memoirs of a Boy Soldier* (New York: Sarah Crichton Books; Farrar, Straus and Giroux, 2007). This lucid book, written by a rehabilitated child soldier brought to the United States, has received considerable critical acclaim and is probably the best first-person account of this issue.
36. See, for example, Douglas Farah, "War and Terror Inc.," *The Washington Post*, September 23, 2007, pp. B1 and B4; on Russian arms entrepreneur Viktor Bout, purportedly "The world's premier gray-market arms provider" and dubbed "Africa's merchant of death" by a senior British cabinet minister because of Bout's many sales to dictators and rebel leaders there.
37. Michael Renner, "An Epidemic of Guns," *Worldwatch Magazine*, July/August 1998, p. 25. Most of the specifics in this "Flashpoint" come from the same article.
38. Michael Renner, "Small Arms, Big Impact: The Next Challenge of Disarmament," *Worldwatch Paper 137*, October 1997, p. 34.

39. Ban Ki-moon, "What I Saw in Darfur: Untangling the Knots of a Complex Crisis," *The Washington Post*, September 14, 2007, p. A13.
40. Mohammed Mamdani, "The International Criminal Court's Case against the President of Sudan: A Critical Look," *Journal of International Affairs* 62, 2 (Spring/Summer 2009), pp. 85–92.
41. Stephanie McCrummen, "Ethiopian Opposition Figures Get Life Terms in Widely Faulted Case," *The Washington Post*, July 17, 2007, p. A17.
42. Karin Brulliard, "U.S. Outreach on Rough Seas off Western Africa; Naval Effort Seeks to Build Stability, Trust in Strategic Region," *The Washington Post*, May 21, 2009, p. A8.
43. This staggering figure cannot be verified because access to the remote areas of the conflict by outside observers has been impossible, and many of the deaths have resulted from disease and famine related to the conflict, rather than from actual combat. Regardless of the exact figure, few Americans are aware of the enormity of this tragedy, a situation that Ted Koppel's ABC *Nightline* program had hoped to correct in September 2001 through a five-part series titled "Still in the Heart of Darkness." Unfortunately, the last four parts of the broadcast were preempted by the September 11 terrorist attacks, but the series finally aired in late January 2002.
44. Stephanie McCrummen, "Prevalence of Rape in E. Congo Described as Worst in World," *The Washington Post*, September 9, 2007, p. A19.
45. Sudarsan Raghavan, "After Shattering Civil War, Liberians See Hope at Polls," *The Washington Post*, September 9, 2005, pp. B-1, 8.
46. Susan E. Rice, "The Africa Battle," *The Washington Post*, December 11, 2001.
47. Ann Scott Tyson, "U.S. Pushes Anti-Terrorism in Africa," *The Washington Post*, July 26, 2005, pp. A1 and A14. The color photograph accompanying this front-page feature story shows U.S. Special Forces trainers using GI Joe action figures to demonstrate tactics to Chadian troops.
48. Walter Pincus, "U.S. Africa Command Brings New Concerns," *The Washington Post*, May 28, 2007, p. A13.
49. Holly Barkhalter, "Blood on the Diamonds," *The Washington Post*, November 6, 2001, p. A23.
50. Stephen McCrummen, "A Better Life Beckons in Africa; U.S. Downturn Drives Immigrant Professionals Back Home," *The Washington Post*, May 26, 2009, p. A6.
51. The World Health Organization (WHO) has long recognized the value of treated mosquito nets in fighting the renewed scourge of malaria in Africa, but even the modest costs of the nets and the needed reapplications of insecticide can be daunting to Africans in poverty. To learn more about the growing phenomenon of the play pumps and to see one in action in South Africa, visit www.playpumps.org.
52. "Keeping Africa's Turnaround on Track," *The Washington Post*, April 9, 2009, p. A 17.

Asia

Joseph N. Weatherby

*And at the end of the fight is a tombstone white
with the name of the late deceased, and the
epitaph drear: "A fool lies here who tried to
hustle the East."*

RUDYARD KIPLING, 1892

INTRODUCTION TO ASIA

For almost 2,000 years, Westerners have looked to Asia. Here, the West has sought a source for luxury goods including spices, porcelain, tea, and silk. Since early times hardy adventurers like Marco Polo and Vasco da Gama have risked hardships and death to gain access to the wealth of Asia. During the past four centuries, profit has been the primary motivation for the rise of Western imperialism in Asia. As early as 1687 this aim was clearly expressed in directions sent to the East India Company's British agent in India. The company is quoted as ordering him to "establish such a polity of civil and military power and create and secure such a large revenue . . . as may be the foundation of a large, well-grounded sure English dominion in India for all time to come."[1]

Throughout most of this period, the West has also had good reason to fear the military power of Asia. On many occasions fierce warriors have ridden out of Asia to crush kingdoms, sack cities, and take slaves.

Names like Attila the Hun, Genghis Khan, and Tamerlane still strike fear in the hearts of Europeans hundreds of years after their invasions took place. When the adventurer *Marco Polo* met Kublai Khan in 1275, the Khan's empire stretched from Korea to Hungary.

It was not until the Europeans developed efficient ships and effective guns that the military dominance of Asia was broken. Technology allowed Western imperialists to dominate large parts of Asia for almost 500 years. Hilaire Belloc's nineteenth-century comment about Africa could also be applied to Western imperialism then taking place in Asia. He is quoted as saying, "Whatever happens, we have got the Maxim Gun and they have not."[2]

Much of the story of modern Asia has been one of the Western search for wealth followed by imperialism that was made possible because of superior military technology. Now that technology is being challenged by the emerging powers of Asia.

Asserting that if the nineteenth century belonged to Britain and the twentieth century was American, the twenty-first century is likely to be Asian is not an understatement. Western investors are already recognizing that fact. In an August 2007 polling report, the majority of investors stated that they expected the United States to lose its economic leadership in the world within a decade. They expected China to bypass America during that period.[3]

A brief review of the information contained in Table 7.1 does much to illustrate the great variety of conditions in Other World Asia. Such diversity makes it impossible to analyze the region state by state. This chapter will briefly discuss geography and then focus on the major states of the area.

GEOGRAPHY

Where Is Asia?

Viewed from space, there is no Asia! Asia is simply a subdivision of a single Afro-Eurasian "island" that stretches from the Cape of Good Hope all the way to Cape Dezhnev (North Cape) in Russia. Within this great landmass, Asia forms the largest part (see Figure 7.1)

The separation of the continent of Asia from that of Africa and Europe is more cultural and historic than geographic. To identify Asia, most geographers arbitrarily draw a line along the Ural Mountains of Russia down through the Caspian Sea. The line then takes in Turkish Anatolia and the eastern shores of the Mediterranean and Red seas to include the Arabian Peninsula. This marks the western boundaries of Asia. All the lands east of that line into parts of the Pacific are considered to be Asian.

The Asian Continent is subdivided into five regions: Southwest Asia or Asia Minor, South Asia, Southeast Asia, East Asia, and Russian Asia or Siberia. Here, we have included Southwest Asia in the chapter on the Middle East and North Africa. Because, as it is defined in Chapter 1, Russia is not part of the Other World, Russian Asia is not discussed here. Admittedly, this definition of Asia is subjective. Places like the former Soviet Republics of Central Asia along with Afghanistan and Pakistan could have been put in several places. Here, the former

TABLE 7.1 Characteristics of Asian Countries

Country	Population (Millions)	Population Growth Rate (%)	Infant Mortality Rate (per 1,000 Live Births)	Population Under 15 Years of Age (%)	Life Expectancy (in Years)	Urban Population (%)	Literacy Rate (%)	Arable Land (%)	Per Capita GDP ($US)
Middle South									
Bangladesh	156.05	1.292	59.02	34.6	60.25	27	47.1	55.39	1,500
Bhutan	.691	1.267	49.36	30.3	66.13	35	47	2.3	5,600
India	1.166.079 Billion	1.548	30.15	31.1	69.89	29	61	48.83	2,800
Maldives	.396	-.168	29.53	22.3	73.97	38	96.3	13.33	5,000
Nepal	28.563	1.281	47.46	36.6	65.46	17	48.6	16.07	1,100
Pakistan	176.242	1.947	65.14	37.2	64.49	36	49.9	24.44	2,600
Sri Lanka	21.324	.904	18.57	23.9	75.14	15	90.7	13.96	4,300
South East									
Brunei	.388	1.759	12.27	26.6	75.45	75	92.7	2.08	53,100
Myanmar	48.137	.783	47.61	25.3	63.39	33	89.8	14.92	1,200
Cambodia	14.492	1.765	54.79	32.6	62.1	22	73.6	20.44	2,000
Indonesia	240.271	1.136	29.97	28.1	70.76	52	90.4	11.03	3,900
Laos	6.843	2.316	77.82	40.8	56.68	31	68.7	4.01	2,100
Malaysia	25.715	1.723	15.87	31.4	73.29	70	88.7	5.46	15,300
Philippines	97.976	1.957	20.56	35.2	71.09	65	92.6	19	3,300
Singapore	4.657	.998	2.31	14.4	81.98	100	92.5	1.47	52,000
Thailand	65.905	.615	17.63	20.8	73.1	33	92.6	27.54	8,500
Vietnam	86.967	.977	22.88	24.9	71.58	28	90.3	20.14	2,800
East Asia									
China	1.338.612 Billion	.655	20.25	19.8	73.47	43	90.1	14.86	6,000
Korea, N	22.665	.42	51.34	21.3	63.81	63	99	22.4	1,700
Korea, S	48.508	.266	4.26	16.8	78.72	81	97.9	19	2,400
Comparison States									
Japan	127.078	-.191	2.79	13.5	82.12	66	99	11.64	34,200
Belgium	10.414	.094	4.44	16.1	79.22	97	99	27.42	37,500
Italy	58.126	-.047	5.51	13.5	80.2	68	98.4	26.41	31,000

Source: CIA World Factbook, 2009.

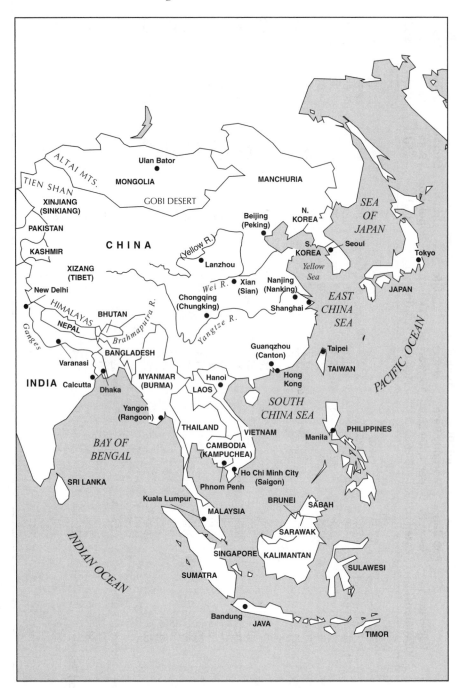

FIGURE 7.1 Political and Physical Characteristics of Other World Asia

Soviet Asian Republics and Afghanistan are discussed in Chapter 9. Because of Japan's unique history of development, it is not considered an Other World state. For our purposes, Other World Asia includes Pakistan as part of South Asia. Southeast Asia and East Asia make up the remaining portions of this chapter.

What Is Other World Asia?

Even limited to South, Southeast, and East Asia, the continent is the world's largest. As might be expected, the land is both physically and climatically complex. Here, there are high mountain ranges, important passageways, vast deserts, tropics, and important rivers. In terms of human geography, for thousands of years important civilizations have thrived in both China and India. Until about 500 years ago, China was arguably the most advanced civilization in the world.

SOUTH ASIA   Most of South Asia is part of a peninsula that stretches from the Himalayas to the southern borders of India. Only Sri Lanka is outside this peninsula. In the north are found the world's highest mountains, with the famous Mount Everest soaring to a height of 29,028 feet. These mountains are part of a continuous highland region stretching west to Switzerland. Here, the range includes the Hindu Kush and the Karakorum separating Pakistan, Afghanistan, and India before becoming the Himalayas of Nepal and Butan. The mountain ranges have made travel in this region difficult.

The Great Deccan Plateau of India lies south of these mountains. This large tableland makes up most of the peninsula. The central parts of the plateau have arid conditions. Below the mountains of the eastern and western Ghats lies a coastal area with tropical forests.

Both India and Pakistan have great river systems that support some major areas of population. The Ganges is considered to be a sacred river by Indian Hindus. Rising in the Himalayas, the river flows past the great cities of Allahabad and Varanasi for 1,560 miles before joining the Brahmaputra to reach the Bay of Bengal. The Indus headwaters are in Tibet. The river flows for 1,800 miles through Jammu and Kashmir into Pakistan, where it eventually reaches the Arabian Sea. The Indus has a number of hydroelectric and irrigation systems that are a source of power for Pakistan. The control of some of these systems has been a source of conflict between India and Pakistan since they were granted independence in 1947.

The major cities of South Asia are Karachi, Pakistan (12,130,000), and Islamabad, Pakistan (780,000). India, the second most populous state in the world, has a number of great cities including Mumbai (Bombay; 18,978,000), Kolkata (Calcutta; 14,767,000), Delhi (15,926,000), and Hyderabad (6,376,000).

SOUTHEAST ASIA   Southeast Asia is the land that lies to the east of India and to the south of China. Most of the climate is tropical monsoon. This means that there is a wet and a dry season. The trees are typical of a warm, humid climate, with palm trees and bamboo common. Rice is grown almost everywhere and is a staple in most of Southeast Asian diets.

The terrain of the region is complex. Mountains separate river valleys, with most people living in the deltas of the region's principal rivers. Southeast Asia has six major river systems: the Brahmaputra, the Irrawaddy, the Salween, the Chao Phraya, the Mekong, and the Hong (Red).

Southeast Asia is a region with large cities. Major Southeast Asian cities include Dhaka with a population of 13,485,000 and Chittagong (4,529,000) in Bangladesh, Rangoon (4,880,000) in Myanmar, Bangkok (6,704,000) in Thailand, and Ho Chi Minh City (5,314,000) and Hanoi (4,378,000) in Vietnam. Finally, Singapore is a city with a population of 4,436,000.

EAST ASIA Other World East Asia is made up of China and Korea. Of these, China is by far the most important. China is the world's most populous and third-largest state in area. One out of every five people on the planet is Chinese. China may be divided into six parts: China, the lands to the east and south of the Great Wall; Manchuria; Inner Mongolia; Sinkiang; Tibet; and Taiwan. Today Taiwan is held by the Nationalist Chinese who were driven from the mainland in *1949*. However, most Chinese in both Taiwan and on the mainland consider Taiwan to be part of "greater" China.

As might be expected, China has a complex geography. High mountains, deserts, and endless forests surround China, except along the 4,000-mile east coast. All of this has contributed to China's historic isolation from the states to the north and west.

In the west the Tibetan Plateau reaches heights of 12,000 feet. The part called Sinkiang (Xinjiang) is an isolated flat land surrounded by mountains. It is dry land inhabited by Turkic-speaking peoples. Here are located some of the world's highest mountains. Much of this region is underpopulated because it is too cold, too dry, too high, and too remote.

The northeast includes Inner Mongolia and Manchuria. This area has cold, long winters. Manchuria was the site of the puppet-state called Manchukuo. Established by the Japanese in 1932, Manchukuo served as a cover for the Japanese occupation of Manchuria and the later invasion of the Chinese heartland. While it existed, the last surviving member of the Manchu Dynasty, Henry Pu Yi, ruled Manchukuo. With the defeat of Japan in World War II, Manchukuo was abolished and China reestablished control. Today Manchuria is known for agriculture, mining, and manufacturing.

Most people live in the Chinese heartland. Although there are many cities here, most people live in the valleys of China's great rivers, the Huang Ho (Yellow), the Yangtze, and the Xi. Two of these rivers, the Huang Ho and the Yangtze, rise in the same area as the Mekong and Brahmaputra. Finally, the Xi is not important because of its length, which is only about 300 miles; rather, it is an important source of river commerce between the great city of Guangzhou and the Macao-Hong Kong areas. Once known as the Pearl, this river was one of the entry points for European imperialists during the nineteenth century.

About 32 percent of China's 1.2 billion people live in urban areas. China has more megacities than any other Other World Asian state. The largest and the most important cities are in order of size: Shanghai (14,987,000), Beijing (11,106,000), Tianjin (9,166,000), Hong Kong (7,206,000), Chongqing (4,900,000), Shenyang (4,828,000), and Guangzhou (3,893,000). The former Portuguese colonial city, Macao, has a population of only 481,000.

OTHER ASIAN NAMES   In Asia different names have been used to describe regions or the continent as a whole during different historic periods. Two examples are the *Orient* and the *Far East.*

THE ORIENT   In ancient times, the Latin root word *Orient* referred to the rising of the sun. Gradually, the word came to mean eastern lands. At times, it could mean anything to the east of Venice. During the eighteenth and nineteenth centuries, Europeans thought that anything along the eastern coast of the Mediterranean to the Pacific to be the Orient. So in old Constantinople (Istanbul), one could cross from "the West to the Orient" while remaining in the city, by crossing the Bosporus Strait. Today, the term *Orient* is usually used to refer to East Asia.

FAR EAST   The *Far East* is simply a designation given to the general area of East Asia by Western imperialists. Like the terms *Near East* and *Middle East,* the term *Far East* designates the distance from the colonial capitals in Europe. Today this term is considered to be offensive to some nationalists.

RELIGION IN ASIA

As might be expected in a region so large, Asia has a complex religious heritage. There are at least five major religions or philosophies that have mass appeal. The major sects of Asia are Buddhism, Confucianism, Daoism (Taoism), Hinduism, and Islam. In addition to these major faiths, a number of others are of local importance.

Buddhism

Both a religion and a philosophy, *Buddhism* was founded by an Indian prince, Gautama, around 550 B.C. Today there are more than 385 million Buddhists worldwide.[4] Buddhism is an acquired rather than a revealed religion like Christianity and Islam. Buddhists view life as a cycle of tribulation. The aim of the believer is to overcome life's suffering through following a series of steps or paths to reach nirvana. To the Buddhist, nirvana is a state of liberation from earthly desires. Buddhists also believe in reincarnation based on one's previous behavior. Although Buddhism began in India, the modern religion has the largest numbers of believers elsewhere. Centers of Buddhist worship are located in Sri Lanka, Tibet, China, and Southeast Asia.

Confucianism

Confucius was born around the same time as Buddha, 551 B.C. He was concerned with how society should be arranged. His ideas of social order have played an important part in the administration of Chinese society for over 2,000 years. Although *Confucianism* was originally a philosophy, temples and a ritual had developed by the first century A.D. Many emperors even proclaimed Confucianism as a state religion. Confucianism declined because of its association with the old imperial regime. Under Mao, Confucian temples were destroyed and believers severely persecuted. In recent years, however, the government of the

People's Republic has been more tolerant of this traditional Chinese system of belief. At the present time there are 6.4 million Confucians.

Daoism (Taoism)

Founded by Latose in the sixth century B.C., like Confucianism, *Daoism* was not supposed to be a religion but a way of finding peace in solitude. Later writers developed an elaborate ritual and built temples around what became the Daoist religion. Over time Daoism involved alchemy, magic, ghosts, saints, and gods. One major aim was to find the secret of immortality. Daoism has absorbed practices from both Buddhism and Confucianism. As a native Chinese religion, Daoism has had a great influence on art and literature. Daoists have survived revolution, Communism, and the modern world to maintain a small foothold in modern China.

Hinduism

Originally a religion of India, Hinduism today has an estimated 837,262,000 believers worldwide, making it larger than either Buddhism or Confucianism. Hinduism is one of the world's oldest religions, reaching back 4,000 years. It has no founder and recognizes numerous traditions and gods, making Hinduism a religion of great diversity. Most Hindus would emphasize that while using different paths, they strive to attain liberation for the soul from a series of lifetimes. The ultimate goal of this cycle of reincarnation is to achieve a purity and union with God. One of the features of Hinduism has been the emergence of a caste system that includes four classes: priests, rulers, peasants, and artisans. Sometimes called a fifth class, the untouchables have been discriminated

The Ganges: The river is of great religious significance. Here at Varanasi, Hindus bathe in its sacred waters.   *Source: EARL HUFF*

against since early times. Author Stanley Wolpert has described the emergence of the untouchables class in India in the following way: "In all probability the sub-class of untouchables emerged in the late Aryan age, recruited first perhaps from those . . . who performed tasks that were considered 'unclean' such as the work of tanners, associated with animal carcasses, and that of sweepers, especially among the ashes of cremation grounds."[5] Although officially outlawed in employment in modern India, the caste system still remains a social feature of Hindu life.

Islam

The basic ideas of Islam are discussed in some detail in Chapter 8. Islam became an important force in South Asia through invasion in the sixteenth century. Traders along *the Silk Road* spread the religion into China. Today there are 869 million Muslims living in Asia. The most important Muslim majority states are Afghanistan, Bangladesh, Indonesia, and Pakistan. However, there are large Muslim minorities in India, China, and the Philippines.

CASE STUDIES

1. The People's Republic of China: The Dragon

The History of Old China

Many in China place an emphasis on fate. People living in China during the past century and a half would be quick to point out that fate has not been kind to them during this period.

In its preface, a Chinese publication states their frustration in the following way:

> The year 1840, the gate of feudal China was opened by the rumble of gunfire in the Sino-British Opium War, turning the country into a semi colonial and semi feudal society that lasted for more than a century.

Writing about the same subject, the author states further:

> Heavy is the heart whenever looking back to this period of history: The corrupted rulers, the endless wars, the slowly developed economy, the people in deep distress, and the foreign policies humiliating the country and forfeiting its sovereignty.[6]

During the nineteenth century, China fought and lost the so-called *Opium Wars*. In these conflicts, Chinese authorities attempted to stop the importation of opium, which was being used by British businessmen to pay for their purchases of tea and other luxury goods. In 1860, during one of these conflicts, the British burned the Emperor's Beijing summer palace in retaliation for the Chinese execution of Western hostages.[7] In 1900, a Nationalist group called the Society of Righteous and Harmonious Fists, or Boxers, moved against foreign missionaries, businessmen, and diplomats in China. The Chinese leadership attempted to take advantage of the Boxer uprising to oust foreign interests from China. The humiliating defeat of the Boxers resulted in a fatal weakening of the imperial government, leading to its complete collapse in 1911.

After the empire, China degenerated into a land of warlords and conflict, culminating in the famous civil war between the Communists and the Nationalists. That war began in 1927 and did not end until the final defeat of the Nationalist forces in 1949. To make matters worse, the Japanese forces took advantage of Chinese disunity to occupy Manchuria in 1931. It was there that they established the satellite state, Manchukuo. In 1937, the Japanese invaded China proper. They did not leave China until the Japanese surrender in 1945.

The civil war between the Chinese Communists and Nationalists continued until the Communists' victory in 1949. The leader Chiang Kai-shek took the surviving Nationalists to the island of Formosa, setting up a dispute over the island's sovereignty that continues to the present day. The civil war and World War II cost untold millions of Chinese lives. These conflicts also set back Chinese economic development for a generation or more.

New China Under Mao

> We communists never conceal our political views. Definitely and beyond all doubt, our future or maximum program is to carry China forward to socialism and communism.[8]
>
> Mao Zedong

In 1949, the Chinese Communists under the leadership of Mao Zedong (Mao Tse-Tung) were able to unify the mainland under one rule for the first time in half a century. Early on, Mao had recognized that the Chinese experience was different from that of Russia. The strength of the party was in the peasants of the countryside, not the urban proletariat! Mao argued that in "semi-colonial and semi-feudal" China, "the broad peasant masses" had simply "risen to fulfill their historic mission to overthrow the rural feudal power." He further stated that, "Every revolutionary comrade should know that the national revolution requires a profound change in the countryside."[9]

With the arrival of Chinese Communist rule on October 1, 1949, struggle and pain for the average person in China did not end. During the rule of Mao, at least three traumatic events overshadowed any accomplishments of the regime. These horrible trials for the Chinese people were the Korean War, the Great Leap Forward, and the Cultural Revolution.

China entered the Korean War against the United States when 2.3 million "volunteers" crossed into Korea on October 25, 1950. Using the slogan "Resist America, Aid Korea," the Chinese fought the United Nations (UN) forces to a stalemate along the 38th parallel until a truce was signed in July of 1953.[10]

The human cost of this conflict was terrible for both the Chinese and the Koreans. Geoffrey Stern has put the losses this way:

> In a war of firepower against manpower, the U.S. put Chinese and North Korean deaths at 1.5 million. If this seems incredible, there are Chinese sources which put it even higher.[11]

The *Great Leap Forward* (1958–1960) was a disaster for the Chinese economy. Mao and the party leadership attempted to bypass the traditional steps of the development process to create a modern industrial and agricultural state overnight. Planners in the cities ordered Chinese farmers to ignore traditional agricultural methods to create communes. Workers in the cities were told to industrialize in ways that were sometimes called "backyard steel mills" by detractors in the West. The result of this misadventure was famine in the countryside and economic disaster in the cities. Mao quietly abandoned this experiment in 1960.

What the Great Leap Forward did to the economy, the *Cultural Revolution* (1966–1976) did to Chinese civilization. This campaign began as an attempt by Mao to purge China of any opposition. It quickly spread to an attack on intellectuals, teachers, artists, professionals, and progressives not adhering to Mao's authority in the party. Before it ended with Mao's death, the Cultural Revolution had resulted in the imprisonment of thousands and the destruction of China's art and architecture.

China After Mao: The "Ka-Ching" Dynasty

To get rich is glorious.

Deng Xiaoping[12]

Deng Xiaoping was fond of the story of the black cat and the white cat to illustrate his change in the economic course of China. He would point out that the color of the cat did not matter so long as it caught the mouse. China was opened to the West for development when Deng began what became known as the second revolution in 1978. In 1979, he led a delegation to the United States with the purpose of increasing trade. In an ever-increasing process, Western business interests embraced the opportunity to do business with China.

To be sure, there have been setbacks in this development. The most serious event was the 1989 suppression of the pro-democracy movement in Tiananmen Square. However, China's admission to the World Trade Organization (WTO) and the selection of China to host the Olympic Games both signal that China will be a major economic player during the first half of the twenty-first century.

Deng's rule can be characterized as one that moved the economy away from the old Communist dogma and central planning toward a more modern free-market mechanism. However, as the Tiananmen Square tragedy demonstrated, he would not tolerate any political reforms that would set in motion a challenge to the rule of the Communist Party.

China today is a paradox. It is still a state controlled by the Communist Party. At the same time China has an economy that is rapidly becoming one of the most "freewheeling, rough and tumble" capitalist systems in the world! How can these two seemingly contradictory positions be reconciled? The position taken here is that the People's Republic is in the transitional stage of moving from a totalitarian to a one-party authoritarian state. In this case, twenty-first century China is following a course already largely completed on Taiwan. The outcome of this process may be something like fascist Spain during the final years of General Francisco Franco's rule. In this case the party will continue to hold on to power by opposing any organization or group that could evolve into a force that might challenge the party organization's grip on power. At the same time the economy will be left largely free to continue to grow at one of the world's fastest rates. Unlike other states in Asia, China is also insulated from world economic downturns because of a huge domestic market with unmet needs.

American companies have been quick to recognize the potential of the Chinese marketplace. In a statement made in 2005, Myron Brilliant, vice president for East Asia, U.S. Chamber of Commerce, said, "The United States ranked second among China's global trading partners in 2004 and China was again the third largest trading partner for the United States."[13] In 2007, China also ranked sixth in world exports behind only the Euro area, the United States, Germany, the United Kingdom, and Japan. This makes China a major world trade player in both exports and imports.[14]

The Silk Road: For centuries, the Silk Road was the only contact that the West had with China. Silks, gunpowder, rugs, and paper passed along this road to the West. This Chinese monument marks the beginning of the road.   Source: *Craig Arceneaux*

Although Chinese exports remain high, serious safety and quality issues emerged in 2007. The American toy maker Mattel was forced to recall a large number of toys made in China because they contained lead paint. Earlier, food products including fish were rejected by American officials because they failed to meet U.S. health standards. Much of China's new prosperity depends on exports mainly to the United States. If Chinese products, as a whole, become suspect, the Chinese economy could be in serious trouble.

To be sure, there are potential sources of unrest. Perhaps the greatest threat to stability is the disparity of income between rural and urban China. However, the euphoria generated by China's admission to the WTO and being selected to host the Olympic Games should buy the authorities time to stabilize the situation before serious problems can develop.

Addressing the problem of inequality, Joseph Caron, Canadian Ambassador to China, said, "There are ongoing debates on change and stability in China." He then stated that,

> Stability is linked to representative institutions and accountability, rule of law and good governance. On the ground, at the level of individuals, this means rights and individual freedoms, equity, justice and probity, the free flow of information and the end of endemic corruption. It also means freedom from undue influence by those in power.[15]

Anyone who has not been to China within the past 10 years cannot imagine the kind of growth that has occurred in places such as Hong Kong, Shanghai, and Beijing. Even provincial towns such as Suzhou and Tai'an have modern high-rise buildings. In China, the Communist Party is attempting to expand economically while keeping a tight grip on all forms of political expression. The question remains, can a modern economy develop while ignoring political expression?

Ambassador Caron also pointed out that, "Among the top twenty developed countries in the world, no country has achieved and sustained its standards of living without respect for individual rights, rule of law, and representative institutions."[16]

Some of China's worst fears occurred in July 2009 with an outbreak of Muslim riots in the Chinese interior. These riots followed similar ones in Tibet that occurred in 2008. The 2009 unrest was the most far reaching since the army ended the Tiananmen Square protest in 1989. These new riots demonstrated to the government that there are still large pockets of unrest in the countryside.[17]

What the Chinese citizens want is stability. Will they be content if the Party remains so long as it provides the kind of environment that will allow them to enjoy the material benefits of the modern world? What they fear is the kind of uncertainty and chaos that occurred with the collapse of Communism in Russia. No one can predict whether this model of political control and economic openness will succeed.

Globalization: Disco sign outside the Hard Rock Café in Tai'in China. *Source: Joe Weatherby*

China and the World Economic Downturn

As stated earlier, China's large, unmet domestic market largely insulates the market system from outside forces. To be sure, the export market has been hurt by the world recession. Thousands of workers have been displaced as their factories closed.

Nevertheless, the economy continues to grow because of a thriving domestic market. The government claims that the overall economy could grow by as much as 8 percent in 2009. Early signs show that this forecast could be accurate.

In January 2009 new vehicle sales in China surpassed those in the United States. In July, the Chinese stock exchange exceeded that of Japan's stock market in value.

Although these numbers will not be sustained for the entire year, they are indicative of what can be expected from China in the future.

Chinese Foreign Policy

In addition to its domestic problems, China also has two difficult security problems that must eventually be dealt with. First and foremost is the problem of a prosperous, democratic Taiwan that might make moves toward formal independence. Here, the mainland party leadership must respond to the concerns of mainland Nationalists who oppose any talk of separation while avoiding provoking the United States into resuming a formal military backing of Taiwan.

A nuclear North Korea is another thorny foreign policy issue for China. Here, a desperate "saber-rattling" Korean leadership could force the introduction of nuclear arms into Japan and South Korea. The specter of a forward-deployed American nuclear force projecting a viable presence off the Chinese coast as the result of Korea's behavior provides additional headaches for Chinese planners. Either of these two issues could resume China's isolation and cause a strengthening to all the economic gains recently made. This could cause social unrest and result in the downfall of the current regime.

2. India: The Elephant

Although Vasco da Gama opened the European route to India, it was the English who were to exercise primary rule over the subcontinent. At first, European penetration of this part of the world was hindered by the previously mentioned Treaty of Tordesillas, which had divided the colonial world between Portugal and Spain. After the Protestant Reformation, however, Holland and England were no longer restrained from challenging the Portuguese and the Spanish monopoly of Asian trade.

Few could have imagined that when Captain William Hawkins sailed his flagship, *Hector*, to India, on the East India Company's first visit, the English would grow in power until they ruled all of southern Asia! The English presence in the region lasted from the *Hector*'s arrival in 1608 until India and Pakistan gained full independence in 1947.[18]

The English arrived in India only a year after the founding of Jamestown in 1607. However, they stayed in India more than 350 years. The British impact on Indian culture is profound. Today India is the world's largest English-speaking nation. Although there are many Indian dialects, English is still the only universally understood language. The schools, universities, hospitals, courts, and even government have an English base.

The British East India Company came to India solely for trade when it established its first factory at Surat in 1612. The first century of British trade in India was accompanied by struggles with both Indian and European leaders. To British thinking, this situation required a military response. This period resulted in the conversion of the East India Company from a mere trading company into the de facto rulers of India. This situation of private company colonial rule was to last until Queen Victoria appointed the first Viceroy of India in 1858.

Under British colonial rule, nineteenth-century India achieved a measure of economic development. In the cities, the emergence of an Indian industrial class was well underway. The British also brought new lands under irrigation, thereby increasing agriculture.

A side effect of this activity was the emergence of a Western-educated Indian middle class. These "new Indians" demanded a greater role in political affairs. In 1885, the self-appointed Indian Congress movement first met to discuss social and political issues. In a manner not unlike the earlier American Continental Congress, these educated Hindu Indians demanded reforms from Britain, not revolution. However, by 1906, a more radicalized national congress was demanding nothing less than self-rule for India. By 1920, even relatively pro-British Indians such as Mohandas Gandhi were openly and actively opposing continued British rule. Gandhi's nonviolent resistance movement provided a base for mass support that complemented the political efforts of the Indian National Congress.

In the same year that the Indian National Congress first demanded self-rule, another organization of nearly equal significance was formed. The Muslim League demanded that the British create a separate Muslim state in Pakistan.

During World War II, India supported the British by sending large numbers of troops to fight for the Empire. At the same time, the Germans and the Japanese tried to foment rebellions in India by attempting to recruit Indian prisoners of war into Nationalist armies of liberation. The Japanese movement was called the Indian National Army and was led by Subhas Chandra Bose. The Germans sponsored a movement called the Free Indian Legion. Although these movements may have had as many as 40,000 volunteers, it is believed that no more than 7,000 ever were committed to combat. These Nationalist movements were discredited by the defeat of fascism and became only a footnote to the history of World War II.[19]

As World War II ended, Britain reluctantly recognized its inability to continue governing South Asia. It announced that it was going to shortly withdraw from the region. In February 1947, amid growing Hindu–Muslim violence, the British Labor government announced a withdrawal date. The Hindus under Mohandas Gandhi and Muslims led by Mohammed Ali Jinnah tried but failed to reach agreement on the establishment of a single Indian state. In August 1947, British India was divided into a Muslim Pakistan and a majority Hindu India. Because large minorities of Hindus and Muslims were caught on the wrong side of the new borders, a population exchange became necessary. During this process, 16 million people were forced to move, while another 500,000 people died in the religious violence that followed independence. This period provokes anger in both India and Pakistan more than 50 years after partition.

The creation of two states did not end communal strife. Just as conflicts between Muslims and Hindus were instrumental in the division of British India into two states, later tensions between the Punjabi of West Pakistan and the Bengalis of East Pakistan resulted in the 1971 creation of a separate state in the east called Bangladesh. Pakistan remains as a Muslim state in the West.

India became free of British rule in 1947. The Chinese mark their independence from colonialism with the establishment of the People's Republic in 1949. At that time most observers would have considered India to be ahead of China. Since that time China has endured major wounds that have resulted in the deaths of millions. Despite these setbacks, why is China economically ahead of "democratic" India today? Several answers should be apparent to the reader. First, China abandoned its state planning in favor of moving toward an open free-market system starting in 1979.

Although late to start, in 1991, India began to reform its creaking, inefficient Socialist system. To be sure, the governmental institutions have not been as friendly to foreign businessmen as China. In spite of hurdles, India has managed to become one of the world's fastest-growing economies. India has expanded from the well-known electronic industry to many areas of high-end manufacturing. Indians are eager to trumpet the recent purchase of British Steel by the Tata Steel Group as an example of the new economic power being developed by the former colony.[20]

India still has a long way to go before challenging China. The per-capita income of India is only one-half that of China. India is still ranked by the World Bank as 90th out of 146 countries on the corruption index.[21] It will be almost impossible to make lasting improvements in India before these problems are addressed.

There are also some positive signs in the domestic economy. India's purchasing power is expected to bypass that of Japan in the future. The explosive birth rate has been reduced to 1.7 percent from a high of 2.2 percent only a few years ago.[22]

The primary difference between the economies of India and China might not be noticeable at first glance. China's economy is based on supplying the developed world with low-cost finished goods. India's economy has concentrated on supplying goods to the domestic market. Most observers believe that India's growth is more isolated from world downturns than that of China.

India's primary domestic economic problem is to broaden the benefits of the new economy to reach more and more of the "left out people." It is in the area of providing economic opportunities to the Indian masses that the Indian economy will ultimately succeed or fail.

The other great internal problem in India is, like it was in 1947, sectarianism. In recent years, a Hindu movement called the "Saffron Tide," the Hindu color, came into prominence. The Hindu Nationalist Bharatiya Janata Party became a rival to the old Congress Party as the ruler of India. Like European Nationalists of the 1930s, the BJP focused on "scapegoats" to gain most Hindu support. The more than 100 million Indian Muslims were particularly targeted, but the movement also singled out Christians and Jews.

After several years of BJP rule, a new coalition called the United Progressive Alliance (UPA) dominated by the old Congress Party gained power. In new elections held in 2009, the Congress-led Alliance almost gained a majority in the Indian parliament. To many, this election confirmed that the old politics of religion and caste, advocated by the BJP, were over.

In foreign affairs, India has been moving away from close political ties with China and Russia toward an association with the United States. President Bush visited India and formalized an agreement to aid in the development of atomic energy for peaceful purposes there. India's moves are seen as an effort to have the United States provide a counterbalance to the ties that China has with Pakistan.

On the domestic front, Congress Party leader Sonia Gandhi recently said, "We are out to repair India's secular fabric." She then added, "We are proud that we are once more a society that celebrates its diversity, led by a government that stands by its commitment to defeating prejudice and discrimination."[23]

Finally, the Indian political system is democratic in name only. Political offices are regularly bought and sold. The courts operate with a system of "rule by law," not "rule of law," making judges and high officials above the law. There is widespread police corruption, rendering many personal freedoms, including the "freedom from fear," meaningless. Until the "world's largest democracy" is ready to address these issues in a straightforward manner, there will be little chance for India to become a major player in world affairs.

India and the World Economic Downturn

Leaders in India, like those in China, are optimistic about the economic future. Recent polls of business leaders ranked India third in world consumer confidence.[24] One might ask why there is such a positive feeling about the economy? First, only a small part of Indian gross domestic product (GDP) relies on exports to survive. About half of India's production is to fulfill domestic needs. For example, India has surpassed South Korea as Asia's third largest vehicle market. With the introduction of the new Tata Nano, this market will allow large portions of the Indian population formerly not served to purchase an affordable automobile.

The recent election victory of the Congress Party–led alliance has encouraged business. The Indian stock market surged in value on news of the Alliance victory.

Finally, Indian banking has remained stable. The banks had little exposure to the problems that faced banks in the developed world. It is now up to the new government to develop policies that will capitalize on the economic advantages that India has.[25]

3. The Four Asian Tigers: Taiwan, Hong Kong, Singapore, and South Korea

Introduction

With one exception—Thailand—the nations of Southeast and East Asia share a common past: colonization by outside powers. Burma, Malaysia, Singapore, Brunei, and Hong Kong were ruled by the British; Indonesia was Dutch; Indochina (Vietnam, Cambodia, and Laos) was French; the Philippines were first under Spanish rule and then under the Americans. In both the nineteenth and twentieth centuries, parts of China were controlled by foreign powers, including Britain, Russia, Germany, Japan, Portugal, and the United States. In the twentieth century, both Korea and Taiwan were occupied by Japan. Typically, boundaries drawn by the colonial powers paid little attention to the ethnic makeup of the lands they administered, so people with well-established cultural identities were often divided. Just as often, diverse ethnic groups were combined into larger political units. This ethnic mix was often complicated by the addition of large Chinese and Indian minorities who were either transported or encouraged to settle there by the colonial powers. Consequently, when the regions were granted independence, the newly formed states often lacked the sense of nationhood in terms of a nation-state. Cohesion, when it existed, was often nothing more than the common impulse to rid the region of the taint of colonial rule. In the process of forming modern entities, these new Asian nations have strongly opposed any outside pressures as interventions into their rights as sovereign states. The memory of the humiliation of colonial rule dies hard. As author Aeba Takanori has put it,

> The negative perception of foreign control remains as if explosive magma flows within the hearts of the people in these regions.[26]

Thus far, four states have been able to channel a new self-confidence in their ability to compete with the best that the developed world now has to offer. Called the Asian Tigers, these states can serve as models for their neighbors still wallowing in anger and self-pity. Their ability to survive the current world economic downturn will test their own economic permanence.

Taiwan

On the mainland, Taiwan is called Chinese Taipei. The confusion over the island's name recalls one of the world's longest-lasting disputes: over which China rules China. Both the People's Republic of China (Communist) and Taiwan (Nationalist) officially endorse the concept that Taiwan is part of China. After more than 50 years, they still disagree over who is the legitimate ruler of China.

When 2 million members of the defeated Nationalists (Kuomintang) fled from the mainland to China's smallest province, Formosa (Taiwan), in 1949, few observers gave them a chance for long-term survival. The United States, their principal supporter, was braced to abandon the Nationalists to their fate. However, when North Korea attacked South Korea in June 1950, the Nationalists received a "new lease on life." The Truman administration recognized that an active Nationalist movement could serve as a sufficient threat to the mainland to check Chinese intentions in Korea. The United

States placed elements of the Pacific Fleet between the mainland and the Nationalists, thus preventing an almost certain Communist occupation of the island.

Since the Korean War, Taiwan has not only survived but also prospered. Economically, the Republic of China's development has been remarkable. Taiwan's economy is made up of textiles, clothing, electronics, processed foods, and chemicals, along with agricultural products and fishing. This means that the average citizen of Taiwan earns as much or more than his counterpart in South Africa, Greece, Portugal, or the Czech Republic. *The Economist of London* Economic Freedom Index ranks Taiwan ahead of rival Japan.[27]

Politically, the Republic of China has evolved from an authoritarian state under martial law headed by the Nationalist Party, to a fairly open democracy where, for the first time, an opposition candidate was elected president in 2000. That president, Chen Shui-bian, was a fervent Nationalist who in the past opposed unification with the mainland. The fact that the Nationalist Party stepped aside and allowed him to take office was seen as a further move toward a more democratic society. Traditional politicians like their mainland counterparts advocated a one-China policy. They simply disagreed over who should run the "one China." The Communist government consistently offered to consider a one-China, two-systems formula similar to the one applied to Hong Kong.

In January 2008, legislative elections carried the old Kuomintang (KMT) Party to power. This could signal much closer ties with the mainland in the future.

Like their counterparts on the mainland, the leaders of Taiwan face a dilemma both politically and economically. Almost half of the Taiwanese people seem to favor more political contact with the People's Republic.

Economically, contact with the mainland is exploding. Since 2002 China has passed the United States as Taiwan's largest trading partner. In 2004, China accounted for 18 percent of Taiwan's foreign trade.[28] According to He Sizhong, director of the economic bureau of the Taiwan Bureau of Affairs of the State Council (PRC), Taiwan-funded businesses in China exceed 65,000. Contracted Taiwan investment in China is more than $82 billion (U.S.).[29]

Many members of the defeated Nationalist Party have grown to accept eventual reunification with the mainland. The United States has attempted to play an important role in resolving this conflict. In 1949, the Nationalists talked of retaking the mainland. Now they talk of defensive engagement with the mainland. The American role is to reassure the Taiwanese that they will remain militarily strong enough to deter an attack, but not so strong as to encourage more talk of independence. The main American hope is that economic integration will, over time, heal the bad feelings and suspicions on both sides, leading to a peaceful settlement.

Taiwan clearly has actually, if not legally, recognized independence. Taiwan maintains political separation while increasing economic integration with the mainland. It is in everyone's interest to continue to maintain the status quo with the "ideal of one China, two systems." The alternative to a peaceful evolution is almost too serious to contemplate. The leaders of the United States, the People's Republic, and the Republic of China have each made the danger of the situation abundantly clear.

In 2001, then President George W. Bush stated on a Cable News Network (CNN) broadcast that while he supported a one-China policy uniting China and Taiwan, the United States would do whatever it took to defend Taiwan from attack. In the same interview, he was quoted as saying, "We need a peaceful resolution. . . . Our nation will help Taiwan defend herself. . . ."[30] With a new president now in office, the American ability to balance the twenty-first century interests of the People's Republic of China and the Republic of China promises to be very interesting indeed.

Taiwan and the World Economic Downturn

Taiwan experienced a serious decline in business during 2008 and 2009. At first, experts predicted that the GDP of Taiwan would decline but still grow at around 2 percent. In January 2009, that forecast was changed to a no-growth GDP. By February, the forecast was revised again to show a negative GDP.

Taiwan's problem is similar to that found in other Asian Tigers, an economy largely based on exports. Without the large populations found in China and India to rely on for consumer purchases, Taiwan must attempt to ride out the downturn. Most economists don't see much improvement in Taiwan's economy before late 2010.

Hong Kong

The story of Hong Kong is one of the most interesting in Asia. When it was ceded to Great Britain by the Treaty of Nanjing in 1842, Hong Kong was a barren island. Before the British arrived, mainly fishermen and pirates had used the harbor. When it became British, Hong Kong's future was assured. Author Trea Wiltshire has described the British arrival in the following way,

> When Hong Kong became one of the spoils of the Opium War, merchant princes such as William Jardine and John Dent were quick to relocate.

Later the author states,

> The secure base enabled the merchants to form banks that would service these rapid developments of the colonial island and its Treaty Port Sisters. It also provided a convenient headquarters for the fledgling consular services that took root in each of the coastal outposts and for the British Army and Navy.[31]

The growth of Hong Kong as a British colony was accelerated by two events. In 1860, Kowloon and Stone Cutters Island were ceded to the colony by China's signing the Beijing Convention. In 1898, the New Territories, a large area adjacent to Kowloon, was leased to the colony for 99 years. The additions of land allowed the inhabitants to expand past the limits of Hong Kong Island.

During the twentieth century the colony prospered as a door to China until the Japanese occupation during World War II. The British reoccupied the colony in 1945.

Many feel that the greatest postwar event contributing to the growth of capitalist Hong Kong was the Communist victory over the mainland in 1949. Why can this be viewed as a positive event in Hong Kong? Simply stated, the Communist victory ended the dominance of Shanghai as China's window to the outside world.

After 1949, China's isolation allowed Hong Kong to become the "transshipment point" for most goods and services passing to and from China. Hong Kong became one of the world's leaders in container shipping and the manufacture of clothing, toys, calculators, radios, travel goods, handbags, and artificial flowers.

In the 1980s it became clear to the British that the lease on the new territories would not be renewed when it ended in 1997. After months of negotiation, the Chinese and the British agreed to Hong Kong's return to Chinese sovereignty under the "one China, two systems" arrangement. Under this arrangement, sovereignty would be transferred from Britain to China, but a great deal of autonomy would remain in the hands of the Hong Kong people for 50 years.

Thus far, one China, two systems has worked, but with mixed results. Economically, the two systems have been able to thrive side by side. Politically, Hong

Kong has had an often bumpy relationship with China. Politically, it is still possible for the U.S. Department of State to report,

> Hong Kong with a population of nearly 7 million remains an international city and one of the world's most open and free economies. Hong Kong residents enjoy a strong respect for the rule of law and civil liberties.[32]

The authorities in China, however, have recently questioned some of the "freewheeling" political protests that occur in the former British colony. Recently, China's President Hu Jintao compared Hong Kong to the more politically subdued Macau, saying that the people of Hong Kong "should summarize your experience, look for your shortcomings, and constantly raise your governance ability." This mild criticism masked the threat of a more heavy-handed Chinese involvement, should Hong Kong politics ever get out of hand.[33]

When the 1997 British handover took place, many businessmen assumed that Hong Kong would slip into economic decline. Even stalwarts like Jardine Matheson moved its corporate headquarters to Bermuda after a 170-year stay in the colony. The most optimistic observers believed that Hong Kong would be eclipsed by a resurgent Shanghai; they were all to be proved wrong!

In 2007 Hong Kong was listed first in the world on the index of economic freedom.[34] By 2009, the world economic downturn dropped the area to fourth behind first place Finland.[35]

Hong Kong and the World Economic Downturn

In 2008, Hong Kong's per capita GDP was $43,000 (U.S.) per year. This ranked Hong Kong GDP income with Switzerland and ahead of both Germany and the United Kingdom.

The year 2009 was bad for the territory. Almost all of Hong Kong's exports are re-exports from the mainland. The export-oriented trade for the first quarter of 2009 fell more than it had in more than 50 years. Mainland China is Hong Kong's largest trading partner. Most Chinese products destined for export are going to the United States. Few observers expect much improvement in Hong Kong's economy until the United States rebounds from its recession.

Thousands of Hong Kong businessmen have expanded into Chinese manufacturing located in centers near Hong Kong. Michael de Goiyer of Hong Kong Baptist University estimated that as many as 250,000 workers cross the border between China and Hong Kong every day.[36]

Hong Kong has been able to reinvent itself as one of Asia's most important centers for service. Today Hong Kong focuses on shipping, banking, and finance. The city is noted for rule of law, efficient service, and freedom from corruption. With exploding economic growth in China, Hong Kong could rival New York and London as financial centers within the coming years. Hong Kong also remains particularly advantaged to capitalize on the resources of China. It will continue to remain a major Asian Tiger in the twenty-first century.

Singapore

According to Dorothy Perkins, the name *Singapore* literally means "the lion city" when translated from the Indian Sanskrit.[37] Modern Singapore is one of the Asian Tigers. Situated at the end of the peninsula of Malaysia, this city-state of 4 million people is one of the world's most important trading centers. Because of its location at the mouth of the Strait of Malacca, which leads from the Indian Ocean, Singapore is called the Gateway to the Pacific.

Although the area now called Singapore had been a trading town in early times, it was only a loosely populated island when the Malacca Sultanate ceded it to the British East India Company in 1819. It was then that the company representative, Sir T. Stamford Raffles, founded the city of Singapore. In 1824, the trading post came under the control of the British government. It was to remain a British colony until 1942 when the Japanese captured it. The British reoccupied the island with the defeat of Japan in 1945. Singapore gained full independence from Britain in June 1959.

When the British first established Singapore as a trading post, few could have guessed that a century and a half later it would be one of the world's most important commercial centers. In 2008, this multicultural city-state had a per capita income of $52,000 U.S. The key to Singapore's success is more than just strategic geography. The political system is noted as paternalistic. Although a republic with free elections, the government keeps a tight hold on public order. The civil rights group, Reporters without Borders, ranks Singapore in the bottom fourth of countries on press freedom. Considering the diversity of Singapore's society both ethnically and religiously, this kind of control is understandable.

Singapore occupies a land area of only 255 square miles. Still, according to the *South China Morning Post,* Singapore ranks as the world's third highest on the Economic Freedom Index.[38] Observers have asked how a city-state with so few resources could become one of the world's centers for business. Kevin O'Conner, market analyst at CLSA Asia-Pacific Markets in Hong Kong replies, "They have to shape up to compete in the environment or die."[39]

Singapore has overcome its environment to create an investment-friendly atmosphere, making it a leader in corporate location, banking, technical manufacturing, and shipping. Past economic forecasts projected a growth rate around 6 percent.[40] Unfortunately, the world economic downturn has caused a decline in growth since those earlier forecasts were made.

Singapore and the World Economic Downturn

Even with Singapore's high per capita GDP, there are social stresses made worse by the economic downturn. Singapore is a multicultural society. Potential social problems made worse by the declining economy include religion, race, and jobs held by foreign workers. Singapore has attempted to overcome these stresses through a unique program called "Tri-partite Partners." This program is designed to unite government with businesses and workers to fairly share the burdens of the economic downturn.

Although many workers lost jobs in 2008 and 2009, more than 70 percent found new jobs within three months. Many workers are heartened that cuts came from all sectors, including foreign workers.[41] Most observers expect Singapore to bounce back economically in 2010. Singapore—not the United States or Japan—is the model for development currently being followed by the People's Republic of China. The Chinese hope to avoid the chaos of post-Communist Russia by keeping a tight hold on politics while letting a free-market economic system develop.

South Korea

Like the other Asian Tigers, Korea experienced both European and Asian colonial rule during the nineteenth and twentieth centuries. In 1900, Tsar Nicholas II ordered his troops into Northern China and Korea.[42] The Russian hold on these territories was strengthened by their participation in putting down the *Boxer Rebellion* in China. However, Russia lost everything when its troops were defeated in the Russo-Japanese War of 1904.

Japanese colonial rule was consolidated by 1910 when Japan annexed Korea. Korea was not to see the end of Japanese rule until their final defeat in World War II. At the Yalta Conference held in February 1945, the Allied Powers agreed to a number of secret provisions regarding Asia that were not made public until 1947. Among the Asian agreements was Russia's commitment to declare war on Japan within three months of the defeat of Japan. In return, Russia would get footholds in Manchuria and Korea to the 38th parallel. Hans Morgenthau graphically pointed out the continuing role that Korea has played in the great power struggle for Asia:

> The rivalry between Japan and Russia for control of Korea ended with the defeat of Russia in the Russo-Japanese War of 1904–1905. Japanese control of Korea, thus firmly established, was terminated with the defeat of Japan in World War II. From then on, the United States replaced Japan as a check upon Russian ambitions in Korea. China, by intervening in the Korean War, resumed its traditional interest in the control of Korea.[43]

The Korean War lasted from 1950 to 1953. Although the first great military conflict of the cold war, it ended in a stalemate with the opposing parties stretched along the 38th parallel in essentially the same place that they were before the war began. The war firmly divided North and South Korea into the separate states that exist today.

South Korea was completely devastated both socially and economically in 1953. The struggle on both fronts to become an important player in East Asia has been difficult for the South. With the exception of its military power, the Communist North is almost a complete failure.

Today South Korea ranks fourth among the Asian Tigers. Considering the recent past, however, fourth is an impressive accomplishment. With an average income of $20,400 U.S., Koreans can boast that their individual earnings exceed those of both China and India in Asia, Argentina and Brazil in the Americas, and Poland and Latvia in Europe. Korea is third of the Asian states exporting products to the United States. Despite the global economic slowdown, South Korea expects to continue to have both growing shipbuilding and automobile industries.

As South Korea enters the twenty-first century, two potential problems loom on the horizon. First, there is the economic threat coming from China in the market for low-cost goods. To compete, Korea must follow the examples of Japan, Taiwan, and Singapore by moving into the fields of high technology where their higher labor costs can be utilized effectively.

The second problem is in the often-hostile relations that the South has with North Korea. The 38th parallel remains one of the most militarized borders existing today. It is clearly in the interests of both parties to move toward a normalization of relations, possibly leading to eventual reunification.

Everyone is familiar with the difficulties that have come with German reunification. The differences between North and South in Korea are far greater than those that existed between East and West Germany. Whether this conflict can be resolved in the foreseeable future is impossible to predict.

South Korea and the World Economic Downturn

Like the other Asian Tigers, South Korea was dealt a major setback in 2008 by the world economic downturn. The South Korean news agency reported that the South Korean economy ranked thirteenth largest in 2008.[44]

After its slow start in 2009, observers were surprised to find South Korea reporting gains in GDP during the second quarter of the year. If these numbers are projected to the entire year, South Korea could experience major GDP growth in 2009. This new growth is attributed to a successful government stimulus program that encourages domestic consumer confidence.

Korean President Lee Myung-Bak called for new measures to further soften the effect of the downturn. First and foremost, he urged government officials to develop new programs that would benefit both the people and small businesses. He also proposed serious planning to prepare the country's economy for life after the world downturn.[45]

FLASHPOINTS

The Wild Card: Pakistan: A Nation in Turmoil

Founded in 1947 when Muslims and Hindus were unable to agree on a single nation, Pakistan was first divided into areas in the west and the east of the Indian subcontinent. In 1971 Eastern Pakistan, with Indian help, successfully became the independent nation of Bangladesh. The former West Pakistan, now Pakistan, remains a republic with major military influence. The government has been unstable for many years. There have been assassinations, coups, and countercoups throughout its history.

As a nuclear state, Pakistan has earned a place as a nation to be taken seriously. At the present, the government is on the front line in the war on terror. Unfortunately, it has only limited influence in the tribal lands that border Afghanistan where most of the terrorists seek sanctuary. Furthermore, the government's hold on the more developed lands in the south is uncertain because many Muslims there are sympathetic to the Afghan rebel's cause. At best, this government's hold on power seems to be tenuous. Pakistan is a place where Western policy is based on the survival of one individual. This is a risky gamble because if the government were to be replaced, a nuclear-armed Pakistan could become one of the Other World's most dangerous hot spots.

PAKISTAN'S DILEMMA: KASHMIR AND INDIA OR THE FIGHT AGAINST ISLAMIC RADICALS

Kashmir

Kashmir has been called the "Switzerland of Asia." This area is probably the most beautiful spot in Asia. Here, there are lush valleys and shimmering lakes surrounded by the rugged mountains of the Karakorums and the Himalayas. It was to this region that the British colonials sent their families during the fever-ridden hot months in India. Like middle-class Americans who relocated to the mountains during the polio epidemics, the English believed that Europeans were safer from the tropical diseases common during the hot seasons if they were in the cool climate of Kashmir. Srinagar became the de facto British capital of India during the summer months.

Kashmir had been a Muslim state since the Mogul empire overran it in 1586. When the British occupied the area in 1846, they recognized Kashmir as a semi-independent state but placed a Hindu prince in charge. Hindus continued to rule locally under British tutelage until British withdrawal from South Asia in 1947.

When India and Pakistan were created out of old British India, most semi-independent states had to choose between joining India or Pakistan. At first the *maharaja* of Kashmir attempted to keep his state neutral, but large portions of the Muslim population revolted, forcing him to flee to India. Once in India, the Hindu *maharaja* declared Kashmir to be Indian against the will of the majority Muslim population. Indian troops were rushed to Kashmir to secure India's claim.

The result was the start of a conflict that continues to the present time. After three wars, Pakistan occupies about one-third and India two-thirds of Kashmir. In the 1980s, Muslim separatists renewed their fight for linking Kashmir with Pakistan. The result has been the continuation of a low-intensity war between the Muslim population, supported by Pakistan, and India. The conflict has ended the tourist trade and devastated the region. Now that both India and Pakistan have nuclear weapons, the small area of Kashmir constantly threatens to ignite a major conflict in South Asia.

In the spring of 2002, the conflict again reached a crisis level as both India and Pakistan alerted their nuclear forces and sent armies to the border. War was averted, but just barely. Everyone knows that a nuclear war in the Indian subcontinent would kill millions and possibly plunge the entire world into an economic depression.

In many ways, the dispute over Kashmir is not unlike the one between Israel and the Palestinians. In both cases the parties to the dispute can cite "chapter and verse" to justify their particular points of view. Until recently, both India and Pakistan used the inhabitants of the disputed territory as the foot soldiers for their larger conflict.

A 2009 return of a coalition with the Congress Party leading remained in power in India. Pakistan continued its support of America in the war on terror. The United States and the allies continued to occupy Afghanistan. These events put a new emphasis on solving the *Kashmir dispute*. To avoid the spread of conflict, the United States made it clear that India and Pakistan should move ahead on breaking the logjam over Kashmir.

The Fight Against Islamic Radicals

Although Pakistan is a Muslim nation, it has serious problems with Islamic radicals along the border with Afghanistan. The dilemma for Pakistan may be stated simply as "How many forces should they keep on Kasmir's frontier, and how many should be committed to the fight against Islamic radicals on the border with Afghanistan?"

Throughout the spring of 2009, the army of Pakistan was involved in counterinsurgency actions against Islamic radicals. This offensive coincided with similar American actions in Afghanistan. The United States has put pressure on Pakistani authorities to continue actions against Islamic radicals inside the country. The problem is that the Pakistani offensive is alienating large sections of the Islamic nation. How long the government can maintain actions in the border territories before domestic opposition builds to a point that it threatens the regime remains a major political question.

The Issue of North Korea

By all conventional measurements, the Democratic People's Republic of Korea is a failed state. The economy has declined from 1990 levels. Large segments of society exist at near starvation levels. If it were not for aid from the United Nations and from China, the system likely would have fallen apart.

Although not a Marxist principal, the North Korean leadership has become hereditary. Today, the founder's son, Kim Jong-il, is the chief of state. Little is known about North Korea's internal politics. It is believed that Kim's third son, Kim Jong-un,

End of Empire: Regimental Plaques on the Khyber Pass, Pakistan.   *Source: Richard Krandzdorf*

has been tapped to succeed his father. If North Korea were not a nuclear-armed state, few outside South Korea and China would be concerned.

Historically, as states became nuclear powers, their rhetoric became muted. Not so with North Korea. In 2009, the state became more belligerent. The North set off a new underground nuclear device. They also fired several long- and short-range missiles. The North Koreans have even made threats against the United States.

North Korea's nuclear ambitions are a direct threat to both South Korea and Japan. If the North persists in its quest, South Korea and Japan will also be forced to go nuclear. Such a growth in unconventional weapons would be a threat to the People's Republic of China.

If a cash-strapped North Korea sells either rocket or nuclear technology or hardware to Iran, all bets are off concerning nonproliferation in the Middle East. In turn, these actions could begin a nuclear arms race throughout the developing world. Any effort to stop or reduce the spread of nuclear weapons would be dead.

For several years, six-sided talks between North Korea, South Korea, China, Japan, Russia, and the United States were touted as the best way to bring the North into the world community. These talks were designed to offer foreign aid and technology transfers in return for the North's agreement to scrap its nuclear program. Unfortunately, the North walked out of the talks, and for the moment, they are dead.

There are fears that an internal failure of the regime could trigger a mass flight of refugees into China. Such an event could destabilize the region. North Korea is and will remain one of the most dangerous spots on earth.

Summary

Asia is the world's largest and most diverse continent. The lands of Asia include the world's highest mountain ranges, great river systems, foreboding deserts, rich agricultural regions, and steaming jungles. China and India are the world's two most populous countries. China and India are also the two major political powers on the continent. The four smaller political and economic "powerhouses" are Taiwan, Hong Kong, Singapore, and South Korea.

Politically, the People's Republic of China is emerging from the political and economic sterility of a Communist command economy into one of the most dynamic states in Asia. With other smaller states matching China's growth, the twenty-first century is likely to be an Asian one.

Review Questions

1. Briefly outline the tension between India and Pakistan.
2. What is the policy of "one China, two systems"?
3. What is the dispute over Taiwan about?
4. Why is North Korea dangerous?
5. Who are the Asian Tigers?

Key Terms

1949—Date that Chinese Communists drove the Nationalists off the Mainland to Taiwan. This date is called "Liberation Day" on the Chinese Mainland.

Boxer Rebellion—A Chinese rebellion at the end of the nineteenth and beginning of the twentieth centuries against foreign influence, provoking military intervention by eight nations.

Buddhism—The only major religion of China that was imported from the outside.

Cultural Revolution—A period under Mao when the party used mob rule to eliminate opposition and, in so doing, destroyed much of the cultural heritage of China.

Daoism—One of the three main religions of China. Along with Confucianism, Daoism is native to China.

Great Leap Forward—A period in the 1950s when the Chinese under Mao attempted to industrialize overnight.

Kashmir Dispute—A conflict between India and Pakistan over the largely Muslim region of Indian Kashmir.

Marco Polo—An early European visitor to China who wrote down his adventures and opened up knowledge of China to Western readers.

Opium Wars—A series of nineteenth-century conflicts fought primarily between China and Britain to force China to trade goods in exchange for Western supplies of opium shipped from India.

The Silk Road—Several land trade routes that were used to carry goods between China, India, and the West.

Useful Web Sites

China: *english.gov.cn*
Taiwan: *english.www.gov.tw*
Pakistan: *www.pakistan.gov.pk*
India: *www.india.gov.in*
Singapore: *www.gov.sg*

For Further Reading

Connor, Mary. *The Koreans: A Global Studies Handbook.* Santa Barbara, CA: ABC-CLIO, 2002.
Feigon, Lee. *Mao: A Reinterpretation.* Chicago: Ivan Dee Publishing, 2002.
Lijun, Seng. *China and Taiwan: Cross-Strait Relations under Chen Shui-Bian.* New York: Macmillan, 2003.
Murthy, Ranjani. *Gender, Poverty, and Human Rights in Asia.* New York: Macmillan, 2003.

Notes

1. *Who Said What When: A Chronological Dictionary of Quotations* (London: Bloomsbury Publishing, 1988), p. 95.
2. Ibid, p. 200. Also note that the Maxim machine gun was the first truly automatic gun. Adopted in 1884, it was the standard British infantry support weapon until after World War I. It, and other guns like it, ended the horse cavalry as a serious instrument of war. See Eric Morris, Christopher Chant, Curt Johnson, H.P. Willmott, *Weapons and Warfare of the 20th Century* (Secaucus, N.J.: 1976), p. 13.
3. The China Syndrome, Polling Report.com, taken from the Brownwood, Texas Bulletin, August 11, 2007, p. 5.
4. Sources for all figures on religion adherents taken from: *The World Almanac and Book of Facts 2009* (New York: World Almanac Books, 2009), p. 682.
5. Stanley Wolpert, *A New History of India,* 5th ed. (New York: Oxford University Press, 1997), p. 32.
6. *A Glimpse of Old China* (Beijing, China: China Pictorial Publishing House, 1995), p. 1.
7. Trea Wiltshire, *Encounters with China: Merchants, Missionaries, and Mandarins* (Hong Kong: Form Asia Books, 1995), p. 42.
8. Chairman Mao Tse-Tung, *Quotations from Chairman Mao Tse-Tung* (Peking: Foreign Language Press, 1966), p. 24.
9. Chairman Mao Tse-Tung, "Report of an Investigation into the Peasant Movement in Human," *Selected Works of Mao Tse-Tung, Vol. 1* (Peking: Foreign Language Press, 1954), pp. 23–59.
10. Dorothy Perkins, *Encyclopedia of China: The Essential Reference in China: Its History and Culture* (New York: Checkmark Books, 2000), p. 259.

11. For more information on Chinese losses in Korea see Geoffrey Stern, *Atlas of Communism* (New York: Macmillan, 1991).
12. Quote attributed to Chairman Deng Xiaoping. J. D. Brown, *China: The 50 Most Memorable Trips* (New York: Macmillan, 1998), p. 532.
13. "U.S. China Economic Relationship," Testimony by Myron Brillant, Vice President U.S. Chamber of Commerce, House Committee on Ways and Means, *Congressional Quarterly,* Washington, D.C., April 14, 2005.
14. See *The Economist Pocket World in Figures, 2007 Edition* (London: *The Economist* in association with Profile Books, 2007), p. 34.
15. Joseph Caron, "The Business of Doing Business with China: An Ambassador Reflects," *Ivey Business Journal Online,* May 2005, University of Western Ontario, Canada, p. 1.
16. *Idem.*
17. See "Beijing's Nightmare: Riots in Xinjiang," *The Economist,* London, July 11, 2009, taken from Lexis-Nexis, the Academic Universe, July 17, 2009.
18. For an interesting account of the Portuguese, Dutch, and English struggle to control trade with India, see Wolpert, op. cit., pp. 135–148.
19. Don McCombs and Fred L. Worth, *World War II: 4,139 Strange and Fascinating Facts* (New York: Wings Books, 1938), pp. 278–279.
20. Jo Johnson, "See India's Steely Drive is Overcoming Jaded Colonial Attitudes," *The Financial Times,* London, England, Feb 3, 2007.
21. *The Economist Pocket World in Figures, 2007 Edition* (London: *The Economist* in association with Profile Books, 2007), p. 26.
22. Gurcharan Das, "Where Society Has Triumphed Over State Comment: One of Indian Government's Harshest Critics Explains Why He Believes It Makes Sense to Invest in India," *The Financial Times,* London, England, Oct 10, 2006, p. 3.
23. "The Ruling Party says Coalition Government A 'Historic Endeavor,'" Indian News Agency PTI. Accessed from Lexis Nexis Academic Universe, May 22, 2009.
24. "Indians Not Blaming Media for Failing to See Recession Coming," India Broadcast Industry website Indian_television.com. June 23, 2009.
25. "Emerging Market CEOs More Upbeat," China Daily website, reported by The Financial Times Ltd., London, January 24, 2008.
26. Aeba Takanori, *Asian Magma and Japan-U.S. Relations: Journal of Japanese Trade and Industry,* 1 May 2001. Accessed from Lexis-Nexis Academic database.
27. *Pocket World in Figures, 2007 Edition* (London: *The Economist* in association with Profile Books, 2007), p. 31.
28. "Taiwan-China Trade Up 33.1 Percent in 2004," *Agence France Press News,* Paris, taken from Lexis-Nexis, the Academic Universe, March 2, 2005.
29. "Mainland Approves Over 65,568 Taiwan-Funded Businesses," Xinhua News Agency, PRC, taken from Lexis-Nexis, the Academic Universe, June 29, 2005.
30. "Bush Says U.S. Will Defend Taiwan," *United Press International Dispatch,* 25 April 2001. Accessed from Lexis-Nexis, the Academic Universe.
31. Trea Wiltshire, *Encounters with China: Merchants, Missionaries, and Mandarins* (Hong Kong: Form Asia Books, 1995), pp. 170–171.
32. "U.S.-Hong Kong Policy Act Report," United States Department of State, U.S. News Service. Taken from Lexis-Nexis, the Academic Universe, April 1, 2005.
33. *Tiger on the Doorstep: Management Today* (London: Haymarket Publishing Services, February 7, 2005).
34. Economic Freedom Index, *Pocket World in Figures, 2007 Edition* (London: *The Economist* in association with Profile Books, London, 2007), p. 31.

35. Dennis Eng, "Asia Loses Top Spot for Business Friendliness, Finland is better than H.K., Singapore, for Companies," South China Morning Post, H.K., p. 2, May 23, 2009. The Heritage Foundation still list Singapore in second place.

36. Peter Godspeed, "Hong Kong Reborn: With a Form of Democracy and a Burgeoning Economy, What's Not to Like About the Hand Over?" *National Post,* Canada, March 12, 2005, p. A13.

37. Perkins, op. cit., p. 466.

38. Dennis Eng, op. cit., p. 2.

39. "How Success Turns Local Heroes Into World Heroes: Companies in Energy and Service Sectors Draw Investors," *International Herald Tribune,* Paris, France, April 9, 2005, p. 16.

40. Chuang Peck Ming, "Singapore's NODX up 1.8 Percent in H1: Full-year Growth Forecast for Non-oil Exports Trimmed to 4–6 Percent," *Business Times Singapore,* Section Singapore, taken from Lexis-Nexis, the Academic Universe, July 18, 2007.

41. Lee U-Wen, "Record 9,410 Workers Lost Jobs in S'pore in Q4; but 70 Per Cent of the Locals Retrenched in Q3; Found Jobs by December," *The Business Times,* Singapore, Top Stories, April 25, 2009.

42. Elizabeth Heresch, *The Empire of the Tsars: The Splendor and the Fall, Pictures and Documents 1896 to 1920* (Vienna: Stroitel Pub., 1991), p. 54.

43. Hans J. Morgenthau, *Politics Among Nations: The Struggle for Power and Peace,* 5th ed., Revised (New York Alfred A. Knopf), pp. 183–184.

44. "Goldman Raises Growth Forecast to Minus 3 Per Cent," *Korea Times,* Korea, April 27, 2009.

45. Dyum Duk-Kun, "South Korean Leader Calls for Unprecedented Measures to Fight Economic Crisis," South Korean News Agency, Yonhap, BBC Monitoring Asia-Pacific, London, June 26, 2009, taken from Lexis-Nexis, the Academic Universe, June 26, 2009.

8

The Middle East and North Africa

Joseph N. Weatherby

My own ambition is that the Arabs should be our first brown dominion, and not our last brown colony.

LAWRENCE OF ARABIA, 1919

Both the East and the West want to corrupt us from within, obliterate every distinguishing mark of our personality and snuff out the light which guides us.

MUAMMAR AL-QADDAFI

Everything in the Middle East changed on September 11, 2001. But the more that things in the Middle East change, the more they stay the same.
There is a saying in the West that the Middle East is a region too important to the outside world to allow it to be governed by Middle Easterners. The Middle East has played a pivotal role in world affairs since ancient times. Forming the land bridge between Asia, Africa, and Europe, the Middle East has the strategic attention of both the East and the West (see Figure 8.1).

The Middle East is also the birthplace of the world's three great monotheistic religions: Judaism, Christianity, and Islam. For more than 1,000 years, Islam has been the religion of about 90 percent of the region's inhabitants. The effect of religion on politics is more pronounced in the Middle East than probably in any other region in the world.

FIGURE 8.1 Political and Physical Characteristics of the Middle East and North Africa

233

The twentieth century witnessed one of the greatest transfers of wealth in history, as vast supplies of oil were discovered in both the Arabian Peninsula and North Africa. This development prompted the bitter Western comment that "where there are Middle Easterners, there is oil." In the twenty-first century, Saudi Arabia, Kuwait, Iran, and Iraq accounted for more than 53 percent of the world's petroleum reserves. This oil is a primary fuel for the industries of Europe, the United States, and Japan. As newspaper headlines indicate, more issues critically important to the future of the United States and the Western world converge in the politics of the Middle East than anywhere else in the Other World.

This chapter offers a brief introduction to the Middle East and North Africa. After a discussion of geography and economics, we trace the history of the Middle East; the story of Islam; and the subsequent rise of nationalism in Egypt, Turkey, Iran, Saudi Arabia, and Israel. The essential aspects of Arab nationalism are also discussed. Finally, the central points of the Arab-Israeli dispute are outlined in the "Flashpoints." The data in Table 8.1 illustrate the vast differences in population, wealth, and conditions of life in the North African and Middle Eastern countries.

Although most Americans can point to a map and identify some countries located in the Middle East, few have any idea what nations are actually included in the region. Even scholars fail to agree on the subject. The U.S. Department of Defense states categorically that there is no precise, generally accepted definition of the region variously called the Near East or Middle East.

Because, at times, all the area from the Atlantic coast of Morocco to Afghanistan has been included in this region, no one term seems to describe adequately the whole. The terms *Middle East* and *Near East* are inadequate, misleading, and culturally biased. They are misleading because they have been used to describe different places at different times in history. Originally, the Near East referred to the lands of the eastern Mediterranean, and the Middle East described the Indian empire controlled by Britain. The terms converged geographically only during World War II, when the British based their Near Eastern and Middle Eastern operations in Cairo. Because the active involvement of the United States in the region began during this period, Americans have tended to use the term *Middle East*, whereas Europeans continue to use the more traditional designation, *Near East*, to describe the same area. Even in the absence of this confusion, the terms *Middle East* and *Near East* are culturally biased from the standpoint of inhabitants of the region. Both terms describe the Other World in ways that are meaningful only in reference to the former colonial powers in Europe.

In an effort to avoid these pejorative labels, writers sometimes use the phrases *the Arab world* and *the Islamic world* as substitutes. Unfortunately, these words often confuse as much as they inform. *The Arab world* cannot accurately describe the region as a whole because the phrase ignores 67 million Iranians, 76 million Turks, and 5 million Jews living in Israel. Much of the same problem arises with the use of *the Islamic world*. Although

TABLE 8.1

Country	Population (Millions)	Population Growth Rate (%)	Infant Mortality Rate (per 1,000 Live Births)	Population under 15 Years of Age (%)	Life Expectancy (in Years)	Urban Population (%)	Literacy Rate (%)	Arable Land (%)	Per Capita GDP ($ US)
MIDDLE EAST									
Bahrain	.727	1.285	4.29	25.9	75.16	89	86.5	2.82	37,200
Iran	66.429	.883	35.78	21.7	71.5	68	77	9.78	12,800
Iraq	29.945	2.507	5.14	38.8	69.94	67	74.1	12.12	4,000
Israel	7.233	1.671	5.41	27.9	80.73	92	97.1	15.74	28,200
Jordan	6.342	2.264	2.72	31.3	78.87	78	89.9	3.32	5,000
Kuwait	2.961	3.547	2.37	26.4	77.71	98	93.3	.84	57,400
Lebanon	4.017	1.107	6.06	25.8	73.66	87	87.4	16.35	11,100
Saudi Arabia	28.686	1.848	2.49	38	76.3	82	78.8	1.67	20,700
Syria	20.178	2.129	25.87	35.9	71.19	54	79.6	24.8	4,800
Turkey	76.805	1.312	25.78	27.2	71.96	69	87.4	29.81	12,000
United Arab Emirates	4.798	3.689	12.7	20.4	76.11	78	77.9	.77	40,000
Yemen	23.822	3.453	54.7	46.2	63.27	31	50.2	2.91	2,400
Algeria	34.178	1.196	27.73	25.4	74.02	65	69.9	3.17	7,000
Egypt	83.082	1.642	27.62	31.4	72.12	43	71.4	2.92	5,400
Libya	6.31	2.17	21.05	33	77.26	78	82.6	1.03	14,400
Morocco	34.859	1.479	36.88	30	71.8	56	52.3	19	4,000
Tunisia	10.486	.98	22.57	22.7	75.78	67	74.3	17.05	7,900
Comparison States									
Canada	33.487	.817	5.04	16.1	81.23	80	99	4.57	39,300
Poland	34.482	-.047	6.8	15	75.63	61	99.8	40.25	17,300
Italy	85.127	-.047	5.51	13.5	80.2	68	98.4	26.41	31,000

Source: CIA World Factbook 2009.

Muslims account for most of the area's population, large Christian and Jewish minorities play pivotal roles. This term also implies a religious unity in Islam, which simply does not exist except on the most superficial level.

Despite these concerns, the terms *Middle East* and *North Africa* will be used in this chapter because of their common usage in the United States. The Middle East will be understood to include the Arab states of Arabia and the eastern Mediterranean, Turkey, Israel, and Iran. It will also contain the North African states of Egypt, Libya, Tunisia, Algeria, and Morocco. This selection may seem arbitrary because it omits Afghanistan, Somalia, the Sudan, and Mauritania, which form transition areas between the Middle East, North Africa, and other adjacent regions.

In the Middle East, one encounters strange-sounding names with a regional significance. The Holy Land, Maghreb, Levant, Judea, Samaria, and the Fertile Crescent are all examples of special places that require more explanation. The *Holy Land* was traditionally associated with pilgrimages and crusades to the sites venerated by Christians because of their association with the life of Jesus. Today, the term also includes sites sacred to Jews and Muslims, most of which are in or near the city of Jerusalem.

The Maghreb is a phrase literally meaning, and implied by tradition, "the setting sun in the west." This term is used to describe the North African countries of Morocco, Algeria, and Tunisia, and some writers also include Libya and Mauritania. Like the Maghreb, *the Levant* signifies a direction, the eastern point of the compass. The Levant is generally understood to include the present states of Lebanon and Israel.

Judea and *Samaria* are ancient Hebrew names currently applied by the government of Israel to the former Jordanian-held territories on the West Bank of the Jordan River. The old biblical names are used to remind the world that Israel claims a historic right to bring Jewish settlers into these Arab-populated territories. These terms are used by those Israelis who support the expansion of the borders of Israel to include all the territories that biblical tradition teaches were promised by God to the ancient children of Israel.

The term *Fertile Crescent* is familiar to many in the West because it is the traditional site of the birthplace of Western civilization. It includes the present countries of Israel and Lebanon as well as Syria and Iraq. Some writers say that the Fertile Crescent arches like a bow from the eastern Nile delta to the mouth of the Shatt al-Arab River in Iraq. Other authorities hold that the western terminus of the bow is Palestine, not the Nile delta. What is important to remember is that this is an area of relatively good agriculture, low population, and a reasonable climate. As in ancient times, this area offers the best hope for the development of a nonpetroleum-based economy.

GEOGRAPHY

Western perceptions of the Middle East are simultaneously accurate and misleading. The greatest expanse of desert in the world exists here, but although there are still camel-mounted Bedouins in parts of the Middle East, most people now live in villages, towns, and cities. Even those Bedouins who have not settled into permanent residences are now likely to be exchanging their "ships of the desert," camels, for Toyota trucks. Like many parts of the Other World, the Middle East is an area of both variety and dynamic change.

In its simplest form, the Middle East can be divided into three distinct geographic regions: the plains of North Africa and Arabia, the Fertile Crescent, and the northern tier. These areas are surrounded by five seas and five straits and are bisected by two of the world's great river systems.

The Plains of North Africa and Arabia

The vast deserts of the Sahara and the Rub al Khali cover more than 95 percent of this region. Because of their immense size, it should not be surprising to learn that the surfaces of these two deserts vary from gravel to rock to sand.

The Qattara Depression, larger than 4,000 square miles, is located near the Mediterranean in Egypt's portion of the eastern Sahara. From time to time, proposals have been made to divert the waters of the Mediterranean over the precipice to the Qattara floor, which is 400 feet below sea level. Engineers estimate that enough falling water could be diverted through generators to create an electric power complex that would rival the Nile's Aswan High Dam. A combination of environmental concerns and a shortage of capital in Egypt have postponed serious consideration of this project for the foreseeable future. There has been another, perhaps more feasible, Qattara proposal to tap an abundant ancient water supply, believed to exist beneath the depression floor, to create a new Nile delta in the desert. Whether the Egyptian government will find the development funds that would be required to attempt either of these ambitious schemes is doubtful at present.

The Rub al Khali of Saudi Arabia is famous for sand mountains that are hundreds of feet high. This desert contains the largest area of sand on earth. The Rub al Khali is about the size of Texas, extending from Yemen in the east

The Sahara: Camels gathered around one of the government-prepared watering holes in the Sahara Desert. *Source: Joe Weatherby*

to the United Arab Emirates in the west. For the first time since the ancient caravan routes flourished, Westerners are again penetrating the unknowns of the Rub al Khali, but this time in modern vehicles and engaged in the search for oil.

The remaining 5 percent of the plains of North Africa and Arabia is a transitional territory that includes two distinct areas: desert scrub country and a rich Mediterranean coastal zone. This zone stretches from the Nile delta westward for most of the length of North Africa and to the Atlantic coast of Morocco as far south as Casablanca. The desert scrub country contains some soil, moisture, and vegetation, and much of it resembles the high plains of the western United States. The conditions that produce desert scrub occur elsewhere in the Middle East, including southern Turkey, western Iraq, western Iran, and parts of Jordan and Syria. The nomads live in the desert scrub with their ever-migrating herds of sheep and goats.

Most of the residents of the plains live in the narrow coastal zone of the Mediterranean rather than in the deserts. The North African coast of the Atlantic and the Mediterranean generally conforms to what is known as the Mediterranean climate. This climate features hot, dry summers, with brown or dormant vegetation, and cool, wet winters, when the plant life has its growth period. In North Africa, this coastal zone ranges from only a few miles in width in parts of Egypt and Libya to as much as 50 miles in Algeria. In Egypt, the coastal zone and Nile valley and delta combined average 2,700 people per square mile, representing one of the world's densest populations. Remarkably, unlike other high-density areas, such as the Netherlands, the people of Egypt are still largely engaged in traditional Other World occupations, including subsistence agriculture (see Box 8.1).

Some of the great cities of Africa and the Middle East are located in or near the Mediterranean coastal zone. Cairo, with a population of over 11.8 million people, is the largest and most important city on the African continent. Other important North African cities are Alexandria, Egypt (4.1 million); Tripoli, Libya (2 million); Benghazi, Libya (1.1 million); Tunis, Tunisia (1.9 million); and Algiers, Algeria (3.3 million). Both Rabat (1.7 million) and Casablanca (3.3 million) are located in the coastal zones of Morocco. Saudi Arabia in the Arabian Peninsula contains the

Water

The greatest shortage in the Middle East is water. Since ancient times, Mediterranean people have used ingenious methods to carry water to the fields. The following are several traditional irrigation methods still used in the region.

The *qanat* is a tunnel sometimes over 10 miles long that taps the groundwater in the foothills and transports it to the fields in the valleys. This system is used in Iran and other mountainous countries in the northern tier.

The *shadoof* is an ancient system using a goat-skin bag attached to a pole that is pivoted from the river to the field. This water system is used extensively along the banks of the Nile River in Egypt. The water wheel is a device used to lift and transport water. This system is usually animal-powered.

The *Archimedes* screw is a portable gear used to raise water from a river or pond to the fields.

historic cities of Mecca (1.3 million) and Medina (1 million). The commercial centers of Jedda (3.2 million) and Riyadh (5.1 million) are also located in Saudi Arabia.

These statistics may have more meaning if we compare the size of North African and Arabian cities with those found in the United States. Cairo has about the same population as New York City; Alexandria and Casablanca are larger than Houston; Tunis and Mecca are the same size as San Antonio; Jedda, Rabat, and Riyadh are all larger than San Francisco.

The North African and Arabian plains contain a number of mountains, including the Atlas and Rif of Morocco and the Tell Atlas of Algeria and Tunisia. The highest point in Egypt is the 8,600-foot Jabal Musa (Mount Sinai), located in the southern Sinai. Tradition holds that God gave the Ten Commandments to Moses on Mount Sinai. The Arabian Peninsula is mountainous in Yemen and Oman. In both places, peaks reach heights of 12,000 feet.[1]

The Fertile Crescent

Perhaps nowhere in the world has so much human history been tied to one single geographic area as in the Fertile Crescent. Everywhere the visitor looks, on the hills or in the valleys, important events in the history of humankind have occurred. Here are the ruins of ancient civilizations, the land of prophets, and the birthplace of Judaism and Christianity. Geographically, the Fertile Crescent includes a narrow coastal zone flanked by the sea on one side and a rather low coastal range of mountains, running north to south, on the other. Along the southern border of Turkey, the Fertile Crescent arches eastward through a gap in the mountains to include the desert scrublands of Syria and Iraq before joining the rich river basins of the Tigris and Euphrates rivers. The region terminates at the northern end of the Persian Gulf.

The coastal zone of the Fertile Crescent is similar in many respects to the coast of California. Although this analogy has limitations apparent to any geographer, it may be useful to consider the following comparisons. If we were to travel the coastal route south from San Francisco to Los Angeles, we would pass through countryside that is similar in many respects to the coastal zone of the eastern Mediterranean, with Beirut being comparable to the Bay Area, Haifa to Monterey and Carmel, the Lebanon Mountains to the California coastal range, the Bekaa Valley in Lebanon to the Salinas Valley, and Tel Aviv to the area between Santa Barbara and Los Angeles.

The cities of the eastern Mediterranean do not rival either those of North Africa or the interior of the Fertile Crescent. Tel Aviv has a population of 3,012,000 and Jerusalem 711,000. Tripoli, the second-largest city in Lebanon, has a population of 245,000 people. The population of Beirut, Lebanon's capital, is 1,777,000.

The two major cities of the Fertile Crescent are Baghdad, Iraq, and Damascus, Syria. Baghdad, with a climate similar to the southwestern United States, has a population of 5,620,000. The population of Damascus is over 2,228,000. Syria and Iraq are the most important states of the Fertile Crescent. Both are considered to have a good chance to develop well-rounded economies, maintain low population densities, and establish reasonable standards of living. Presently, their problems are mainly political, not geographic or economic.

The Northern Tier

The northern tier is an area of mountains and plateaus linked to a mountain system that stretches from the Alps in the west to the Himalayas in the east. Although Afghanistan and Pakistan are often included in this region, this discussion of the northern tier is limited to Turkey and Iran.

Both countries are located on high plateaus surrounded by mountains. Turkey is situated on a peninsula jutting out into the Mediterranean. Turkey is about the size of Texas and Arkansas combined. The Anatolian Plateau, a high, dry region about 3,000 feet above sea level, is located in the center of Turkey. Here, the Turks produce most of their wheat and cereals. Two mountain ranges run east to west along the edges of the plateau. The Pontic Mountains are located on the north and the Taurus Mountains on the south of the peninsula. Eastern Turkey is extremely mountainous along the Iranian border. Mount Ararat, the traditional site of the landing of Noah's ark, is near this border. Turkey has a long, varied coastal region that includes both a Mediterranean climate along the south and west and a wet area near the Black Sea city of Rise. This city receives as much as 100 inches of rain a year. With such climatic variety in the coastal zone, Turkey raises a number of crops, including tea, tobacco, and cotton. Although most people live in villages, Turkey has several large cities. Istanbul, with a population of 10 million, is the largest. Ankara, the capital, has a population of 3.7 million, and Izmir has 2.5 million people.

Nature has played a cruel trick on Iran. Larger than Alaska, Iran consists of a high desert surrounded on all sides by rugged mountains that prevent moisture from penetrating into the interior. The Zagros Mountains run along the length of the eastern shore of the Persian Gulf, and the Elburz Mountains are located along a line parallel to the southern coast of the Caspian Sea. The jewel of the Elburz is a partially snowcapped volcano 18,376 feet high. This volcano, Mount Damavand, is clearly visible from Tehran. Tehran is built in the foothills of the Elburz and has a setting and climate closely resembling Salt Lake City, Utah.

Most of the interior of Iran consists of two terrible deserts, where some of the world's highest temperatures have been recorded. The Dasht-i-Kavir, or "Salt Desert," and the Dasht-i-Lut, or "Sand Desert," popularly called the "Desert of Death," are largely untraveled even today. The hostile environment in Iran's interior has caused over 70 percent of the country to remain uninhabited. The people of Iran live either along the narrow coastal plain of the Caspian Sea or in scattered urban centers in the north and west. Tehran, the capital, totally dominates these urban centers with a population of over 7.3 million people. The nation's second-largest city, Meshed, has a population of 2 million.[2]

Strategic Geography

The Middle East contains two of the world's great river systems: the Nile and the Tigris and Euphrates. The area also has two lesser waterways that are important in the politics of the region: the Suez Canal and the Jordan River.

Flowing 4,037 miles, the Nile is the world's longest river. Rising in Ethiopia and Uganda, it crosses the Sudan, enters Egypt at Lake Nasser, passes through the dam at Aswan, and flows past Cairo to the delta and the Mediterranean. If there is a central feature to Egypt, it is most certainly the Nile, which has been the life-support system for this nation's residents for more than 5,000 years. The need to secure the Nile in upper and lower Egypt is as important today as it was when the pharaohs ruled the nation in ancient times. As in the past, today's Egyptian leaders pay particular attention to politics in the Sudan. To the Egyptian, the fate of the Sudan still affects the security of the Nile.

Both the Tigris and the Euphrates begin their journey to the sea in central Turkey. The Euphrates passes through Turkey, Syria, and Iraq, and the Tigris through Turkey and Iraq. The Karun flows from Iran to join with the Tigris and the Euphrates, forming a new river called the Shatt al-Arab just before reaching the northern shore of the Persian Gulf. It is in this meandering delta of the Shatt al-Arab near Basra where much of the war between Iraq and Iran was fought during the 1980s.

The Suez Canal has been strategically important since its opening in 1869. One hundred and one miles long, the canal joins the Red Sea with the Mediterranean, saving ships the costly and time-consuming trip around the tip of southern Africa when traveling from the Persian Gulf and points further east to and from Europe. For further information on strategic waterways, see the "Flashpoints" section at the end of this chapter.

The Jordan River and its system of lakes and seas are historically significant as the site of many events sacred to Christians and Jews. The Jordan is also politically important because it is the disputed border between Jordan and Israel. The river flows through a valley for about 80 miles between the Sea of Galilee (Lake Tiberias) and the Dead Sea. The Jordan's economic significance is limited. Ranging from 50 to a few hundred feet in width, its potential for irrigation cannot possibly meet the exaggerated hopes for agricultural development of either the Arabs or the Israelis.[3]

No area of the globe is as strategically located as the Middle East. For centuries, it has been the invasion route of Egyptians, Persians, Romans, Christians, and Muslims. Today, its important location as a passageway between Africa, Europe, and Asia is without challenge. Five easily traversed seas surround the Middle East: Arabian, Red, Mediterranean, Black, and Caspian. There are three gulfs of importance: the Gulf of Aden, located at the tip of the Arabian Peninsula; the Gulf of Oman, situated between Oman and Iran; and the famous Persian Gulf. Entry and egress to all but two of these bodies of water are controlled by narrow straits: the Straits of Gibraltar, controlling the western Mediterranean; the Dardanelles and the Bosporus, dominating entry to the Black Sea; the Bab el Mandeb, controlling the southern end of the Red Sea and the Suez Canal; and the Straits of Hormuz, which must be passed to enter the Persian Gulf. Strategic straits do not dominate the Arabian Sea, which is part of the Indian Ocean, and the Caspian Sea, which has no outlet.[4]

PEOPLE

A popular misconception is that there is a homogeneous race of people in the Middle East. This notion is fostered by some of the region's religious institutions, whose traditions allude to Arab, Jewish, or even Aryan races. These terms, however, have little meaning in the Middle East today, unless they are limited to linguistic or cultural associations.

Although there are no recognizable groupings about which everyone would agree, authorities acknowledge that the region contains Semitic, Turkish, and Persian-speaking people. Of the Semitic-speaking population, the Arabs are the most numerous. Although there are many dialects, written modern standard Arabic is understood by educated Arabs everywhere. Arabic is spoken from the Atlantic coast of Morocco to the shores of the Persian Gulf. By this definition, approximately 200 million Arabs live in the region. Although there is a single Arab nation in theory only, the common bond of language has meant that unification is an aspiration of many of the region's inhabitants.

The other large Semitic group lives in Israel. Reviving a formerly ritualistic language as a symbol of their nationalism, the more than 5 million Jews living in Israel have again made Hebrew a living language.

The ancestors of the 60 million Turkish-speaking people in modern Turkey came to the Anatolian Peninsula in the eleventh and twelfth centuries from central Asia. They have lived in a single identifiable state since the Turkish Republic was created from the breakup of the Ottoman Empire following World War I.[5]

Persian is an Indo-European language written with a modified Arabic alphabet. There are about 36 million Persian-speaking Iranians in Iran. Finally, the region also contains people who speak different languages, including the Kurds, Armenians, and Greeks.

RELIGION

Two great forces are shaping the character of the modern Middle East. One is the Islamic religion and the other is nationalism.

Islam is the youngest of the three great monotheistic religions that arose in this region; the other two are Christianity and Judaism. Islam has been the dominant religion in the Middle East for more than 1,000 years. Today less than 10 percent of the population is non-Muslim. To understand the Middle East, therefore, one must have some knowledge of Islam.

First, however, a distinction should be made between what is often referred to as the popular or folk religion and the formal religion of mosque and church. Generalizing about Middle Eastern folk religions is next to impossible except to point out that the popular practices of Christians, Jews, and Muslims are similar. All have their local saints, sacred places, and symbols. Many of these traditions spill over from one religion to another. For example, people of all religions in the Mediterranean traditionally paint the doors and shutters of their homes blue to ward off the evil eye. The distance between this popular practice and the formal religion of the scholars is often as great as that of the Pentecostal snake handler in the Appalachian Mountains and the pope in Rome. This inquiry will be limited to the formal religious practices of the majority religion, Islam.[6]

Much of the universal appeal of Islam is found in its straightforward simplicity. Unlike Christianity, there are no priests dispensing sacraments, no catechism, and no complicated theology. Islam demands a belief in only one God, called *Allah* in Arabic. Muslims believe that *Mohammed* is the prophet of God. The word *Islam* means "submission"; thus, a Muslim is a believer who has submitted to the will of God. This simple theology may be summarized as belief in the oneness of God, the prophecy of Mohammed, judgment day, and life after death.

Islam is more than a religion, as that term is generally understood in the West. It is a way of life, 24 hours a day, 7 days a week, 365 days a year. Muslims do not concern themselves with what is the truth because truth is contained in the profession of faith and the word of God as revealed through Mohammed in the Koran. The great questions of Islam are centered on how a good Muslim should live and relate to others, not what a Muslim should believe to enter paradise. Although it is easy to make a profession of faith in Islam, it is difficult to live the life of a good Muslim. As a guide for living, Muslims observe five religious obligations, called the

North Africa Door: Popular culture in North Africa holds that either the "hand" door-knocker represents the hand of Mohammed's daughter, Fatima, or that the fingers represent the Five Pillars of Islam. *Source: Joe Weatherby*

Five Pillars of Islam: professing faith, observing ritual prayer, giving alms, fasting during the month of Ramadan, and making a pilgrimage to Mecca.

The Profession of Faith (*Shahadah*)

Muslims believe that there is no god but God and that Mohammed is his prophet. The implications of this profession are threefold. First, in contrast to most Christians, who believe that there is one God, expressed as Father, Son, and Holy Spirit, Muslims hold to an uncompromising *monotheism*: "There is no god but God." Second, Muslims believe that although other prophets, including Jesus, have received revelations, Allah's words as revealed through Mohammed are the final, complete message from God to humankind. Third, Muslims believe that this message is contained, in full, in a book called the Koran.

Prayer (*Salat*)

Traditionally, Muslims pray at five prescribed periods a day: in the morning before sunrise, noontime, afternoon, sunset, and late evening. The prayer is ritualistic and keeps the believers in constant contact with God. Islam differs from those forms of Christianity in which believers pray through mediators inasmuch as Muslims believe that they have direct access to God.

Alms Giving (*Zakat*)

Muslims believe that they are obliged to pay a percentage of their income to the poor and needy. They do not believe that poverty is a crime. For Muslims, there is little or no stigma attached to this system of voluntary religious welfare. Many Muslims give to Islamic charities that then provide help for people who are in need. In recent years, the West has accused some Islamic charities of providing cover for the funding of international terrorism.[7]

Fasting (*Sawm*)

During Ramadan, the ninth month of the Islamic calendar, all Muslims are called on to observe the fast by abstaining from all food, drink, and other earthly pleasures during daylight hours. This month-long fast, longer than anything practiced in either Christianity or Judaism, teaches Muslims self-denial and moderation.

Pilgrimage to Mecca (*Hajj*)

If possible, all Muslims are enjoined to visit the Great Mosque in Mecca at least once. Here, facing the Ka'bah and wearing the same ritual white, Muslims from every station in life, from every country in the world, both male and female, pray as equals before God.[8]

Holy Struggle (*Jihad*)

Many consider the *jihad*, or holy struggle, to be almost a "sixth pillar of Islam." This duty, often misunderstood in the West, has two meanings: one inner and one external. The inner meaning calls on Muslims to fight constantly against their own evil inclinations. The external command offers salvation to those Muslims who fight to promote a universal Islamic doctrine. The confusion concerning *jihad* arises because the term has been used in a political manner by some Islamic leaders to further their own purposes.

The Muslim community is governed by a hierarchy of principles expected to guide the faithful in all matters of life. These principles, or authorities, are collectively called the *Shari'ah*, or "the path to be followed." This path includes, in descending order of importance, the Koran, the tradition (*Hadith*) of how Mohammed lived, consensus (*Ijma*) of the religious scholars on issues, and deduction (*Qiyas*) where there is no precedent. Not all Muslim communities accept this hierarchy in its entirety.

The great split in Islam began because of a dispute over how the successor (caliph) to Mohammed should be selected. The Shi'ia branch of Islam is centered in Iran. Shi'ites believe that the first caliph should have been Ali, the son-in-law of Mohammed, and that successive caliphs should have come exclusively from the descendants of Ali. Sunnis, who make up approximately 80 percent of the world's Muslim population, believe that the caliphs should have been chosen by election of the faithful from members of Mohammed's tribe. Over the centuries, many other differences have developed between these two branches, and their disputes still color Middle Eastern politics hundreds of years after the original split occurred.

HISTORY

Since the seventh century, the history of the Middle East has been inexorably bound to the history of Islam, which includes at least five distinct Sunni periods: the life of Mohammed, the *rightly guided caliphs*, the Umayyads, the Abbasids, and the Ottomans.

The Life of Mohammed (A.D. 571–632)

Mohammed was born in A.D. 571 in the city of Mecca. Orphaned as a child, he was reared by a grandfather who was a leader of the Meccan Quraysh tribe. Mohammed is traditionally believed to have traveled with caravans to other parts of the Middle East as a young man. His visits may have exposed him to other religions. When he was 40 years old, he started receiving revelations commanding him to tell the world that there is one God, that Mohammed is his prophet, and that there will be a judgment day. These revelations were revolutionary ideas that threatened the existing society in Mecca. In the summer of 622, opposition from the Meccans forced Mohammed to flee from Mecca 200 miles north to the city of Medina. The date of Mohammed's flight, called the *Hijra*, marks the beginning of the Islamic calendar. After converting Medina to Islam, Mohammed lived to see not only Mecca but also the entire Arabian Peninsula become Muslim before his death in A.D. 632. Muslims do not ascribe divine qualities to Mohammed. He is considered to have been a human being who, while living a perfect life, served as a messenger from God.

The Rightly Guided Caliphs (A.D. 632–661)

Mohammed's death left the movement without a clearly designated successor. This vacuum initiated a struggle for power that ultimately led to the Sunni-Shi'ia split. Although some of the faithful believed that Ali had been designated by Mohammed as his successor, Abu Bakr (the prophet's father-in-law) was chosen to be the caliph. After only two years, Abu Bakr chose Umar to be the caliph, and under Umar's leadership, Islamic armies conquered the Fertile Crescent, Persia, and Egypt. Much of what is familiar to Westerners about Islam, including the veiling of women and the ban on alcohol, was institutionalized during Umar's tenure. Uthman succeeded Umar, who was assassinated in 644, but he too was assassinated 12 years later. Ali was finally selected as the fourth caliph, only to be challenged by the powerful Umayyad family from Mecca. The Umayyads backed another leader named Mu'awiyah. There was a civil war between the Umayyads, who had the support of Muslims in Syria, and the Muslims who supported Ali. Eventually, Ali was assassinated in 661. Shi'ites still maintain that Ali was the only legitimate successor to Mohammed.

Muslims look with fondness at the period of the first four caliphs as a time when the religion had a purity of purpose that ultimately was lost. Modern Muslims tend to stress the exertions of the period, the justice, and the humanity, and ignore the disturbing reality that three of the four "rightly guided caliphs" were assassinated. Nevertheless, if there ever was a time that Muslims long to return to, it is this one.

The Umayyad Dynasty (A.D. 661–750)

Under the first Umayyad caliph, Mu'awiyah, the election of leaders was ended in favor of a dynastic approach, and the political capital of Islam became Damascus. During the almost 100 years that the Umayyads ruled, the Islamic faith spread to three continents. It was only a question of time, however, until the non-Arab elements of the empire began to believe that they were being treated as second-class members of the Damascus state. In 750, the non-Arab dissidents of the empire arose and ended the Arab domination by destroying the Umayyads. In place of the Umayyads, a new multicultural system was established, called the Abbasid dynasty.

The Abbasid Dynasty (A.D. 750–1258)

With the rise of the Abbasids, the so-called Golden Age of Islam began. The empire's new capital in Baghdad saw Muslims lead the world in philosophy, literature, mathematics, and medicine. Many developments that were to bear fruit in the explosion of the arts and sciences during the Renaissance in Europe originated in the streets of Abbasid Baghdad. The rule of the Abbasids came to an end in the year 1258, when Mongol armies from central Asia conquered Baghdad. After the fall of the Abbasids, no single power was able to dominate the Middle East until the Ottoman period.

The Ottoman Empire (A.D. 1453–1918)

Tradition holds that the *Ottomans* came to Anatolia from central Asia in the early Middle Ages. By the mid-1300s, they were in the process of establishing an empire that would again extend Muslim control to parts of Europe, Africa, and the Middle East. Although it is difficult to generalize about an empire that lasted for over 600 years, one may safely state that many of the conditions found in the modern Middle East began in the practices of the Ottomans. For example, the Ottomans were able to rule a diverse multicultural empire stretching over much of the Mediterranean world because they established a system of religious and cultural autonomy called the Millet. Sectarian separation was institutionalized and even encouraged by the Ottomans as long as loyalty and taxes were paid to the caliph. This system of religious toleration resulted in the survival of small Christian and Jewish groups, which otherwise would have disappeared. Middle East groups still divide along sectarian lines after the fashion of the Millet.

During the eighteenth and nineteenth centuries, Ottomans were in retreat in the face of increasing Western power. Many of the negative stereotypes that Westerners have about the Middle East come from this period of Ottoman weakness. The Ottomans survived the nineteenth century but collapsed with the defeat of the Central Powers in World War I. The subsequent partition of the non-Turkish elements from the empire resulted in the creation of the modern Turkish Republic.

Shi'ite Islam

Most people in the West see Islam as monolithic. In reality, Islam is no more monolithic than Christianity. Like most Christians, Muslims agree on a few fundamental beliefs, but after that there is diversity.

The Shi'ia are the largest minority in Islam. They have a different history and traditions. First the Shi'ites argue that upon the death of Mohammed, Ali should have been selected caliph. Second, Shi'ites believe that the Shi'ia Imam (caliph) must be a direct descendant of the Prophet Mohammed and Ali, the first Imam. Most believers recognize 12 Imams in history. The twelfth Imam, called "the Lord of the Age," has been "hidden" but will eventually return at the end of the world to establish a perfect and just society.

Until the twelfth Imam returns, his successor, called a *Mujahid* or *Ayatollah*, has the right to interpret religion for the Shi'ite community. Most believe that, because the Ayatollahs are successors of the twelfth Imam, their decisions have special force over the community of believers.

Unlike Sunni Islamic leaders, Ayatollahs continually make religious and political pronouncements. This explains how the religious leadership in places like Shi'ite Iran can "veto" the actions of elected secular leaders. This tradition gives extraordinary power to the senior religious leadership in Shi'ite Islam.

Islam Today

Much has been written in recent years concerning the resurgence of Islam as a unifying force in the Middle East. Although most would agree that Islam is not a form of nationalism, Islamic attitudes and symbols clearly are used and

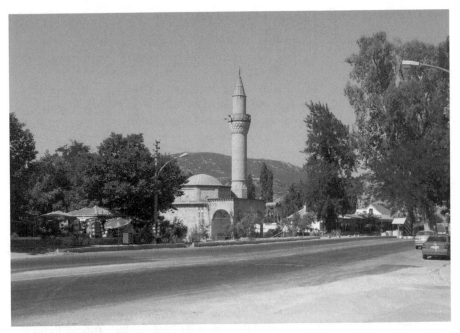

Islam Today: With about 128,424,000 adherents, Islam is one of the world's fastest growing religions. This mosque is located in Turkey near the ruins of the ancient city of Ephesus. *Source: Joe Weatherby*

manipulated by nationalists in the Middle East to legitimize their respective political objectives.

Muslims have certain important attitudes concerning non-Muslims. Islam victoriously entered the world scene over 1,400 years ago and remained so for almost 1,000 years. This long period of dominance has led to a collective mind-set that is reflected in the commonly used Muslim expression "Islam dominates and may not be dominated." Thus, for Muslims, some religions may be tolerated, but none will be allowed parity, much less dominance, if there is power to prevent it.

Although some Muslims view the defeats of the recent past with the rationalization that "Islam gains strength with every testing," there is no denying that it is particularly galling to have unbelievers dominating believers after all these centuries. This attitude is reflected in the responses of many people from the Middle East when they come in contact with the outside world. In the nineteenth century, the early military defeats administered by the West were rationalized on the grounds of Middle Eastern technological inferiority. Attitudes eventually evolved into a conspiratorial view of history in which the West was blamed for every problem in the region.

In the twentieth century, continuing defeats, both external and internal, led to a further sense of helplessness that is reflected in an almost irrational rage against anything Western or modern because it is believed to represent colonialism in a new form. This attitude can be seen in a number of ways, including the actions of students studying in the West, Islamic resurgence movements in the region, and the return to conservative Islamic dress by many university-educated women. Although forecasting the direction these frustrations will take is difficult, one may safely say that they have a real basis in fact and can only become a major unsettling element in Middle Eastern politics.

Generally, one focuses on "Islamic fundamentalism" when referring to the resurgence of Islam in the Middle East. What is often ignored is that fundamentalist movements exist in all major religions. Like their counterparts in Christianity and Judaism, the fundamentalist movements in Islam represent only a fraction of the total number of believers.

Political Islam

Throughout the history of Islam there have been groups that have held extremist views when compared with those of the majority of Muslims. This deviation from orthodoxy has occurred in most religions.

What cannot be ignored since the September 11, 2001, attacks is the reality that while there is not a monolithic fundamentalist movement using world terrorism as a strategy, there are many well-financed and organized fundamentalist groups that do. Furthermore, many Muslims who would not engage in terrorism do provide a fertile field of support for those fundamentalists advocating violence as a solution to Other World problems.

Islamist political movements have received positive receptions in many parts of the Middle East where the inhabitants have suffered the experiences of colonialism and neocolonialism, social injustice, poverty, and governmental ineffectiveness. These Muslims resent the harsh life, lack of jobs, and the culture of corruption that has created a wide gap between the rich and the poor. The fundamentalist movements offer hope for change and a new sense of worth to an often-bankrupt society tired of experimenting with imported solutions to problems. Fundamentalists have won many friends by taking leading roles in assisting the sick, the widowed, the poor, and the unemployed. They have been active in reforming the schools and universities. They have even been involved in such diverse activities as blood drives and providing financial aid for funerals. All these fundamentalist movements call for a moral sense of purpose that offers alternative solutions to the ones advocated by the secular nationalists and the traditional Muslim leaders who currently make up the Middle Eastern establishment.

The situation in Islam today is different. Almost all Muslims in the Other World have a memory of the excesses of Western colonial domination. These humiliations are constantly emphasized through the various forms of mass communication. In this way extremists can get wide exposure in the general population.

American and other Western military and political support for Israel coupled with Israeli victories and expansion are seen by Muslims as unjust. The Western military occupation of Iraq and Afghanistan can be easily translated into a new form of imperialism by the local mass media. The result is that while only a few in the Middle East are terrorists, many sympathize with their activities. The West through 200 years of action has lost the hearts and minds of many Muslims in the Other World.

The lesson of the Iranian revolution should now be clear to everyone. The Islamic reformers captured that revolution from secular nationalists because they offered the masses a chance to put an end to the evils of the past. The Iranian revolution should serve as a warning to the establishment in every state of the Middle East. If the injustices of the past are not addressed, there will be a rise in militant Islamic fundamentalist movements throughout the region.

In part, the Islamic resurgence has occurred because Islam avoided the stigma of failure that accompanied the secular philosophies. In the twentieth century, capitalism, Socialism, Marxism, and secular nationalisms have all been tried, and each has ended in failure. Only Islam offers hope for a renewal of Middle Eastern society without the taint of defeat, corruption, or association with colonialism. In whatever form it takes, Islam is today, as it has always been, the central factor in the lives of millions of people.

THE COLONIAL EXPERIENCE

For the better part of 1,300 years, Christians from Europe have fought Muslims from the East. During the last 200 years, this traditional conflict has been worsened by the impact of Western colonialism. It began with the French invasion of Egypt in 1798. Although this occupation was cut short by the British victory over the French fleet at the battle of Aboukir Bay,[9] it signaled a growing European interest in the area. Soon Britain, France, Italy, and Spain pursued their imperial objectives. Germany and Russia were absent only because their ambitions were frustrated by the British and the French. The British began their imperial adventure on the periphery of the Middle East by developing a series of strategic colonies on the shores of the Persian Gulf. By the opening of the Suez Canal in 1869, Britain controlled colonies stretching from Aden, at the mouth of the Red Sea, across southern Arabia all the way to India. Later, the British leased the Ottoman island of Cyprus and used it as a naval base to check the Russian attempts to enter the Mediterranean.

The British military occupied Egypt in 1882 because of a fear that the Egyptian government would not pay debts owed to foreign investors. This occupation was considered to be temporary, but the British did not leave Egypt until 1956. They were also interested in expanding their influence along the Red Sea. After much fighting, the Anglo-Egyptian forces occupied the Sudan in the last decade of the nineteenth century. By this time, Britain was the European country with the most extensive presence in the Middle East. When the Ottoman Empire was disbanded at the end of World War I, the British gained custody of Iraq, Palestine, and Transjordan. Semi-independent, these territories were administered by the British as mandates until the end of World War II. For the most part, British colonies in the Middle East were established as strategic colonies either to protect the lifeline to India or to create a stable environment for business investment.

After earlier French occupation of Egypt, French imperial activity was limited to the establishment of a colony in Algeria in 1830. Throughout the nineteenth century, French settlers expanded this colonial bridgehead until it included a large portion of North Africa. In the twentieth century, these holdings grew to include the southern portion of Morocco. France gained control of Syria and Lebanon as part of the partition of the Ottoman Empire. Regardless of their official status, the French administered these territories as colonies.

Spain and Italy developed imperial ambitions in North Africa during the early part of the twentieth century. Italy began a military occupation of Libya in 1911, when the territory was taken from the Ottomans. Building on several ancient enclaves, the Spanish joined the French in the partition of Morocco by occupying the northern portion in 1912. Although established largely for prestige purposes, these colonies proved difficult to completely pacify and expensive to maintain. Whether these colonies ever justified the blood and treasure required to hold them is doubtful.

Although Germany never actually controlled any territory in the Middle East, it did play an active political role as a participant in the great power struggles of the nineteenth and twentieth centuries. Before World War I, it sent military advisors and agents to both the Ottoman Empire and to Persia. It also participated in the planning and partial construction of the Berlin-Baghdad railway. Because the Germans were only in the Middle East in a financial or advisory capacity, and because they were opposed to the British and French, they were the most admired Europeans active in the region.

With the exception of the Navy in the war against the Barbary pirates, the United States avoided involvement in the Middle East until the end of World War II. Before President Truman played a leading role in the establishment of the state of Israel, the United States escaped the colonial stigma applied to most other developed countries. Since that time, the United States has been blamed for almost every ill that plagues the region.

During the past 200 years, almost every area in the Middle East has suffered under colonial occupation. Many of these areas fell under European control after World War I. As a result of this experience, the worst forms of imperialism are well remembered. At times, the Western powers have denied that they were officially in the Middle East in an imperial capacity. Nowhere in the Other World was Western imperialism implemented in a more hypocritical or cynical fashion.

There is no question that American intervention against Iraq in the two wars has heightened regional suspicions about the intentions of the United States. To many in the Middle East, American actions look very much like the past colonial activities of Britain and France.

GOVERNMENT

By the last quarter of the twentieth century, the countries of the Middle East had received formal independence. The end of colonialism resulted in the creation of one of the most politically complex regions in the Other World, containing democracies, authoritarian civilian states, military-dominated regimes, and monarchies. Morocco, Saudi Arabia, Jordan, and the Arab states of the Persian Gulf are authoritarian monarchies. Libya and Syria are regimes in which the military plays an important role. Egypt, Tunisia, and Turkey are civilian authoritarian states. Iraq, at this writing, is under an American military occupation arguably not unlike periods of British colonial rule during the twentieth century. Iran is an Islamic republic. In the past, both Israel and Lebanon have been considered Western-style democracies, but a civil war, Palestinian intrigues, Syrian military intervention, and the 1982 Israeli invasion combined to kill any short-term hope for an independent democracy.

By 2005, both Israel and Syria had officially withdrawn from Lebanon. By 2009, the Lebanese held what was termed by many as the first free elections in many years. In this election, the radical Islamic forces were soundly defeated. There is still much foreign intrigue being played out in Lebanon. Only time will tell if the Lebanese can truly return to the active democracy that once existed.

Since independence, few Middle Eastern regimes have demonstrated a sustained commitment to constitutional government. During periods of crisis, decision making has often reverted to informal systems that exist outside the formal mechanisms of government. Personalities and politics, therefore, rather than law, dominate the Middle East, as it is understood in the West, where following procedure is more important than winning. Middle Eastern government institutions must be considered as only a part of a greater cultural whole that is involved in political decision making. Traditional social, cultural, and religious institutions still play a disproportionate role in the politics of the region.

ECONOMICS AND NATURAL RESOURCES

One may generally state that with the exception of petroleum there are no significant mineral deposits in the Middle East. Although it is true that the resources of the region are limited, it is also true that much of the Middle East has not been thoroughly surveyed. Nevertheless, important mineral resources have been found in limited areas. Phosphate deposits are mined in Morocco, the former Spanish Sahara, Tunisia, Jordan, and Egypt. Iron ore is found in both North Africa and Turkey. Some gold has been discovered in Egypt and Saudi Arabia.

Clearly, oil is the great natural resource of the region. The Persian Gulf states provide significant amounts of the oil needed by Europe, Japan, and the United States.[10] What is perhaps more important is the realization that the oil states of the Middle East and North Africa control more than 60 percent of the world's proved reserves of oil and 25 percent of the reserves of natural gas. Because of these resources, this region will play an important economic role in world affairs for a very long time.

There is a vast contrast between oil-rich states with low populations and non-oil-producing states with high populations. For example, the United Arab Emirates' per capita gross national product (GNP) is about $43,400 (U.S.); that of the most populated Arab country, Egypt, is only $3,900. This discrepancy is a destabilizing element for the entire region. Former Iraqi President Saddam

Hussein cited economic inequity as a justification for his 1990 invasion of Kuwait:

> The malicious Westerners intentionally multiplied the number of countries with the result that the Arab nation could not achieve the integration needed to realize its full capability. When fragmenting the Arab homeland, they intentionally distanced the majority of the population and areas of cultural depth from riches and their sources.[11]

In an effort to redress some of this economic inequity, Saudi Arabia donated more than $120 billion in aid to the Other World during the last half of the twentieth century. This aid went to a total of 70 states, including 38 in Africa and 25 in Asia. The principal dollar recipients were friendly, poor Arab states.[12] In 2007, the *South China Morning Post* reported that the Kingdom is the world's leading donor of foreign aid with 5 percent of Saudi's GDP used for this purpose.[13]

The scarcity of water is the most serious impediment to improving agricultural production in the region. In an experiment, the Gulf States and Saudi Arabia have made great strides, at high cost, to start an agricultural industry. There have been calls from some of the poor states to use Arab oil money to make the non-oil-producing states breadbaskets for the region. This pan-Arab agricultural vision for the present is still a dream.

Turkey, with a better supply of water than the Arab states, has a well-developed agricultural system. The Turks rank among the top 20 nations in the world in the production of wheat, potatoes, barley, olives, tomatoes, sunflower seeds, cotton, tea, and wool. Iran produces wheat and grapes, and Egypt is famous for its high-quality cotton and oranges. Grain products and oranges are also produced in the Levant.

Case Studies

On Middle Eastern Nationalism

Despite their diversity, the countries of the Middle East underwent similar experiences that shaped their attitudes toward the outside world. All of them felt the humiliation of Western colonialism in one form or another. As was the case elsewhere in the Other World, reaction to the colonial experience served as a spark that ignited the fires of nationalism. Much of the force of Middle Eastern nationalism has centered on a resistance to Western colonialism.

Over the years, the competing nationalism of the Turks, Iranians, Egyptians, and Israelis has resulted in irredentist claims against one another. When one looks at the territorial aspirations of Turks, Kurds, Iranians, Iraqis, Israelis, Palestinians, Jordanians, Egyptians, and Libyans, it becomes obvious that if all their hopes are to be realized, the people of the Middle East will have to stack countries on top of one another. Reaching a satisfactory solution for these competing nationalistic objectives is one of the great political problems of the twenty-first century.

The traditional goal of Middle Eastern nationalism has been to achieve independence. Certainly, here, as elsewhere in the Other World, there is no agreement about what independence means or how it can be realized. The case studies in this chapter demonstrate that Middle Eastern nationalists have used a variety of approaches to achieve their objectives. Some have totally rejected the political and religious institutions of the past, as in Turkey, whereas others have sought independence by returning to what they believe to be the traditions of early Islam, as in Saudi Arabia and Iran. Finally, some nationalists have sought to chart a middle course similar to that of Egypt.

Although included in this discussion, the experience of Israel cannot readily be identified with other nationalism in the region. Israel is a settler state based on Western traditions. The Israeli experiment, however, is interesting because the Zionist form of nationalism is becoming more sectarian and Middle Eastern in its point of view.

In Chapter 2, nationalism was described as it has developed in the West. Among the features discussed were exclusivity and suspicion of others. Nationalism also supported the establishment and maintenance of the modern nation-state. We will see from the case studies in this chapter that this process also occurred in the Middle East. Some Middle Eastern nationalism, however, is moving in new directions, making it difficult to categorize in traditional terms. Some nationalistic movements no longer identify with the state boundaries that currently exist. They favor a new unification through supranational units such as the Levant or the Maghreb.

Many of the new nationalists view their own governments as illegitimate, and they almost repudiate those goals of their fathers 40 or 50 years ago. At that time, nationalistic efforts were directed at the overthrow of the colonial rule of Britain and France. Some Islamists who express their opposition to Israel, the United States, and the Arab establishment have articulated this changed attitude. They are voicing opposition to Arab governments of the left and right, and they are hoping to use the Islamist revolution as a catalyst to spread change to all the states of the Middle East. Recently, this point was forcefully made by the popular dissident Saudi cleric Sheik Hamoud al-Shuaibi. When asked about Arab governments that cooperate with the United States, he replied, "I don't specify any person or group of persons. But everyone who supports America against Islam is an infidel, someone who has strayed from the path of Islam."[14]

Middle Eastern nationalistic sentiments are primarily products of the urban centers. In much of the countryside, people still have loyalties similar to those found in prenationalistic Europe. To these people, the first contact with the authority of the state is often a point of contention and not an expression of loyalty. The villagers' contact with the government is limited to paying taxes and watching the state take their village sons away to the army. In many of the rural areas, the values of the central government have little or no legitimacy.

Traditional nationalism has failed to fulfill regional aspirations, so it is being either modified or discarded. In the past, nationalistic goals included political unity and freedom from both colonial and neocolonial domination. Arab nationalism also hoped to establish a classless society, a democratic political system, and an effective challenge to Israel. After years of formal independence, these stated goals remain unfulfilled dreams.

1. Turkey

Emerging from the Ottoman defeat of World War I, Turkish nationalism drew on the struggles and writings of the previous 50 years to create a movement based on the unifying aspects of the Turkish language and Turkish identification. This idea succeeded in ways in which the similar Young Turk movement had failed. In the nineteenth century, the Young Turks failed because the multinational character of the old Ottoman Empire rendered the appeal of being Turkish ineffective. Modern Turkish nationalists succeeded because the geographic limits of the new Turkish republic coincided with areas where people identified with being Turkish instead of Ottoman.

The new movement was led by a military hero named Ataturk (Mustafa Kemal). He was determined to break Turkey out of the backwardness of the Ottomans by creating a modern, secular Eastern European republic that could compete on equal terms with any country in the West. At the time, Ataturk's revolution was expected to be as significant as those of his contemporaries: Hitler, Mussolini, and Lenin. Seventy years after the founding of modern Turkey, Ataturk's reforms are not considered as revolutionary as they once were. Since the 1950s, Turkish nationalism has abandoned some of its more controversial themes. For example, Islam is a resurgent force in what was once considered to be a secular state. Nevertheless, as they have done for a half-century, Turkish nationalists still turn away from the Middle East and look toward Europe for their future. We should remember that the central feature of Turkish nationalism has been the rejection of the failed institutions and solutions of the past to create an entirely new system.

Throughout the second half of the twentieth century, Turkish politics continually revolved around heated disputes between competing civilian forces, often interrupted by military takeovers. After the passions of the moment cooled, the military would return to the barracks until the next time. During this period the military even removed Suleyman Demirel, the seven-time prime minister, from office on two occasions.

In domestic affairs, Turkey is a state with a population that is 99 percent Muslim. Most Turks still support the move to Westernize the country and join the European community. They fear fundamentalist movements like those that developed in Iran and Afghanistan. They do not want to see a civil war like the one taking place in Algeria. This paradox between Islam and Westernization forces the government to walk a fine line.

The fears of the secularists came true in the spring of 2000 when the "near Islamist" Justice and Development party came to power. In spite of a dispute with the United States over using Turkish bases for the invasion of Iraq in 2003, this party is more popular than ever. This triumph of the conservative Muslims over the traditional secular leaders represents a real shift in Turkish politics.

In their years of power, the Justice and Development Party has witnessed unprecedented growth and prosperity. The major beneficiaries of this prosperity have been the rural areas of central Turkey. The new middle class of this region is religious, is conservative, and supports the Justice and Development party. This breaks a more than 80-year tradition of power held by the urban secular middle class. In the summer of 2009, this shift of political power was confirmed when the Justice and Development Party was reelected by an overwhelming vote.

Turkish foreign policy focuses on four issues. First, the Turks hope to see more positive moves by the European Union toward setting a specific time for their admission to the Union. Second, the government believes that a positive vote on peace in Cyprus can be achieved. Third, the Turkish authorities want the United States to move to restrict the activities of Kurdish terrorists over raiding in Turkey from safe havens in Iraq. Finally, Turkey sees itself as a "bridge" between the Middle East and the West.

The European Union

Recently, these foreign policy goals have been frustrated. EU membership has been put on indefinite hold because of the opposition of France, Germany, and Austria. Failure in the quest to join the European club could cause Turkey to move closer to the Arab Middle East. The European Union dreams were further delayed in 2009 when the president of the Republic of Cyprus, Demetris Christofias, threatened to block any Turkish membership as long as Ankara occupied part of the island of Cyprus.

Loss of hope of ever joining the European Union also hardens the stand of those who believe that Turkey must defy European opinion and oppose the reunification of Cyprus. Under the present circumstances, there is little Turkish sympathy for compromising this issue.

The Kurds remain a problem for Turkey. As the Americans face more opposition in Iraq, the chances of a semiautonomous "Kurdistan" are increasing. This causes real concern in Turkey because of the continuing dirty war with the Turkish-based Kurds who often use Iraqi Kurdish territory for a safe haven. The possibility of a Turkish incursion into Iraqi Kurdish land is an increasing possibility.

Although Turkish importance to the West may not be what it was during the cold war, it is still important for several reasons. Although this relationship is sometimes a "rocky one," Turkey is still democratic and secular. In March 2005, President (then foreign minister) Abdullah Gul signaled that there would be little change in Turkish policy when he said, "We do not plan to have an agenda that includes Islamic policies and laws."[15] The question that could be asked in 2009, Is the preceding statement still correct?

Cyprus

In 1974, an Athens-supported *coup d'état* overthrew the multicultural government of Cyprus in an attempt to link the island to Greece. This action provoked a Turkish military intervention. The Turkish victory divided the island between Greek and Turkish *Cypriots*.

The Turks justify their action by pointing out that the London treaties of 1959 and 1960 allowed Turkish action. The treaties also prohibited Cyprus from joining any other state or group of states without the consent of all the interested parties, including Turkey.[16]

Starting in 2001, more contact between Greeks and Turks on the island occurred. The Turks opened their border with Greek Cyprus in 2003. In 2004, the majority of Turkish Cypriots accepted the UN-sponsored reunification plan. Although the Greek population rejected the proposal, there still remained hope that some form of agreement might eventually take place. In the meantime, a divided Greek Cyprus became a member of the European Union in 2004.

In spite of many difficulties, the Turkish-backed Cypriot president, Mehmet Ali Talat, hinted that there could be a referendum on peace as early as 2010. He and the Greek Cypriot president have been engaged in talks aimed at holding just such a vote.[17]

Kurdistan

Kurdish aspirations for independence pose threats to several states, including Turkey, Iran, Iraq, and Syria. In the case of Turkey, low-intensity conflicts with the Kurds have been taking place for years. Many Turks are fearful that the American defeat of the government of Iraq could lead to the establishment of a Kurdish state in northern Iraq. If that event were to occur, that conflict would almost certainly spread to eastern Turkey.

For years, The Kurdistan Workers Party (PPK) had been accused of mounting terrorist attacks on Turkey from safe havens in Kurdish Iraq. In October 2007, the Turkish Parliament took action to stop these actions by giving the military authorization to mount cross-border operations against the PPK. Forces in Iraq vowed to oppose any Turkish incursion into their territory. If a serious military conflict were to occur on this border, it could easily spread from an Iraqi and Turkish dispute to involve Kurdish lands in both Syria and Iran.[18]

2. Iran

Like the Ottoman Empire, the Persian Empire (Iran) was an Islamic monarchy, except that Shi'ite Islam was the state religion. Iranian nationalism developed during Anglo-Russian interventions in Persia in the early days of the twentieth century. The history of nationalism in Iran can be divided into three periods: the reign of the Pahlavis, the Mossadeq crisis, and the Islamic Republic.

The first Pahlavi, Reza Shah, was an army officer who seized power in 1921 and had himself crowned king (*Shah*) in 1925. His rule lasted from 1925 to 1941. Reza Shah believed that a modern state, like Turkey, could be created in Iran. Although many proposed changes emulated those of Ataturk in Turkey, Iran was far less Westernized and change came slowly. Unlike Ataturk and Lenin, who destroyed the old to create a new system, Reza Shah wrapped himself in the traditions of the old Persian monarchy to establish his legitimacy. In the late 1930s, he indicated a sympathy for Adolph Hitler that provoked a Russian-British-American intervention in Iran once World War II began. Reza Shah was deposed, and with the approval of the Western powers, his young son, Mohammad Reza, was placed in power.

Mohammad Reza's reign was uneventful until the Iranian oil crisis of 1951. At that time, a popular nationalist leader, Mohammed Mossadeq, formed a political organization known as the National Front. He gained control of the government and then nationalized the British-owned Anglo-Iranian Oil Company. The Western oil powers responded by boycotting Iranian oil. Deprived of oil revenue, by 1953 the Iranian economy was in such bad shape that the Shah used this crisis to attempt to have Mossadeq removed. The Shah's action failed, and he was forced into exile in Switzerland. In one of the most interesting periods in modern history, supporters of the Shah were persuaded—it is now believed, with CIA help—to stage a counterrevolt.[19] Mossadeq's allies failed to respond effectively, and the Shah was returned to power within days. The downfall of Mossadeq ended the rule of one of the only truly popular, secular nationalist leaders in modern Iranian history. Returned to power, the Shah ruled in an increasingly arbitrary manner until he was forced into exile in 1979.

When the Ayatollah Khomeini assumed power in Iran, he enjoyed the support of both the secular nationalists abroad and the religious nationalists at home. The Western-educated elites, who accompanied him on his return flight from exile in France, carried foreign passports. Khomeini's first cabinet was made up of these secular nationalists. Many of these officials expected him to bring liberal democratic rule to Iran. Within three years, all of these officials had disappeared from the political scene. Ayatollah Khomeini built his political base among the poor and the dispossessed who also happened to be the religious conservatives. In this way, he was able to shape the Iranian revolution into a struggle that was both religious and class oriented.

Totally reversing two millennia of Iranian monarchy, the Islamic Republic of Iran has represented a temporary victory for the religious nationalists over the secular nationalists of the 1950s. The leaders make effective use of the symbols of Shi'ite Islam to maintain authority over the Iranian people. According to the rhetoric of the regime, this movement represents an attempt by Shi'ism to gain the leadership of the Islamic world. The progress of the Islamic revolutionary model developed by Iran is being watched with interest by many states of the Other World.

In 1997 a moderate Shi'ite cleric was elected president of the republic, gaining almost 70 percent of the vote. Although this victory was confirmed in Mohammad Khatami's reelection four years later, the struggle between reformers and traditionalists continues. In a blow to the reformers, Iran elected a hard-line president, Mahmoud

Ahmadinejad, in 2005. Preceding the election, the opposition had largely been marginalized by the conservative religious leadership called "the guardians." Dozens of opposition politicians were disqualified and their newspapers were closed before the election took place. *New York Times* columnist David Sanger stated that "the Bush administration declared the process rigged."[20]

Since ascending to the presidency, Mahmoud Ahmadinejad has played an active role in challenging the West in general and the United States in particular. He has stepped up Iran's nuclear research and development. He has begun the modernization of Iran's military, including the development of a credible missile capability. He has proved to be a destabilizing factor in the region by supplying anti-Israeli and anti-American forces in Syria and Iraq.

The real power in Iran is not held by the government or its officials; it is welded by the conservative clerics or guardians under the leadership of the Supreme Leader of the Islamic Revolution, who is elected for life, Ayatollah Sayyed Ali Khamenei. He controls the political apparatus of the country and, in practice, overrules the president and the assembly. The presence of an American army on the borders cannot help but remind the clerics of the repeated Western interventions into their country during the last century. They are playing a very dangerous game as the leaders of Iraq found out.

The power structure of the ruling elite of Iran was shaken to the core during the disputed presidential election in 2009. The "losing" candidate, Mir-Hossein Mousavi, challenged the re-election of Mahmoud Ahmadinejad.

Literally thousands of Iranians from all over the country engaged in protracted election protests. Finally, the supreme leader, Ayatollah Ali Khamenei, ordered a crackdown on the protestors. In spite of that order, some demonstrations were still taking place a month later.

Although the protests have largely been suppressed, the ruling powers have lost a great deal of legitimacy. With a population largely made up of people under 25 but ruled by old men, it is only a question of time before the opposition reasserts itself. Next time the unrest could threaten the survival of the regime.

The real test for the long-term success of the Iranian revolution depends on the ability of the state to make measurable improvements in the lives of most Iranians while, at the same time, avoiding a conflict with the United States. This revolutionary balancing act will not be an easy one to accomplish.

3. Egypt

Egyptian nationalism emerged as a reaction to Napoleon's invasion in 1798. The national movement is almost as old as the French Revolution. Experiencing both peaks and valleys during the nineteenth century, nationalists later championed the call to end the British occupation of Egypt that had begun in 1882. In the 1920s, a middle-class anti-British political movement called the Wafd emerged to dominate Egyptian politics until the rise of Nasser in 1952.[21]

Probably no man in the history of the modern Middle East has successfully captured the hearts and minds of Other World peoples of all social classes and political philosophies as did Gamal Abdel Nasser. Espousing a militant nationalism of Arab Socialism and social reform at home, Nasser also called for independence from foreign domination, opposition to Israel, and Arab unity abroad. He is best remembered by Middle Easterners for his successful challenges to the policies of the United States and the former colonial powers of Western Europe. Nasser's continuing contribution to Egyptian nationalism is symbolic and transcends specific successes or failures of his policies while he was the country's leader. Following Nasser's death in 1970, Anwar el-Sadat assumed control.

Anwar el-Sadat's 11-year rule over Egypt is extolled in the West as an example of what an enlightened Other World nationalist can accomplish. Sadat expelled the Russians in 1972, fought Israel to a standoff in 1973, and then went to Jerusalem to begin a process that resulted in the 1979 peace agreement with Israel. Sadat's assassination in 1981 is still viewed in the West as a great setback to peace efforts in the region. Surprisingly, Egyptians rarely discuss the tenure of Sadat. In Egypt, he is considered to have frustrated the cause of Arab unity by stressing the separateness of Egypt and peace with Israel over the greater good of the Arab people. Sadat's virtual surrender of the Egyptian economy to Western investment raised new fears of a return to neocolonial status. The danger of an erosion of independence, whether direct or indirect, has become central to the thinking of many Egyptian nationalists who were opposed to Sadat.

President Hosni Mubarak sought to develop a nationalism that steered a middle course between the economic excesses of Sadat and the political adventurism of Nasser. He worked hard to end Egypt's isolation in the Arab world. Expelled after the Camp David agreement, Egypt was restored as a member of the Arab League and the league's headquarters was returned to Cairo. The Egyptians continued to honor the peace agreement with Israel. They reestablished diplomatic relations with Russia and remained a close Arab ally of the United States. The thrust of all of these diplomatic efforts was aimed at establishing Egypt as a bridge between competing states in the region.

In domestic policies, Mubarak remains firmly entrenched in power. When he first assumed the role of president after Sadat, Mubarak asserted that he would remain in office until the end of his term. In 2005, he announced that he would stand for election again. He won that election handily. In 2009, there were rumors that he planned to eventually pass the office to his son.[22]

A new development in the Egyptian opposition movement has occurred among the young. This involves the Internet. Today it is estimated that there could be as many as one in nine Egyptians with Internet access. Facebook has become a vehicle for young political activism throughout the Middle East. As with recent events in Iran, the Internet could become a political force among the young in Egypt.[23]

There is no question that elections in Iraq, Lebanon, and Palestinian territories has put pressure on the Egyptian authorities to make changes. In allowing limited opposition to Mubarak, they faced enormous difficulties, not the least being more than 24 years of political stagnation. The problems of Egypt were accelerated by a series of terrorist attacks on the infrastructure of the tourist industry. One of the most serious of these attacks occurred at Sharm el Sheikh, where more than 80 people were killed in July 2005. These terrorist operations represent a major threat to the continued domestic stability of the regime. Egypt is one place where the rise of a radical Islamic movement strong enough to unseat the present pro-Western authoritarian leadership remains a distinct possibility.

In 2009, Egyptian foreign policy was directed at convincing Israel that no normalization of life would be possible until both the Palestinian situation and the status of Jerusalem were resolved satisfactorily. At the same time, Mubarak tried to convince the Americans that no peace in the Middle East would occur without forceful leadership from the United States. To successfully pursue these often-contradictory policies, Mubarak had to avoid offending the United States while recognizing that the majority of people in Egypt were anti-Israel.

In a sense, Egyptian policy toward the United States is schizophrenic. On the one hand, the media mouths a political rhetoric that is anti-American. At every opportunity, the United States is portrayed as the protector of Israel. Furthermore, American interest in the Arab world is limited to easy access to low-cost oil. On the other hand,

Egyptian economic interests are closely tied to maintaining good external relations with the United States. Egypt cannot afford to ignore the major aid package dispersed every year by the Americans. Egyptians learned in 2003 when they backed the European Union's position against the importation of American beef into Europe that the United States can "bite back." The United States abruptly suspended talks on a U.S.–Egypt free trade agreement. The message was clear. The neocolonial phrase "one should not bite the hand that feeds you" still applies.

In the Arab world, Egypt still tries to maintain a leadership role as Arab spokesman. Again, however, the American invasion of Iraq clearly demonstrated the limits of Egyptian persuasion when a major power decides that its national interests are threatened.

Of all the states of the Middle East, Egypt is the one that authorities speak of in the most pessimistic terms. Beset by a population explosion that is uncontrollable without using unacceptably draconian measures, no Egyptian government can hope to make significant improvements in the lives of the people in the foreseeable future. The question being asked by all who look at Egypt's problems is: How long will the Egyptian masses wait before turning to more radical solutions to their problems? Because Egypt is the most populous Arab state, the direction that it takes will determine the future of much of the Middle East. Is time for Egypt growing short? Egypt's leaders have many problems and few solutions. The miracle is that Egypt continues to limp on, surviving each gloomy forecast.

4. Saudi Arabian "Bedo-Nationalism"

One often speaks of the British royal family as "the family business." Perhaps no better example of a family business exists than that of the House of Saud. Since the alliance between a clan chief, Muhammad ibn Saud, and a religious leader, Muhammad ibn Wahhab, in 1744, the House of Saud has played the defining role in Arabian politics. Whether in or out of power, Sauds have always been a force to be reckoned with.

The modern story of Saudi Arabia began in 1901, when the famous leader, Abdul-Aziz ibn Abdul Rahman Al-Saud (ibn Saud), rode out of desert exile in Kuwait to capture the fortress of Riyadh. From that base he gradually increased his hold on the Arabian Peninsula until he was able to unite all the major tribes and their territories to create the present state of Saudi Arabia (called the Kingdom) in 1932.

In 1933, ibn Saud rejected British advice and granted a 60-year petroleum concession to Standard Oil of California. When a great pool of oil was discovered, this arrangement became one of the most profitable business deals in history. The oil company first evolved into the Arabian American Oil Company (Aramco) and later, under Saudization, into Saudi Aramco.

Ibn Saud's greatness was in his ability to first win military victories and then consolidate power by linking his family through marriage and alliances to the other major families in the region. This tribal linkage has remained intact to the present day. Furthermore, he was able, in his international politics, to skillfully balance his role as an Arab leader with that of a world leader.

Using the Kingdom's vast oil wealth, he and his sons were able to wrench the Arabian people out of the Bedouin system into the modern world. All of this was accomplished without sacrificing the region's traditional values. Saudi Arabia became the world's best example of the premise that a state did not have to be Western to be modern. Because of the leadership from the House of Saud, residents of the Kingdom were able to enjoy the benefits of the modern world while remaining true to the religious and cultural traditions of their Bedouin roots.

At first glance the Saudi government is authoritarian. However, this view dismisses the complexity of Arabian politics by substituting Western models of government. Politics in Arabia are true to the traditions of that region. The West separates religion from government and focuses on problem-solving strategies. The Kingdom combines religion and government by placing all issues within an Islamic context. These issues are dealt with on the basis of personal relationships backed by family honor.

Although updated many times in this century, the Kingdom is organized around the complex interaction of powerful tribes and families, often having blood ties to the House of Saud. At each level from district to province, there is room for input offered to local leaders through an unstructured meeting called the *majlis*. In the "bedo-democracy" of a *majlis*, the leader is the first among equals. Appointed governors called *amirs* repeat this process at provincial levels. The national Majlis al-Surah is composed of 150 members who advise the king. The king rules; he does not reign as in the English monarchy.

There is a modest change taking place, however. King and Prime Minister Abdallah ben al-Aziz Al Saud is a hereditary ruler. Arrangements have been made creating a committee of Saudi princes who will select the future kings.

Under the King, Saudi government is still silent family government. Consequently, there are questions about how much real influence is exercised by the formal governmental apparatus. It is known that there are factions within the family itself, but little is known about how important decisions are actually made.

In October 2003, the government announced the intention to develop a process for electing half of the Majlis al-Surah. As of fall 2009, no elections had been held. There has also been a movement for holding local elections, but no action has been taken. Instead, the tribal tradition of choice is still observed. In 2005, there were some elections held at the municipal level.

Socially, women are segregated from men in schools and the workplace. This is a costly and inefficient system. But because of the high level of education throughout the Kingdom, it works. There have been other attempts at modernizing society that have yet to succeed. Most apparent of these reform measures are attempts to change the rules that prohibit women from driving cars or voting in elections.

Because of the linkage of the state with Islam, the Kingdom does not have a constitution in the Western sense. The Koran is the constitution of Saudi Arabia. The state does have a basic law that covers many items found in Western constitutions. These provisions include general rules for the organization of the financial system, the eligibility for succession to king, and the organization of the judiciary. The basic law also provides for a citizen's bill of rights, the protection of private property, and the protection from arbitrary punishment.

The Future for Bedo Nationalism

How long can this system of tribal leadership last? Demographics indicate that the future for the system is not promising. Like the king, who was born in 1924, most of the Saudi leadership comes from the 2.4 percent of the population that is over 65 years in age. At the same time, almost 60 percent of the population is under 25! To many observers, there is a clear separation between the old and one of the fastest growing youth populations in the world. This disconnection is complicated by a decline in economic opportunity within the kingdom. Between 13 percent and 25 percent of Saudi males are unemployed. It is only a matter of time before the Saudi young, both male and female, demand a greater voice in Saudi affairs. Will the current system be able to reinvent itself to meet these new demands or will another system emerge to guide Saudi Arabia through the first half of the twenty-first century?

Attempts at reform in Saudi Arabia have been uneven. In 2009, the King replaced some conservative members of high councils dealing with law and education. He also pledged $12.5 billion to establish a new, more open technical university for both men and women. This new university is expected to be free from conservative religious influence. Its endowment, one of the world's largest, is designed to attract the best and brightest instructors from all over the world.

At the same time, the government announced that the local elections that were held in 2005 and scheduled to be repeated would be delayed for two years. This delay in the fledgling attempts at democracy discouraged many Saudi reformers.

September 11 exposed a dark side of the Saudi story. A significant number of the terrorists who bombed the World Trade Center that day were Saudis. When the United States traced the plot back to Saudi Osama bin Laden's organization in Afghanistan, more Saudi involvement was found. The question of why Saudis and others from the wealthy Gulf states would actively participate in terrorism needs an answer.

The Arabian Peninsula has been very religious since the time of Mohammed. In the eighteenth century, the Sauds adapted Wahhabism. The Wahhabi interpretation of Islam is probably the most conservative in the Muslim world. For most of this time, Arabia remained isolated and poor. In this environment it was easy for a ruler to impose a conservative system.

The problem started to occur with the discovery of oil in Arabia. This influx of wealth also brought foreigners and other ideas along with technical expertise. Saudis welcomed the wealth but not the Western ideas on cultural and political issues. Rationalizing the contradiction between Wahhabi religious zealotry and opposition to materialism, while at the same time acquiring great wealth, was a problem. The House of Saud maintained its power by saying one thing abroad while saying something different and catering to religious conservatives at home. Domestically, the government tolerated no formal political or religious dissent. They established state-supported mosques everywhere. The clerics were required to remain supportive of government policy. Through this strategy, the House of Saud was able to walk a fine line between being supportive of the West abroad while maintaining a certain tolerance for the radical elements of Saudi society at home.

Two events have brought this policy into question. First, the Russian war in Afghanistan mobilized large numbers of Saudis to go and fight there. However, when the veterans returned to their homes, many were committed to adopting a military solution to solve their social problems.

The second problem occurred as a by-product of the Western intervention in the effort to expel Iraq from Kuwait. When the war was over, the Americans did not go home. The fact that America, Israel's greatest supporter, continued to base large numbers of troops in the region is a source of great resentment to many Saudis.

Working through religious clerics who remain largely outside the state religious establishment, an underground of radicals emerged. These militants often were wealthy, and many were Afghan war veterans. All saw that the oil business had corrupted the purity of Islam. Saudi and Gulf leaders were compromising their principles to deal with the West. Typical of the radical clerics who have inflamed these militants is Sheik Hamoud al-Shuaibi. He calls for every Muslim to stand up with the Afghan people and fight against America.[24] Because the normal political and media outlets are closed to them, the religious militants have coalesced around "house mosques."

Clerics like Sheik al-Shuaibi remain outside the official religious establishment. Although not yet powerful enough in Saudi Arabia to threaten the survival of the government, these militants can cause social unrest if the government attempts to implement the serious crackdown that America would like to see. Saudi Arabia today has a young, potentially volatile population. Whether the Saudi version of Bedo Nationalism can survive the rise of these Muslim militants remains to be seen.

In the aftermath of the events of September 11, the war in Afghanistan, and the invasion of Iraq, American support of the ruling regime of Saudi Arabia has been severely shaken. American troops have been redeployed outside the Kingdom. American press accounts of some Saudi involvement in terrorist acts against the United States have shaken the "special relationship" between America and the Kingdom.

The Kingdom faces many other challenges. The birthrate is one of the highest in the Middle East. There are far too many guest workers taking jobs that Saudis should be prepared to occupy. The Kingdom must broaden the economic base before the oil revenue declines. Finally, Saudi Arabia's geographical location dictates that the Kingdom must be prepared to play a major role in the Gulf long after the Americans have sailed over the horizon.

5. The Arabs

Political scientist Karl Deutsch once said, "A nation is a group of people united by a common dislike of their neighbors and a common misconception about their ethnic origins."[25] If one looks at the spirit of the nation from the perspective of the Arabs, it is clear that Deutsch's observation applies to the Middle East.

Arab nationalism is often characterized as xenophobic, negative in international outlook, and dependent on a historical past that is often more myth than fact. Arabs are suspicious of others because of what they perceive to be more than 200 years of lies and deceit by the colonial powers. Throughout the nineteenth century and well into the twentieth, this pattern repeated itself with cynical regularity. For example, the British promised the Arabs independence during World War I, only to carve up the region into colonial mandates when the war was over. Arab nationalists from Gamal Nasser to Osama bin Laden have seen this event as a treacherous act, ensuring that the Arabs would remain a divided people who could be controlled by outsiders. Many Arab nationalists see both American support for the state of Israel and the occupation of Iraq as fresh attempts to divide and dominate the Arab people.

The history that forms the basis of Arab nationalism is characterized by the gap between aspiration and reality. The aspiration is the reestablishment of a single, united Arab nation similar to the nation that existed during the early days of Mohammed. The reality is that this kind of unity never existed. Even during its early days, the Islamic state was characterized by civil wars and assassinations. In modern times, the aspiration has been to free the Arab people from foreign domination. The reality has been a reliance on foreign influence, aid, and military support to accomplish Arab political goals. For example, Arab opposition to Israel caused nationalists to embrace almost any outside power that was perceived as being willing to aid in this effort. The reality of this approach has been to mortgage Arab sovereignty to external obligations. Finally, the aspiration that oil can be used to achieve Arab economic independence has clashed with the reality that Arab oil must be sold abroad for hard currency. Instead of unifying the Arabs, wealth generated by oil has divided rich and poor Arabs across the region. Although Arab nationalism is a potent force, it has failed to meet the aspirations of those who seek the rebirth of a great, unified Arab nation.

6. Israel

Israel may be described as a state with a European ideology transplanted into the Middle East. This impression may be less true today than it was in the past. Modern Israel is more conservative, militaristic, sectarian, and Middle Eastern than it once was. With U.S. financial aid more important than ever before, Israel reflects many of the same neocolonial fears and suspicions that are found in other Middle Eastern states.

Founded in Basel, Switzerland, in 1897, modern political *Zionism* is a form of nationalism that calls for the establishment and maintenance of a Jewish state in Palestine. The return to Palestine is based on Jewish traditions that go back 2,000 years. The specifics of this call have been modified to fit the changing needs of the movement. Today, Zionism generally means that the survival of the State of Israel must be guaranteed as a symbol of refuge for Jews everywhere, whether they choose to immigrate or not.

Over the years, two factions of nationalists emerged to contend for power. The Israeli Labor Alignment represented secular nationalists who were interested in the establishment of a modern state with viable borders. These nationalists included some of the great names of Israeli history, such as David Ben-Gurion, Golda Meir, and Abba Eban. They represented the ideas of the European founders of Israel, and their party alignments dominated the policies of Israel from the nation's founding until 1977.

In 1977, the demographic changes in the Israeli population tilted politics in favor of non-European Jews. Continuing Palestinian hostilities and new demographics created conditions that brought a conservative coalition, called the Likud, to power. The Likud represented the second direction taken by the Zionists. Their view argued for the creation of a "Greater Israel" or a "Promised Land" that would include those portions of the Middle East that tradition held were promised by God to the ancient Hebrews. In recent years, non-European Jews who had experienced Arab domination also tended to support Likud's hard-line policies toward the Arabs.

In the new century, Israeli nationalism is in a state of transition. No one can predict with certainty the final direction that the movement will take. On the one hand, Israel can pursue the maximalist goal of recovering and then holding all of "the land of Israel." To the outsider, this course seems to be not only impractical but also sure to doom the state to entering into an endless cycle of debilitating wars with the Arabs, followed by costly occupations. To many, this is a process in which Israel cannot hope to prevail.

The other nationalist approach is accommodation with Israel's neighbors. This choice is also dangerous and difficult. It involves making painful concessions on issues that are of primary concern to most Israelis. This course is made all the more difficult because it means that Israel will have to give up the most when exchanging "land for peace." It is analogous to sacrificing several chess pawns in order to win the game. Here, winning for Israel is survival as a Jewish state with secure borders and peaceful neighbors.

The Palestinians and Israelis seriously discussed a negotiated settlement in the summer of 1999 only to have the Palestinian leader Yasser Arafat reject the peace plan at the last minute. To outsiders, this plan had possibilities because it offered Palestinian statehood, a return of most of the West Bank and Gaza, plus a foothold of some kind in Jerusalem. In return, the Palestinians would have had to give up all disputed claims in Israel and agree to a permanent peace. In short, the Palestinians would have largely gained politically what they had lost on the battlefield.

Following this disappointment, a hard-line Likud, under the leadership of Ariel Sharon, took power in Israel. Many observers stated ruefully that "the Palestinians had never missed an opportunity to miss an opportunity." Certainly, the deal offered by the

Israelis in 1999 would not likely be repeated. This deadlock ushered in the beginning of years of low-intensity conflict that embittered parties on both sides.

Following the death of Yasser Arafat in 2004, Ariel Sharon announced to the world that Israel would impose a "temporary" solution by extending an already begun wall of separation in the West Bank and by a total withdrawal from Gaza. The withdrawal from Gaza was complete in the summer of 2005.

Israel bought some time by withdrawing from Gaza. Still, the major problems separating Palestinians and Israelis remained: the future of the West Bank and Arab Jerusalem. These issues are so great that any major moves by the Israelis to meet Arab demands could result in domestic unrest in Israel itself.

Politically, the Labor Party had been largely marginalized since the failure of the 1999 peace talks. Likud, however, threatened to split over what had to be done to achieve peace with the Palestinians in Gaza. On November 21, 2005, Ariel Sharon, the former war hawk, turned Israeli politics upside down when he announced that he was resigning from Likud and forming a new center political party dedicated to a peaceful settlement of the conflict. Shortly after the founding of his centrist party, Kadima, Prime Minister Sharon suffered a massive stroke. He was replaced by Ehud Olmert, as acting Prime Minister and the Kadima head. Kadima won the election held in March 2006. The party followed the path laid out by Sharon. In the absence of the settlement with the Palestinians, Israel threatened to establish unilaterally a border between the two parties. They extended the security wall that they were building to enclose all the West Bank of the Jordan that they intended to hold. All Israeli civilians were eventually to be relocated to permanent settlements within the wall. The Israeli army continued to remain active in those areas evacuated. Kadima leaders called this a civilian disengagement with a military buffer remaining in the abandoned areas.

Kadima's plans were severely shaken by two events. In the summer of 2006, Israel responded to a Hezbollah attack originating in Lebanon with a heavy bombing and shelling campaign. For the first time, the Israeli Defense Force was not quickly victorious. Rather than incur the heavy losses expected in a new occupation of Lebanon, the Israelis were forced to accept a stalemate with the United Nations border guarantees. The perceived Israeli military invincibility was severely shaken both at home and abroad. To many, Israel was seen as having fought a campaign with little or nothing gained. The second event occurred when elections were held in the winter of 2006 in the Palestinian territories. The Palestinians chose a Hamas-led government over their previous Fatah leadership. This result provoked a Western boycott of aid normally sent to the Territories. In 2007, Hamas seized power in Gaza, and the Fatah held on to control of the West Bank. In effect, Israel was now faced with the problem of dealing with two mutually hostile Palestinian entities.

There are the secular Israelis who want a return to normalcy. The sectarian nationalists in the Likud settlement movement want no further concessions made to the Palestinians. Some even threaten violence against their own government if more concessions are made.

By 2009, many Israelis had become skeptical that any settlement could ever be made with the Palestinians as they're presently constituted. Following new elections, the hard-line Prime Minister Benjamin Netanyahu was selected to create a rightist government.

Prime Minister Netanyahu's comments on Jerusalem–West Bank settlements in a two-state solution with the Palestinians placed his government in direct conflict with the Obama administration's policy on the Palestinian question. The new Prime Minister was pressured by the United States to acknowledge that a future Palestinian state might be possible. However, he placed so many restrictions on his plan that it was immediately rejected by the Palestinians. The Israeli Prime Minister's hard line was reinforced when he was quoted as saying, "United Jerusalem is the capitol of the Jewish people and the State of Israel. Our sovereignty over it cannot be challenged."[26] The Prime Minister's statement was a "deal breaker" for the Palestinians. All Palestinians demand that parts of East Jerusalem (the Arab quarter) shall become the capital of any future Palestinian state.

For the time being, the Netanayahu government is trying to shift American attention toward Iran. At the same time, it continues to isolate the Jerusalem Palestinians while expanding Jewish settlements in the West Bank. Peace may have been close in 1999. In 2009, a lasting peace between the Palestinians and Israelis seems further away than ever.

Looking Ahead

Trust everybody, but cut the cards.

Finley Peter Dunne

As we shall see in the "Flashpoints" section at the end of this chapter, many of the region's conflicts are indigenous and based on long-standing cultural and geographic factors. On the surface, each of these issues should stand alone. In the Middle East, however, the Arab-Israeli conflict and the Western occupation of Iraq dominate the politics of the region.

What are the prospects for peace? Two scenarios illustrate the difficulty in attempting to forecast the future for any political issue in the Middle East.

The Pessimistic Scenario

It is not the big armies that win battles; it is the good ones.

Maurice De Saxe, Marshal-General of France

Without a settlement to the Arab-Israeli dispute, those parties on both sides who prefer the status quo to peace can be expected to continue their present policies. The status quo benefits those Israeli factions that believe that any settlement will force Israel to make concessions in territory. Palestinians are fearful that the Arab states might be willing to sacrifice the Palestinian nation to regain territory previously lost to Israel. Many Arab leaders continue to use their dispute with Israel as an excuse to prepare for war abroad and to avoid reform at home.

If the deadlock continues, acts of terrorism will increase. The Arabs will accelerate the arms race to achieve qualitative military parity with the Israelis. This military development will be achieved at the expense of funds that could be made available for social development. The likely result of this scenario will be the continuation of Arab regimes that are volatile and unstable.

If the American and allied efforts fail in Iraq, the outcome is almost too grim to contemplate. There could be a collapse of central authority followed by a civil war. The more numerous Shi'ia will likely separate and move in the direction of the Iranian model. Those Sunnis who survive such a conflict will link with Syria. An "independent" Kurdish region will almost certainly provoke a Turkish invasion followed by an occupation. Iraq will cease to exist, and the balance of power in the Middle East will be fundamentally changed.

The Optimistic Scenario

> God willing, there will be peace.
>
> A Palestinian Expression

The 2003 Iraq War involved hundreds of thousands of American soldiers. In this conflict, the Arab–Israeli dispute was a secondary but important aspect. If not understood before, that the issues in the Middle East are interrelated became obvious. This event shattered the complacency of those in the Bush administration who had wished to avoid direct involvement in the affairs of the Middle East. Badly frightened at the prospect of a permanent Vietnam, many Americans became active in attempts to eliminate the conditions that could lead to an extended American military involvement in the region. The result was that the United States applied pressure on all the parties involved to force them to negotiate.

The end of the cold war also freed the hands of those leaders in the West who had used the policy of containing Communism as a test for dealing with the governments in the Middle East. For the first time, there was agreement that it was in the interest of Russia, the United States, and the other Western powers to encourage a settlement between Arabs and Israelis. The major powers combined with a majority of other states in the world to encourage the parties of the region to talk seriously about peace. Although Palestinians and Israelis continued to play the game of attack and reprisal, there was still some hope. Both the Israelis and Palestinians had nowhere to go. There was no plan B. Eventually, the issues dividing the parties would have to be resolved if either party is to survive in peace.

In Iraq, a successful democratic state in the heart of the Arab world would energize democratic movements everywhere. An oil-rich, stable, and peaceful Iraq would exert great positive influence on the entire region. The result would make the blood and treasure expended by the West worth the price.

FLASHPOINTS

Palestine

At the beginning of the twenty-first century, a twentieth-century problem is still the central feature of Middle Eastern politics. This dispute is between Jews and Arabs over the control of Palestine. Since 1948, the Palestinian focus has been on opposition to the state of Israel. At the same time, Israeli Jews have consistently opposed the creation of a Palestinian state. The result has been a series of Arab, Palestinian, and Israeli conflicts fought in 1948, 1956, 1967, 1973, 1982, 2006, and 2009. In addition, there have been a number of continuing low-intensity conflicts that are characterized by the cycle of attack and retaliation. Israelis call Palestinian bombers and hijackers "terrorists"; Palestinians call the attacks by the Israeli military and settler shootings and bombings acts of "state terrorism."

Before discussing the specifics of the dispute, we need to make several assumptions. First, the leaders on both sides have raised their demands to the heights of irreducible principles. This has had the effect of painting both parties into ideological corners that ensure that peace is impossible without ideological surrender of the other side.

Second, the ongoing conflict has resulted in both sides suffering grievous injuries at the hands of their opponents. Peace requires a new way of thinking where these past injustices are forgiven if not forgotten.

Third, because Israel has been victorious, all of Palestine has fallen to the Jewish state. Israel still controls most of the land. Thus far, Israel has not been prepared to take the draconian step of expelling the millions of Palestinians who live there. Peace will require that Israel give up the most to end the conflict.

Fourth, Israel can win the military battles, but without peace, Israel is in danger of losing the demographic war with the Palestinians. In a recent editorial, the *New York Times*, citing Israeli sources, stated the following:

> The real argument lies in the demographics which become increasingly clear for a state that seeks to define itself as Jewish. There are 3.2 million Palestinians in the West Bank and Gaza, with an annual growth rate of 4.2 percent.

The editorial later states,

> In Israel itself there are 1.3 million Arabs and 5.4 million Jews living between the Mediterranean Sea and the Jordan River. By 2020, Jews will be a minority.[27]

The doomsday scenario is an Israeli evolution into a new South Africa, with a Jewish minority attempting to maintain political control over a majority Palestinian population. Without peace and stability, few Jews on the outside can be expected to move to Israel. The failure to attract American and European Jews to live in Israel could be a demographic time bomb for Israel.

Finally, Palestinians and Israelis must cooperate for either of the two cultures to prosper. Without continued outside aid, neither entity can succeed on its own. There is no place for Palestinians and Israelis to go.

The same issues that confronted the peacemakers in 2000 remain. The areas of dispute blocking peace are not hard to identify. The first of these issues will be land. How much will be returned to the Palestinians and how much needs to be retained for Israel's military security? A complicating factor is the numerous Israeli settlements that are now part of the Palestinian landscape.

The second issue is water. There is not enough water for everyone. The desert is worthless without water. At present, the Israelis take most of the water for their own use, starving many of those Palestinian farmers who remain in the West Bank.

The third issue is refugees. Almost half a million Palestinians either fled or were forced from their homes in 1948. In every war since that time, more Palestinians have gone into exile. Their future status was one of the deal breakers in the 2000 negotiations. It is unreasonable to expect Israel to absorb the millions of Palestinians whose families once lived in what is now Israel. To obtain peace, however, a form of compensation that is fair to those who lost their homes and businesses must be found.

The fourth issue involves the repatriation of Palestinians in Israeli jails. This is an explosive issue that in part drove the Second Intifada. To the Israelis, many of these people are terrorists. To the Palestinians, the prisoners are freedom fighters working to free their homeland. This issue can be resolved. A prisoner release program has been successful in Northern Ireland, and it can be in the Middle East.

Fifth is the issue of Jerusalem. Here, religion has become mixed with nationalism on both sides. This makes retreat from the stated demands of Israelis and Palestinians almost impossible. The issue is complicated by the size of the area that is the subject of most of the dispute, the Old City. The walled portion of the Old City is approximately 1,000 by 1,500 meters. Christian, Jewish, and Muslim holy places are literally stacked one on top of the other. No Palestinian or Israeli leader can negotiate away claims to the Old City. For peace to occur, a way must be found to provide for a Palestinian presence, if only symbolically, in the Old City.

Currently, there are "two unofficial states" on the ground in the territories. Gaza is controlled by Hamas. This homegrown political terrorist organization won the last parliamentary elections that were held in the territories in 2006. Then the organization seized power in Gaza by a coup de' état. These actions provoked economic and political isolation by most Western states and Israel.

The West Bank is still controlled by Fatah. There are plans proposed by some in the West to support the Fatah organization to provide a bulwark against further Hamas expansion.

Finally, the creation of a Palestinian state must occur. At present, the territories nominally under Palestinian control are so "Balkanized" that a viable state is impossible. Some solution to the statehood aspirations of the Palestinians must be reached if peace is to be achieved.

The negotiations held in 2000 made a great deal of progress toward a comprehensive peace. Outsiders can easily see what needs to be done to achieve a final settlement. New thinking, however, by Palestinians and Israelis will be required if the parties are to escape the endless cycle of violence.

At the present time, many Palestinians refuse to pay more than "lip service" to the idea of coexistence with a permanent Israeli state. At the same time, many Israelis cannot let go of the idea that a "greater state" of Israel, including large parts of the West Bank territories, should be created.

The Iron Laws of the Arab–Israeli Conflict

Israelis say that the Palestinians can make peace with the terrorist groups, such as Islamic Jihad and Hamas, or they can make peace with Israel, but they cannot do both. Palestinians say that Israel can have the occupied Palestinian land, or they can have peace with Palestinians, but they cannot have both.

All conflicts eventually come to an end. Historians tell us that even the Hundred Years War and the Thirty Years War in Europe came to an end. Palestinians and Israelis have two choices. They can continue this seemingly endless conflict of attack and retaliation until both sides are devastated and exhausted or find creative ways to resolve this dispute.

Most outside observers agree that peace will require short-term beginning compromises from both sides. In the long run, the right to a Palestinian state living in peace side by side with Israel will have to happen. The borders of the two states will largely be the old ones that existed in 1967. Parts of Jerusalem will be shared between the parties. Many Israeli settlements, but not all, will have to be abandoned. Palestinians will have to accept the idea that for most of them, the dream of returning to modern Israel to live is gone in favor of a fair compensation. Finally, Palestinians must truly accept the reality of a permanent Israeli state. One can hope that these conditions for peace are realized sooner rather than later.

The Palestinians

The Palestinians are an ancient people who claim to trace their origins to Roman times or earlier. After the Arab conquest, their sense of national consciousness remained dormant until World War I, when they began again to speak of a Palestinian people. During the negotiations that preceded the creation of the state of Israel, serious proposals were also made in the United Nations (UN) for the creation of a Palestinian state. The Arab side rejected the UN proposal. Unfortunately, any further hope for the establishment of a state that would parallel the one created in Israel was lost with the Arab defeat in the 1948 war. Since that time, all the parties to the Arab–Israeli dispute attempted to manipulate the aspirations of the Palestinians. The Palestinian Liberation Organization (PLO; Fatah) claimed to represent the interests of the Palestinian people. When the leadership of the PLO agreed to an autonomy agreement, they took a chance that measurable results could be achieved before the opposition to a limited agreement could grow. Many Palestinians, especially those exiled abroad, believed that the current agreement would never lead to Palestinian sovereignty. Furthermore, they charged that limited autonomy permanently surrendered the lands taken from the Palestinian people in 1948. The slow pace of events since the signing of the accord has strengthened the opposition to a settlement with Israel.

The decline of PLO fortunes after 1993 resulted in the corresponding rise of the Islamic fundamentalist organization Hamas. Unlike the PLO, Hamas was opposed to any peace talks with Israel. By active participation in the Intifada, Hamas earned the respect of many Palestinians. Hamas was a "home-grown" organization rising out of the occupied territories. Unlike the PLO's leaders, Hamas leaders were not intellectuals imported from the Palestinians living abroad. Furthermore, the Hamas opposition to Israel was clear and uncompromising. To a people forced to live under Israeli military occupation, this hard line struck a responsive chord. Facing Hamas, moderate Palestinians were placed in a no-win position. When they moved to compromise with the Israelis and the West, they weakened their position with the Palestinians they claimed to represent. To the chagrin of both the PLO and the Israeli authorities, Hamas is now a major player in Palestinian politics.

Israel has repeatedly tried to break the Hamas hold on Gaza. In response to repeated Hamas-inspired rocket attacks on Israeli settlements, the Israeli army invaded and devastated parts of Gaza in January 2009. Since that time, an Israeli embargo has prevented the importation of materials that could be used to rebuild the destroyed parts of Gaza.

Now that Hamas remains in power in Gaza and the PLO (Fatah) in the West Bank territories, there are questions about the ability of the Palestinians to ever become a legitimate, internationally respected government. Can these two organizations get past their rhetorical and physical violence and evolve into a force that can deal with Israel and the rest of the world? And just as important, can Israel and the rest of the world be convinced enough to trust what the Palestinians say? If no lasting agreement can be reached, political and financial support for Palestine will permanently end. The Palestinian people will then be condemned to continue with the misery that they find themselves in today. Palestinian disunity takes the pressure off Israel to make any further concessions for peace.

For their part, the Palestinians have endured a political and social tragedy that colors their politics. They fear that a grand peace may be negotiated by the great powers at their expense. This concern was raised to a higher level in April 2009 when President Obama made solving the Israeli-Palestinian dispute a major part of his administration's agenda.

By their often-violent actions, the Palestinians have attempted to ensure that their cause will not be ignored. The result is a Palestinian problem that is influencing issues everywhere in the Middle East.

The Iraqi Disputes

Iran

If it is true, as the old saying goes, that "the bones of the Middle East were buried by the dogs of British imperialism," the Iraq–Iran dispute is a case in point. The British who favored the Ottomans over the Persians created the border as a result of a nineteenth-century mediation. The object of this effort was to keep Russia out of the Persian Gulf by giving control of the Shatt al-Arab River to the British-backed Ottomans. Although the Persians objected to the location of the border on the east bank of the river instead of the usually accepted main channel, it was not until 1975 that Iraq, the Ottomans' successor, agreed to use the navigable channel as the border. In return, the Shah of Iran agreed to stop aiding the Kurdish rebellion against Iraq. After the Shah's demise, Iraq unsuccessfully attempted to restore the old border by invading Iran in 1980. The result was one of the more terrible wars in modern history. When the fighting ended, the battle lines were in approximately the same location as the prewar border. To free troops for service in Kuwait in 1990, the Iraqi authorities conceded all their major war gains to Iran.

The 2003 Invasion of Iraq

After Iraq's 1991 defeat in Kuwait, the UN-imposed sanctions, restrictions on oil sales, and international scrutiny of their every move, the Iraqi authorities remained defiant. In response, the Iraqi authorities gambled that a sustained resistance to UN restrictions would eventually force an end to the sanctions followed by a Western withdrawal from the Persian Gulf region. That gamble failed in the spring of 2003. The Iraqi regime engaged and was defeated by the United States, the United Kingdom, and other forces who quickly occupied the entire country. Since the end of the Iraqi War and the elimination of Saddam Hussein, the American leadership has been confronted by a series of issues, many of which overwhelmed the British almost a century ago:

- In Iraq, it is much easier to win a conventional war than establish a secure peace.
- Iraq is an artificial country where Iraqis hold traditional loyalties to religion, region, tribe, and family in higher regard than the conventional nationalistic loyalties to the state so valued in the West.
- In 2009 America, the coalition allies, and their Iraqi friends face the reality of building a modern state while fighting a clandestine war fueled by both internal and external supporters.

If Iraq is to succeed as a product of the 2003 coalition victory, several issues must be satisfactorily resolved in the Iraqi government:

- Can Iraqis implement and agree to a constitution that guarantees the status of the majority Shi'ia while protecting the autonomy of the Sunni minority and the Kurds?
- Are Iraqis willing to secure the established rights of women? If they are unable to follow through with this reform, the leadership of Iraq is likely to lose Western political support.
- While acknowledging a pivotal role for Islam, the authorities must not move Iraq into a religiously intolerant state if Western political support is to continue.
- Like other societies, Iraq must devise a scheme in which the state's vast oil resources are spent for the greater good of all Iraqis and not for just one sectarian group.

None of these issues are resolved at this time. Iraq is clearly at a crossroads. If Iraqis are able to fairly resolve the issues raised here, the present conflict will be only a bump in the road toward a modern, prosperous state in the Middle East. If they fail, the alternative could be civil war followed by the breakup of the present Iraqi state.

A start toward full Iraqi sovereignty was made in the summer of 2009, when American and the remaining coalition troops pulled out of the major cities, leaving local forces to maintain order. It is now up to the Iraqi authorities to make the difficult decisions necessary for Iraq to emerge as a successful democracy.

Strategic Waterways and Oil Pipelines

The Turkish Straits

The Dardanelles and Bosporus are narrow straits, between 1 and 4 miles wide, that dominate the Russian-controlled Black Sea. The straits have been a point of conflict between Russia and Turkey for centuries. The continued Turkish control of the Dardanelles and Bosporus is a source of irritation because it has frustrated repeated Russian attempts to gain easy access to the Mediterranean Sea. At present, Russian access to this area is governed by treaty. Should the Turks again attempt to block access, they will provoke a major international conflict.

The Suez Canal

Opened in 1869, the *Suez Canal*, including the Great Bitter Lake and Lake Timsah, is 101 miles long. It serves as the only direct sea passage from the Mediterranean to the Indian Ocean. Much of the history of the modern Middle East has involved struggles for the control of this strategic waterway. Although the canal is at sea level, requiring no complicated, easily sabotaged system of locks, its location near unstable, hostile neighbors makes its access uncertain at times. For example, in the summer of 1984, an unknown terrorist organization was able to mine parts of the canal and the Red Sea to prevent ships from using the waterway. Because of its importance to Europe, threats to close the Suez Canal always raise the possibility of conflict.

The Persian (or Arab) Gulf

The question over name—Persian or Arab Gulf—implies a more serious conflict over control of the single most important waterway in the world. It is through the Persian Gulf (Arab Gulf) that two-thirds of the world's oil is exported. The conflict between Kuwait and Iraq raises the possibility of seizure of the Strait of Hormuz by an unfriendly power bent on shutting off oil shipments to the West. Because the United States is committed to keeping the oil flowing from the Gulf, any closure will immediately provoke a great-power intervention with all its dangers.

Oil Pipelines

One of the major problems associated with Middle Eastern oil is getting the product to the consumer. Pipelines are an efficient alternative to ships for the movement of petroleum products from the Persian Gulf and Saudi Arabia to Europe. For many years, some pipelines have connected Saudi Arabia with Lebanon and Israel, and others have linked Iraq with the Mediterranean through both Syria and Turkey. The chief problem of relying on pipelines is their vulnerability to sabotage that often occurs in the lands they cross during periods of political instability. For example, the pipeline through Israel has been closed since 1948, and the pipeline from Iraq to the Mediterranean was closed by

Syria for the duration of the Iran–Iraq war. Until the political situation in the Middle East changes, the potential of moving oil by pipeline remains an unfulfilled dream.

OPEC and the Politics of Oil

Through the first decade of the twenty-first century, the world faced record prices for oil. Some forecasters fear that as the huge populations of China and India modernize, the demands for oil will explode. Will civilization as we know it come to an end because a shortage of oil is becoming one of the major questions of our time?

Other analysts, such as Professor Mukul Sharma of the Department of Petroleum Engineering at the University of Texas, do not think so. He says, "By and large, articles are written by people who know very little about the oil and gas business. It is largely because the media are dominated by people in New York, so they go to energy experts at Harvard and MIT. What the hell do they know about energy, especially the oil and gas business?"[28] A colleague of his, Professor Scott Tinker, Director of the University of Texas Bureau of Economic Geology, points out that today "when the well goes dry by these (current) methods, drillers have only recovered, on average, 30 percent of the oil that is there; it's hardly dry."[29] The Cambridge Energy Research Associates have used a field-by-field analysis to project that global oil production capacity will exceed global demand by 7.5 million barrels a day by the end of the decade.[30]

Should we take seriously the comments of the "experts" at the University of Texas? Will the fossil fuel business remain, as it always has been, an artificially controlled cartel of both producers and distributors? Even Saudi Arabia, the world's key oil power with over a third of the reserves of the Middle East, predicts that it will double its proved reserves in the near future. As Muhammad Ali Zainy, London Center for Global Energy Studies, puts it, "Since these OPEC countries are closed, the only information available is available to themselves alone. So they can come up with a new reserves figure and the rest of the world will just have to take it."[31] Could it be just another example of how in the past the cartel has encouraged the idea of future shortages to keep the price of oil artificially inflated?

In 1901, a Western adventurer, William D'Arcy, received a concession to explore for oil in Iran. At almost the same time, an Armenian, C. S. Gulbenkian, obtained a similar concession from the Ottoman Empire. Less than 50 years later, these concessions had grown into a vast oil cartel controlled by seven Western companies: Exxon, Mobil, Standard Oil of California, Texaco, Gulf, British Petroleum, and Shell. Called the Seven Sisters, these companies gained a virtual monopoly on the production, refinement, and distribution of Middle Eastern oil.

Designed to present a united front when negotiating prices with the oil companies, the Organization of Petroleum Exporting Countries (OPEC) was organized in 1960 by Iraq, Saudi Arabia, Iran, Kuwait, and Venezuela. Subsequently, OPEC membership grew to include Qatar, Libya, Indonesia, Algeria, Nigeria, Ecuador, Gabon, and the United Arab Emirates.

The OPEC cartel was only marginally effective until the October 1973 Middle East war. At that time, the sale of petroleum products was linked by the Arab members of OPEC to the support for their cause against Israel. The selective withholding of oil caused an energy crisis in the West. During the next decade, OPEC oil rose from a pre-1973 price of around $3 a barrel to over $30 a barrel. This oil shock was difficult for the developed world, but it destroyed the hopes of many Other World states that were depending on low-cost energy to finance development. Ignoring 50 years of Western oil cartel exploitation, newspapers in Europe and the United States were filled with articles editorializing on the "evils" of OPEC. Today, more than 30 years after the first oil crisis in the 1970s, Western observers admit that although the economic impact of OPEC has been considerable, it is a political force in the Other World far out of proportion to its size.

If high prices cause the developed world to convert to other energy sources, it will have serious implications for every state in the region. Like Haiti with sugar and Brazil with rubber, Middle Eastern oil could become just another surplus commodity that is a victim of production elsewhere.

There is little doubt that the competition for these resources will increase with the industrial rise of China and India. This will tempt producers to keep prices high as long as the OPEC cartel can. However, as the price of oil passes $60 to $70 (U.S.) a barrel, brand new methods of recovery once thought too expensive become possible. The developed world has the resources to exploit novel recovery methods for the 70 percent of remaining oil in old wells. At $40 a barrel, the West has the technology to profitably recover energy from oil shale, which exists in vast quantities in North America. Other exotic fuel sources also become practical at these prices, including methane or natural gas, oil from coal, and liquefied natural gas. Professor Sharma pointed out that the world has enough coal unmined that can be converted to fuel current energy needs for the next 2,000 years.[32] All it takes to make these conversions possible today is continued high prices to justify the investment.

Finally, at a conference in South Africa, Exxon Mobil's president Rex Tillerson stated that some estimates said there were more than 7 trillion barrels of oil yet to be discovered. He further added that 3 trillion barrels could be recovered from conventional fields, oil sands, and other sources that are "more than twice all the oil recovered up to now in all of human history."[33]

Summary

Geographically, the Middle East and North Africa can be divided into three distinct regions: the plains of North Africa and Arabia, the Fertile Crescent, and the northern tier. The Middle East is an area of contrast, including some of the world's most famous deserts, mountain ranges, and rivers. Oil is the most important natural resource of the region. A scarcity of water limits agricultural development throughout most of the Middle East. The monotheistic religions Judaism, Christianity, and Islam have developed in the Middle East. Today, Islam is the professed religion of 90 percent of the population, and most political activity in this part of the Other World is affected by religion.

Nationalism is a second feature of Middle Eastern politics. Case studies in this chapter describe the various forms of nationalism that have developed in Turkey, Iran, Egypt, Saudi Arabia, and Israel. A brief description of Arab nationalism is also included. These case studies illustrate the directions that nationalists have taken in this part of the Other World.

Review Questions

1. Discuss some of the features of Arab nationalism.
2. List the Five Pillars of Islam.

3. What role does oil play in Middle Eastern politics?
4. Why is Islam called a way of life?
5. Compare the nationalisms of Turkey, Iran, Egypt, and Israel.

Key Terms

- **1798**—The date of the French invasion of Egypt which is considered to be the beginning of the modern European colonial period.
- **Allah**—The name of God in the Arabic language.
- **The Fertile Crescent**—The historic land stretching up the eastern Mediterranean and along the southern border of Turkey to exit through Iraq into the Persian Gulf.
- **Monotheism**—The belief in one God.
- **Mohammed**—Considered by Muslims to be a human being who lived a perfect life and was a prophet of God.
- **The Ottomans**—A tribe that came to what is now Turkey, in the Middle Ages, and established a great empire that lasted from 1453 to 1918.
- **The Rightly Guided Caliphs**—The first four successors to Mohammed: Abu Bakr, Umar, Uthman, and Ali.
- **Shah**—Persian word for king.
- **The Suez Canal**—Opened in 1869, the Canal provides a passage from the Mediterranean Sea to the Red Sea.
- **Zionism**—Founded in 1897, Zionism is a Jewish form of nationalism calling for the establishment and maintenance of a Jewish state in Palestine.

Useful Web Sites

Israel: *www.gov.il*
Iraq: *www.cabinet.ig*
Turkey: *www.tccb.gov.tr*
Egypt: *www.egypt.eg*
Iran: *www.president.ir*

For Further Reading

Goodwin, Jan. *Price of Honor: Muslim Women Lift the Veil of Silence on the Islamic World*. New York: Penguin, 2003.

Humphreys, R. Stephen. *Between Memory and Desire: The Middle East in a Troubled Age*. Berkeley: University of California Press, 2001.

Laqueur, Walter, and Rubin, Barry. *The Israel-Arab Reader: A Documentary History*, 6th ed. New York: Penguin, 2001.

Mansfield, Peter. *A History of the Middle East*, 2nd ed. New York: Penguin, 2004.

Selfa, Lance. *The Struggle for Palestine*. Chicago, IL: Haymarket Books, 2002.

Shehadeh, Raja. *Strangers in the House: Coming of Age in Occupied Palestine*. South Royalton, VT: Steerforth Press, 2002.

Sonkin, Michael. *Against the Wall: Israel's Barrier to Peace*. New York: New Press Publishers, 2005.

Weinberger, Peter. *Coopting the PLO: A Critical Reconstruction of the Oslo Accords, 1993–1995*. New York: Bowman and Littlefield Publishers, 2006.

Zuhur, Sherifa. *Egypt: Security, Political, and Islamist Challenges*, Carlisle Barracks, Carlisle, PA: Strategic Studies Institute, U.S. Army War College, 2006.

Notes

1. Madeline Miller and J. Lane Miller, *Harpers Bible Dictionary* (New York: Harper & Row, 1973), p. 688.
2. Population figures taken from *The World Almanac and Book of Facts 2009*, (New York: World Almanac Books, 2009).
3. For more information on the politics of water, see Adam Kelliher, "Thrust for Peace Is on Water," *Times* (London), 3 August 1991, p. 6.
4. Lawrence Ziring, *The Middle East Political Dictionary* (Santa Barbara, Calif.: ABC-CLIO Information Services, 1983), p. 415.
5. Lord Kinross, *The Ottoman Centuries* (New York: Morrow Quill, 1977), p. 85.
6. For more information on the Pentecostal Holiness Church, see Ed Housewright, "Faith on a Deadly Scale," *San.*
7. For an example of a charity accused of aiding terrorism see Mary Beth Sheridan, "U.S. Raids Islamic Charity in Va; Immigration Charges Filed Against Worker," *The Washington Post*, Washington, D.C., July 26, 2005, p. Metro BO1.
8. The Ka'bah is a cubelike building located in the courtyard of the Great Mosque in Mecca. According to Moslem tradition, it was the first house of worship built by the prophet Abraham. *San Francisco Examiner, 2* March 1995, p. A8.
9. Sometimes called the Battle of the Nile, British Admiral Nelson defeated the French on August 1, 1798, J. R. Hill, *The Oxford History of the Royal Navy* (Oxford, England: Oxford University Press, 1995), p. 111.
10. For pre-1991 Gulf War petroleum export figures, see Richard Teitelbaum, "Where Do We Go from Here?" *Fortune*, September 1990, p. 30.
11. Edward Mortimer and Michael Field, "Nationalism, the Steel of the Arab Soul," *Financial Times* (London), 18/19 August 1990, sec. 11.
12. Alfred B. Prados, *Saudi Arabia: Post Issues and U.S. Relations*, C.R.S. Issue Brief No. 1B93113, Congressional Research Service, The Library of Congress, Washington, D.C., 1996.
13. Robert Lynam, "Kingdom Opens Up to the World," *South China Morning Post*, Hong Kong, September 6, 2007, Supplement, p. 1.
14. Douglas Jehl, "To Some Saudi Clerics, It's Infidels vs. Islam: Harsh Anti-Western Opinions Resonate Among Citizens," *The Dallas Morning News*, 6 December 2001, p. 19A.
15. Islamic Policies, not in Turkish Government's Agenda, comments made on Turkish NTX Television, reported by the *Financial Times Information Service*, London, accessed from Lexis-Nexis, the Academic Universe, March 14, 2005.
16. "Turkey and Europe," *Turkish Daily News*, Ankara, Turkey. Accessed from Lexis-Nexis, the Academic Universe, November 16, 2001.
17. "Cypriot Leader Eyes Peace Referendum Next Year," Turkish Semi-Official News Agency Anatolia, Taken From Lexis-Nexis, the Academic Universe, April 13, 2009.
18. "Northern Iraq Raid Wins vote" *Turkish Daily News*, online edition, Ankara, Turkey, October 18, 2007.

19. Although never officially acknowledged by the U.S. Government, there is little doubt about the CIA involvement in this episode. See Kermit Roosevelt, *Countercoup: The Struggle for the Control of Iran* (New York: McGraw-Hill 1979), Chaps. 11, 12, 13; and R. G. Gant, *MI 5, MI 6; Britain's Security and Secret Intelligence Services* (New York: Gallery Books, 1989), pp. 113–114.

20. David Sanger, New York Times correspondent, "Election Advances Iran's Nuclear Future," *The Dallas Morning News*, Dallas, Texas, World Section p. 15 A, June 26, 2005.

21. Shortly after World War I, nationalists formed the Egyptian Delegation (Wafd al-Misri) to pressure for independence. This group eventually became the Wafd party.

22. "Mubarak Said to Quit Office, Call for New Election in the Next Few Days," Al-Sha'b Newspaper, Egypt, June 9, 2009, reported by BBC Worldwide Monitoring, London, taken from Nexis-Lexis, the Academic Universe, June 10, 2009.

23. Ibid.

24. Jehl, op. cit.

25. Mortimer and Field, op. cit.

26. Howard Schneider, "Netanyahu Upholds Plan to Build in East Jerusalem," The Washington Post Foreign Service, USA. July 20, 2009, taken from Lexis-Nexis, the Academic Universe, July 20, 2009.

27. "The Middle East Math," *The New York Times, Late Edition*, Editorial Desk, Section A, p. 30, Col. 1, Sept. 12, 2003.

28. Avrel Seale, "How Long Do We Have?" *The Alcade*, Vol. 93, No. 6 Texas Exes, Austin, Texas July/August 2005, p. 42.

29. Avrel Seale, op. cit., p. 43.

30. Sudcep Reddy, "Putting a Cap On Oil Supply Worries," *The Dallas Morning News*, June 22, 2005, Sec. D, p. 1.

31. Saeed Shah, "Oil Reserves Are Double Previous Estimates Says Saudi," *The Independent Online Edition*, London, September 28, 2005.

32. Avrel Seale, op. cit., p. 44.

33. Saeed Shah, op. cit.

9

Central Asia and the Southern Near Abroad

Olga D. Novikova-Carter

We live in a moment of history where change is so speeded up that we begin to see the present only when it is already disappearing.

R. D. LAING

What man calls civilization always results in deserts.

DON MARQUIS

During much of their past, nations of Central Asia and the Southern Near Abroad have received little attention from the outside world. For many, this part of the world is most strongly associated with the remote historical times of Genghis Khan, Tamerlane, or the great Silk Road. For most of its history, this region was not a coherent nation, but a geographically defined area of independent political entities and tribal groups. This territory has been a cradle of several empires, as well as a target for numerous invasions and massive migrations, which had an impact on the population's composition, language formation, cultural similarities, and distinctions.

After the collapse of the Soviet Union in 1991, the geopolitical atmosphere of Central Asia has fundamentally changed. The weakness of the newly independent states has created a political vacuum, and world powers have competed with each other to fill it.

The current military operations against terrorists, competition among oil companies for control of energy resources, future strategic pipeline routes of the region, and revival of the nuclear power industry fueled by the fear and anticipation of high oil prices has led to an increased interest in the affairs of this region's countries and has contributed to the recognition that this region occupies a new and increasingly important position in world affairs.

WHAT IS CENTRAL ASIA AND THE SOUTHERN NEAR ABROAD?

One does not argue on terms, they are to be agreed upon.

AN ANCIENT GREEK MAXIM

As mentioned in Chapter 7, the subdivisions of Asia are, to a great extent, subjective, contingent on the purposes of the given discussion, and can be described by employing different terms.

For the purpose of our analysis, we included in the definition of Central Asia all former Soviet republics of Central Asia, such as Kazakhstan, Kyrgyzstan, Tajikistan, Turkmenistan, and Uzbekistan, as well as a bordering, landlocked Afghanistan. We use the expression the *Southern Near Abroad* in reference to Armenia, Azerbaijan, and Georgia.[1] Although there might be numerous arguments for suggested subdivisions, you may also find that some countries are referred to as the Caucasus, Transcaucasia, Southeastern Europe, or West Asia. We adhere to an Ancient Greek's saying that "one does not argue on terms, they are to be agreed upon"; thus, the focus of our attention will be on the substance of issues pertaining to this part of the world, rather than on terminology. See Table 9.1 for recent data on the countries that make up Central Asia and the Southern Near Abroad.

GEOGRAPHY

Where Is Central Asia and the Southern Near Abroad?

Central Asia and the Southern Near Abroad make up a landlocked territory on the interior of the Asian continent stretching for hundreds of miles from the Black Sea to the Caspian Sea in the west, to Chinese borders in the east, and from the southern border of Eastern Russia to the borders with Pakistan and Iran. These territories include the Caucasus Mountains, the Aral-Caspian lowland with its vast deserts of Karakum and Kizilkum, and the basins of two great rivers Sir-Darya and Amu-Darya, which flow into the Aral Sea.

This region is situated in the geographic center of the Eurasian continent and is full of contrasts: perpetually snow-capped mountains, Great Steppe, and sand deserts to impetuous rivers, picturesque lakes, and landlocked seas. Large parts of

TABLE 9.1 Central Asia and the Southern Near Abroad

Country	Population (Millions)	Population Growth Rate (%)	Infant Mortality Rate (per 1,000 Live Births)	Population Under 15 Years of Age (%)	Life Expectancy (in Years)	Urban Population (%)	Literacy Rate (%)	Arable Land (%)	Per Capita GDP ($US)
Afghanistan	33.610	2.63	15.2	44.5	44.6	243	28.1	12.1	800
Georgia	4.616	-0.33	16.2	16.1	76.3	53	100	11.5	4,700
Armenia	2.967	-0.03	22.21	18.2	72.63	64	99.4	17	6,400
Azerbaijan	8.239	0.76	54.6	23.9	66.66	52	98.8	18	9,000
Uzbekistan	27.606	0.95	23.3	28.1	71.9	37	99.3	9	2,600
Kazakhstan	15.399	0.39	28.3	21.8	67.22	58	99.5	8.3	11,500
Turkmenistan	4.885	1.14	45.3	28.9	67.8	49	98.8	4.5	6,100
Tajikistan	7.349	1.89	41	34.3	65.3	26	99.5	6.2	2,100
Kyrgyzstan	5.432	1.35	31.3	29.7	69.4	36	98.7	6.5	2,100
Mongolia	3.041	1.49	39.8	28.1	67.5	57	97.8	0.8	3,200

Source: Population, Infant Mortality Rate, Population Under 15 Years of Age, Urban Population, Life Expectancy, Literacy Rate, Arable Land, and Per Capita GDP from *The World Almanac and Book of Facts, 2009.* Population Growth Rate and Life Expectancy from CIA *World Factbook, 2009.*

FIGURE 9.1 Political and Physical Characteristics of Central Asia and the Southern Near Abroad

this region are highly seismic, with frequent earthquakes, whose destructive power has wiped centers of great civilizations from the face of the earth over the centuries. Most importantly, the diverse geography determines the nation's natural conditions and thereby its economic development and culture (see Figure 9.1).

Mountains

> More beautiful than mountains
> Could be only mountains,
> Which you have not seen yet.
>
> VLADIMIR VYSOTSKY

The mountains of the region are as unique and diverse in character as the people who live in these areas. It is difficult for an outsider, especially for an urban dweller, to distinguish and appreciate all the shades of beauty of these natural "monuments." Mountains dominate the landscape. Great and Small Caucasus,[2] forming a skeleton of Georgia, Armenia, and Azerbaijan in the west, account for almost 60 percent of their territory. These mountain systems are young in geological terms and are still in the process of active formation, which leads to frequent and powerful earthquakes, such as the most recent one in Armenia in 1988, which razed several cities and cost more than 45,000 human lives, and the earthquake in Baku, Azerbaijan, in 2000, which measured between 5.9 and 6.3 on the Richter scale.[3]

This area is also sadly known for its mud volcanoes and mud slides. If we start our mountain journey beginning from its northwest part, in Kazakhstan, we would see that its edges are adjoined by the round-topped old geological system of the Southern Ural Mountains, which is connected on the northeast with the Altai Mountains (14,700 feet), both being nature's treasury in terms of deposits of coal, iron ore, manganese, chrome, nickel, cobalt, copper, molybdenum, lead, zinc, bauxite, gold, and uranium.

The eastern and southern borders of the region are ringed by the highest, and one of the youngest, geological mountain formations on the planet. This mountain division is the subject of ongoing discussion and disagreement among members of the geographic scientific community. The most studied of those mountain systems is the Pamir Mountains, which are referred to by all neighboring nations of the region as the "Roof of the World." At its westernmost extension of the Tien-Shan (21,000 feet), the Hindukush system, Karakorum, and Himalayas hone their peaks reaching more than 22,960 feet.[4]

There are several stories about the origin of the term *Hindukush* (translated as Hindu Killer). The first one suggests that the mountains memorialize the Indian slaves who perished in the mountains while being transported to the Central Asian slave markets; the second suggests that the name came from a corrupted pre-Islamic name of the mountains *Hindu Koh*, which divided Hindu of the southern Afghanistan from Hindu in the north; the third one points to the possibility of the name being a posited Avestan appellation meaning "water mountains."

Kyrgyzstan, Tajikistan, Uzbekistan, Turkmenistan, and Afghanistan are privileged and burdened by being mountainous countries. While in Uzbekistan and Turkmenistan, mountain areas cover only southern parts of the territory, or approximately 20 percent; in other countries, like Azerbaijan and Afghanistan, mountains occupy almost 50 percent of the land. In Tajikistan, mountains cover 93 percent of the country.[5]

The majestic beauty of the mountains of Central Asia has as its hidden cost unexpected and vicious earthquakes. The history of earthquakes became an integral and often tragic part of the ancient and modern history of nations of this part of the world. The world community will never forget the massive earthquakes in Ashgabat (Turkmenbashi), Turkmenistan, in 1948, which destroyed most of the city, and the powerful earthquake in Tashkent, Uzbekistan, in 1966.[6]

Mountain terrain is an important determinant of the location and development of industries, agriculture, transportation, and tourism. Numerous high passes that transcend the mountains are forming a strategically important interconnected network for the transit of caravans. The completion of tunnels and roads has decreased travel time between major centers from a few days to a few hours. At the same time "old communication arteries," high passes, are still in use for drug trafficking and smuggling of illegal goods because they are difficult to control. The growth and formation of these great mountain systems, which separates the inland area from the Indian Ocean, resulted in the dry climate and the formation of the Karakum and Kizilkum sand deserts in Uzbekistan and

Turkmenistan. The remoteness from the oceans and the impact of mountain barriers to the moisture penetration into the region has significant effects on the climate of Central Asia, as well as on the nature of waterways of the region.

Climate

The "continental" climate of the region is typical for arid and semiarid steppe, with cold dry winters (January temperature varies from 28° to −13°F) and hot summers with temperatures between 86° and 104°F.

In intermountain plateaus, a northerly dry wind, known as the "wind of 120 days," blows during the summer months of June through September. This wind is usually accompanied by intense heat, drought, and sand storms, bringing rough times to the inhabitants of the desert and steppe land.

Mountain areas represent another distinct climate zone, with the main precipitation in the form of snow. Permanent snow covers the highest mountain peaks. Because Armenia is 90 percent mountainous and Georgia is 80 percent, their climate is consistent with the general characteristics of this zone, with a few subtropical "implants" on the coast of the Black Sea.

The climate of the Turkistan Plains represents a transition between mountain and steppe. Aridity increases and temperatures rise with descending altitudes, becoming the highest along the lower Amu-Darya and in the western parts of the plains, closer to the Caspian Sea. The climate of Azerbaijan and Georgia varies from subtropical dry in central and eastern Azerbaijan to subtropical and humid in the south, while in Georgia it is subtropical dry.[7]

Lunch? A meat market in Kazakhstan.   *Source: Olga Carter*

Water Resources: Rivers, Lakes, and Seas

The common statement that "water is life" has been a nondisputed notion for all times and all nations in this part of the world. Although the vast territory of Central Asia and the Southern Near Abroad possesses many rivers, river basins, and lakes, the demand for water for agricultural, industrial, and urban development has always been greater than its limited supply. The blueprint of river systems has undergone numerous changes over time. For example, in ancient times the Amu-Darya flowed into the Caspian Sea, and only much later changed its course into the Aral Sea. The Amu-Darya's changing character has had an impact on life in these basins in Afghanistan and Uzbekistan. Many rivers and streams simply empty into arid portions of the region, spending them through evaporation without replenishing; others flow only seasonally. Eight large rivers flow from the Caucasus mountain ranges into the central Kura-Aras lowland, alluvial flatlands, and delta areas along the seacoast.

The beauty of mountain-surrounded lakes has been an inspiration to the greatest poets of all time. Among those inspirational "eyes of the earth" well known all over the world are the Armenian Lake Sevan, Lake Balkhash, and Issyk-Kul in Kazakhstan. The fate of an ecologically threatened Central Asian water basin the size of California depends on the ability of countries of the region to adopt preservation strategies. The heart of the basin is Lake Balkhash, the third largest fresh water lake on earth, located in the southeast corner of Kazakhstan. Rivers flowing through neighboring Kyrgyzstan and China replenish water in the lake. For decades, diversion of waters to local factories and farms threatened Lake Balkhash with the same fate as the notorious Aral Sea. Environmental organizations have been highly critical of China's "Go West" policy, sponsoring massive population migration into the territory of the basin, with as many as 40 million new inhabitants. A dam has been built to reverse the flow of rivers feeding Lake Balkhash, and waters have been drained into nearby rice and sugar farms. According to representatives of the European Commission, the executive branch of the European Union, who have studied the basin, these farms consume twice the water that European and American operations require.[8]

A special place in the water resource system of Central Asia and the Southern Near Abroad should be devoted to two uniquely similar yet distinctly different large, salt-water natural reservoirs: the Caspian and Aral Seas. Although these landlocked geological formations look like big lakes, they meet some of the characteristics and criteria of a sea.

CASPIAN SEA REGION

Weep not that the world changes—did it keep a stable, changeless state, 'twere cause indeed to weep.

WILLIAM CULLEN BRYANT

Energy Resources of the Caspian Sea

The Caspian Sea region, which includes the sea and littoral states, is an important player in the world energy markets. It has the potential to become one of the major oil and natural gas exporters over the next decade, if not for a number of complications, such as a lack of adequate export infrastructure, disagreement over new export routes, and border disputes.

The Caspian Sea region is defined to include Azerbaijan, Kazakhstan, Turkmenistan, as well as parts of Russia, Iran, and Uzbekistan, which, although not a littoral state, is the region's largest natural gas producer. The Caspian region of the 1990s was like an old, once wealthy city neighborhood gone to seed and then suddenly rediscovered and made fashionable again by a new generation; it was a time of high expectation and change caused by oil.

Oil is not a new phenomenon here; its abundance was noted by Marco Polo 700 years ago. What is new is the politics of the Caspian region. Three new littoral states, Azerbaijan, Kazakhstan, and Turkmenistan, have emerged from the ruins of the Soviet Union and opened the door to the world energy community to share in what was once a Russian monopoly.

How much oil is left in the Caspian basin is unknown. Some estimates suggest there are nearly 200 billion barrels, approximately as much as the proven reserves of Iran and Iraq combined. Other sources suggest a range between 17 and 49 billion barrels, which is comparable to OPEC member Qatar on the low

Black Gold: The Bibi Oil Field in Azerbaijan is the oldest in the world. Out of 11,000 wells, only half are producing. Over 200,000 tons of oil have been spilled on the ground, causing an environmental disaster area. *Source: Olga Carter*

end and the United States on the high end.[9] In 2008, regional oil production reached 1.9 million barrels per day, comparable to annual production from South America's second-largest oil producer, Brazil.

By the year 2010, the countries of the region are forecast to produce between 2.4 and 5.9 million barrels per day, which exceeds the annual production of South America's largest oil producer, Venezuela, in 2007. Actual production in the region at the moment is far more modest—about 1.1 million barrels a day or 1.9 percent of the world's total.[10] This is due mainly to a difficult economic and political transition period associated with the collapse of regional trade and cooperation after the break-up of the Soviet Union. The power struggle among internal political structures makes this process even less manageable. Measured in 1995 U.S. dollars (the year chosen as a basis of comparison for prices), the region's gross domestic product (GDP) remains below 1992 levels in Azerbaijan, Kazakhstan, and Turkmenistan. It has had a detrimental effect on the standard of living of the population of the region: 24 percent of the citizens of Azerbaijan and 14 percent of citizens of Kazakhstan (two major oil-producing states) were estimated to be living below the poverty level in 2005. The most realistic way of improving the situation is through the successful development of the region's oil and natural gas potentials.

One of the first steps on the way to this goal, especially in the face of world economic recession, is achieving a multilateral agreement on division of the Caspian Sea's resources between the five littoral states: Azerbaijan, Iran, Kazakhstan, Russia, and Turkmenistan. Currently, only a trilateral agreement has been signed by Azerbaijan, Kazakhstan, and Russia regarding subsurface boundaries and collective administration of the sea's waters. According to this agreement, these countries have divided the northern 64 percent of the Caspian Sea into three unequal parts: Kazakhstan, 27 percent; Russia, 19 percent; and Azerbaijan, 18 percent. Turkmenistan has signed a bilateral agreement with Iran to cooperate in dividing the Sea according to different ratios. Currently, Turkmenistan has disputes with Azerbaijan over the rights to develop oil and gas fields that Turkmenistan considers its own.

Russia, Kazakhstan, and Turkmenistan have signed an agreement regarding construction of a new gas export pipeline from Central Asia to Russia. The pipeline that originated in Turkmenistan and skirts the Caspian coast on the way north to Russia through Kazakhstan will be capable of transporting up to 20 billion cubic meters of gas a year, and will strengthen Russia's negotiating power in dealing with Ukraine and European Union.[11]

In the northern Caspian state of Azerbaijan, oil production is up 70 percent since 1992. Here, there are major oil development projects at Azeri, Chirag, and deepwater Gunashli. The beginning of Kazakhstan's Tengiz oil field in 1992 marked a historic breakthrough for the Western oil industry. Chevron was the first to invest in Tengiz, followed by Exxon Mobil, British Petroleum, and Russian LUKOIL. Not only is Tengiz huge, but it holds an estimated oil reserve of 6 to 9 billion barrels of oil, with a production potential of more than 1 million barrels a day. This "Second Caspian oil rush" has contributed to an increase in foreign investment activity in these regions.

The Caspian Sea region has even more growth potential in the natural gas arena. According to some experts, estimates of the regional natural gas reserve are around 232 trillion cubic feet (Tcf)—comparable to those in Saudi Arabia. In 2007, natural gas production in the Caspian Sea region was approximately 4.5 Tcf, comparable to the production of South America, Central America, and Mexico combined. Although the exploration, development, and operation (including construction of an export infrastructure) of a natural gas industry is more capital intensive, this industry has a fast-growing pace because of an increased demand for its product, considered to be one of the most effective energy sources.

In July 2003 two Russian oil and gas giants, LUKOIL and Gazprom (Russian State natural gas monopoly), formed a joint venture with Kazakhstan's state oil company, KazMunaiGaz, to develop a promising hydrocarbon structure located on the border of the Russian and Kazakhstani offshore sectors with estimated recoverable reserves of 20 Tcf of natural gas. LUKOIL reported the launch of a drilling program for 2004 to 2010; production started in 2005.

Turkmenistan's natural gas production and export have been affected by the competition with Gazprom because the pipeline system connecting the region to the world markets is owned by Gazprom and routed through Russia. Uzbekistan—one of the world's top 10 natural gas-producing countries—has chosen an alternative export strategy: concentrating on domestic consumption and neighboring natural gas markets and avoiding Russia's pipeline systems. On April 9, 2009, a pipeline blast occurred on the Davletbat-Dariyalyk pipeline near the Turkmenistan-Uzbekistan border. Turkmenistan has accused Russia's energy behemoth of engineering the pipeline explosion that disrupted export from this Central Asian nation. Russian experts have attributed the incident to Turkmen lack of maintenance of a worn-out infrastructure. This blame game has rocked the Caspian Basin's key energy relationship, creating a looming "gas war" for Russia on its southern front. Some experts are wondering if Turkmenistan, being an energy treasure-house with the world's fourth largest natural gas reserves, is attempting to devise a multivector approach to energy exports, including possible commitments to the U.S.-backed Trans-Caspian Pipeline. To some degree, such a move is of a political nature, and indicated that Gasprom could soon lose control over Turkmen gas export. In a broader context, it implies that Russia is losing some of its position in Central Asia.

The region has exceptional potential for economic development and growth, although it will need considerable investment in its infrastructure to realize this potential in full. If we take a closer look at the Caspian oil- and gas-producing countries' export routes, we note several changes in the region's energy flow. First of all, there is a significant shift to an east-west axis toward Europe and away from an existing south-north axis toward Russia. One of the main complicating factors slowing production is the development of the largest part of the new pipeline system.[12] Can the Bosporus Straits, already a major checkpoint for oil tankers, manage additional tanker traffic in an environmentally safe manner? Of great geopolitical significance is the alternative pipeline, Baku-Tbilisi-Ceyhan (BTC) 1,087 miles long, which was put into operation in 2006. It transports crude oil from Azerbaijan through Georgia to Ceyhan, which is on the coast of Turkey, bypassing the Bosporus Straits.

Extremely fast growth in China's demand for oil and natural gas during 1995–2008 brought up strong support for the consideration of an east-west flow for oil and natural gas. In Europe, oil demand over the next 10 to 15 years is expected to grow by approximately one-tenth of that of China over the same period of time. State-owned China National Petroleum Corporation (CNPC) paid $780 million (U.S.) to construct the 1,000-mile pipeline, which provides a direct route to China for oil from Kazakhstan fields. CNPC is currently negotiating with Kazakhstan for more acreage in the Caspian Sea area for further expansion in this region.[13]

There is also a proposal for the development of a Southern axis through either Afghanistan or Iran to supply oil and natural gas to Asian markets. After the Taliban's removal from power in Afghanistan in December 2001, proposals to build a Trans-Afghan natural gas pipeline and the Central Asian Oil Pipeline have reemerged. In 1997, Turkmenistan and Iran completed the $190 million pipeline, connecting those two countries and allowing them to be engaged in low-volume "swap" deals. Under this arrangement, oil in tankers is delivered to refineries in Iran's northern regions in exchange for similar volumes of crude oil from Iranian ports in the Persian Gulf.

Central Asia has benefited from the skyrocketing 2000–2008 energy demand worldwide. Rich uranium mines in Kazakhstan and Uzbekistan have caught the attention of countries turning to nuclear power generation as an alternative to oil and gas. Kazakhstan's uranium reserves of 472,000 tonnes account for 15 percent of the world's total and are second only to those of Australia, according to the World Nuclear Association. By 2010, the country plans to increase its 4,300 tonnes-a-year production four times, which would place it above Canada and Australia (28 percent and 23 percent of the world's uranium production, respectively) to become the world's largest uranium producer.[14]

Uzbekistan holds 3 percent of the world's uranium reserves. Kyrgyzstan's reserves are smaller but are still quite attractive to investors. Russia is trying to regain control over the region's atomic energy industry that it enjoyed during the Soviet era.

Regional Conflicts in the Caspian Region

Regional conflicts in the Caspian region and surrounding countries are by far the most serious consideration in determining export pipeline routes. For the sake of brevity, we will discuss only the most complicated conflicts.

1. Afghanistan is still in the category of a war zone unsuitable for substantial investments, despite the change in central power.
2. The Azerbaijan–Armenian war over the Armenian-populated Nagorno-Karabakh enclave in Azerbaijan has not yet been resolved, thus prohibiting development. Armenia's victory in 1994 in this vicious war has led to its economic blockade of this landlocked country by Azerbaijan and Turkey. Armenian economic growth, fueled by financial aid from America and Armenian *diaspora*, generated much of the recent wealth in the hands of local *oligarchs* and a high level of corruption. Russian troops still patrol Armenian borders, justifying its long-term military presence in the area.

Azerbaijan fears that Nagorno-Karabakh might declare independence and win international recognition, as happened with Kosovo and South Ossetia.

3. Russia's long and bloody war in Chechnya resulted in hundreds of thousands of casualties and refugees in neighboring countries, destabilizing the region and creating a rising support of Islamic fundamentalism in the region.

4. The civil war in Tajikistan from 1990 to 1997 between the progovernment forces and Islamist rebels had a lasting effect on a current composition of political forces in the country. Thirty percent of seats in the government were given to the Islamic United Tajik Opposition as a part of a peace treaty.

5. Separatist conflicts in Abkhazia and South Ossetia, Georgia's autonomous republics, led to Georgia's loss of control over parts of its territory, dominated by the Soviet-style ruling clans and supported by Russia. The Russia-Georgia 7-day war, which started on August 8, 2008, was an open military phase of a long preparation for a war by all sides—Russia, Georgia, South Ossetia, and Abkhazia. Georgia's attempt to regain control over the separatist region of South Ossetia ended in a humiliating defeat from Russian troops and in declaration of South Ossetia's independence. The less-visible result of this war, according to some experts, was Russia's defeat in its attempt to gain a strategic position in the region by ruining plans to stop construction of Nabucco, the competing gas pipeline to the Russian pipeline project, "Southern Stream."[15] Nabucco's projected capacity is 31 billion cubic meters of natural gas per year, connecting the Caspian region, Middle East, and Egypt via Turkey, Bulgaria, Romania, and Hungary with Austria and further on with the Central and Western European gas markets. The pipeline's length is approximately 1,900 miles starting at the Georgian/Turkish and/or Iranian/Turkish border, respectively, leading to Baumgarten in Austria.[16]

Despite Georgia's defeat and territorial loss of South Ossetia and Abkhazia, Russia came out of this war with much higher losses with more and more countries joining the Nabucco project. New countries, like Turkmenistan and Azerbaijan, are expressing their interest in supplying their natural gas for Nabucco. Europe is tired of the disruption of the natural gas supply from Russia every winter. Russia's old political game of "divide and conquer" is still in action but not always working flawlessly.

This information is key to an accurate interpretation of the political climate of this geopolitical area. Political analysts view the statement "Follow the oil (natural gas)" as a useful principle for a safe navigation in the ocean of political problems of the region.

RELIGION

Islam

We might as well give up the fiction that we can argue any view.
For what in me is pure conviction, is simple prejudice in you.

PHYLLIS MCGINLEY

The conventional view of Central Asia as a Muslim territory requires some clarification. During the last two millennia, this region was under the influence of several political and religious doctrines. Islam is the latest religion to arrive and be assimilated by Central Asia. It was brought to the region by Arabs in the seventh century and introduced by the force of arms and gifts. Since that time, Islam has become an integral part of the cultural makeup of nations of the region.

The indigenous belief systems of Tengri and Shamanism, which co-existed with Zoroastrianism and Buddhism, not only "broke the equation that Arab equals Muslim" but also has altered the character of Islam there. In the eyes of the native population, religion and culture are tied together.[17] However, because of the religious oppression of the Soviet system, the vast majority of people have never read the Koran or been to a mosque. People do not practice strict orthodox Islam as practiced by most Arabs in the Middle East. Instead, in most of Kazakhstan, Kyrgyzstan, Tajikistan, and other countries, people practice Folk Islam. They mix superstition with Muslim practices.[18] They fear the evil eye, which is perceived to be a destructive force resulting from people's envy and ill will. They are wary of spirits, which may cause physical or mental illness. Kazaks, for instance, visit the graves of Muslim saints to try to gain blessing or favor. In many cultures Muslims commonly wear *tumars*, which are charms with a Koranic scripture written on them, to try to protect themselves from evil. Appealing to fortunetellers and faith healers when ill is still a common practice. Folk Islam has also played an important role in the survival of Islam among the urban population.

Soviet Influence

Islam has been "paganized" by native cultural practices similar to Christianity in new mission fields and by the political realities of the Soviet era. The Soviet authorities did not prohibit Islam entirely but oppressed its practices in overt and covert manners.[19] In doing so, they achieved various levels of secularization of Islam in most Central Asian countries. They tried to use religious traditions to placate a population, by creating and approving a Muslim Board of Central Asia that acted as a governing agency of the Muslim faith with headquarters in Tashkent, Uzbekistan. The grand mufti, who headed the board, had extensive international contacts with other countries, but the very nature of all his activities and leadership were carefully screened for political reliability. All Islamic movements or networks outside the control of the state were severely suppressed. The Soviet efforts led to the widening of the gap of understanding between Muslims and others and contributed to the emergence of competing Islamic ideologies among the Central Asians themselves.

During the first years of independence, newly emerged states of Central Asia have been experiencing the resurgence of a more secular form of Islam. This form of Islam relates to the population more in traditional and cultural terms than in religious ones. Many support a revival of religion's status only as an element of national revival. They do not attend mosque services, even occasionally, but adhere to popular Islamic traditions, such as life-cycle events like births, weddings, and funerals. At the same time, governments are making a calculated effort to recapture their national history and culture by supporting a growing interest in Islamic teachings and an open, state-sanctioned observance of religious holidays and practices. Since 1991, hundreds of mosques and religious schools have been built or restored and reopened. The impact of Islam on Central Asian culture is not a growing concern of the world, but the rapid politicization of Islam is. History has demonstrated that political involvement of religious establishment (as in Afghanistan during and following the Soviet invasion) moved Islam from the position of being a total way of life to the condition of no distinction between religion and state.

The vast majority of Uzbeks, Kyrgyz, Turkmens, Tajiks, and Kazakhs, like their kin in Afghanistan, are Sunni Muslims. There are fewer Shi'a Muslims, the other main branch of Islam, and the Shi'a religious practices of Azerbaijan and Kurdish minorities are not politicized. Such a situation is consistent with the proportion of each branch among the world's Muslims.

The historical division of Islam into Sunni, or orthodox Islam, and the Shi'a was a result of political disagreement over successors rather than doctrinal differences. Sunni communities have no clerical hierarchy: Each individual stands in a personal relationship to God, needing no intermediary. Any adult versed in the form of prayer is entitled to lead prayers. Shi'a, on the other hand, have a highly structured hierarchy of divinely inspired religio-political leaders.

Christianity

The next largest religious community in the region is Christianity. The leading position has been occupied by the Russian Orthodox Church, the historic faith of many Russians and Ukrainians, followed by Roman Catholics. Most Catholics were Germans, relocated into exile during World War II from European territories of the USSR. Baptists and Seven Day Adventists also live in the region. Other religious groups include small numbers of Jews.

In Azerbaijan, the most significant religious minority group is represented by the Zoroastrian religion, which is a legacy of the early Persian influence.[20] Zoroastrianism is known mostly as a cult of fire; the various rites of this religion center on the eternal flame in the Temple of Fire. Later forms of the Zoroastrian religion teach that through good deeds the righteous person earns an everlasting reward, namely integrity and immortality, as well as resurrection of the dead as a way of the renewal of the world.

The religious composition of Armenia, Azerbaijan, and Georgia has been influenced greatly by their location as a meeting point of southeastern Europe with the western border of Asia. Azerbaijan's population is predominantly Shi'a Muslim. Only 4.8 percent of the population is Christian, and a small percentage is Jewish. The dominance of Christianity in two other countries of the Caucasus region is overwhelming. Ninety-nine percent of the population in Armenia and 83 percent of the population in Georgia is Christian.[21] These countries accepted Christianity in the early fourth century. The millennium-long history, as well as the history of repression during the Soviet period, encouraged the incorporation of a Christian religious identity into a national identity.

PEOPLE

Oh the times! Oh, the customs! (O tempora! O mores!)

CICERO

When you visit a foreign country the most interesting things are not its nature or architecture. The most interesting thing is people.

NIKOLAI GOGOL

The cultural diversity and complexity of the people of the Southern Near Abroad could be compared with the multicolor carpets, which are famous for their designs all over the world, whether they are made in Turkmenistan, Uzbekistan, Afghanistan, or elsewhere in the region. Although cultures of the region are not homogeneous, there are some commonalities:

1. A search for the historical past of each nation, which is currently a subject of reassessment
2. A reinforcement of a sense of national identity and national pride
3. A declining position of the Russian language as a second language and a means of intercultural communication
4. Kinship and tribal relations retaining a strong influence over the social and political structure of each country
5. A shift from open hostility to a cautious official sanctioning of religion in the social life of each society
6. Cultural values that emphasize honor, solidarity, hospitality, mutual support, shame, and revenge, which determine social order and individual responsibility
7. The respect for elders being great in rural and urban areas
8. The marriage celebration, as well as other life-cycle events, possessing great importance and arranged according to old customs
9. The role of women in most of the region's societies that has never conformed to Western stereotypes about Muslim women. With the exception of Afghanistan, the division of labor remains very strict. Women usually are not visible actors in political affairs outside the home. They never wear the veil or practice strict seclusion.

LANGUAGE

After all, when you come right down to it, how many people speak the same language even when they speak the same language?

RUSSELL HOBAN

The dominance of the Turkic language group is one of the most visible features of the region.[22] The spoken languages of Kazakhstan, Uzbekistan, Turkmenistan, Kyrgyzstan, and Azerbaijan belong to different branches of Turkic language that have been influenced by a diverse history of nations. Language still remains a foundation of cultural interconnectedness. A high degree of language loyalty was reflected in the populations' claims of native language. For instance, 99.4 percent of Turkmen in Turkmenistan claimed Turkmen language as their native language in a 1989 census. Among the group, represented for the most part by educated urban dwellers, 28 percent claim Russian as their second language. Only 3 percent of Russians in this republic spoke Turkmen. This language distribution is consistent throughout the region.

During the Soviet period, written forms of many languages of the region underwent several reforms, being changed from Arabic script to the Latin alphabet to Cyrillic script. The independent language policy has been marked by a determination to establish native language as the official language and to remove the heritage of a Russian-dominated past. In some countries, specifically in Turkmenistan and Azerbaijan, where the Cyrillic-based alphabet was officially replaced by the Latin-based script, English has been moved ahead of Russian as the "second state language." Nevertheless, Russian does remain a key language in government and other spheres. In the past, Russian language policies created a barrier and a discriminatory factor for nonnative speakers, especially middle-aged professionals, in terms of social status and position, job retention, promotion, social acceptance, and prestige.

The Tajik language *Farsi*, which traditionally has been called *Persian*, belongs to the Iranian language group. Many Persian language writers were called *Tajiks*. Based on instructions of the Soviet central political leadership, they had been identified in that way, although they had not lived in Central Asia.

There are several eastern Iranian peoples of the Pamir Mountain area in Tajikistan. Because of their geographic isolation, they have not been assimilated by their Persian or Turkic-speaking neighbors and have managed to preserve their distinct identities. Only at the end of the Soviet era did the central government allow some form of education and media sources to operate in native Pamiri languages.

The Armenian and Georgian languages grew in different directions. Armenian developed from a combination of Indo-European and non-Indo-European language stock with an alphabet based on the Greek. Georgian, unrelated to any major world languages, uses a Greek-based alphabet that is different from Armenian.

The Afghan language mosaic is the most colorful in the region. It is home to a multiplicity of ethnic and linguistic groups, with a considerable degree of cultural homogeneity, as a result of cultural assimilation. The largest ethnic group, Pushtun, speaks several mutually intelligible dialects of Pushtu. Some also speak Dari. Both of the languages belong to the Iranian branch of the Indo-European language family. Among other language and ethnic groups in Afghanistan, the most prominent positions are occupied by Tajik, Uzbek, Turkmen, and Hazara.

HISTORY

A thousand years scarce serve to form a state: an hour may lay it in the dust.

LORD BYRON

The Southern Near Abroad's location at the meeting point of southeastern Europe with the eastern border of Asia greatly influenced the histories of the people forming its present-day republics. Their people were subject to invasion and control by the Ottoman, Persian, Mongol, and Russian empires. The starting points and the outside influences that formed cultures of the region were quite different.

A legacy of the early Persian influence in the Southern Near Abroad countries as well as a later conquest and centuries of occupation by the Ottoman Empire has added Turkic influence on different aspects of secular culture, most notably in language and art.[23] The diverse people of Central Asia underwent different degrees of displacement and, at different times, experienced growth and decline. The times of independence enabled civilizations to flourish and to individualize their forms of art and literature.

Archaeologists working in the deserts of Turkmenistan have discovered evidence of an ancient, literate civilization that existed in Central Asia more than 4,000 years ago.[24] According to experts, traces of lost civilizations suggest that the ancient people of Central Asia were not as isolated as previously thought, but rather had continent-wide connections. New excavation sites are a real goldmine for archaeologists. A baked-clay statue found in southern Turkmenistan was similar to a Bactrian one found in Northern Afghanistan and Mesopotamia, which led experts to suggest that a high-level civilization was prospering approximately 3,000 years ago and was a direct heir to Mesopotamian civilization.

Between 700 B.C. and A.D. 250 Central Asia witnessed the emergence of the Achaemenid Empire, the invasion of Alexander the Great (who set up at least eight cities in the region between 334 and 323 B.C.), and the rise and fall of nomadic and sedentary[25] civilizations, of which the most flourishing were the Bactrian Kingdom and the Kushan Empire. Their high level of social and cultural organization gave rise to a rich and prosperous trade through the Silk Road linking China to the West. The route took its name from silk, the commodity most in demand in Europe.

The period of A.D. 250 to 750 has been referred to as a crossroad of civilizations. It witnessed complex political events as the result of the arrival of warring dynasties and ethnic movements, as well as far-reaching social, economic, and cultural upheavals. This was the time of nomadic migrations and the constitution of steppe empires that swept over these sedentary populations and not only left their imprint on social and political life but also added a new ethnic component to the population. These multicultural societies had assimilated to a various degree the great religious traditions of Buddhism, Zoroastrianism, Christianity, and Shamanism. The arrival of Islam at the end of this period brought fundamental changes to all aspects of life.

During the eight centuries of A.D. 750 to 1500, the new faith of Islam gradually spread, affecting much of Central Asia; many mosques and madrassas were built in the Uzbekistan cities of Samarqand, Bukhara, and Khiva. These were the centuries in which nomadic and military empires arose in the heart of Asia, impinging on the history of adjacent cultures to an unparalleled extent. The most destructive period was the invasion of Genghis Khan in 1220. This left most of the cities in ruins. His descendant Timur, also known as Tamerlane, resurrected once-famous cities by using the labor of slaves and artists captured during successful crusades. The formation of the Turco-Mongol Golden Horde had a major, enduring influence on the course of the region's history.

The history of Central Asian civilizations from about 1500 to about 1850 was a period that witnessed the last phase of nomadism as a viable system of social organization. The shift of the main lines of international trade from the Great Silk Route to the oceanic routes reflected the early impact of colonialism, notably British and Russian.

Beginning in the eighteenth century, the Russian Empire constantly probed this region for possible expansion toward the Black Sea, the Caspian Sea, and India. These efforts involved Russia in a series of wars with the Persian and Ottoman empires, both of which by that time were decaying from within.

The Colonial Experience

To be ignorant of what occurred before you were born is to remain always a child. For what is the worth of human life, unless it is woven into the life of our ancestors by the records of history?

CICERO

Borders are scratched across the hearts of men by strangers with a calm, judicial pen.

MARIA MANNES

The Russians lacked colonies, but there was a world to win on their southeastern frontier. Internal colonialism as an *annexation* of adjacent territories was the most practical way for Russia to extend its territory and influence, and then change the balance of powers in this area. As soon as the Russian conquest of the Caucasus was completed in the late 1850s, an intensive incorporation of Central Asian states into Russia began. It took different forms, from fairly peaceful colonization, as in the case of Kazakhstan with the assembly of Kazakh's elders supporting the decision to join Russia in 1731, to a military conquest in the case of Turkistan in 1873. There, the Turkmen put up the stiffest resistance against Russian expansion. By 1876, the territory known today as Uzbekistan either had fallen under direct Russian control or had become a protectorate of Russia.[26] According to the treaty signed by the Khanate of Bukhoro with Russia, khanates retained control over internal affairs, while Russia controlled foreign relations of these states. This form of colonialism gave Russian merchants significant concessions in foreign trade.[27]

A few years later, the Russians signed an agreement with the Persians and established what is essentially the current border between Turkmenistan and Iran. In 1897, an agreement was signed between the Russians and the Afghans.

In the second half of the nineteenth century, a new type of border had been formed in Central Asia. These borders were different from the European meaning of the term *border*. Distinctive sociohistorical environments predetermine the type of geopolitical or state border. In this context, we need to distinguish between two types of borders: European or Western types, and Asian and

Eastern borders. Even in the middle of the nineteenth century, two types of borders existed. There were constant borders of a sedentary population and flexible, constantly changing borders with the nomadic tribes. The constant borders were the internal borders of the permanent agricultural oases. The flexible borders, similar to the notion of frontiers, reflected the lifestyle of the nomadic populations.[28]

The importance of colonization of the area was based not only on the value of this territory to Russia, as a main source of cotton at the time, but also on its position in the formation of new political realities in the world. Turkistan had been swallowed by Russia unnoticeably, while India was perceived as a real colonial goal. Although India is separated from the Russian Central Asian periphery by Afghanistan, it is just a perception; the reality is that, in strategic terms, Afghanistan played the role of the border zone between Russia and Great Britain.

During the first period of Russian presence in the area, daily life for Central Asian people did not change much. The Russians did not mix with the indigenous people beyond the needed interaction for cotton production. This Russian separateness led to a nonprejudicial but rather patronizing relationship between Russian numeric minority and local majority groups that was similar to the position of the British in India.

The most significant social and economic changes produced by the era of Russian rule can be summarized as follows:

1. Moscow absorbed the greatest part of the wealth of Central Asia with an increased emphasis on cotton cultivation.
2. To operate successfully in remote colonial places, the development of the infrastructure was crucial, including the construction of railroads, communication links, smelting plants, and cotton-ginning machinery.
3. Military hospitals and schools were built to provide adequate training and services to the labor force.
4. There was an expansion of economic relations with Russia. A barter system was created.
5. There was an introduction of a Russian system of administration in the territories.
6. Military-supported bases were created on the borders.
7. An agrarian policy brought about a gradual shift in the proportion of nomads to a more settled population.
8. Industrial capitalism has been accompanied by a pronounced social differentiation between Russians and the native population.

The reasons for Russian expansion toward Transcaucasian states were slightly different. From 1773, Georgian rulers began efforts to gain Russian protection from the Turks of the Ottoman Empire. The Russian occupation of parts of Georgia turned the country into an arena of Russian-Turkish rivalry for decades. The impact of the colonization of this area can be seen in these social processes:

1. Russian education and ranks of nobility were introduced.
2. Russification intensified as time passed.

3. The Georgian Orthodox Church lost its independent status in 1811.

4. A rebellion against intensified Russification became more pronounced.

From the moment of a seemingly easy conquest of Central Asia, Russia's image was transformed from being an Asia in Europe to becoming a Europe in Asia.

The Sovietization Process

Sporadic antitsarist revolts occurred during the years immediately preceding the 1917 Russian Revolution. This unrest swept through the whole region and was later transformed into an armed resistance to Soviet rule known as the Basmachi Rebellion.[29] Its impact was the strongest in small towns throughout the region between 1920 and 1930.

In the process of creating the new republics of Soviet Russia in the 1920s, the central political leadership arbitrarily defined national identities and national borders, which until that time had little political importance. These nonetheless became a stumbling block and a source of national armed conflicts. One example is the conflict between Armenia and Azerbaijan.

In 1924 Central Asia was divided into distinct political entities. The process of the establishment of Russian control over these states was a lengthy and costly one. To maintain control, the Bolsheviks used rhetoric appealing to the people of the area: Decolonization and national sovereignty were pledged to non-Russians.[30]

Efforts of the Soviet state to undermine the traditional way of life resulted in significant changes in family structure and political relationships, observances of religious holidays, economic activities, and the migration of a rural population into industrial centers. The massive *collectivization* of the 1920s and 1930s is remembered in the history of Soviet nations as the largest manmade social disaster. The essence of this policy was to introduce the advantages of the collective cooperative agricultural units that were opposed by individual operations. The process of collectivization was supposed to be voluntary and gradual; however, neither of these ideals was realized. Stalin's central government required a fast collectivization and suppression of all resistance. Creation of collective farms and agricultural entities was marked as the bloody period of genocide. Individual property was confiscated, owners were imprisoned in concentration camps for decades, and many were killed. Their families were expelled from the traditional lands and had a mark (similar to a birthmark) of the "enemy of the nation" for life. They were discriminated against in all areas of life, such as access to higher education, desirable jobs, and social recognition.

Local *intelligentsia* who were openly critical to such policies were labeled as "bourgeois nationalists" and shared the fate of other persecuted categories. National intellectuals were purged for being nationalists. This was a loosely defined offense that could be applied to any form of opposition to central government policies.

Stalin and Lavrenti Beria, his chief of secret police from 1938 to 1953, were both Georgians. Stalin's oppressions, however, were as severe toward Georgian intellectual opposition as toward any other group. The best-known manifestation of this was the execution of 5,000 nobles in 1924 and the purge of Georgian intellectuals and artists from 1936 to 1937.

This was the darkest page in the Soviet history of the region. As much as the rest of the Soviet era has been marked by the same political realities, the intensity of social control and oppression never reached the same magnitude. During the later part of the Soviet period, there was strict control of religious freedoms, entrepreneurship activities, press censorship, and individual correspondence. Loyalty to regime and Russification were the prerequisites to obtain any position on the social ladder.

Russification is one of the social phenomena requiring an objective analysis. As a successor of the tsarist policy of Russification, the Soviet era added a number of new dimensions:

1. A significant number of Russians and other Slavic and non-Slavic peoples were relocated to the region as part of the state policy of industrialization.
2. An urban concentration of immigrants predetermined the role of Russian language as the major language of communication.
3. Russian was the language of the state, and all official documentation was maintained in Russian. Local officials who participated in the regime did so on Russian terms.
4. In the majority of public schools in urban settings, the educational process was conducted in Russian.
5. Some native language schools existed as a display for the international community. In reality, they were only exotic oases of native culture.
6. Because the majority of native speakers lived in rural areas, native languages had been relegated to the position of peasants, second-class languages. Every family that had desires for their children to advance in social structure made enormous efforts to provide Russian language instruction for their children as a key to their futures.
7. The funding of native arts and folklore was based on a "leftover" approach, meaning the budget would be provided from local budgets after all other social programs were fulfilled.
8. Russian officials occupied key leadership positions in all spheres of social, political, and economic life. One of the hypocritical realities of that time was the practice for a leader of any entity to be a native, with a Russian national deputy as a must for close control on the issue of loyalty.

Only 18 years later, after the declaration of independence of the Republic of Tajikistan, its current president Emomali Rahmon introduced a draft of the new "Language Law." All official correspondence and communication with the government agencies and institutions must be maintained in the official language of the country—the Tajik language. The Russian language would remain as a language of international communication. "The greatness of the nation," said Emoli Rahmon, "can be judged, first of all, on the basis of the respect and care of people to their native language. It is time for us, similar to other developed and civilized countries, to take care of the purity of our national language."[31]

An independent observer may ask whether there were other positive and/or negative aspects of the impact of the Sovietization process on the

Central Asian region. To be fair, in our assessment of the sociopolitical development, we should mention some other social changes occurring during that time:

1. There was intensive industrialization, which contributed to the development of the industrial establishment and energy sectors in each of these countries. This policy, however, resulted in a degree of dependency on central decision making.

2. There was the intensive exploration of natural resources, such as oil, coal, iron ore, and underground water resources in Kazakhstan; natural gas and salt in Uzbekistan and Turkmenistan; and gold and silver in Kyrgyzstan.

3. There was a centrally planned migration of the labor force as a mandatory requirement for all higher education professionals. The required time frame of such job assignments after graduation from the university was set at three years. For most young people, this is the time of building relationships and starting families, which was a key factor causing them to stay in Central Asia for life. That's why such a large segment of the Russian-speaking population exists in all former republics of the Soviet Union. This is also why they find themselves unprepared to operate in native languages and now experience severe job and social discrimination.

4. There was an ongoing ethnic integration; intermarriages were at the highest level in industrial centers, such as Alma-Ata, Tashkent, Bukhara, Ashghabad, and Dushanbe. The overall level of prejudice against the non-Russian minorities in the area was generally insignificant.

5. There was a restructuring of the agricultural production in favor of monocultural specialization, with cotton dominance at the expense of sufficient food production by local agricultural state enterprises.

6. There was the development of a highly politicized standardized system of education, with high academic standards.

7. There was an enormous improvement of the health care system with the mandatory immunization of the whole population and eradication of epidemics that had killed hundreds of thousands of people in the past.

8. There was a development of a social welfare system providing inexpensive and high-quality daycare facilities, free school uniforms, books, lunches for children from big families, free medical services, 12 weeks of paid maternity leave and one year unpaid with a guaranteed work place, retirement for women at the age of 55 and for men at the age of 60, 25 working days of paid vacation per year, free higher education, inexpensive summer camps for children, resort vouchers for adults, and numerous privileges for families with more than four children.

9. Scientific research institutions were created. The first space ship's launch site, cosmodrome Baikonur, was built in Kazakhstan.

10. State governments depended on funding coming from the center in Moscow, which contributed to the tension between the center and the periphery.

The Aftermath of Soviet Rule

In view of the 70-year period of the oppressive Russification and central dominance, the "pendulum of the grandfather's clock" not surprisingly moved not only to the point of reconstruction of national identities but also even further to an extreme position, giving rise to an open nationalism and discrimination against Russian-speaking minorities. Even Kazakhstan, which maintains close economic and political ties with Russia, is moving ahead with plans to replace Cyrillic script with the Latin alphabet, following the experience of Azerbaijan, Turkmenistan, and Uzbekistan.

The economic logic of continued ties to Russia during the post-Soviet period, with the predominant dependency of newly independent states on exports of primary products, raw materials such as oil, gas, and cotton, with prices set by Russian monopolies below world prices, created a resistance against participation in new treaties, political unions, and integration blocks where Russia was a dominant member. The native professionals of every state commonly understood that such economic cooperation would preserve Central Asia's *de facto* colonial position within Russian industry.

That's why some of the countries of the region, including Uzbekistan, rejected an offer to be a part of the Commonwealth of Independent States (CIS), an organization of states of the former Soviet Union. They are working on the integration of their nations into a broader context of the world's economic and political communities. In 2001 a regional security organization, the Shanghai Cooperation Organization (SCO), was founded. Its members include China, Kazakhstan, Kyrgyzstan, Tajikistan, Uzbekistan, and Russia. The organization is making joint efforts to consolidate mutual political trust, pushing pragmatic cooperation to a higher level, playing a greater role in safeguarding members' interests, and ensuring regional peace and stability. At the latest summit of the organization on June 25, 2009, in Yekaterinburg, Russia, the SCO reiterated the strong commitment of all members to fight terrorism and drug trafficking. One of the new issues on the agenda was to broaden economic cooperation and work together to overcome the global financial crisis and to contribute to the development of favorable conditions for regional trade and stabilization in the region.[32]

GOVERNMENT

> A leader is best when people barely know that he exists, Not so good when people obey and acclaim him, worst when they despise him.
>
> LAO TZU

Any state that emerged from the ruins of the USSR would have proclaimed its intent to create an open society and to build a democratic secular state according to the Western model. Nevertheless, in almost all the former Soviet Republics of the region, the established order could be best described as an *authoritarian political model*, based on the power of the individual at the top. This description is fully applicable to the countries of Central Asia and the Southern Near Abroad. Presidents of these countries awarded themselves with the functions and powers typical of the former secretaries of the Communist Party of the Soviet era, adding some of the characteristics of Asian rulers from feudal times. This could be seen in the proposition to restore the Halifat, an Islamic medieval feudal state structure in Uzbekistan.

The late president of Turkmenistan, Saparmurad Niazov, was awarded the lifelong position of president and the official title of Turkmenbashi, that is, "The Head of the Turkmen."[33] His death in December 2006 sparked an intense speculation among Western analysts about the future of the most isolated of former Soviet republics, called by one analyst in the mid-1990s, "Central Asia's North Korea albeit minus the nukes." While the newly elected Turkmen President Gurbaguly Berdymukhammedov inherited Niazov's apparatus largely intact, he did not inherit his megalomaniacal ego. On February 11, 2007, running against five other candidates, Berdymukhammedov won 94 percent of the vote. A few years later, assessments are at best mixed. The atmosphere in Ashgabat has been transformed. The Turkmen authorities no longer refuse to discuss openly sensitive issues. In June 2008, the European Union and Turkmenistan held their first "human rights dialogue" in Ashgabat. A new constitution was adopted in September 2008 which increased parliament's powers. President Berdymukhammedov has begun to dismantle his predecessor's bizarre personality cult: Months of the year were returned to their original names; mandatory readings of Niazov's spiritual book *Ruhnama* at schools was abolished. The new president has pardoned several political prisoners, authorized broader access to the Internet for the public, restored the right to 10 years of education, and reinstated pensions.

Kyrgyzstan gives us another illustration of the *personality cult* phenomena: In 1991 the first president of Kyrgyzstan, Askar Akayev, was awarded the title of "The Supreme Khan of the Kyrgyz."[34] As much as it may sound unusual for a democratic state, such symbolism played a stabilizing role during times of political crisis, following the failed coup d'état in Moscow in 1991. When the Kazakh ruling party won all 98 seats at stake in the August 18, 2007, elections, President Nursultan Nazarbaev suggested that democracy and pluralism would not suffer under a one-party system. One-party politics is a clear step backward—to Soviet-style rule.

Today all countries in the region claim to have a multiparty system, freedom of the press, and other features of developing democracies. At the same time, the following characteristics can be found in each of them:

1. Political power has been monopolized by presidents and their allies.
2. Newspapers of the political opposition have been closed.
3. Corruption has affected all areas of life.
4. The use of antidemocratic ways to make amendments to the constitution has occurred, especially during election campaigns.

What are the reasons for the "authoritarian transformation" of the political regimes in the region? First, it is a result of the painful transition process from the authoritarian Communist model to a Western model; it is a disease of "growth." Second, the local traditional cultural environment is tearing away foreign elements of the liberal democratic institutions from the West. Third, it is a combination, or synthesis, of two systems. The process of integration of these opposing components could be best illustrated through the analysis of one of the countries of the region.

CASE STUDIES

Kyrgyzstan

Every generation needs a new revolution.

Thomas Jefferson

Several colorfully named revolutions have succeeded over the past few years in the region: the Rose Revolution in Georgia in 2003, the Orange Revolution in Ukraine in 2004, and the Tulip Revolution in Kyrgyzstan in 2005. Was it a "revolutionary bug" that had come to Kyrgyzstan, or had the local environment generated objective conditions for the protest movement to grow and to erupt in the form of revolution? To understand what happened and the challenges Kyrgyzstan is yet to face in rebuilding the economy and democracy, one must take a look back into the recent past of this country.

The territory of Kyrgyzstan is approximately 200,000 square kilometers. Its population is slightly above 4.5 million people. Forty percent of the population lives below the poverty line, according to official statistics. Foreign debt is now approaching $3 billion.[35] Kyrgyzstan has valuable natural resources: gold, silver, uranium, other rare metals, and oil. In addition, this small country has the third-largest gold mining industry after Russia and Uzbekistan. Its annual production of gold is more than 20 tons; 40 percent of gold export is done by a Kyrgyz–Canadian joint venture, Centera Gold Inc. The Canadian-based uranium/gold concern, Cameco Corporation, has a controlling interest in Centera. The revision of the ownership structure of Centera Gold, Inc., in April 2009 increased the Kyrgyz government share to 33 percent. In return for the share transfer, Cameco received rights to mine 25,000 additional hectares in the field and face a less-complicated tax structure. This deal put to rest all talks of nationalization. It was also a step toward restructuring the mining industry and meeting long-standing demands for Kyrgyzstan's greater control over its most lucrative assets, creating more jobs for local people.

During the Soviet period, Kyrgyzia held the largest number of livestock. Today, out of what was once 11 million sheep, only 4 million remain. Unemployment has skyrocketed because 70 percent of the industrial enterprises are closed. The rate of migration to Russia and other countries is worrisome.[36] However, in a time of global financial and economic crisis, Kyrgyzstan may have to absorb thousands of young surplus laborers. The risk of social and political upheaval may grow.

The World Bank has labeled Kyrgyzstan among one of the three most corrupt post-Soviet countries. Corruption is defined as "the abuse of public office for private gain." It takes many forms. Land redistribution based on favoritism and *privatization*— selling state property for pennies to former state and Communist party leaders who became businessmen overnight—runs rampant. "One morning they woke up being millionaires," one analyst stated. Allegedly more than 3,800 enterprises were sold for next to nothing. Another form of corruption is manipulation of government contracts, licenses for energy resources, and brokerage service.[37]

Among numerous examples of corruptive practices by the government were scandals around the license issued to Cameko, and the fraudulent gasoline transaction of the United States–Kyrgyz joint venture titled "Vostok." Redistribution and misappropriation of international economic aid became one of the new forms of corruption. Because of the country's claimed democratic image, in the past Kyrgyzstan has received international funds three times higher per capita than any post-Communist country in Central Asia. From 1992 to 1998 Kyrgyzstan was awarded foreign loans totaling $1.3 billion by various international organizations and donor countries. In most cases these were 30-year loans with 2 percent interest, the cheapest money ever; however, as a result of the country's corruptive practices, providing financial support was like pouring water through a sieve. The lives of the citizens did not improve.[38] Today the World Bank and the International Monetary Fund are negotiating terms and conditions of a debt reduction program with Kyrgyzstan. Successful participation in the debt reduction program, launched by the World Bank and the IMF, could diminish Kyrgyz foreign debt by $800 million.

During the past 18 years, the political climate of Kyrgyzstan has been under the influence of two forces, an old state party *nomenklatura*[39] and a new elite that emerged as a result of Mikhail Gorbachev's *perestroika*. This contradiction between old and new elite is just the tip of the iceberg. Its base is determined by a historic conflict between the aristocracy of northern Kyrgyzstan, which had a strong tribal structure, and the nonaristocratic South, with family groups as its power base. During the Soviet period, the party leaders were recruited from the South. Northerners were more urbanized, more secularized, and Russianized. Under the strong influence of Uzbekistan, southerners were representing agrarian regions where traditions of Islam were the strongest.[40]

Most indicative of the victory of the tribal political groups and clans is that of the former president Askar Akayev, the first popularly elected president, who resigned on March 24, 2005. He belonged to the largest and most powerful northern tribe, Sari-Bagysh, and, through his wife, was supported by the most aristocratic clan, the Djegetins. In this culture where every person knows seven generations of his predecessors, clan-family relationships play a crucial role. Admitted by the former president's press secretary, Kamil Bayalinov, "It is not a secret that, in general, high officials of the government are coming from one clan or another.[41] This is reality." "In our small republic, wherever you turn, everybody is somebody's man."[42]

In the 1990s, the essence of transition of political power was not so much the transition from a Communist to a democratic regime, but, in reality, it reflected the redistribution of power among the ethnic elite and regional political centers. One form of this process was incorporation of traditional institutions into a modern social system. Perhaps the most highly criticized by the International Human Rights Organization was the Kyrgyz government's decision to grant legitimate status to Aksakal Courts. They were allowed to make decisions related to local issues, and this provision resulted in some unexpected consequences because some of the Aksakal Courts made death penalty decisions that were carried out immediately.

The traditional norm of tribal solidarity prohibits rank-and-file members from contesting their own tribal leadership and compels them to offer maximum support in their struggle with leaders from other tribes. The logic of this practice is simple: The larger the gain of the tribal elite, the larger the share that will trickle down in the form of investments, subsidies, jobs, and government projects.

Political power allowed members of the tribal elite to control the majority of the Kyrgyz energy complex, transportation, communication, production of alcohol products, commercial aviation, and the cotton and sugar cane industries. From the Western perspective, such an informal relationship of political power and ownership interests is called corruption.

Not many experts predicted that the protest against corruption and dynastic succession of Ascar Akaev, motivated by two rounds of flawed parliamentary elections, could take the form of uprising. Unlike peaceful events in Ukraine, this uprising prompted the president of Kyrgyzstan to break the pledge of nonviolence. Although the police force was fewer in numbers, it behaved brutally enough to enrage protesters, many of whom were women and teenagers who had come from the nearby villages. For two nights after the uprising, looters targeted businesses they thought belonged to the Akaev family.[43] Some of the desperate business owners put up signs saying, "We are with the people." Despite the fact that the president himself fled to Russia and eventually agreed to sign a letter of resignation, there were practically no anti-Russian sentiments or looting against ethnic Russian businesses (although Turkish and Chinese businesses were damaged).

The revolt in March 2005 left Kyrgyzstan with two parliaments, both of which initially sat in the same building. The Supreme Court of the country favored the old parliament, which had nominated the former prime minister, Kurmanbeck Bakiev, as acting president. Most observers believed the election in July 2005 was fair for the most part, and, as first results were announced, the favorite, Bakiev, had clearly won a resounding victory.

In this regionally divided country, in which the south is separated from the north by a mountain range and contains a large Uzbek minority with a devout adherence to Islam, it was the south that became the scene of the largest demonstrations. These eventually snowballed into a mass movement called the Tulip Revolution.

The true revolution, however, is not about throwing out one ruler and replacing him with another. The goal of democratic revolutions is to support democratic institutions and market reforms in society and to fight corruption. The world was wondering: "Would Kyrgyzstan be able to rise to such a challenge?" Five years later, observers regard Kyrgyzstan's progress as measurable and promising. However, the next contested presidential election in July 2009 demonstrated the fragility of democratic gains and weakness of democratic institutions. The presidential opposition was denied an equal access to the state television, Central Election Commission data, and law enforcement agencies in their campaigns. The allegedly corruptive electoral practices led protesters to the streets of Beshkek and Balikchi on election day. Special forces units were ordered to use tear gas and clubs against peaceful protesters. The victory of the incumbent president Bakiev came out with tears, indeed—this time, unfortunately, not with tears of joy for the progress of democracy.[44] However important, political processes don't constitute the whole picture of the present and future developments of the country. For many Kyrgyz, the hidden power in Bishkek that wields the most influence in the Central Asian region is China. Chinese immigration into Kyrgyzstan is emerging as a politically sensitive topic. Soon after the time of Bishkek's accession to the WTO in 1998, Chinese products and traders flooded into the country. A new report by the French Institute of International Relations (known by its French acronym IFRI) says the volume of bilateral Chinese-Kyrgyz trade almost tripled between 2004 and 2007, from $602 million to $1.64 billion. In 2007, Chinese exports made up 94 percent of cross-border commerce.[45] In contrast to Russian investments, Chinese investments don't have visible strings attached, although Kyrgyzstan's growing dependence on a heavyweight neighbor may provide Beijing with leverage over the Kyrgyz political system in the future. Kyrgyzstan's powerful neighbors, Russia and China, are playing their hidden games, pursuing different goals. China is pursuing economic influence, whereas Russia is pursuing both political and economic influence, openly and unapologetically.

FLASHPOINTS
Domino Effect and the Clash of Interests

The "ghost of revolution" is rambling throughout the vast fields of Central Asia and the Southern Near Abroad. Georgia, Ukraine, and Kyrgyzstan are just the beginning of the march of democratic forces in the area that Russia once considered to be its political playground. Even though the Russia-controlled environment rarely yields surprises, the contested elections in Armenia in February 2008 held a number of the surprises. Serzh Sarkisian, the prime minister, announced victory in an election that allegedly was far from being free from intimidation and fraud. The opposition protested, took to the streets, and was shut down by brute force. The world media turned its attention away from the long-predicted results to the unexpected bloodshed in Armenia. Eight people were killed in clashes between special forces and demonstrators, who were protesting against alleged election fraud, corruption, and local mafia. "An election won with some blood" was the headline that ran in a leading newspaper.[46]

The sequence of revolutions and protests against antidemocratic corruptive election practices may create a domino effect among other corrupt post-Soviet political regimes. Some of them today have to make the tough decision between two evils: to accept Russian "help" and become politically manipulated by Moscow to strengthen their rotten autocratic structures or to maintain an independent course and be crashed by a growing democratic opposition force. Since 1991 these old post-Soviet powers have tried to balance the United States, the West, and Russia. They now recognize that the only way to prolong their existence is to accept help on Moscow's terms.

After September 11, 2001, a U.S. air base, Manas Air Base, was established near the capital of Kyrgyzstan Bishkek, to support operations in Afghanistan; this has been a proverbial "thorn in Russia's side." Kyrgyzstan offered coalition forces unrestricted overflight rights to aircraft flying for combat, humanitarian purposes, and search-and-rescue missions for a period of one year, with the possibility of extension during the antiterrorism campaign, for which much hope and hard work has been put forth by American men and women in uniform. There were about 2,000 American and European troops there.[47] The U.S. Army in Kyrgyzstan was not only building airfield facilities, but was also constructing bridges of understanding and friendship with local people by helping them to rebuild local hospitals and schools; by providing computers and training for teachers; by generating jobs for local construction workers, translators, doctors, and security officers. However, for the Kyrgyz top politicians, this was a small measure, unlike Russia's direct transfer of $150 million to Kyrgyzstan on April 1, 2009, as part of a $2 billion financial aid package. Another less-publicized aspect of this package involved a debt-for-asset swap. In exchange for writing off most of the Kyrgyz debt to Moscow, Russia has offered to acquire a 48 percent stake in a Dastan munitions' plant, which had always been dependent on orders from Russia.[48] This development has thrust the geopolitical competition between Moscow and Washington back into the news. In October 2003, Russia created its own air base in Kant, near the capital city of Bishkek, as a response to the U.S. and coalition forces' air base. To emphasize its strategic importance, then Russian president Vladimir Putin arrived in Kyrgyzstan to attend its official opening. According to some in Moscow, Kyrgyzstan was another blow to Russia in the competition for influence in the former Soviet Union after Georgia and Ukraine. Moscow used all its resources to change the balance of power in the area in its favor. In February 2009, the Parliament of Kyrgyzstan voted to terminate their lease of Manas Air Base to the United States. This required Americans to vacate the base within six months. U.S. officials remain hopeful that there may be still room for negotiations.

In Moscow's view, the closure of Manas Air Base is a small fragment of the bigger principal geopolitical challenges to Russia: the expansion of NATO influence in the region and the drift away from Moscow. These challenges are seen as interrelated because the expansion of NATO influence encourages the drift away from Moscow, and the drift facilitates NATO expansion. An area of interest in this regard is the Caucasus state of the Caspian area, Azerbaijan.

Azerbaijan

Azerbaijan's strategic position in the center of the Caspian and its key role in the realization of projects of exploration and transportation of Caspian energy resources determine its increasing significance as a major player in the region. The capital of Azerbaijan, Baku, with a population of 2.1 million, is one of the oldest oil fields in the world. The clear line in the establishment of an alliance with Turkey and the West makes Azerbaijan an attractive candidate as leader in the Caucasus region. It is viewed as a possible base for the strengthening of the American influence in the region. Azerbaijan is extremely interested in developing close ties with NATO. There has been much official discussion in Azerbaijan about the possibility of either the United States or Turkey acquiring military bases in Azerbaijan. Every taxi driver in the city enthusiastically speculates that Baku might request the closure of the Russian early warning station at Gabalinskaya. The main justification for Azerbaijan wanting NATO bases has been seen in the existence of close political and military relations between Russia and Armenia. The presence of Russian military bases in Armenia, particularly as the Nagornyy Karabakh conflict between Armenia and Azerbaijan, remains unresolved.[49]

The Russian-Armenian close political, military, and economic partnership in some way counters the decline of Russian influence in the region. To regard Russia as irrelevant to the region is a mistake. Russia has the power to influence the region's policies in the foreseeable future. The skills and art of the regional political players will be seen in their ability to pursue policies that will enhance the independence of the newly independent states under the balanced relationship with both the West and Russia. Democratically elected Azerbaijani President Ilham Aliev has taken this challenge, giving priority to stabilizing the investment climate in the country, strengthening the army, liberating occupied lands, and improving the living standards of people. Under President Aliev, Azerbaijan is fast becoming the Kuwait of the former Soviet Union. The transformation of Azerbaijan into the main transport corridor of the region has elevated the strategic significance of this country.

The Aral Sea: An Environmental Disaster

> Civilization is being poisoned by its own waste products.
>
> Willam Ralph Inge

In many instances, one of the contributing factors to the many so-called natural disasters is the consequence of inadequate development of policies and practices. The shrinking Aral Sea, located on the border of Kazakhstan and Uzbekistan, has become a dual symbol, first of the destructive power of the Soviet central planning system in the area of water management, and, second, the Central Asian government's inability to cooperate on a crucial regional issue. According to UN experts, if left untouched, this symbol of one of the worst human-created ecological disasters in history will likely not exist by 2020.

Specialists estimate the Aral Sea's surface is now only 25 percent of the surface that existed before Soviet central planners, in 1970, implemented a poorly researched and ill-calculated project of diverting the flow of the sea's two main rivers, the Amu-Darya and Syr-Darya, to agricultural irrigation schemes, to turn Central Asia into the Soviet Union's primary cotton region. The Aral Sea is actually divided into three parts: the Northern Aral Sea (NAS) and the Southern Aral Sea (SAS), which consists of two sections along the north-south axis. Thousands of tons of salt and sand from the dried-up seabed are being scattered by winds across a 300-mile radius. The president of Kazakhstan, Nursultan Nazarbaev, called the sea's shrinkage a "global disaster," noting that salt and sand from the sea affects the environment as far as the Arctic Ocean.[50]

With the help of the World Bank, Kazakhstan is trying to secure the survival of the northern segment of the Aral Sea by constructing a closure dike and stimulating additional flow of water into this part of the sea. The complex set of measures targeting the improvement of ecological and environmental conditions of the delta area would result in a higher volume of water channeled into the NAS. After construction of the dike, the surface area of the NAS would increase by between 20 and 25 percent. This, however, will not solve the whole problem. The preservation of the Aral Sea is not just a matter of general improvements to the landscape of the region. UN experts are urging the Kazakhstani government to stop spending money on restoration of the Aral Sea and direct the main part of the immediate spending on evacuating people from an ecological disaster area.

The Aral Sea basin contains some 35 million people, with 2.5 million of them living in the disaster zone, which encompasses most of the two regions of Uzbekistan, the Northern regions of Turkmenistan, and the south-central Kazakh province of Kyzyl-Orda. Public attention was drawn to this tragic situation for the first time during Gorbachev's perestroika and glasnost period. The analysis of experts at that time emphasized the dramatic effect of the disappearance of the Aral Sea on the health of the people in the region. Disease, malnutrition, and birth defects caused by the spread of salts containing high concentrations of pesticides and residues of chemical fertilizers are at deadly levels.[51] Experts and practitioners are unanimous in their opinion that rehabilitating the depleted sea would be practically impossible without the international community's support. This critical situation has led to regional cooperation and to the search for practical, cost-effective solutions for more efficient water management strategies.

The rising impact of disasters is becoming a commonly cited indicator of unsustainable development. These risks, however, can be managed, and people can be made less vulnerable to natural phenomena.

Soviet Nuclear Testing Site in Kazakhstan

The nation that destroys its soil destroys itself.

Franklin D. Roosevelt

The means by which we live have outdistanced the ends for which we live. Our scientific power has outrun our spiritual power. We have guided missiles and misguided men.

Martin Luther King, Jr.

The second of the two gravest environmental threats to Kazakhstan is radiation contamination in Semipalatinsk, where the Soviet Union has tested almost 500 nuclear weapons. Experts' estimates suggest that more than 1.5 million people in Kazakhstan today, almost every tenth citizen, have been affected by the nuclear tests. The radiation continues to adversely affect the health of the local population. There is now a reported seven-degree difference between the temperature of the soil in Semipalatinsk and in neighboring areas.[52] According to the Semipalatinsk prenatal center, only 10 percent of pregnant women in some rural areas nearby are healthy; the rest have problems because of weakened immune systems. Some members of the opposition to the government's environmental policy are raising the issue of compensation to the huge number of civilians who were harmed by nuclear testing during the Soviet era. The issue of compensation is a sensitive one because the former officials of the Soviet KGB and the Interior Ministry are receiving additional compensation, while common people receive nothing.[53]

Kazakhstan's experts suggest that more than $1 billion would be required to clean up nuclear contamination, resources that could not be found easily even with international support. There was an alternative proposal to generate resources through the development of a highly profitable project for the establishment of nuclear waste depository facilities for imported nuclear waste. The criticism of this proposal was so sharp that for a while it was taken off the discussion table. But for how long?

The Status of Women in Central Asia

The level of development of society can be determined by the role and position of women in it.

Frederick Engels

What is a woman? I assure you, I don't know . . . I do not believe that anybody can know until she has expressed herself in all the arts and professions open to human skill.

Virginia Woolf

Only the educated are free.

Epictetus

The members of the Central Asian family, as well as members of the Caucasus family, occupy carefully graded positions according to age and sex. As in many other traditional cultures, all understand that the daughter leaves the family when she marries. It is perceived, however, as a loss of productive labor; therefore, this transfer to the family of her husband should be compensated. So the training of daughters in obedience to men and in household activities begins early. Emphasis on a traditional extended family provides encouragement for having a large number of children. The current Central Asian proverb, "A home with children is like a bazaar,[54] and a childless home is like a tomb (nazar)" demonstrates this cultural value. Attitudes and practices concerning marriage, family planning, and women's roles are part of the larger issue of family.

Bride Price

As part of its campaign to emancipate the women of Central Asia, the Soviet government bitterly fought, by law and propaganda, the old customs and traditions related to the role and position of women within the family and society. One of the customs that was prohibited was the custom of paying the bride price, *kalim*. Article 196 of the Criminal Code stated that paying *kalim* "entails correctional labor for a period up to one year" for both the donor and the recipient. The basis for Soviet opposition to the custom was the Russian misconception of the role of the bride price in Central Asian marriage. The Russians did not understand the nature of the marriage agreement in Central Asia, which in fact bypasses not only the bride but also the groom. From the point of view of European Russians and other Slavic cultures, the payment of bride price meant that the woman was being sold as a *chattel*, or slave, to the family of the groom. This practice, as well as other traditional customs of Central Asia, was considered among the "feudal survivals of old customs degrading to women."

To the Central Asian, the bride price is not only a payment to the bride's family for having raised the girl but also a protection for a woman in case she returns home because of mistreatment by her husband. Bride price is still paid today, but in many instances it is little more than a symbolic payment.

Education and Equality

Soviet family policy in Central Asia was aimed at bringing the family closer to a contemporary Russian model. Despite the official suppression of old traditions, the Central Asian family has not changed as rapidly or as markedly as the Western family. The Soviet regime was aware that the fastest and surest way to change traditional societies in Central Asia and the Caucasus was by getting women out of the family and into schools and other outside activities. To this end, the constitutions of each of these republics contained a paragraph dealing with women's rights, including the caution that ". . . the drawing of women into study, into agricultural or industrial production, into the governing of the state or into social or political activities is punishable by law."[55]

In all fairness to the Soviet system, the process of the elimination of illiteracy among the women of Central Asia was an enormous success story. Families were accountable for sending school-aged children to get free public education at all levels, including high school. It was not an easy process for those parents in rural areas, who did not object in principle, but whose livelihood depended on children's labor in small private gardens and on collective farms. The whole tobacco, cotton, and rice industries rested on women and children. So, the quality of education was significantly lower in rural areas than in cities.

The practice of marrying off girls at the traditional marriage age, which was 14 and up, was prohibited by law. Nevertheless, the practice existed sporadically and was a reality of life in remote areas. There was also a category of parents in some places who kept girls out of school at an early age to get a higher bride price from the groom's family. An unspoken rule was that an uneducated wife-to-be would be at a high demand because she would be more dependant and submissive and would keep traditional cultural norms unchanged.

The regime was encouraging women to participate in different public activities. Even after many years of official pressure, however, the residues of traditional behavioral patterns and basic customs were seen in rural areas, among working-class groups, and at some meetings, plays, and movies. Women often sat separately from men in public. There were even women's sections in some local government offices.

The Soviet socialist ideology emphasized equality of women. The Soviets created a variety of social programs to encourage women to participate in industrial and social development. They opened up wide-ranging educational and job opportunities for women. Though the number of women in all professions and at all educational levels was the highest in Soviet Asia compared to other Asian and African countries, there was still a notable lack of Central Asian women in public life. Since the collapse of the Soviet Union in 1991, women in all countries of the Southern Near Abroad region have experienced a great decline of living standards, along with a great shrinkage of career opportunities. Since the declaration of independence by each of these countries, political leaders have promoted a state-managed revival of Islamic and traditional cultural values. They view such policies as a crucial component of a broader strategy of establishing distinct national identities. As a result, some of the gains made by women during the Soviet era have eroded since 1991. For example, literacy rates have slid from above 90 percent to around 60 percent.

As a result of severing connections with the other countries of the former Soviet Union and the reduction of government funding and social programs, industrial and agricultural production has shrunk by as much as 60 percent. The skyrocketing unemployment rate, combined with corruption, instability, and little respect for human rights, hit women hard. Women were the first to lose their jobs and to face discrimination, harassment, and violence. Because an independent existence has become almost impossible, women are under enormous pressure to get married.

Drug Trafficking and Human Trafficking

Central Asia is a major transit area for drug traffickers moving their products from Afghanistan to markets in Russia and the West. When up to 80 percent of the population of the region lives below the poverty line, and families are caught in a hand-to-mouth existence, women become scapegoats. There is evidence that girls' education is being curtailed, and domestic abuse of women has emerged as a serious problem. In such a desperate economic climate, a growing number of women have resorted to illicit activities, including prostitution and drug smuggling, to subsist. Large numbers of drug traffickers in Tajikistan, for example, have used women as couriers, assuming they would attract less scrutiny at border checkpoints. There is much anecdotal evidence that some women involved in drug trafficking are not even paid in cash, but instead get paid with flour or other essential goods that they need to feed and care for their families, as reported by representatives of the International Harm Reduction Development Program, a nongovernmental project that works on addiction-related issues. Drug addiction among women in Tajikistan has exploded. Addiction among women was virtually unheard of before 1991. Recent data compiled by the same agency, however, indicate that women now make up to 3.2 percent of the total number of registered addicts in the Tajik capital of Dushanbe. Their incarceration creates even more problems, contributing to a growing number of abandoned and homeless children and exploitation of children.[56]

But drug trafficking is only one facet of the larger picture; human trafficking is on a steady rise. Comparing the trafficking problem among the countries of Central Asia, we can see similar circumstances in all of them, such as a high rate of unemployment, corruption, and poverty. While in Tajikistan, the issue of labor exploitation in trafficking is more of a problem, in Uzbekistan and Kazakhstan it is more of an issue of trafficking for sexual exploitation. There is a different context, but the scope of the problem is pretty much the same.[57]

HIV/AIDS

International organizations report a frightening increase of women contracting HIV/AIDS. Of those who contract HIV/AIDS in the Kyrgyz Republic, 55 percent are thought to be female, although the majority of those officially registered with the disease are males. In about 80 percent of cases of female HIV/AIDS in Kyrgyzstan, husbands have infected their own wives. There are several reasons for such a picture. The most typical, according to experts, are lack of sex education, low awareness of sexually transmitted disease, revival of old traditions of kidnapping future wives, unofficial polygamy, and increased extramarital sex, often with prostitutes.[58]

The chilling cases of several hospitals in Southern Kyrgyzstan that left more than 200 children and their mothers infected with HIV by using the same catheters on 10–15 people reveal severe social and economic problems: a lack of medical supplies, combined with negligence, greed, and corruption in the health care system, and crippling poverty.[59]

To combat HIV/AIDS and other health-related problems, such as high maternal and infant mortality rates, society needs to address the larger issues of gender equality, power reduction, and social protection. Currently, the effort of the international community is to engage women in addressing these problems through women-operated nongovernmental organizations.

One of the positive developments in this direction can be seen in Kazakhstan, where women take an active role in almost 40 percent of small- and medium-sized businesses. The Kazakh legislature was the first to address and implement a government-supported program for small- and medium-sized women's businesses. In 2008, 150 million KGS—Kyrgyzstani som (equivalent to $3.5 million U.S.)—were allocated for the development of this type of businesses; in 2009 the sum was doubled. Though this is a sign of progress in Central Asian women's rights and conditions, there is a long way to go. Hope comes from the fact that despite women's unequal treatment in Central Asia, they have demonstrated great strength, flexibility, and openness to change in the post-Soviet transition.

Afghanistan

It is your concern when the wall next door is on fire.

Horace

The lands that currently make up Afghanistan have been at a crossroads since ancient times. Here, historic figures, including Alexander the Great, Cyrus and Darius the Great, Ghengis Khan, and Tamerlane all fought for control of this important crossroads of Asia. The region has been important because it was an area surrounded by contending states rather than having value itself. As a buffer area, Afghanistan has always had strategic importance. During the nineteenth century, both the Russians and the British were repeatedly involved in Afghan intrigues called the "Great Game." Frederick Hartmann emphasized the buffer status of nineteenth-century Afghanistan this way:

> Afghanistan has played such a role ever since British power was expanded up to its southern borders in India and the Russians established a common frontier with the Afghans on the north. There is an old Afghan saying that defines the role of mountainous Afghanistan: "This goat separates the lion from the bear."[60]

Rouhollah Ramazani made a similar comment:

> Russia's direct agreements (usually after territorial conquest) with the Northern Tier states in the nineteenth century largely provided the basis for her present long boundaries with these states. Furthermore, her direct negotiations with Great Britain as in the case of Afghanistan, and her collaboration with Great Britain as in the case of Iran and Turkey, were influential in defining the boundaries of these latter states with each other.[61]

During the twentieth century, Britain, Russia, Germany, Iran, China, Pakistan, India, and the United States all played their parts in the destabilization of Afghanistan.

Afghanistan maintained the status of a buffer state during the cold war. Both the United States and the Soviet Union vied for influence by extending aid to the Afghans. In 1973, King Zahir Shah was overthrown by the Afghan military. A military government, headed by General Mohammad Daud Khan, ruled until 1978. In 1978, a coup d'état brought a Marxist government to power in Afghanistan. Splits within the Afghan Communist Party over both Islam and Socialist reforms soon threatened the very survival of the Marxist revolution. It was this volatile situation that caused the Soviets to intervene on the night of December 24, 1979. The Afghan prime minister was killed, and in his place the Soviets installed Babrak Karmal. Soviet forces eventually swelled to around 120,000 before their withdrawal in 1989.

The Soviet intervention provoked open civil war. A number of loosely organized resistance fighters calling themselves the *mujahedeen* (holy warriors) were able to tie down the Soviet military for a decade. Soviet policy throughout much of the Other World was subjected to harsh criticism until the "new thinking" of Mikhail Gorbachev brought a Soviet withdrawal, coupled with military and economic support for the last Soviet-installed government, led by former Afghan Secret Police Chief Najibullah. Tainted by its association with the Soviets, that government failed to establish legitimacy either at home or abroad. More than 5 million refugees fled Afghanistan, most settling in Pakistan near the Afghanistan border.

A stalemate that characterized the final years of Soviet intervention continued for a time after the Soviet withdrawal; however, the combatants looked for support from outside states, including the former Soviet Union, China, the United States, Pakistan, Saudi Arabia, and Iran. Given the drastic changes that occurred in the international environment, such support soon diminished as other priorities emerged. In April 1992, the Najibullah government collapsed, and several *mujahedeen* rebel groups entered Kabul, the capital. In the months and years that followed, the nine *mujahedeen* factions that waged war against the old Soviet-installed governments increasingly turned their weapons on one another.

A tenth faction appeared in early 1995. The new faction, known as the Taliban, or "Seekers," was originally made up of students of Islam from the southeastern city of Kandahar. This faction's avowed aim was to end Afghanistan's internal conflicts and lawlessness and to institute an Islamic government in that state. With covert support from Pakistan, the Taliban gained control of 8 of Afghanistan's 28 provinces within a few months. Within the next few years, the Taliban extended their control to Kabul and most of the remainder of Afghanistan. In an effort to reform society to conform with their version of Islamic law, they proceeded to ban all music except for religious songs and eventually banned movies, television, and videocassettes. Severe restrictions were also placed on women's clothing and activities. Meanwhile, armed resistance continued in the countryside.

Although unrest and a fitful civil war continued for years after the Taliban gained control of most of the country, it was the September 11, 2001, terrorist attacks in the United States that propelled Afghanistan from the shadows to the "center stage" of world events. Western analysts deduced that the attack on the United States was either mounted or supported by the Al Qaeda terrorist organization of wealthy Saudi Arabian Osama bin Laden. Al Qaeda and bin Laden received sanctuary from the Afghan Taliban.

When the Taliban government refused to meet the American demands to turn over bin Laden and the Al Qaeda leadership, along with several Americans and

Europeans being held for allegedly preaching Christianity, U.S. and British forces aided opposition forces in a military campaign in Afghanistan. This campaign resulted in a total Taliban defeat in December 2001. Even before the Taliban government collapsed, there were moves to end more than 20 years of civil war with the establishment of an interim council that would serve until more permanent political arrangements could be made. Meeting in Bonn, Germany, under the sponsorship of the United Nations, most of the rival Afghanistan factions agreed to take steps that, if successfully implemented, could lead the country toward a peaceful future.

The Bonn agreement provided for a series of steps intended to result in an acceptable post-Taliban government. Most of them have been implemented over the years. The first general and open democratic election was successfully held for the first time in the history of the country on October 9, 2004. A crucial step toward the future unification of the conflicting groups in the society was the fact that a majority Pashtun leader, Hamid Karzai, became the country's first-ever democratically elected president. Afghans voted for peace and democratic change and for the rebuilding of their war-torn country against extremists of all kinds.

Afghanistan's political process since presidential and parliamentary elections has been disappointing but not disastrous. The government's activities have produced little in the way of legislative changes. One of the important accomplishments, however, was the signing of a new constitution into law by President Karzai in January 2004; this constitution determines the new strategic vision for Afghanistan development. Article 43 of the constitution, for example, states that education is the right of all Afghan citizens, and it is provided free of charge by the state up to the level of a bachelor's degree. Such strong emphasis on the importance of equal and accessible education reflects government-wide understanding of the role of education in the development of a stable and self-sufficient society. In just two years—2007 and 2008—in the Uruzan province, the birthplace of the Taliban leader, Mullah Omar, and dominated by conservative ethnic Pashtuns from whom the Taliban draw their strength, there were a number of changes: The number of children in school rose from 12,000 to 50,000; 100 health centers were built; the number of medical doctors rose from 2 to 30. Although the infant mortality rate of 152 deaths per thousand live births is still horrifying, it fell from 166 per thousand in 2005. Even with these positive changes, the illiteracy rate is well over a staggering 70 percent of the population.[62]

Rebuilding Afghanistan requires assistance not only in educational sectors but also in every sector of its society, including, first of all, rehabilitation of agriculture. The Afghan Agricultural Ministry and the United States Agency for International Development (USAID) have held several conferences and fairs, sharing their knowledge and offering incentives to farmers to switch from growing poppies to a variety of alternative crops, including pomegranates, wheat, and corn. As a result, some visible progress has been made. According to UN experts, 18 out of 34 provinces are now poppy-free, which is up from 13 in 2007. Ninety-eight percent of Afghan poppies are grown in just seven, highly unstable, Southern provinces,[63] in which the Taliban and drug mafia are intertwined. Drug trade provides financing for the Taliban, while the drug mafia has a vested interest in the insecurity that encourages poppy cultivation. The main obstacle in the way of developing Afghanistan's agriculture includes lack of fertilizers and suitable machinery and technology, poor road networks, shortage of electricity, and few storage facilities.

Improving health care, creating jobs, rebuilding the infrastructure, empowering women, and most importantly, reducing endemic corruption are the areas of critical importance for the healthy future development of Afghanistan. One must accept that Afghanistan has never seen a government without corruption and bribery in its history.

Glad to be Going Home: Soviet special force troops leaving Afghanistan. *Source: Olga Carter*

Should we go or stay: The question of US troops remaining in Afghanistan was a major political issue in 2009. *Source: John Stuart*

Even the army is not free from corruptive practices: In order for a member of a minority ethnic group, Hazar, to be promoted, he is expected to pay a bribe to his superior, a Tajik. As one sergeant claimed: "I can't get promoted to sergeant-major because I can't pay the necessary bribes."[64] Only gradual institutional reforms, job creation, and growing stability can effectively fight this internal enemy.

The past internal conflicts among different ethnic groups and warlords will not disappear overnight; in fact, they manifest themselves in armed conflicts from time to time, but most of all in growing corruption. Current problems in building a unified democratic society in Afghanistan stem, to some extent, from the artificial historic nature of the Afghan state. Although Afghanistan has had a form of independence since Ahmad Shah unified the tribes in 1747, the current borders are largely the result of the nineteenth-century rivalries of Russia and Britain. Again, author Rouhollah Ramazani addressed this point:

> In the case of Afghanistan and Iran, Great Britain assisted through arbitration in providing a basis for their present boundary. And in the case of Afghanistan and the part of India that is now Pakistan, Great Britain established the controversial Durand Line, which cuts between ethnically related tribal groups.[65]

Afghanistan is surrounded on all sides by neighbors that are hostile to each other. In the past, all these states have attempted to exploit the tribal and religious differences that already existed because of the arbitrary way that Afghanistan was shaped in the first place. One can say that "the Great Game" in Central Asia still continues, only with different players.

In the immediate aftermath of the Taliban fall, the effort of the international community was concentrated on two main issues—security and reconstruction—and much has been accomplished. The Afghan Army is at last emerging as a credible fighting force. In 2007 more than $7 billion went into training and equipping it as well as the police force. Every week now, a Kandak (a 650-man battalion) finishes training and takes to the fields. The size of the Afghan National Army (ANA) is around 80,000. It is now better equipped with body armor, M-16 assault rifles, and the latest model of Humvee armored vehicle. The desertion rate has dropped considerably from 30 percent just three years ago to 7 percent.[66] NATO specialists stress that the comprehensive approach in which military actions are backed by political and economic progress will eventually allow Afghan forces to be at the forefront of the fight.

Some progress can be seen in the capital of Afghanistan, Kabul, and a few areas in the north of the country, where Afghan businesses and markets are thriving. Women are increasingly confident that they can walk down the streets without heavy cloth, or *burkas*.[67] One million refugees have returned to rebuild their homes and lives, and many roads are being repaired, yet much work remains. Security and reconstruction are still huge challenges. Today Taliban fighters are not the same people who fought during the U.S.–led bombing campaign in 2001. They are new recruits, drawn from the poor *madrassahs* (Islamic religious schools) of neighboring Pakistan. These groups receive support from influential religious fundamentalists in Pakistan and other countries. One such fighter said that he was paid $55 (U.S.) in Pakistan to come and fight the holy war against the Americans and their Afghan surrogates. The Taliban is using the media to manage its image, to be viewed as freedom fighters. An increase of attacks linked to Taliban fighters on newly opened schools for girls and government and humanitarian agencies, the refusal of warlords to disarm and relinquish territory, and an increase in opium production and drug trafficking to the world markets will not stop plans to complete a constitution, hold elections, and rebuild the country. International effort is focused on working with local partners to provide water and health care services to millions of people. In some areas of Afghanistan, these agencies are engaged in community-based education, large-scale agricultural projects, sanitation, and health education.

The problem of fighting the "war of necessity" in Afghanistan, as Barack Obama likes to put it, however, is more serious than just a shortage of troops, disjointed mini-campaigns of U.S. and NATO allies, and different aid policies resembling a "pot-luck dinner where every guest is free to bring his own dish," as a recent report by the European Council of Foreign Relations put it.[68]

The State Department acknowledges that though the gains are tenuous, failure is not an option in Afghanistan. The goal is to implement President's Obama's strategy "to reduce the capability and will" of insurgents and extremists, including Al Qaeda. The situation in Afghanistan is "serious, but success is achievable and demands a revised implementation strategy, commitment and resolve, and increased unity effort," the commander of U.S. and NATO troops in Afghanistan said, assessing the eight-year-old conflict.[69] Some experts point out that this war cannot be won just inside Afghanistan. Going after the enemy that we really need to fight would make our strategy winnable. How long it will take to build a terrorist-free, peaceful Afghanistan remains to be seen. Many others have tried and failed to bring stability to this part of the world. One should not forget the warning that Rudyard Kipling issued 100 years ago to outsiders who ventured into this part of the world:

> One sword-knot stolen from the camp will pay for all the school expenses of any Kurrum Valley scamp who knows no word of moods and tenses. But, being blessed with perfect sight picks off our mess-mates left and right.[70]

Summary

More than any other time in the region's history, Central Asia and the Southern Near Abroad face a crossroads. One path leads to the development of social and political institutions of these countries compatible with the Western system. The other leads to the restoration of national identities through revitalization of traditional social norms. There is a hope that the wisdom of generations of these nations will help to constructively integrate the two.

Deeply woven into the fabric of Central Asian and world economic cooperation, the region is becoming an important component of peace stabilization in the area. The war in Afghanistan, lasting since the early 1980s and the impact of the U.S. military presence in the region, predetermine a serious interest in the analysis of the recent developments and different aspects of life in the nations of this part of the world. It indicates that the new century is indeed becoming an Asian one.

Review Questions

1. What are the main oil- and natural gas-producing countries of the region?
2. What are the political and economic implications of the "gas war" for the stability in Central Asia? For European Union countries?
3. What are the main uranium-producing countries of the region?
4. What factors contributed to the environmental disasters of the Central Asian region?
5. Describe the commonalities and differences in social changes in Central Asian countries under Russian rule and Soviet rule.
6. What are the specific characteristics of the process of transition to a democratic society and market economy in countries of the region?
7. What was the essence of the Soviet policy of Russification in Central Asia and the Southern Near Abroad countries?

8. What was the goal of the Soviet policy regarding the role of women in society in Central Asia, and in what way has it been affected since the disintegration of the former USSR?

9. What are the reasons for the tension in Armenia-Azerbaijan relations?

10. What were the consequences of the Russia-Georgia 7-day war?

11. How have changes in the political environment of Kyrgyzstan contributed to the foreign investment activities in the country?

12. What goals are being pursued by China in Kyrgyzstan? By Russia in Kyrgyzstan?

13. Why can Afghanistan be called an artificial country? What are its crucial problems at the present time?

14. What are the causes and consequences of increased drug trafficking in Central Asian countries?

Key Terms

- **annexation**—A process of the permanent incorporation of an adjacent territory with the national domain.

- **authoritarian political model**—An order based on an absolute and unlimited power of the individual at the top of the political pyramid; common for all Central Asian countries in the past. Current political models in these countries have a strong resemblance with those in the past.

- **collectivization**—The process of a forceful merger of private farms into large agricultural enterprises in the former USSR in the 1930s, accompanied by the massive confiscations of private land, livestock, and property of those who declined to join such units voluntarily. Massive persecutions, imprisonment in concentration camps for farmers, combined with the ineffective management of the confiscated property, led to a significant decline in agricultural production in the country.

- **confiscation**—A transfer of ownership by the government, which does not involve compensation to the owner.

- **diaspora**—People settled far from their ancestral homelands.

- **feudalism**—A social and economic system in which social position was based on land ownership. In Central Asia, feudalism created a form of personal dependency of peasants on their landlords in all areas of life.

- **intelligentsia**—A group of people with a substantial level of education and ability to think critically interested in improvements of learning and cultural values of society. This term originated in the Russian revolution to differentiate the intellectual classes from the bourgeoisie and proletariat.

- **oligarch**—A member of a wealthy elitist governing group that exercises control of political processes.

- **perestroika**—Perestroika translates from Russian as "reconstruction," a new ideology introduced by the leader of the Soviet Union, Mikhail Gorbachev, in 1986. According to this innovative set of views and new regulations, more decision-making power was delegated by the central government to the local governing agencies; elements of market economy were encouraged; people of the Soviet Union were allowed to create small private business enterprises; more foreign visitors were allowed to visit the country and more

Soviet people were allowed to travel abroad; and freedom of the press was the leading force to a new openness in society.

- **personality cult**—Practice by which a leader is elevated to a preeminent status through a propaganda campaign in order to reinforce his or her power.
- **privatization**—The transfer of ownership from the government to private companies and individuals, including foreign investors.
- **Russification**—The process of forceful implantation of Russian language as the language of official communication and education, suppression of local traditions, and implementation of Russian cultural elements.
- **urbanization**—The process of the growth of cities and development of a specific lifestyle associated with accumulation of wealth and power in big cities.

Useful Web Sites

Central Asia: *www.centralasiadaily.com*
One World.net: *www.oneworld.net*
EurasiaNet: *www.eurasianet.org*
Global Security.org: *www.globalsecurity.org*
Business Information Center for the Newly Independent States: *www.bisnis .doc.gov*
Afghanistan: *www.afghan-web.com*
Armenia: *www.armtown.com*
Azerbaijan: *www.azerbaijan.az*
Georgia: *www.nationsonline.org*
Kazakhstan: *caspiannews.kz* OR *http://kazakhstannews.com*
Kyrgyzstan: *loc.gov*
Tadjikistan: *http://topix.com/world/tajikistan*
Turkmenistan: *www.turkmenistan.ru*
Uzbekistan: *www.mfa.uz* OR *www.einnews.com/uzbekistan*

For Further Reading

Bransten, Jeremy. "Kyrgyzstan: A Democracy Only for the Rich." RFE/RL, October 14, 1997.
Brydon, Diana. "Commonwealth or Common Poverty?" *Kunapipi: Special Issue on Post-Colonial Criticism,* 11–1 (1989).
Huskey, Eugene. "Between Democracy and Authoritarianism: Askar Akayev." Paper, Presented at the ASN 4th Annual Convention. Columbia University, April 15–17, 1999.
Idinov, Narynber. "Kyrgyzstan: Politicians Wrangle over Gold Production." RFE/RL, February 6, 1998.
Johnson-Odim, Cheryl. "Common Themes, Different Contexts: Third World Women and Feminism," *Third World Women and the Politics of Feminism,* Bloomington and Indianapolis: Indiana University Press, 1991.
Kostyukova, Irina. "The Towns of Kyrgyzstan Change Their Faces: Rural-Urban Migrants in Bishkek," *Central Asian Survey,* 13, 3 (September 1994), p. 428.

Mederoy, Sultan. "Analyses of Privatization in Kyrgyz Republic, Its Main Result and Further Strategies," *Journal of Economic Cooperation Among Islamic Countries,* 18, 1–2 (1997), p. 35.

Murzalin, Ahanbolat. "Central Asia: Are There Limits to Authoritarian Development?" *The Times of Central Asia,* 2, 23(66), June 8, 2000.

Osmanalieva, Raya. "Tribalism in Kyrgys Society," *Central Asia Monitor,* 5 (1999), pp. 10–11.

Pryde, Iam. "Kyrgyzstan: Secularism vs. Islam," *The World Today,* 48, 11 (November 1992), p. 208.

Sangari, Kumkum. "The Politics of the Possible," *The Nature and Context of Minority Discourse.* Abdul Jan Mohammed and David Lloyd (eds.). New York: Oxford University Press, 1990.

The Times of Central Asia, February 23, 2000.

Notes

1. The spelling of the name of each country is as officially registered by the government at the United Nations.

2. The expression *Caucasian racial group* (used almost exclusively in North America to refer collectively to the people of European, Middle Eastern, South Asian, and North African ancestry) was first proposed by the German scientist Johann Friederich Blumenbach (1752–1840). His studies based the classification of the Caucasian race primarily on skull features, which he claimed were optimized by the Georgians, a people living in the Southern Caucasus.

The name *Caucasian* stems from the Caucasus mountains, the region imagined to be the location where, according to Biblical legend, Noah's Ark eventually landed after the Deluge. From this area, known as Mount Ararat, Noah's son Japheth, traditional Biblical ancestor of the Europeans, established his tribe prior to its supposed migration into Europe. Even though the mountain is located in Turkey (approximately 18 miles south of Armenia), Ararat is the national symbol of Armenia.

3. "1988: Death Toll Rises in Armenian Earthquake— On This Day, 10 December," BBC News. Accessed at http://news.bbc.co.uk/onthisday/december/10.

4. For more information on the mountain systems of Asia, see http://www.mazalien.com/himalayan-pilgrimage.html.

5. For more information on the territories covered by mountains in each country of the region, see Library of Congress Country Studies at http://lcweb2.loc.gov.

6. "Seismic Activity of the Turkmenistan in 1992." *Seismology Report of Turkmenistan.* (Ilim, 1994), N 2, pp. 83–92.

7. These are technical terms that the ordinary reader may not know: The *steppe* refers to a vast plain devoid of forest and is one of the largest plains in Russia and Kazakhstan. A *continental climate* is typical for an interior of a large landmass, such as Central Asia. Such regions usually experience hot summers and cold winters, being far away from the moderating influence of the ocean. A *climate zone* refers to a region characterized by a certain average temperature, rainfall, and dryness. A *subtropical climate* is typically a middle-temperature region with moderately dry summers and very wet, overcast winters.

8. Ilan Greenberg, "Talks Stall over a Central Asia Water Basin," *International Herald Tribune,* March 8, 2007, p. 8.

9. For more information about oil reserves in the region, see "Country Analysis Brief: Caspian Sea Region" at http://www.eia.doe.gov.
10. Bernard A. Gelb, CRS report for Congress, September 8, 2006, "Caspian Oil and Gas: Production and Prospects."
11. News in Brief, *Petroleum Economist*, August 3, 2007. Accessed from Lexis-Nexis Academic database.
12. The Caspian Pipeline Consortium project (CPC) connects Kazakhstan's Caspian Sea area oil production fields with Russia's Black Sea oil tankers' port of Novorossiysk. The oil is then taken by tankers to the world markets.
13. "Central Asia: History Repeats Itself," *Petroleum Economist*, November 3, 2006. Accessed from Lexis-Nexis Academic database.
14. "Central Asia: Competition Heats Up for Uranium," *Petroleum Economist*, November 3, 2006, Accessed from Lexis-Nexis Academic database.
15. For more information on Nabucco pipeline project, see http://www.nabuccopipeline.com.
16. Sergey Ilchenko, "Russia and Georgia One Year After the War," Commentary, July 24, 2009. www.comments.ua.
17. R. N. Frye, "Zoroastrier in der islamischen Zeit," *Der Islam* (Berlin: 1965) p. 41; idem, "The History of Ancient Iran" (1958); idem, *The Heritage of Persia* (1963).
18. Gavin Hambly, ed., *Central Asia* (London: 1969). First English Edition.
19. Gelene Carrre d'Encaussee, *Decline of an Empire: The Soviet Socialist Republics in Revolt* (New York: 1979); Paul B. Henze, "Marx on Russians and Muslims," *Central Asian Survey, AACAR Bulletin*6, (1987).
20. Mary Boyce, "Zoroastrians: Their Religious Beliefs and Practices" (1984); idem, *A History of Zoroastrianism* (1975–1991): 3 Vols. (Vol. 3 with Franz Grenet).
21. For more information on the religious composition of the countries in the region, see Library of Congress Country Studies at http://lcweb2.loc.gov.
22. Kasgarli Mahmuc, *Kitab Diwan Lugat at Turk.* Completed ca. A.D. 1074/1077. *Editio Princeps* by Kilisli Rifat (3 Vols.) (Istanbul: 1917–1919). English translation by R. Dankoff with J. Kelly as *Compendium of Turkic Dialects* (3 Vols.) (Cambridge, MA: 1982–1984).
23. Beatrice Forbes Manz, *The Rise and Rule of Tamerlane* (Medford, MA: Cambridge University Press, 1989).
24. *Tourism,* 1 (2, 2001), pp. 26–27.
25. An unsettled lifestyle of a tribe or nation is known as *nomadism;* this term implies a constant movement from one territory to another. Without a domestication technology, people must follow their food supply. Such a lifestyle is in direct contrast with a *sedentary lifestyle* in which people are living in permanent or semi-permanent settlements. People within this lifestyle commonly have well-developed agricultural technology.
26. Z. V. Togan. "On the Origins of the Kazakhs and the Ozbeks," H. B. Paksoy, ed. *Central Asia Reader* (New York: M. E. Sharpe, 1994).
27. George J. Demko, "The Russian Colonization of Kazakhstan 1896–1916," *University Uralic-Altaic Series Vol. 99* (Bloomington, IN, 1969). Soviets also made land demands on other nationalities and took land by military force, including in the Baltic region.
28. A. Lamb, *The Sino-Indian and Sino-Russian Borders: Some Comparisons and Contrasts/Studies in the Social History of China and South-East Asia* (Cambridge University Press, Cambridge, MA, 1970), pp. 135–152; J. L. Wieczynski. "The Russian Frontier," *The Impact of Borderlands upon the Course of Early Russian History.* (Charlottesville: University Press of Virginia, 1976).

29. "The Basmachi (Turkistan National Liberation Movement)," *Modern Encyclopedia of Religions in Russia and Soviet Union*, Vol. IV (Academic International Press, Gulf Breeze, FL 1991), pp. 5–20; Idem; "Zeki Belidi Togan's Account: The Basmachi Movement from Within," H. B. Paksoy, ed.; *Central Asia Reader* (New York: M. E. Sharpe, 1994). The term *Basmachi* was used as a derogatory reference toward the Turkestan national liberation movement against Soviet annexation of Central Asia between 1920 and 1930.

30. R. L. Cansfield, "Soviet Gambit in Central Asia," *Journal of South Asian and Middle Eastern Studies*, 5, 1.

31. Aleksandr Reutov, "Russkiy Yazik Ostalsia Bez Dela," *Kommersant*, 124, 24 (July 2009). www.kommersant.ua.

32. Manmohan Singh, "Speech to Members of Shanghai Cooperation," *Real Clear World*, June 25, 2009. www.realclearworld.com

33. R. Grankin, "Saparmurad Niyazov (Turkmenbashi)," *Secretniye Materiali 20 Veka*, No. 12 (114), June 2003, international newspaper.

34. The *khan* title, which refers to the supreme leader, has been used throughout history in traditional Kyrgyz society.

35. For more information on Kyrgyzstan's economic indicators, see *The World Fact Book*: http://www.cia.gov

36. Fred J. Hill and Andrew Wad, "Kyrgyzstan," *Nations of the World: A Political, Economic and Business Handbook*, 4th ed. (Millerton, NY: Grey House Publishing, September 2003), p. 812;

37. A. Turchinov, "Tenevaya Economika i Tenevaya Politika," *Demoni Mira I Bogi Voini. Cotsialnije konflikti v Postkommunisticheskom Mire* (Kiev: Politichna Dumka, 1997).

38. Timirbayev Viacheslav, "Sprut po Imeni Korruptsija," *Vecherniy Bishkek*, 1999; Grigory Shulgin "Akayev," *Secretnye Versii* (Kyiv, Ukraine), No. 7, July 2003, p. 11.

39. The term *nomenclatura* refers to a system of relationships in the former Soviet Union under which appointees of a high level of the government or Communist party were rotated within the highest level of the system. It is a reflection of the corrupted form of bureaucracy of the former USSR.

40. James Critchlow, "Corruption, Nationalism and the Native Elites in Soviet Central Asia," *The Journal of Communist Studies*, 4, 2 (1988).

41. A kinship group whose members are believed to be descended from a common ancestor far enough in the past that they cannot trace their specific genealogical ties to one another is known as a *clan*. Clan members can usually trace their ancestry up to seven generations back.

42. V. E. Hanyn, "Conflicts in Kyrgyzstan," *The Word of Kyrgyzstan* (Bishkek, Kyrgyzstan), July 15, 1995.

43. "Order Sought in Kyrgyzstan," *The Dallas Morning News*, March 26, 2005.

44. Bek Orozaliev and Mikhail Zigar, "Kurmanbek Bakiev Pereizbralsia Dosrochno," *Kommersant* 124 (Kyiv, Ukraine), July 24, 2009. www.kommersant.ua.

45. Umed Erkinov, "Kyrgyzstan: Is China the Hidden Power in Beshkek?" *EurasiaNet*, March 18, 2009. www.eurasianet.org.

46. "Troubling News from the Caucasus," *The Economist,* March 8, 2008.

47. "Manas International Airport, Ganci Airbase, Bishkek, Kyrgyzstan," June 8, 2004. Accessed from www.globalsecurity.org.

48. Irina Tezz, "Kyrgyzstan: Russia Set to Take Major Stake in Kyrgyz Torpedo Plant," *EurasiaNet*, April 1, 2009. Accessed from www.eurasianet.org.

49. R. Orudzhev, "Armiane Oskorbliaut Genseka Soveta Evropi," *Ekho Plus*, July 23, 2005.

50. Elina Karakulova, "Prirodoohrannie NPO v Kazahstane Okazivaut Vsio Bolshee Vlijanie na Politileu, vcura sianez," *Kazakhstan Daily Digest,* August 20, 2003. www.eurasianet.org.

51. "Kazahkstan: Dyke Project to Save Part of the Aral Sea," *IRINews Asia,* August 20, 2003. www.centralasiadaily.com.

52. "The Caspian Sea Level Changes and Its Influence on the Seismicity of the Western Turkmenia," *Inducing of Earthquakes by Underground Nuclear Explosions: Environmental and Ecological Problems.* (Moscow: Nauka, 1994) p. 69; "A Possibility of Seismic Activity Induction by Technogenic Processes in Kara Bogas-Gol Gulf," "Earthquakes Induced by Underground Nuclear Explosions," *Environmental and Ecological Problems, NATO ASI Series* (Spring, 1995), pp. 383–390.

53. Ina Lankulova, "Kazakn Senator Seeks Compensation for Nuclear-Test Victims," *Kazakhstan Daily Digest,* August 20, 2003. www.eurasianet.org.

54. A traditional type of an open market in Asian societies is called a *bazaar.* It is known for its art of bargaining; it is very noisy and highly entertaining.

55. Nuria R. Ismagilova, "Women in Mind: Educational Needs of Women in Central Asia, General Problems, and Strategies for Development, Khujand, Tajikistan," February 1, 2001. Accessed from www.mtnforum.org.

56. Press Release: Justin Burke, "Women Likely to Suffer Most in Central Asia's Turmoil." *Women's News,* October 7, 2003. Accessed from Lexis-Nexis Academic database.

57. "Trafficking in Person in Central Asia: The Scope of the Problem and the Appropriate Responses." Regional Central Asia Conference, "Combating Trafficking in Human Beings—Regional Response." Jointly organized by the OSCE and the Republic of Kazakhstan. Astana, Kazakhstan, May 18–19, 2006.

58. "HIV/AIDS Rates Among Women," September 16, 2003, Bishkek, Kyrgyzstan. Accessed from OCHA IRIN database.

59. Abdujalil Abdurasulov, "Kyrgyzstan: Victims Still Seeking Justice for Infant HIV Outbreak," *EurasiaNet,* March 12, 2009. www.eurasianet.org.

60. Frederick H. Hartmann, *The Relations of Nations,* 5th ed. (New York: Macmillan, 1978), p. 331.

61. Rouhollah Ramazani, *The Northern Tier: Afghanistan, Iran, and Turkey* (New York: Van Nostrand, 1966), p. 50.

62. Tirin Khot, "The Dutch Model," *The Economist* (London), March 14, 2009, U.S. Edition Special Report Section.

63. "Bring On the Pomegranate," *The Economist* (London), November 29, 2008, U.S. Edition Special Report Section.

64. "Good News from Arghandab," *The Economist* (London), August 2, 2008, U.S. Edition Special Report Section.

65. Ramazani, op. cit., p. 50.

66. "Good News from Arghandab," *The Economist* (London), August 2, 2008, U.S. Edition Special Report Section.

67. *Burkas* are the traditional dress style of women in some Islamic countries; they cover women's faces completely with a mesh fabric at the eye level for visibility and air circulation.

68. "Paddy Re-enlists," *The Economist* (London), January 26, 2008, U.S. Edition Special Report Section.

69. Jason Straziuso, "U.S. General Calls for New Strategy against Taliban," August 31, 2009, Associated Press; accessed from Yahoo News. www.yahoo.com.

70. Quoted by Valerie Pakenham, *Out in the Noonday Sun: Edwardians in the Tropics,* (New York: Random House, 1985), p. 194.

INDEX

A

Abbasid Dynasty, 246
Afghanistan
  government, 313
  history, 311–316
  internal conflicts, 314
  rebuilding of, 313–316
  Taliban, 82–83, 312–313
  terrorist threats, 3
  turmoil in, 6–7
  U.S. military action, 5
  women's burka, 82–83, 315
Africa
  African Union (AU), 197
  civil strife, 6
  False Start in Africa, 58
  North Africa. *See* North
    Africa
  rule of law, 82
  sub-Saharan. *See* Sub-
    Saharan Africa
AFRICOM (Africa Command),
  165, 194
Agriculture
  colonialism and, 29
  forests, 86
  Indian exports, 60
  land reform, 80
  in Latin America, 102, 103,
    113–114
  Middle Eastern water issues,
    238, 253
  modernization, 85–86
  slash and burn, 102, 103
  Stolen Harvest, 80–81
  Sub-Saharan Africa
    domestication of
      cattle, 151
    exploitation of land, 167
    food shortage, 143
    geographical problems,
      146, 148
Ahmadinejad, Mahmoud,
  257–258
AIDS. *See* HIV/AIDS
Akayev, Askar, 303
Al Qaeda, 193–194
Al Saud, Abdallah ben
  al-Aziz, 261
ALBA (Bolivarian Alliance for
  the Americas), 116, 118
Ali, 246
Allah, 242–243, 275
Al-Qaddafi, Muammar, 232
Angola, 185
Anna, Kofi, 159
Annexation, 295, 317

Apartheid
  in Africa, 148–149, 175, 198
  defined, 198
  global class apartheid, 66
Apollo spacecraft, 5
Arab world, 234, 236
Arabia. *See* Saudi Arabia
Arab-Israeli conflict, 269
Arabs, 263
Arafat, Yasser, 264–265
Aral Sea, 306–307
Arceneaux, Craig, 96–141
Arms Export Control Act, 128
Artificial states, 27, 43
Asia
  Central Asia. *See* Central
    Asia
  China, 211–216
    China after Mao, 213–215
    China under Mao, 212–213
    foreign policy, 216
    geography, 208
    history, 211–212
    Ka-Ching Dynasty, 213–215
    oil demands, 288
    world economic
      downturn, 215–216
  geography
    characteristics of countries,
      205
    East Asia, 208
    Far East, 209
    location, 204, 207
    the Orient, 209
    physical characteristics,
      206
    South Asia, 207
    Southeast Asia, 207–208
  Hong Kong case study,
    221–222
  India case study, 216–219
  Islamic radicals, 226
  Kashmir, 225–226
  North Korea, 226–227
  overview, 203–204
  Pakistan, 207, 225
  political characteristics, 206
  religion, 209–211
    Buddhism, 209, 228
    Confucianism, 209–210
    Daoism (Taoism), 210, 228
    Hinduism, 210–211, 218
    Islam, 211
  Singapore case study,
    222–223
  South Korea case study,
    223–225

Taiwan case study, 208,
  219–221
AU (African Union), 197
Authoritarian political model,
  300–301, 317
Authoritarian transformation,
  301
Authority as power, 48
Axis of evil, 39
Ayatollah, 247
Azerbaijan, 306

B

Bachelet, Michelle, 119
Bakr, Abu, 246
Balance of power
  military domination, 34–35
  as motive for colonialism, 24
Balance sheet of
  development, 58–63
Ban Ki-Moon, 47, 87
Bandaranaike, Sirimavo, 83
Barber, Benjamin, 67
Barre, Mohammed Siad, 188
Bayalinov, Kamil, 303
Bedo-Nationalism, 260–263
Beijing Declaration and
  Platform for Action, 89
Berdymukhammedov,
  Gurbaguly, 301
Beria, Lavrenti, 297
Berlin Conference, 152, 198
Bhutto, Benazir, 83
bin Laden, Osama, 262, 312
Black Hawk Down, 188
Blair, Tony, 164
*Blowback: The Costs and
  Consequences of American
  Empire*, 70
Bolívar, Simón, 96, 97–98, 133
Bolivarian Alliance for the
  Americas (ALBA), 116, 118
Bolivia, 96–98
Bonn agreement, 313
Borders, 295–296
Botha, P. W., 173–174
Boxer Rebellion, 223, 228
Brazil, 60–61, 122–126
Bride price, 308–309
Brilliant, Myron, 213
Britain. *See* England
Brokers, 62, 72
Bryant, William Cullen, 284
Buddhism, 209, 228
Burka, 82–83, 315
Bush, George W.
  Africa policy, 165